D1594765

CAMBRIDGE GREEK AND LATIN CLASSICS
IMPERIAL LIBRARY

GENERAL EDITORS

PROFESSOR E. J. KENNEY
Peterhouse, Cambridge

AND

PROFESSOR P. E. EASTERLING
University College London

DIO CHRYSOSTOM

ORATIONS

VII, XII AND XXXVI

EDITED BY

D. A. RUSSELL

*Emeritus Professor of Classical Literature
and Emeritus Fellow of St John's College, Oxford*

CAMBRIDGE
UNIVERSITY PRESS

Published by the Press Syndicate of the University of Cambridge
The Pitt Building, Trumpington Street, Cambridge CB2 1RP
40 West 20th Street, New York, NY 10011-4211, USA
10 Stamford Road, Oakleigh, Victoria 3166, Australia

First published 1992

Printed and bound in Great Britain by
Woolnough Bookbinding, Irthlingborough, Northants

A catalogue record for this book is available from the British Library

Library of Congress cataloguing in publication data
Dio, Chrysostom.
[Speeches. Selections]
Orations VII, XII, and XXXVI – Dio Chrysostom; edited by D. A.
Russell.
p. cm. – (Cambridge Greek and Latin classics. Imperial
library)
Includes bibliographical references (p. 248) and indexes.
Contents: Euboicus (VII) – Olympicus (XII) – Borystheniticus
(XXXVI).
ISBN 0 521 37548 7 (hardback). – ISBN 0 521 37696 3 (pbk.)
1. Speeches, addresses, etc., Greek. 2. Speeches, addresses,
etc., Greek – History and criticism. I. Russell, D. A. (Donald)
PA3965.D2 1992
885'.01 – dc20 91-36260 CIP

ISBN 0 521 37548 7 hardback
ISBN 0 521 37696 3 paperback

CONTENTS

CONTENTS

PREFACE

The narrative part of Dio's *Euboicus* has always been popular; I recall using it many years ago as a confidence-building text with first- and second-year undergraduates. The opening narrative of the *Borysthen-iticus* has similar charms. The rest of this volume illustrates other sides of Dio's art: his moral and theological earnestness and his epideictic virtuosity. I hope that the selection here offered will thus make an attractive introduction not only to Dio, but to some important aspects of first-century thought and literature in general – the prevailing philo-sophical religiosity, the linguistic and historical classicism, and the burgeoning sophistic exuberance that mark this phase of Graeco-Roman culture.

My debts are many. Various friends in various places where I have worked on this project – at Chapel Hill and Stanford as well as Oxford – have helped me enormously by discussion and advice. Dr M. B. Trapp read and commented on the whole, and made many useful contribu-tions. Rachel Woodrow and Stephen Colvin made my manuscript readable. Susan Moore's invaluable copy-editing made it ready for the typesetter. Dr. D. C. Innes read the proofs, and saved me from much error. The editors of the series have been a source of help and encouragement from beginning to end. The flaws and faults that remain are all my own work.

D.A.R.

ABBREVIATIONS

Arndt–Gingrich	W. F. Arndt and F. W. Gingrich, *A Greek–English lexicon of the New Testament,*[4] Cambridge 1957.	K–G	R. Kühner, *Ausführliche Grammatik der griechischen Sprache*[3] II, revised by B. Gerth (Hanover 1898–1904)
Blass–Debrunner	F. Blass and A. Debrunner, *Grammatik des neutestamentlichen Griechisch*[8], Göttingen 1949.	*NTG*	L. Radermacher, *Neutestamentliche Grammatik,* Tübingen 1925.
FGrHist	F. Jacoby, *Die Fragmente der griechischen Historiker,* Leiden 1923.	*RAC*	*Reallexikon für Antike und Christentum,* Stuttgart
G	W. W. Goodwin, *A Greek grammar*[2], London 1894.	*SVF*	H. von Arnim, *Stoicorum Veterum Fragmenta,* Leipzig 1903–24 (reprint Stuttgart 1964)
GMT	W. W. Goodwin, *Syntax of the moods and tenses of the Greek verb,* London 1897.	WS	H. Weir Smyth, *Greek grammar*[2], Cambridge, Mass. 1956.
Inscr. Olb	T. N. Knipovič and E. I. Levi, *Inscriptiones Olbiae,* Leningrad 1968.		

INTRODUCTION

1. DIO'S WORLD

Of the three speeches in this volume, the work of the foremost Greek orator of the first century A.D., one (36, *Bor.*) was delivered in his native city, Prusa in the Roman province of Bithynia, one (12, *Ol.*) at the great Hellenic religious centre of Olympia, and one (7, *Eub.*) probably, though not certainly, in Rome (see on 7.145). This neatly symbolizes the three loyalties that Dio, like Plutarch and many others of his contemporaries, felt and reconciled. To his native city, he owed the duties of advice and generous use of his means and abilities for the public good; to Hellas at large the duty to proclaim its values and nurture its pride, even in its subjection to Rome; and to the Romans, the duties of a client and an educator. Inseparable from these, there was for Dio – as, again, for Plutarch – an obligation often felt to address all his audiences in a philosophical mode, imparting moral and theological doctrines of universal concern and relevance.

In all this, Dio is typical of the Greek men of letters who practised in the world of the Roman Empire, though not all, of course, shared his moral seriousness. They addressed themselves both to Greek and to Roman audiences. This had been going on for a long time. Since the second century B.C., it had been common ground that Greek was a necessary part of the education of Romans of standing. As patrons and figures of power, such people naturally became the addressees of Greek poets, philosophers, and historians. Indeed, many of them (like Dio's Stoic mentor, Musonius Rufus) themselves wrote in Greek as well as in Latin. The literature of the Empire is thus bilingual: Dio belongs to the same literary culture not only as Plutarch, but as Pliny and Tacitus.[1]

It is important to keep in mind that, on the Greek side, this culture expressed itself, both linguistically and in choice of subjects, in very classical terms. At least since the time of Dionysius of Halicarnassus, who taught rhetoric and wrote history at Rome under Augustus, the

---

[1] This perspective is now clearly seen in the synthesis by A. Dihle, *Die griechische und lateinische Literatur der Kaiserzeit* (Munich 1989; Eng. translation in preparation).

principal vehicle in which Hellenic *paideia* was conveyed was a studied reproduction of the language and style of the Attic orators, historians, and philosophers of the fifth and fourth centuries. In varying degrees, most of the Greek authors of the following period tried to write like Xenophon, Plato, Demosthenes, or Thucydides, while Homer and classical drama were assumed to be 'what every schoolboy knows'. Dio is one of the closer followers of classical models – very different in this from Plutarch – and he clearly had a marvellous ear for the cadences and idioms of fourth-century prose. It is entirely characteristic that he is supposed to have taken two books only on his wanderings: Plato's *Phaedo* and Demosthenes' *On the false embassy*. In fact his debt to other works of Plato – especially *Republic* and *Laws* – and to Xenophon is more conspicuous; but the story is well invented none the less, and much in the taste of the sophists of the second century, of whose linguistic purism Dio is, in some ways, a precursor. Dio also quotes the poets – we shall hear him on Homer and Euripides – but not more recent ones. In his only extant work that deals with rhetorical teaching (*Or.* 18), he emphasizes Xenophon, and only very tentatively suggests some modern orators for study 'because we are not enslaved in our judgement before we approach them'. This is odd, and stands out as something controversial.

This use of an ancient idiom, removed from ordinary speech and to some extent also from the speech of the cultured in academic contexts, did not prevent these writers from presenting moral and social lessons appropriate to their own time. Archaism is as old as Greek literature, and was never in itself a bar to profundity or originality of thought. For Dio and his classicizing or archaizing contemporaries, some 'dressing up' of contemporary things was demanded, as it were, by the genre-rules: Roman governors were 'satraps', the emperor *basileus* with overtones of the Persian monarchy. But Dio, like most of his fellow orators, was involved in local and sometimes in imperial affairs, and was as acutely conscious as, say, Seneca or Tacitus, of the moral, political, and ideological issues of the age.

Yet 'Longinus' – probably Dio's contemporary, and certainly a sharer of his broadly Stoic philosophy – complains of the 'cosmic dearth' of any kind of literature that he could call 'sublime'.[2] And he was surely

---

[2] *De sublimitate* 44.

right. It is in the calmer reaches of humour, epideictic, and *belles lettres*, that this period excels. Dio himself, when he is serious and intense, is an exception; there are parts of our *Olympicus* and *Borystheniticus* that 'Longinus' could easily have acclaimed as ὑψηλά, both for the grandeur of the subject and the Platonic eloquence of the language.

2. DIO'S LIFE

Who was this Dio? He appears in history, apart from his own works and texts derived from them, in a short exchange of letters between Pliny, when he was governor of Bithynia, and Trajan, written in A.D. 110–11 (*Epist.* 10.81–2). Cocceianus Dio, a prominent citizen of Prusa – modern Broussa, a less important place in ancient times than later – has been accused by a political opponent of allowing the graves of his wife and son to be sited in the same building as a statue of Trajan. The accuser wishes to get Dio convicted of *maiestas*. Trajan very reasonably observes that Pliny need not have hesitated: it was an invidious and provocative charge, which it would be discreditable to admit. Dio was perfectly willing to have the accounts of the public works he had undertaken examined; his enemy's political manoeuvre should be left to fail.

At this time, Dio was quite elderly; he had long resumed the public career in his own city which his background called for, but which had been interrupted by the long exile which coloured all his subsequent life and literary career.

The date of his birth is not known; estimates vary between A.D. 40 and A.D. 60, the earlier part of that period being slightly more probable. His grandfather was a Roman citizen (*Or.* 41.5) and his own citizenship probably derived from his family. The name *Cocceianus* implies a connection with one of the Coccei, but, though he claimed friendship with Nerva, it need not be from this that the name, or the citizenship, derived. In any case, he was a prominent and reasonably wealthy member of the ruling élite of Prusa – his father and grandfather had presided in its βουλή – and he never relinquished his obligations to the city. He also had an inheritance of culture. He tells us (46.3) that his maternal grandfather, having lost one fortune on public benefactions (εἰς φιλοτιμίαν), acquired a new one ἀπὸ παιδείας καὶ παρὰ τῶν αὐτοκρατόρων, 'from culture and from the emperors'. Imperial favour, it seems, was conjoined with a reputation as a teacher, orator, or philosopher; it is difficult to be precise. That philosophical interests could well have formed part of Dio's background is important to notice. He was certainly influenced by the Roman Stoic, C. Musonius Rufus,[3] who was exiled under Nero, and the likeliest period for Dio to have had contact with him is the late sixties. All this is typical of his age and class: local wealth, elaborate education, literary success, a client relationship with influential Romans.

The circumstances of Dio's exile are not clear. Domitian, probably early in his reign (perhaps in 82), banished him from Italy and Bithynia. Dio (13.1) tells us that his crime was friendship with a great noble who was disgraced: the common conjecture is that it was Flavius Sabinus, Domitian's cousin.[4] We shall see in the story of the hunters of Euboea (7.11–12) how the fall of a great man ruined his dependants all down the line to the peasant farmer or herdsman: Dio may well have his own experience in mind in creating this story. Banishment lasted until Domitian's death: according to Philostratus (*VS* 488) he was actually with Roman troops when news came of the emperor's murder, and he checked their disorder by his eloquence, like Odysseus casting off his rags and appearing in his true person. Like Pliny and Tacitus, and perhaps with better reason, he could praise the *felicitas temporum* of the new régime.

Yet, in some way, the exile was crucial to Dio's career and literary development. Its effect has been the main subject of discussion about his life since ancient times. Its importance was emphasised especially by the Christian moralist Synesius of Cyrene, writing in the early fifth century. Synesius admired Dio;[5] he knew and approved the nickname χρυσόστομος, 'golden tongue', which had become attached to him, for his fluent eloquence.[6] He also disapproved of the way in which

[3] See A. C. van Geytenbeek, *Musonius Rufus* (Assen 1963) 14–15.

[4] Cf. Suet. *Dom.* 10.4. But note that another victim was a Salvius Cocceianus, a relative of Otho.

[5] Synesius' *Dio* is reprinted in von Arnim, de Budé, and the Loeb Dio (vol. v). Critical edition by N. Terzaghi (Rome 1944); commentary by H. Treu (Texte und Untersuchungen 71 (1958)).

[6] See Menander Rhetor 390.1 Spengel, with Russell–Wilson (1981) *ad loc.* *Fluency* seems important: cf. Cicero's characterization of Aristotle (in his exoteric works), *aureum fundens flumen orationis* (*Ac.* 2.110). Malice later made out that Dio's nickname was a euphemism to indicate his bad breath (Arethas: Loeb Dio, vol. v p. 414).

Philostratus, the author of *Lives of the sophists*, had included Dio among his subjects. Philostratus, he thought, had failed to see that Dio's experiences in exile had converted him from 'sophistic' to 'philosophy'. In Synesius' view, the exile was decisive. He noted that the titles of some speeches included the words 'Before exile' or 'After exile', and he thought that editors should make this distinction for them all. In his earlier days, according to Synesius, Dio wrote specifically 'sophistic' pieces, like the *Encomium of the parrot* or the ecphrasis of Tempe or the statue of Memnon; he also attacked philosophers in polemical works. None of the pieces Synesius quotes survives, and we are thus dependent on him for an estimate of their 'sophistic' character (Tempe, in particular, was a standard theme; it is possible that Aelian, *VH* 3.1 depends in some way on Dio). It is also clear that his interpretation of the πρὸς Μουσώνιον as a serious polemic against the Stoic moralist was controversial. In any case, the 'conversion' theory of Dio's development, which owes its origin to Synesius, has dominated discussion ever since. It is the basis of most authoritative accounts of his career, and especially von Arnim's. It was elegantly and modestly stated by Henri Weil (Clerc (1915) 195): 'un bel esprit ambulant, il devint un sermonneur ambulant'.[7] But it is of course largely speculative and certainly too simple. Without going as far as Moles ((1978) 100) and calling the 'conversion' a 'fraud', it is right to have great reservations.[8]

The basis of the theory is what Dio says in *Or.* 13, a speech delivered in Athens at an unknown date. Here Dio expounds what he says was his reaction to the sentence of exile. It was to review mythical and historical *exempla* – Odysseus, Orestes, the advice of Apollo to Croesus – and to ask the Delphic oracle what he should do. He was told to go on doing what he was doing 'till he came to the ends of the earth'. So he put on poor clothes, 'chastened' himself (κολάσας ἐμαυτόν) and went on his wanderings. Some of those he met called him a beggar or a vagrant, some a philosopher. These would ask him 'what seemed to him good or evil', and he found himself forced to answer them. He thus became a sort of Socrates.

If we can take this literally, then Dio's moral conscience was first

---

[7] See also, e.g., S. Dill, *Roman society from Nero to Marcus Aurelius* (London 1904; repr. N.Y. 1957) 334–83; A. D. Nock, *Conversion* (Oxford 1933) 173.

[8] So also Desideri (1978) who rightly emphasizes the continuity in Dio's career.

aroused at this time. But the signs of a studied performance and the adoption of a recognized pose are evident. The application to Delphi is modelled on Socrates; and the rest of the speech in which this story is told is heavily indebted to the Socratic tradition, especially Plato's *Apology* and *Clitophon*. It is perhaps close to the truth to say that he used his exile (which was after all no disgrace) to refashion his literary career, using his great gifts of classical eloquence and his thorough training in λόγοι to convey a morally acceptable message to the educated in every city he visited. The vagrancy of his exile is the setting of many pieces – our *Eub.* and *Bor.* among them – and it is clear that, even after his return home, Dio maintained the same *persona* of the visiting preacher, distinct in appearance and message from the σοφισταί he attacks: witness especially the *prolalia* of *Ol.*, which is certainly 'post-exilic'. Travelling speakers and teachers were a common phenomenon in the Roman world, and the spectrum of their interests was wide, from declaimers to moralists and professional philosophers. Their audiences too were various; Dio at least addressed himself strictly to the well-educated, who would be attracted by his classicizing language, and could understand it. When we hear him addressing the crowd at Olympia on theology, we think of St Paul on the Areopagus, a generation before. When we read his moral and social advice in *Eub.*, we think of the rich Cypriot, Demonax, Dio's close contemporary, who gave up wealth to be a moral teacher, and whose life by Lucian throws so much light on the culture to which Dio belonged.[9]

Dio is often regarded as a Cynic, on the ground that he used Diogenes as a model, and that his discourses on kingship have many Cynic features (Moles (1978) 94). But his philosophical beliefs were mainly Stoic, as our three speeches clearly show; and, though he adopted something of the simplicity and homeliness of the Cynic preacher, there was clearly a difference between him and the 'barking dogs' like Demetrius.[10] His rags, his beard, and his vehemence were all, we may suspect, well under control.

For most of the corpus, we have no clear evidence of date.[11] Perhaps

---

[9] The historical validity of Lucian's *Demonax* is widely accepted, even by Anderson (1976) 64–6; see also Jones (1986) 90–98.

[10] On Demetrius and other Cynics, see M. Billerbeck, *Der Kyniker Demetrius* (Leiden 1979) and 'La réception du cynisme à Rome', *A.C.* 51 (1982) 151–73. Dio sometimes distances himself from the Cynics (*Or.* 34.2).

[11] Jones (1978) 133ff. offers a speculative chronology.

this does not matter very much. If the foregoing considerations are just, and Dio's attitudes and culture were formed in his youth, and merely modified and exploited by exile and subsequent fame, 'Before exile' and 'After exile' would not be as meaningful as Synesius hoped.

3. DIO'S WORKS

The corpus of Dio's works, as we have it, consists of about 80 pieces. It lacks, as we have seen, some that were known to Synesius; and his important historical and geographical work, *Getica*, is also lost.[12] On the other hand, we have many pieces which Synesius does not mention, and the collection undoubtedly includes some *spuria*. Photius' ninth-century list, however, is precisely what we have, though in an order distinct from that of most of our manuscripts and of modern printed editions. Only the sixteenth-century Meermannianus – an important witness despite its late date – has Photius' order (see below p. 24). But this order does make some sense, and indicates some editorial policy. There seem to have been five main groups:

(i) speeches on kingship, addressed to Trajan (*Or.* 1–4), with the curious 'Libyan myth' (*Or.* 5) which belongs with them;

(ii) pieces featuring the Cynic Diogenes, who, with Socrates and Odysseus, was a rôle-model for Dio in his wanderings (*Or.* 6, 8–10);

(iii) speeches believed to have been delivered elsewhere than in Bithynia: *Or.* 11–13, 7, 31–7. This is a very miscellaneous collection; and the place of 7 (*Eub.*) was clearly in dispute (in some MSS it comes after 6, in others near the end, after 77/8);

(iv) speeches delivered in Bithynia, *Or.* 38–51;

(v) a mixed bag (52–80, 14–30) including some obituary encomia (*Melancomas, Charidemus*) and a large number of short dialogues and essays, some plainly incomplete.

This classification of course gives a very imperfect view of Dio's production. Our three speeches, different as they are from one another, all figure in group (iii); nor is any distinction made between Dio's politi-

---

[12] On *Getica*, see von Arnim's edition (1896) II iv–ix; he also lists the lost works with the evidence for them. Photius' evidence (with Synesius' and Arethas') is reprinted in the editions (conveniently in Loeb, vol. v).

cal and moral discourses and those which have a more literary content. Yet these last are important: especially *Or.* 11 (*Troica*), which argues sophistically that Homer did not tell the truth about the Trojan War; *Or.* 52, a comparison between the treatments of the Philoctetes theme by the three great tragedians; and *Or.* 55, 57, 58 all on matters concerned with Homer. The collectors of the corpus evidently had many problems, not only the introduction of *spuria* (*Or.* 37 is certainly the work of Favorinus), but the existence of so many manifestly incomplete scraps. We must remember that most of the works really were speeches; very few have the form of written compositions, intended, like letters, for distant addressees, like most of the essays collected as Plutarch's *Moralia*. An exception, conspicuous for this reason, is *Or.* 18, in which Dio, in the rôle of a serious teacher of rhetoric, advises a Roman notable on a course of useful reading. *Eub.*, *Ol.*, and *Bor.* are all speeches; and, as we shall see, only *Bor.* is free of serious structural problems, strongly suggesting that our texts are an imperfect reproduction of what Dio said. He was famous as an improviser; improvisation in classical style and language, without putting a foot wrong in grammar, syntax, or word-choice, was a much admired skill; and, though no doubt much was done before every performance by way of private μελέτη, including writing up special passages, we should imagine him as speaking largely impromptu. The resulting texts – perhaps in part the product of note-taking by the audience – often have a spontaneity which compensates the reader for the failures in coherence which he is all too likely to notice.

4. *EUBOICUS*

Our first speech, *Eub.* (= *Or.* 7), is the longest in the whole corpus. It is also the best known, because of the obvious charm and interest of the narrative of Dio's shipwreck (§§1–80). But was he really shipwrecked on Euboea, and did he really meet these hunters? Von Arnim's answer, 'possibly', is as far as one can go. An important consideration is the repeated reflection of the wanderings of Odysseus: also shipwrecked, also concerned with killing a stag (*Od.* 10), also entertained by humble but hospitable people (Eumaeus). Odysseus was certainly one of Dio's rôles (Jones (1978) 46–51), and both his wisdom and his mendicancy were used as models by the Cynics. The setting seems to be the exile (despite the alleged σπουδή, 'urgent business' (§6); at any rate the introduction does not exclude an exile setting, see note on §1), and we may compare the more obviously fictitious episode related in *Or.* 1.50–84 where Dio loses his way on the road to Olympia and encounters a Doric-speaking prophetess, who foretells his future and tells a story of Heracles. What kernel of real experience there was does not much matter; the many parallels that can be adduced (Hunter (1983) 66–7, Anderson (1976) 94–8) between this narrative and the pastoral romance of Longus or Lucian's treatment of Anacharsis or Polyphemus and Galatea cannot demonstrate that the whole thing is fiction.[13] Nor is it particularly helpful to stress the influence of New Comedy (Highet (1973)) or to try to determine the genre of this narrative in relation to the novel. What we have here is a carefully-structured narrative, using many pastoral topics (note especially the culture-shock of the country-man in town: cf. Virgil, *Ecl.* 1 and Calpurnius Siculus, *Ecl.* 7) but directed at specific moral ends. Naturally we think of Theocritus, and of Longus – and of Rousseau[14] or *Paul et Virginie*, and again of parts of *I Promessi Sposi* – but the essential point is the professed lesson: that poverty is no bar to hospitality, nor, in general, to a good and happy life.

The narrative itself includes a story within the story: the hunter's account (§§22–63) of his earlier visit to the neighbouring city and the debate in the assembly concerning his alleged failure to pay his rent. This of course points the contrast between rural honesty and urban chicanery; but the story is developed and enlarged for its own sake – it has potentialities for humour and paradox – because Dio and his audience knew their classical orators and enjoyed a parody which lightly mocked the teaching of the rhetorical schools. There are resemblances also to some famous fictitious debates: Euripides, *Orestes* 867–952 and Menander, *Sicyonius* 169–271 (Highet (1973) 35–40).

The second part of the speech (§§81–152) begins by asserting that the preceding part was not a digression, but was undertaken as an illustration of the thesis that the poor can live as well as, or better than, the rich, especially in their readiness and ability to succour strangers. This discourse is, formally, a discussion of a text from Euripides' *Electra* (424–31: see on §82) which it seeks to refute. Rhetors would call this an

---

[13] E.g. Dio 65 ~ Longus 3.8.2; 71 ~ Longus 3.39.2; 24 ~ Lucian, *Anacharsis* 23; 53 ~ Lucian, *Dial. deorum* 10(4).2.

[14] F. Boll, 'Hellenismus und Orient', in *Kleine Schriften* (1950) 296.

ἀνασκευή, 'demolition'; it was a recognized exercise.[15] It is thus clear that the narrative, as we have it, cannot have been the beginning of the original speech. Von Arnim (1891) clearly showed that some kind of *propositio* or prooemium must have preceded it, and it is idle to fight against this conclusion.

In §§81–102, Dio addresses himself fairly steadily to this theme. He draws mainly on Homer (§§83–96), but comes back to his text from Euripides in §102. This use of poetical texts to introduce moral precepts is characteristic of the culture of the age; one does not teach literature without using it to teach about life. Indeed, the practice goes back to classical times. Dio can appeal (§102) to the usage of Cleanthes (not mentioned by name, but clearly intended) but there are many earlier instances, notably Socrates' discussion of some lines of Simonides in Plato's *Protagoras* (339Aff.). The best extant collection of such material is Plutarch's *De audiendis poetis*, written within a few years of these speeches of Dio's; but it is written from a Platonist and not a Stoic point of view, and its aim is to offer justifications of the classical texts used in education, whereas Dio is prepared to argue against what the poets say. This may seem an unexpected contrast, because it is the Stoic tradition to allegorize and justify, and the Platonic (based on the *Republic*) to condemn – and yet it is Plutarch who justifies and Dio who condemns. The reason is that Dio takes the stance of a philosopher, distancing himself from poets and sophists, whereas Plutarch takes that of an educator determined to use poetry as preparation for philosophy. Plutarch addresses the young through their teachers; Dio the grown men who need to be disturbed or reformed. At the same time, there is a lighter element in all this. As we see from Dio's other works (especially the 'Trojan speech' (11), in which he gratifies the citizens of Ilion by rejecting most of Homer's version of the Trojan War), he and his audiences enjoyed paradoxical revaluations of the classics, especially Homer, whom they all knew best. It is difficult to get the balance between seriousness and fun quite right; but, in *Eub.* at least, straight-

---

[15] ἀνασκευή, 'destructive analysis' : e.g. Aphthonius, *Progymnasmata* 5; D. L. Clark, *Rhetoric in Greco-Roman education* (N.Y. 1957) 190–2. On Dio's use of the technique in *Or.* 11, see W. Kroll, *Rh. Mus.* 70 (1915) 607–10, with useful general remarks.

forward moral concern seems to predominate. In any case, an element of 'play' is perfectly compatible with an earnestness of purpose.

In §103, Dio again looks back at his argument. His manner of doing so – 'so much for the life of farmers, hunters, and shepherds' – is not very apt as a summary of §§1–80, though the characters of the story were once shepherds and are now subsistence farmers and hunters. Still less is it appropriate to §§81–102. A transition is now made, clumsily enough, to a discussion of acceptable and unacceptable occupations for the urban poor. How can they be guided to a life as satisfactory as that of their rustic counterparts? This discussion fills the rest of the speech as we have it (§§105–52). Dio proves vague on what trades are acceptable – they are defined negatively (§112) as not involving an idle or unhealthy life – and confines himself to the point that there is nothing to be ashamed about in honest physical labour (§§114–16). It is only when he comes to list the unacceptable that his writing becomes energetic and colourful, in condemning all the arts of ornament (§§117–18), acting and dancing (§§119–22), auctioneers and advocates (§123). These are easy targets: a long moralizing tradition, especially among Stoics, as well as much popular prejudice, lies behind this list (Brunt (1973)).[16]

At this point, Dio pulls himself up yet again. He disclaims the purpose of constructing an ideal city, which his recent proposals may have suggested. This is not a new *Republic* or *Laws*. The disclaimer in fact advertises the *mimesis* of Plato which is evident in many details of the language, and which the connoisseurs in the audience will have savoured. He repeats instead that the question at issue is the proper employment of people of modest means. Anything that contributes to this, even if it involves following a fresh trail, is appropriate to a philosophical discussion. This promises more than what follows: for what we have (§§133–52) is simply a vigorous, imaginatively written attack on prostitution, adultery, and finally, and with most insistence, homosexuality. The speech ends abruptly on this satirical and aggres-

---

[16] Note especially Cic. *De officiis* 1.150–1, who lists *portitores*, *faeneratores*, all trade (except on a very large scale), and all the arts that minister to pleasure, as unsuitable for the free citizen. He is of course concerned with the well-to-do, not with Dio's urban poor.

sive note. We began in the world of Theocritus; we end in the world of Juvenal.

It is very hard to believe that all this adds up to a speech actually delivered on some one occasion. It is not only very long (though not too long for a single performance by the standard, say, of Aelius Aristides) but it has much less unity than *Bor.* or *Ol.* or many of Dio's other pieces. Moreover, von Arnim's conclusion (1891) is surely right in essence: it is actually incomplete, both beginning and end being lost. One has the impression too that some of the intervening sections have been developed to excessive length, whereas other topics have been omitted. We have to remember both Dio's fame as an improviser, and his self-representation as a mere talker, an ἀδολέσχης, because that is what philosophers in the Socratic tradition were supposed to be. The rigid limits and structures imposed by the law courts and the rhetoricians were alien both to his talents and to his professed stance and technique. Those who edited his speeches may have had to combine versions originating in different performances. The polish and elegance of the narrative, in particular, suggest that it was worked up for its own intrinsic interest; and it has been thought that Philostratus knew it on its own, since he took *Eub.*, like the *Encomium of the parrot*, as 'sophistic' and not serious in content (*VS* 487). Synesius' critique, on the other hand, assumes the whole speech, or something very like it. 'If you deny the seriousness of *The Euboean*', he writes,

it would be difficult to regard any of Dio's works as philosophical.[17]

This speech, he continues,

is a sketch of the happy life, a text of great value for rich and poor alike. It deflates the swelling pride of wealth by showing the happiness of the opposite state, and lifts the dejection of poverty, rescuing it from humiliation, first, by a narrative that charms every ear and might have persuaded Xerxes that a hunter in the mountains of Euboea, eating his millet, was happier than he, and, secondly, by excellent moral precepts, which will stop anyone feeling ashamed of poverty even if he cannot avoid it.

[17] *Dio* 2, 38c. Text in von Arnim II 316.25, Loeb v 576.

Synesius, of course, is pleading a case; but he is quite right to insist that the function of the narrative is moral. The virtue of the hunters' rural life lies in its conformity to nature and its tendency to make people kindly, honest, and faithful. In this sense, the two halves of the extant speech complement each other; and the debate in the Euboean city, with its emphasis on corruption, depopulation, and irresponsibility, anticipates something of the corruption of urban life which the 'precepts' which follow endeavour to redress. It would, however, be unsafe to infer from this observation that the 'debate' was part of the original plan, or indeed to conjecture by what stages the speech has come to be in its present form. Place and occasion are also unknowable; it is clearly a great city, and the most obvious venue – in view especially of the remarks on sexual morality at the end – is Rome itself.[18]

This speech has often been used as evidence for economic and social conditions in Euboea, or in Greece generally.[19] It is true (see note on §37) that the proposals made in the fictitious assembly are very like schemes for the settlement of land and the recovery of rural prosperity which were in vogue under Nerva and Trajan. Dio very likely has this in mind; but much of his description of country life, and of the city, is timeless and conventional. What he says of urban vices in the second part of the speech is historical evidence to the same extent that Lucian or Juvenal may be so used, not more. Nevertheless, with due allowance made for the large literary element in a speech full of mimesis of Plato and the orators, we can still hear the voice of the preacher directing himself to contemporary evils and propounding solutions which may have a political as well as a moral ring. Dio was a political animal,[20] and even when he seems to be romancing there may be more in it than meets the eye.

---

[18] Von Arnim (1898) 457; H. Fuchs, *Der geistige Gegenstand gegen Rom* (Berlin 1938) 53; Brunt (1973) 16 thinks the rejection of music and dancing (§§118–22) also suggests Rome. But §122, which refers to 'persons who will blame us because we are finding fault with what is most important among the Greeks', is not decisive evidence against a Greek city audience. See comm. on 7.104, 106, 122.

[19] See e.g. A. A. Larsen, *Economic survey of ancient Rome*, ed. T. Frank (1938) IV 479ff.; E. Meyer, *Kleine Schriften* I 164–8.

[20] This is, rightly, a major theme of Desideri (1978).

5. *OLYMPICUS*

Ol. was, for Wilamowitz (1928) 382, 'the most beautiful speech, to which one is always glad to return'. It is indeed a splendid *tour de force*, with some of Dio's finest writing. *Eub.* showed us Dio as a social moralist, advocate of the simple life and castigator of vice. In *Ol.* he is a religious teacher, addressing the crowd at Olympia, expounding the greatness of Zeus, and justifying Phidias' sculptural expression of divine grandeur and clemency. And here too there are political overtones: Dio's Stoic assertion of divine providence implies a recognition of the world-order established on earth by the empire.

The structure of the main argument is based on the tradition, largely Stoic and popular with Roman thinkers (see notes on §§39–48), of a 'theology in three parts' (*theologia tripertita*), in which human attempts to comprehend and express the power of god are classified under three heads: the teaching of poets, of lawgivers, and of philosophers. But Dio does not simply follow this through. He says little of philosophers, but much of artists: and he combines the theme with the profounder one of our innate sense of god, the basis of all belief, which the teachers merely interpret. This is deep matter for a festival audience; to prepare the way, Dio offers an elaborate *prolalia* in which he contrasts himself, the drab and unpersuasive philosophic owl, with the peacock sophists; and he does this in a highly sophistic way. It is indeed a *tour de force*.

It was a classical tradition that famous orators should speak at the great festivals. Gorgias, Hippias and Lysias all did so. Gorgias and Lysias had a political theme, Hellenic unity in the face of outside threats. Dio's discourse is clearly not in this line: it has been described as a 'hymn' to Olympian Zeus (Burgess (1902) 178), foreshadowing the prose hymns of Aristides, and akin to the festival speeches for which Menander Rhetor later prescribed. This would no doubt also be in itself nothing very original. Philostratus' account of the visit of Apollonius of Tyana to Olympia (*VA* 4.27–31), even if wholly fictitious, contains a revealing conversation, in which a young man invites Apollonius to attend a recitation of his λόγος εἰς τὸν Δία, which dealt with 'seasons, things on the earth and over the earth, winds, and stars'. Apollonius flattens the young encomiast by eliciting from him that he has not written a speech on his own father, because he respected him too much: how then could he dare to write in praise of Zeus? Dio goes deeper. His

Stoic conviction of the providential government of the world makes him portray Zeus in effect as the One God and sole creator; but his perception that the quality of divine governance involves mercy and clemency leads him to represent Phidias as presenting a worthier Zeus than Homer, for whom the god was primarily a god of storm and battle. Moreover the most important part of the speech, Phidias' defence, raises large questions of aesthetics, in particular the relation between visual and verbal arts.

The speech was, it is evident, delivered within sight of the great statue of Zeus. We may again think of Philostratus' Apollonius (*VA* 4.28): when he looked at the statue he said Ἀγαθὲ Ζεῦ, σὺ γὰρ οὕτω τι ἀγαθός, ὡς καὶ σαυτοῦ κοινωνῆσαι τοῖς ἀνθρώποις, 'O good Zeus, thou art so good as even to share thyself with men.' This is presumably an echo of the Platonic cliché (*Timaeus* 29E) that God, being ἀγαθός, does not grudge good things to any being; but it is also perhaps an interpretation of the statue as expressing the god's φιλανθρωπία. If that is so, it is relevent to Dio's interpretation.

The statue was overwhelming: a seated figure on a throne, about forty feet high, all ivory and gold (the core was hardwood), coloured and carved with all manner of myths and patterns. Coins and Pausanias' description (5.11) give us a general idea. On Zeus's right hand stood a gold and ivory figure of Victory, in his left was a sceptre with an eagle on it. Shoes and himation were of gold; the throne was covered with representations of myth. Awe and amazement would seem the natural reaction; but the emotions expressed by critics and philosophers vary somewhat. For some (Sen. *Contr.* 10.5.8) Phidias fashioned the Thunderer; Epictetus (2.8.25) saw in the fixed stare of the eyes the expression of the irreversible decisions of Zeus, which never deceive and cannot be changed; but in several texts *pulchritudo* is the key word (Quintilian 12.10.9, Plin. *NH* 36.18) and this suggests something gentler and less harsh (Pollitt (1974) 426). Dio, and perhaps Philostratus, seem specially impressed by the sense of fatherhood and beneficence which the work evoked.

No doubt many sermons were preached around this statue (cf. Clerc (1915) 222); two themes were particularly important. One – which is prominent in Dio – was the story that Phidias tried to reproduce the effect of Homer's lines about Zeus's 'nod' (*Il.* 1.528–30: see note on §26). The other was the notion that Phidias had in mind a perfect image of beauty (*species pulchritudinis eximia quaedam*) by which he guided his hand; this was, says Cicero (*Orator* 9–10), what Plato called the idea of beauty. This interpretation was common in Neoplatonists – Plotinus (5.8.1) says that Phidias 'made his Zeus on no sensible model, but by conceiving what Zeus would be like if he wished to appear to us in visible form' – and was influential in Renaissance theory. It was not available to the Stoic Dio, though he comes near to it (§70) when he makes Phidias stress the difficulty of making the εἰκών remain in the craftsman's mind at the time he is working on the hard and difficult stone.

The date of *Ol.* has been much discussed: the three possible Olympiads – 97, 101, 105 – have all had advocates.[21] Of these 97 seems the least likely: the timetable of Dio's movements in the year after Domitian's death (see notes on §§16–20, and on 36.1) hardly allows for him to be at Olympia for the festival. But the references in §§16–20 to preparations for war would apply to either of the other dates, since Trajan's first attack on Dacia was in 101/2, the second in 105/6. It is best to leave the question open. It is certainly unsafe to draw an inference from *Or.* 1.52ff., where Dio (speaking probably in 100) tells a story about his getting lost on the way to Olympia: his wanderings may have taken him there more than once.

Analysis[22]

Close analysis of the *prolalia* (§§1–16, see notes) is difficult. Its colourful self-presentation, however, makes a vivid impression. No doubt Dio's appearance, the studied scruffiness of the hairy, ill-clad figure, itself made the main point; the difference between the philosophers, in the tradition of Socrates and the Cynics, and the elegant and vain sophists whom the audience expected. The content of the passage, too, prepares the hearer for serious discourse, and its skill and versatility foreshadow the bravura and exuberance of Phidias' speech. None the less, the *prolalia* has a certain independence. It could be reused; *Or.* 72, a piece preserved on its own, is very like it (see note on 12.1–16).

---

[21] E.g. Pohlenz, W. Schmid, and Döring (1979) accept 97; von Arnim, Otto Kern, M. Szarmach are for 105; for 101, see especially Jones (1978) 53.

[22] Brief analysis in Kennedy (1972) 575–8.

The specific introduction (§§16–20) follows. Dio has returned from a distant journey. He has witnessed the preparations for a war of conquest, and has also seen the defenders preparing to fight for freedom. He has put his religious duty, the fulfilment of a vow, above curiosity and other interests. Things divine are more urgent than things human; instead of talking about his travels and the lands and peoples he has visited, he proposes to speak of Zeus, in whose presence he and his audience stand. But what is the really appropriate way of doing this (§§23–6)? Should he deliver a hymn like Hesiod's? Or merely admire the cult and art, especially the statue which Phidias made in rivalry with Homer? Or – and this is clearly the real *propositio* – should we inquire how the human mind came to form a conception of the divine at all, and concentrate wholly on this philosophical theme, except of course for paying due attention to the athletics (see note on §26)?

Mankind has in fact an innate and universal understanding that there is a divine ruler of the kosmos. Early man was closer to him than we are, and saw the universe as a temple in which god's mysteries were revealed. Even animals share this vision; how foolish are the Epicureans who shut their eyes and ears to it (§§26–37)!

It is when we try to relate this so far coherent statement to what follows that we begin to see difficulties. The attack on the Epicureans is signalled as a 'digression' (§38), and Dio turns from it, to what he describes as a 'second' source (πηγή, §39) of religion. This is 'that which is "acquired" by argument or myth or habit', whether from anonymous teachers or named ones: some such 'acquisitions' are voluntary (those derived from the poets), others obligatory (the instruction of lawgivers). They all presuppose our innate understanding; and as this is related to our natural affection and respect for parents, it is probable (and nice to believe) that the poets' approach preceded that of the lawgivers. It is, presumably, more in accordance with our rational nature to absorb the principles of belief with pleasure than to have them hammered into us. The implication of this – like that of the earlier statement that primitive men were closer to god – is that there was a golden age, and there has been a decline. At §44, however, Dio seems to adopt a different scheme. Instead of (A) natural and (B) acquired sources of religion (subdivided into two), we find apparently a list of four sources: *(a)* natural, *(b)* poetical, *(c)* legal, and *(d)* artistic. This last is of course to be the main subject, and it is a wholly reasonable addition to the 'acquired' sources. But it is puzzling then to find (§47) that there is another 'fourth', and superior, contributor, the philosopher, who is apparently to be added to the three interpreters identified with the poets, lawgivers, and artists, making now *four* sub-classes under (B) in the original classification. This particular awkwardness can be removed by von Arnim's deletion of δίχα γε; but the more serious difficulty remains that the philosopher, barely mentioned, fades out of sight almost at once. The promise (§48) to bring forward one example of each class (barring the lawgiver) is not fulfilled. Only the sculptor Phidias really appears, though his discussion of Homer indirectly fulfils the requirement of bringing forward a poet. The view (Pohlenz (1949), Pépin (1958)) that Dio means us to identify the philosopher's contribution with our innate conception of a paternal god can hardly be right: on any reading of §47, the philosopher is an 'interpreter' (ἑρμηνεύς), and his function must therefore be to clarify and expound the basic instinct; he does not give it us in the first place. It is possible to speculate about what Dio's philosopher would have offered if he had been allowed to appear: probably a Stoic exposition of the 'creative fire' and the workings of providence, on the line of Cleanthes' *Hymn to Zeus* and Dio's own account in *Bor.*

It seems difficult to avoid the conclusion that the transition from the account of natural religion to the episode of Phidias' imagined trial is confused, either because Dio did not trouble to integrate the various threads of his argument, or because we have a garbled version, perhaps containing elements from more than one performance. As in *Eub.*, it is the transitional passages that raise these nagging but perhaps trivial problems, whereas the main episodes are more coherent.

The 'trial' of Phidias contains some of the best and most suggestive writing in Dio. The accusation is that he represented Zeus in human form so marvellously that all mankind's concept of the god is thereby fixed for ever: was not this presumptuous (48–54)? His reply is that he found men's views already fixed by the poets (55–7); that the human form is not only the natural vehicle to express mind and intelligence but arouses in us feelings of affection and dependence which it is proper to feel towards the gods (58–61); that Homer was even more blatantly anthropomorphic, attributing all kinds of human feelings to the gods, and having at his command a much greater repertoire of words and devices to inspire whatever emotions he will (61–9), whereas the sculptor labours under many constraints in his material and conditions of work (70–2); and finally that Homer's god is one of power and battle, and his own one of Fatherhood and kindness (73–9). Only Zeus himself, he concludes, is competent to weld the elements into the marvels of the universe; he is the supreme craftsman (80–3). Dio's conclusion (84–5) surprises: first a résumé of the themes which have come up in the speech, then a striking prosopopoeia in which Zeus thanks the Greeks for his festival, but grieves to see the country's old age and squalor.

Ol. is Dio's most 'philosophical' speech, and it conveys clear lessons in theology and in aesthetics. It is a defence of anthropomorphic images, and an assertion of a predominantly Stoic view of the providential control of the universe. At the same time, it states important thoughts about the nature of art: that the artist forms an image in his mind, holds it there, and brings forth its reproduction in his medium; that the stone contains, potentially, the statue to come out of it (§44); and that the conditions of poetry and the visual arts are radically different. None of these ideas is new, and all have a long subsequent history. It is odd that Dio is so seldom mentioned by those who clearly shared these ideas. Whether Michelangelo was influenced by him has been debated (see note on §44), but remains unsure. In Lessing's *Laokoon*, which is largely concerned with the same issues, the story of Phidias' dependence on Homer is important; but it is not Dio but Valerius Maximus (3.7 ext. 4) whom Lessing cites as his authority. This is an illustration of the fact that Dio, unlike Plutarch or Seneca or Epictetus, never affected the main stream of European literary culture; his *Nachleben* indeed has never been thoroughly studied, but it is clearly much less rich than that of the other moralists of his age.

6. *BORYSTHENITICUS*

Unlike *Eub.* and *Ol.*, *Bor.* gives no immediate impression of incompleteness or incoherence. It is carefully structured in successive episodes, and its colourful diversity is subordinated to a single theme: harmony, good order, and regular and predictable change on earth as in heaven. The title under which it goes in our tradition includes the words 'which he read in his own city'. This could just be inference from the *post eventum* prophecy of safe return (probably from exile: see notes on §1) in §24, or from the use of a similar analogy between cosmic and human concord in *Or.* 40 (§§35–41), which was addressed to the citizens of Prusa some time after his return, to counsel peaceful relations with the neighbouring city of Apamea. More probably, it is independent information. In any case, it is significant for the interpretation of the speech that its audience is distinct from the fictional audience of Borysthenites whom Dio represents himself as addressing.

Analysis

(A) Dio recalls an occasion at Olbia, when he was walking outside the city by the Hypanis (Bug). He tells his audience all about this isolated Hellenic outpost, which he calls by its old name Borysthenes: its situation, its trade, its decline due to successive barbarian attacks, its present limited extent, far less than the traces of its ancient grandeur (§§1–6). He meets some of his Borysthenite friends, including the handsome young Callistratus, who rides up in full Scythian gear. To tease him – because Callistratus, like all his fellow citizens, is a devotee of Homer and a worshipper of Achilles, whose cult was important in all this region – Dio questions the superiority of Homer over other poets, and suggests that the couplet of Phocylides which asserts that 'a small city on a rock, well governed, is better than Nineveh in her folly' is more valuable than all the martial lays of the epic. Callistratus is not pleased, but agrees to a discussion of Phocylides. There had been a Scythian raid the day before, and the town was on alert; none the less there was an audience – under arms – ready to listen to Dio by the river. He suggests however (§16) that they should go into the city, on the plea that is would be easier to find a suitable auditorium there. Of course, it is also safer.

(B) So they go to the temple of Zeus (§17). The change of scene marks a new topic. This is a common dialogue technique – notably exploited by Plutarch in *De Pythiae oraculis* – and a reminder that this speech is, in effect, a dialogue, with the same kind of interplay of argument and character that we find in that genre. Dio is gratified by his bearded audience – only one man is clean-shaven, and he is unpopular as a collaborator with the Romans (see note on §17) – and proposes a discussion περὶ πόλεως, beginning with the definition of πόλις as a 'collection of men dwelling in the same place, administered by law'. He explains, in Stoic terms, that there is no completely good πόλις on earth, for it is only the city of the blessed gods in heaven that is free of strife;

human beings are, as it were, immature citizens of this city, like children in our earthly communities (§§10–23).

(C) At this point, there is an interruption. An elderly listener, later named as Hieroson (see note on §28), politely proposes, in view of the city's cultural starvation and his own love of Plato, that they should take advantage of Dio's visit (if the barbarians give them a little peace) by hearing his views, not on the earthly city, but on the heavenly one. Dio acquiesces (§28): as he would have done his best to fight the enemy with them, so he will now accede to their request, though he disclaims rivalry with Plato, despite Hieroson's compliments (§27) There follows an exposition of the Stoic concept of the kosmos as a community of gods and men, under law, in which Zeus, as the poets – Homer and Hesiod – dimly understood, is the father and king (§§29–38).

(D) But there is a further secret myth about the kingship of Zeus, which comes from the Magi, who learned it from Zoroaster. There are two parts to the 'barbaric song' as Dio apologetically calls it (§43, cf. §§42, 57). The first states that the movements of the universe are due to four Horses, who symbolize the elements: the Horse of Zeus, who is Fire; the Horse of Hera, who is air (HPA = AHP: see note on §45): the Horse of Poseidon (water); and the Horse of Hestia (earth). Generally, they pull the chariot in accord, all pivoting round the Horse of Hestia, who does not move; but periodically the Horses of Zeus and Poseidon get out of control, and subject Earth to alternate disasters by fire and flood, remembered in the Greek traditions of Phaethon and Deucalion. Many think these are arbitrary catastrophes, but that is not true, for they come about in accordance with the intention of the saviour and steersman of the universe (§§42–50).

And this is not all. There is another change in the Four Horses, which has much more awesome consequences. At certain long intervals, they are all melted into one like so many wax dolls, by the fire of the Horse of Zeus; and after this total absorption of everything into the pure flame, when the desire for creation arises again in what is now the pure intellect of the world, a new kosmos comes into being, fairer and brighter than the old; and its creator and father rejoices to behold it (§§50–60).

Such is Dio's speech to the Borysthenites. In §61, he returns abruptly to his present audience, and excuses his lofty flights of imagination on the ground that the Borysthenites expected them.

.

Each part of the speech raises questions – which are discussed as they arise in the Commentary – about the relationship of Dio's account to philosophical or religious speculation.

(i) How far is his description of Olbia to be believed? It is perhaps the most vivid account of such a city that we have, and the details (e.g. the risk of taking trees for ships as you sail in, §3) look like the genuine observation of an eyewitness. Archaeologists have generally trusted it, even when they are unable (as with the site of the temple of Zeus) to confirm it on the ground.

(ii) How far is his 'Magian' myth genuinely Iranian? Opinions have long been divided. At least since the work of Christoph Meiners in the eighteenth century, there have been powerful advocates of the view that Herodotus, Xenophon, Plato, and the Stoics account for the whole thing: the Persian setting is mere cosmetic colouring, like (e.g.) the references to the Magi in Plato's *Alcibiades* or the pseudo-Platonic *Axiochus*. But students of Mithraism have often been tempted to use Dio as a source, and have sought confirmation of his accuracy in the monuments: so especially the greatest Mithraic scholar of this century, Franz Cumont (see particularly *Les Mages hellénisés* (1938)). Scepticism however seems justified. Dio's periodic partial and total world-catastrophes cannot be reconciled with the Mithraic scheme of successive planetary ages, of which the sun (Apollo or Mithras) dominates the last. Not only classicists like Max Pohlenz (1949) II 454, but Mithraic experts like R. L. Gordon (1971) take a sceptical position. What needs to be explained then is Dio's curious insistence on the αὐθάδεια and ἀτοπία of his 'barbaric song'. The image of the chariot and the horses, essentially derived from Plato's *Phaedrus*, has clearly been coloured by reminiscences of Persian cult (see on §§42–7); but the 'absurdity' of the 'wax doll' image is wholly Greek, and derives either from a paradoxical statement of Zeno or Cleanthes or from conventional criticism of the doctrine of *ekpyrosis* (see on §51).

It may be that reflection on the occasion and the dramatic circumstances may help us to see a way round this difficulty.

Like most of Dio's other speeches, *Bor.* is not mere entertainment; it carries a lesson appropriate to its occasion. What this is, is matter for conjecture. It seems to have to do (a) with being 'Hellenic', (b) with concord and regeneration.

(a) The Borysthenites claim to be 'Hellenic'. They complain of the 'barbarism' of some of the Greek traders who visit them. But they are by no means idealized. Their Milesian origin displays itself in their practice of homosexuality, not something of which Dio (despite his Platonic stance) is at all tolerant (cf 7.148–52). They are also anti-Roman; and Dio, despite his exile, was never that. They admire Homer, which is in itself admirable (cf. 18.8: Ὅμηρος ... καὶ πρῶτος καὶ μέσος καὶ ὕστατος παντὶ παιδὶ καὶ ἀνδρὶ καὶ γέροντι, 'Homer ... first, middle and last for every boy and man and old man'), but they do not see that the heroic *ēthos* exemplified by Achilles is no basis for political life. It seems to be with a view to their needs that Dio embarks upon his 'bizarre' myth and emphasizes its strangeness (αὐθαδῶς §42, ἄτοπος §43, τολμῶσιν §51, οὐκ ἀποτρέπονται §46), as though to show them that truly Greek 'songs' are not only charming but sober and rational. But of course all this is reported to the citizens of Prusa: what lesson is there in it for them? They are perhaps assumed to be wiser than the Borysthenites, and to have a sounder and more modern conception of their Hellenic heritage and their place in the Roman world. The implicit comparison flatters them.

(b) In *Or.* 40, also (as we saw) addressed to Prusa, Dio clearly uses the Stoic concept of cosmic order and cyclical change as an analogy with the political world, an argument for concord.[23] Is this true also of the double myth in *Bor.*? There are good reasons for keeping the possibility open. The assertion of the monarchical government of the universe by Zeus Basileus is an obvious defence of earthly monarchies (1.39 = 12.75 (q.v.), and notes on 36.39–61); and the picture of the world's renewal after destruction is an appropriate figure for the felicity of the new order that Nerva and Trajan inaugurated, and that enables Dio to return to his ruined home in Prusa.

7. TEXT

This is not a critical edition, and what is said about the manuscript tradition is based on the editions of Emperius (1844), von Arnim (1893–6) and de Budé (1915–19) and on the work of François (1922)

[23] See especially Bodson (1967).

and Wenkebach (1908, 1940, 1944). None the less, the notes and apparatus indicate the nature of the textual problems that face Dio's readers. A great deal has been done by scholars from Casaubon to von Arnim and beyond, especially by Reiske and Emperius; yet much remains. There is no doubt that a fresh examination of the manuscript tradition is needed, and it would probably clear up some minor problems. But much of what troubles us is not small-scale scribal error but major stumbling-blocks in the structure and coherence, especially of *Eub.* and *Bor.*[24] These are due to the circumstances of the delivery and preservation of the speeches in ancient times. Such difficulties are very unlikely to yield to any new evidence (except perhaps a papyrus find).

The manuscripts on which editors mainly rely are these:

U = Urbinas 124, eleventh century.
B = Parisinus 2958, fourteenth century.

These two have readings in common which are not found elsewhere. They represent a common text, which was that available to Arethas, whose *prolegomena* they contain.

M = Meermannianus Lugdunensis 67, sixteenth century.
P = Palatinus 117, fifteenth century.
H = Vaticanus 91, thirteenth century (omits *Eub.* 103–32 and 151–end; does not have *Bor.*)

These last two codices represent a different tradition from UB and M.

Modern editions – von Arnim, de Budé, and the Loeb editions – all print the important texts of Synesius, Photius, and Arethas which give us an insight into the history of Dio's text in Byzantine times. On this subject, see especially Brancacci (1986).

One modern commentary must be singled out: Geel's *Olympicus* (1840), a mine of information, and still the only extensive attempt to deal systematically with problems of interpretation in an entire speech.

Eub., much the most popular of Dio's works, has been recently annotated by E. Avezzù (1985); the narrative part is included in Wilamowitz' *Griechisches Lesebuch* and there is a school edition by W. K. Prentice (Boston 1897). There is even a verse translation, H. Hommel's German hexameters (Zürich 1959).

[24] See on 7.103–4, 125–6; 12.1–16, 33–48, 84–5; 36.39–61, 42.

8. MANUSCRIPTS AND EDITIONS

U   Urbinas 124, s. xi
B   Parisinus 2958, s. xiv
M   Meermannianus Lugdunensis 67, s. xvi
P   Palatinus 117, s. xv
H   Vaticanus 91, s. xiii
T   Marcianus 421, s. xv

F. Morel, Paris 1604 (has Casaubon's *Diatriba*).
J. Wolf, Anecdota Graeca, Hamburg 1722, II 217ff. (has Selden's annotations).
J. J. Reiske, Leipzig 1784.
J. Geel, *Olympicus*, Leyden 1840.
A. Emperius, Brunswick 1844.
L. Dindorf, Leipzig 1857.
H. von Arnim, Berlin 1893–6.
G. de Budé, Leipzig 1916–9.
J. W. Cohoon and H. Lamarr Crosby, Loeb edition, 1932–51.

DIO CHRYSOSTOM
ORATIONS
VII, XII AND XXXVI

ΕΥΒΟΙΚΟΣ

1 Τόδε μὴν αὐτὸς ἰδών, οὐ παρ' ἑτέρων ἀκούσας, διηγήσομαι.
ἴσως γὰρ οὐ μόνον πρεσβυτικὸν πολυλογία καὶ τὸ μηδένα
διωθεῖσθαι ῥαιδίως τῶν ἐμπιπτόντων λόγων, πρὸς δὲ τῶι
πρεσβυτικῶι τυχὸν ἂν εἴη καὶ ἀλητικόν. αἴτιον δέ, ὅτι πολλὰ
τυχὸν ἀμφότεροι πεπόνθασιν ὧν οὐκ ἀηδῶς μέμνηνται. ἐρῶ   5
δ' οὖν οἵοις ἀνδράσι καὶ ὅντινα βίον ζῶσι συνέβαλον ἐν μέσηι
σχεδόν τι τῆι Ἑλλάδι.

2 Ἐτύγχανον μὲν ἀπὸ Χίου περαιούμενος μετά τινων ἁλιέων
ἔξω τῆς θερινῆς ὥρας ἐν μικρῶι παντελῶς ἀκατίωι. χειμῶνος
δὲ γενομένου χαλεπῶς καὶ μόλις διεσώθημεν πρὸς τὰ Κοῖλα   10
τῆς Εὐβοίας· τὸ μὲν δὴ ἀκάτιον εἰς τραχύν τινα αἰγιαλὸν ὑπὸ
τοῖς κρημνοῖς ἐκβαλόντες διέφθειραν, αὐτοὶ δὲ ἀπεχώρησαν
πρός τινας πορφυρεῖς ὑφορμοῦντας ἐπὶ τῆι πλησίον χηλῆι
κἀκείνοις συνεργάζεσθαι διενοοῦντο αὐτοῦ μένοντες.

3 καταλειφθεὶς δὴ μόνος, οὐκ ἔχων εἰς τίνα πόλιν σωθήσομαι,   15
παρὰ τὴν θάλατταν ἄλλως ἐπλανώμην, εἴ πού τινας ἢ
παραπλέοντας ἢ ὁρμοῦντας ἴδοιμι. προεληλυθὼς δὲ συχνὸν
ἀνθρώπων μὲν οὐδένα ἑώρων, ἐπιτυγχάνω δὲ ἐλάφωι
νεωστὶ κατὰ τοῦ κρημνοῦ πεπτωκότι παρ' αὐτὴν τὴν
ῥαχίαν, ὑπὸ τῶν κυμάτων παιομένωι, φυσῶντι ἔτι. καὶ μετ'   20
ὀλίγον ἔδοξα ὑλακῆς ἀκοῦσαι κυνῶν ἄνωθεν μόλις πως διὰ

4 τὸν ἦχον τὸν ἀπὸ τῆς θαλάττης. προελθὼν δὲ καὶ προβὰς
πάνυ χαλεπῶς πρός τι ὑψηλόν, τούς τε κύνας ὁρῶ
ἠπορημένους καὶ διαθέοντας, ὑφ' ὧν εἴκαζον ἀποβιασθὲν τὸ
ζῶιον ἁλέσθαι κατὰ τοῦ κρημνοῦ, καὶ μετ' ὀλίγον ἄνδρα,   25
κυνηγέτην ἀπὸ τῆς ὄψεως καὶ τῆς στολῆς, τὰ γένεια ὑγιῆ,
κομῶντα οὐ φαύλως οὐδὲ ἀγεννῶς ἐξόπισθεν, οἵους ἐπὶ
Ἴλιον Ὅμηρός φησιν ἐλθεῖν Εὐβοέας, σκώπτων ἐμοὶ δοκεῖν
καὶ καταγελῶν ὅτι τῶν ἄλλων Ἀχαιῶν καλῶς ἐχόντων
οἶδε ἐξ ἡμίσους ἐκόμων.   30

5 Καὶ ὃς ἀνηρώτα με, Ἀλλ' ἦ, ὦ ξένε, τῆιδέ που φεύγοντα

31 ξένε U corr., B : ξεῖνε

29

ἔλαφον κατενόησας; κἀγὼ πρὸς αὐτόν, Ἐκεῖνος, ἔφην, ἐν
τῶι κλύδωνι ἤδη· καὶ ἀγαγὼν ἔδειξα. ἑλκύσας οὖν αὐτὸν
ἐκ τῆς θαλάττης τό τε δέρμα ἐξέδειρε μαχαίραι, κἀμοῦ
ξυλλαμβάνοντος ὅσον οἷός τε ἦν, καὶ τῶν σκελῶν ἀποτεμὼν
τὰ ὀπίσθια ἐκόμιζεν ἅμα τῶι δέρματι. παρεκάλει δὲ κἀμὲ   5
συνακολουθεῖν καὶ συνεστιᾶσθαι τῶν κρεῶν· εἶναι δὲ οὐ
6 μακρὰν τὴν οἴκησιν. Ἔπειτα ἔωθεν παρ' ἡμῖν, ἔφη, κοιμηθεὶς
ἥξεις ἐπὶ τὴν θάλατταν, ὡς τά γε νῦν οὐκ ἔστι πλόϊμα. καὶ
μὴ τοῦτο, εἶπε, φοβηθῆις. βουλοίμην δ' ἂν ἔγωγε καὶ μετὰ
πέντε ἡμέρας λῆξαι τὸν ἄνεμον· ἀλλ' οὐ ῥάιδιον, εἶπεν,   1
ὅταν οὕτως πιεσθῆι τὰ ἄκρα τῆς Εὐβοίας ὑπὸ τῶν. νεφῶν
ὥς γε νῦν κατειλημμένα ὁρᾶις. καὶ ἅμα ἠρώτα με ὁπόθεν
δὴ καὶ ὅπως ἐκεῖ κατηνέχθην, καὶ εἰ μὴ διεφθάρη τὸ πλοῖον.
Μικρὸν ἦν παντελῶς, ἔφην, ἁλιέων τινῶν περαιουμένων,
7 κἀγὼ μόνος ξυνέπλεον ὑπὸ σπουδῆς τινος. διεφθάρη δ'   1
ὅμως ἐπὶ τὴν γῆν ἐκπεσόν. Οὔκουν ῥάιδιον, ἔφη, ἄλλως·
ὅρα γὰρ ὡς ἄγρια καὶ σκληρὰ τῆς νήσου τὰ πρὸς τὸ
πέλαγος. Ταῦτ', εἶπεν, ἐστὶ τὰ Κοῖλα τῆς Εὐβοίας λεγόμενα,
ὅπου κατενεχθεῖσα ναῦς οὐκ ἂν ἔτι σωθείη· σπανίως δὲ
σώιζονται καὶ τῶν ἀνθρώπων τινές, εἰ μὴ ἄρα, ὥσπερ   2
ὑμεῖς, ἐλαφροὶ παντελῶς πλέοντες. ἀλλ' ἴθι καὶ μηδὲν
δείσηις. νῦν μὲν ἐκ τῆς κακοπαθείας ἀνακτήσηι σαυτόν·
εἰς αὔριον δέ, ὅ τι ἂν ἦι δυνατόν, ἐπιμελησόμεθα
8 ὅπως σωθῆις, ἐπειδή σε ἔγνωμεν ἅπαξ. δοκεῖς δέ μοι τῶν
ἀστικῶν εἶναί τις, οὐ ναύτης οὐδ' ἐργάτης, ἀλλὰ πολλήν   2
τινα ἀσθένειαν τοῦ σώματος ἀσθενεῖν ἔοικας ἀπὸ τῆς
ἰσχνότητος.
Ἐγὼ δὲ ἄσμενος ἠκολούθουν· οὐ γὰρ ἐπιβουλευθῆναί
9 ποτε ἔδεισα, οὐδὲν ἔχων ἢ φαῦλον ἱμάτιον. καὶ πολλάκις μὲν
δὴ καὶ ἄλλοτε ἐπειράθην ἐν τοῖς τοιούτοις καιροῖς, ἄτε ἐν ἄληι   2
συνεχεῖ, ἀτὰρ οὖν δὴ καὶ τότε, ὡς ἔστι πενία χρῆμα τῶι ὄντι

8–9 καὶ μὴ ... φοβηθῆις post κατειλημμένα ὁρᾶις (12) uel post οἴκησιν (7)
transponenda coni. von Arnim.   10 εἶπεν : fortasse εἰπεῖν   25 πολλήν von
Arnim : ἄλλην   29 ἄτε οὐδὲν ἔχων ἢ φαῦλον ἱμάτιον post εἰπόμην (31, 2)
codd. : del. Reiske.

ἱερὸν καὶ ἄσυλον, καὶ οὐδεὶς ἀδικεῖ, πολύ γε ἧττον ἢ τοὺς τὰ
10 κηρύκεια ἔχοντας· ὡς δὴ καὶ τότε θαρρῶν εἰπόμην. ἦν δὲ
σχεδόν τι περὶ τετταράκοντα στάδια πρὸς τὸ χωρίον.
Ὡς οὖν ἐβαδίζομεν, διηγεῖτό μοι κατὰ τὴν ὁδὸν τὰ αὑτοῦ
πράγματα καὶ τὸν βίον ὃν ἔζη μετὰ γυναικὸς αὑτοῦ καὶ 5
παίδων. Ἡμεῖς γάρ, ἔφη, δύο ἐσμέν, ὦ ξένε, τὸν αὐτὸν
οἰκοῦντες τόπον. ἔχομεν δὲ γυναῖκας ἀλλήλων ἀδελφὰς καὶ
11 παῖδας ἐξ αὐτῶν υἱοὺς καὶ θυγατέρας. ζῶμεν δὲ ἀπὸ θήρας
ὡς τὸ πολύ, μικρόν τι τῆς γῆς ἐπεργαζόμενοι. τὸ γὰρ χωρίον
οὐκ ἔστιν ἡμέτερον οὔτε πατρῷον οὔτε ἡμεῖς ἐκτησάμεθα, 10
ἀλλὰ ἦσαν οἱ πατέρες ἡμῶν ἐλεύθεροι μέν, πένητες δὲ
οὐχ ἧττον ἡμῶν, μισθοῦ βουκόλοι, βοῦς νέμοντες ἀνδρὸς
μακαρίου τῶν ἐνθένδε τινὸς ἐκ τῆς νήσου, πολλὰς μὲν
ἀγέλας καὶ ἵππων καὶ βοῶν κεκτημένου, πολλὰς δὲ ποίμνας,
πολλοὺς δὲ καὶ καλοὺς ἀγρούς, πολλὰ δὲ ἄλλα χρήματα, 15
12 ξύμπαντα δὲ ταῦτα τὰ ὄρη. οὗ δὴ ἀποθανόντος καὶ τῆς
οὐσίας δημευθείσης – φασὶ δὲ καὶ αὐτὸν ἀπολέσθαι διὰ
τὰ χρήματα ὑπὸ τοῦ βασιλέως – τὴν μὲν ἀγέλην εὐθὺς
ἀπήλασαν ὥστε κατακόψαι, πρὸς δὲ τῇ ἀγέλῃ καὶ τὰ
13 ἡμέτερα ἄττα βοΐδια, καὶ τὸν μισθὸν οὐδεὶς ἀπέδωκε. τότε 20
μὲν δὴ ἐξ ἀνάγκης αὐτοῦ κατεμείναμεν, οὗπερ ἐτύχομεν
τὰς βοῦς ἔχοντες καί τινας σκηνὰς πεποιημένοι καὶ αὐλὴν
διὰ ξύλων οὐ μεγάλην οὐδὲ ἰσχυράν, μόσχων ἕνεκεν, ὡς ἂν
οἶμαι πρὸς αὐτό που τὸ θέρος. τοῦ μὲν γὰρ χειμῶνος ἐν τοῖς
πεδίοις ἐνέμομεν, νομὴν ἱκανὴν ἔχοντες καὶ πολὺν χιλὸν 25
ἀποκείμενον· τοῦ δὲ θέρους ἀπηλαύνομεν εἰς τὰ ὄρη.
14 μάλιστα δ' ἐν τούτῳ τῷ τόπῳ σταθμὸν ἐποιοῦντο· τό
τε γὰρ χωρίον ἀπόρρυτον ἑκατέρωθεν, φάραγξ βαθεῖα καὶ
σύσκιος, καὶ διὰ μέσου ποταμὸς οὐ τραχύς, ἀλλ' ὡς ῥᾷστος
ἐμβῆναι καὶ βουσὶ καὶ μόσχοις, τὸ δὲ ὕδωρ πολὺ καὶ 30
καθαρόν, ἅτε τῆς πηγῆς ἐγγὺς ἀναδιδούσης, καὶ πνεῦμα

---

15 καλοὺς δὲ καὶ πολλοὺς codd. : corr. Dindorf   20 ἀποδέδωκε PH
28 ἀπόρρητον M m.pr. : ἀπόρρηκτον von der Muehll : κατάρρυτον Casaubon

τοῦ θέρους ἀεὶ διαπνέον διὰ τῆς φάραγγος· οἵ τε περικείμενοι
δρυμοὶ μαλακοὶ καὶ κατάρρυτοι, ἥκιστα μὲν οἶστρον
15 τρέφοντες, ἥκιστα δὲ ἄλλην τινὰ βλάβην βουσί. πολλοὶ
δὲ καὶ πάγκαλοι λειμῶνες ὑπὸ ὑψηλοῖς τε καὶ ἀραιοῖς
δένδρεσιν ἀνειμένοι, καὶ πάντα μεστὰ βοτάνης εὐθαλοῦς δι' 5
ὅλου τοῦ θέρους, ὥστε μὴ πολὺν πλανᾶσθαι τόπον. ὧν δὴ
ἕνεκα συνήθως ἐκεῖ καθίστασαν τὴν ἀγέλην.
    Καὶ τότε ἔμειναν ἐν ταῖς σκηναῖς μέχρι ἂν εὕρωσι μισθόν
τινα ἢ ἔργον, καὶ διετράφησαν ἀπὸ χωρίου μικροῦ
παντελῶς, ὃ ἔτυχον εἰργασμένοι πλησίον τοῦ σταθμοῦ. 10
16 τοῦτο ἐπήρκεσεν αὐτοῖς ἱκανῶς, ἅτε κόπρου πολλῆς
ἐνούσης. καὶ σχολὴν ἄγοντες ἀπὸ τῶν βοῶν πρὸς θήραν
ἐτράπησαν, τὸ μὲν αὐτοί, τὸ δὲ καὶ μετὰ κυνῶν. δύο γὰρ
τῶν ἑπομένων ταῖς βουσίν, ὡς δὴ μακρὰν ἦσαν οὐχ ὁρῶντες
τοὺς νομεῖς, ὑπέστρεψαν ἐπὶ τὸν τόπον καταλιπόντες τὴν 15
ἀγέλην. οὗτοι τὸ μὲν πρῶτον συνηκολούθουν αὐτοῖς,
ὥσπερ ἐπ' ἄλλο τι· καὶ τοὺς μὲν λύκους ὁπότε ἴδοιεν,
ἐδίωκον μέχρι τινός, συῶν δὲ ἢ ἐλάφων οὐδὲν αὐτοῖς ἔμελεν.
17 εἰ δέ ποτε ἴδοιεν τῶν ἄρκτων τινὰ ὀψὲ καὶ πρώι,
συνιστάμενοι ὑλάκτουν τε καὶ ἤμυνον, ὥσπερ ἂν εἰ πρὸς 20
ἄνθρωπον ἐμάχοντο. γευόμενοι δὲ τοῦ αἵματος καὶ συῶν
καὶ ἐλάφων καὶ τῶν κρεῶν πολλάκις ἐσθίοντες, ὀψὲ
μεταμανθάνοντες κρέασιν ἀντὶ μάζης ἥδεσθαι, τῶν μὲν
ἐμπιπλάμενοι εἴ ποτε ἁλοίη τι [σίτου], ὁπότε δὲ μή,
πεινῶντες, μᾶλλον ἤδη τῶι τοιούτωι προσεῖχον καὶ τὸ 25
φαινόμενον ἐδίωκον πᾶν ὁμοίως καὶ ὀσμῆς ἀμηγέπηι καὶ
ἴχνους ἠισθάνοντο καὶ ἀπέβησαν ἀντὶ βουκόλων τοιοῦτοί
τινες ὀψιμαθεῖς καὶ βραδύτεροι θηρευταί.
18   Χειμῶνος δὲ ἐπελθόντος ἔργον μὲν οὐδὲν ἦν πεφηνὸς αὐτοῖς
οὔτε εἰς ἄστυ καταβᾶσιν οὔτε εἰς κώμην τινά· φραξάμενοι 30
δὲ τὰς σκηνὰς ἐπιμελέστερον καὶ τὴν αὐλὴν πυκνοτέραν
ποιήσαντες, οὕτως διεγένοντο καὶ τὸ χωρίον ἐκεῖνο πᾶν

11 τοῦτο C (= Parisinus 3009) : τοῦτό τε uel τοῦτό γε   19 ἄρκτων Schwartz:
ἀνθρώπων   24 [σίτου] del. Emperius

εἰργάσαντο, καὶ τῆς θήρας ἡ χειμερινὴ ῥάιων ἐγίγνετο·
19 τὰ γὰρ ἴχνη φανερώτερα, ὡς ἂν ἐν ὑγρῶι τῶι ἐδάφει
σημαινόμενα, ἡ δὲ χιὼν καὶ πάνυ τηλαυγῆ παρέχει, ὥστε
οὐδὲν δεῖ ζητοῦντα πράγματα ἔχειν, ὥσπερ ὁδοῦ φερούσης
ἐπ' αὐτά, καὶ τὰ θηρία μᾶλλόν τι ὑπομένει ὀκνοῦντα· ἔστι δ' 5
ἔτι καὶ λαγὼς καὶ δορκάδας ἐν ταῖς εὐναῖς καταλαμβάνειν.
20 οὕτως δὴ τὸ ἀπ' ἐκείνου διέμειναν, οὐδὲν ἔτι προσδεηθέντες
ἄλλου βίου. καὶ ἡμῖν συνέζευξαν γυναῖκας τοῖς ἀλλήλων
υἱέσιν ἑκάτερος τὴν αὐτοῦ θυγατέρα. τεθνήκασι δὲ
ἀμφότεροι πέρυσι σχεδόν, τὰ μὲν ἔτη πολλὰ λέγοντες ἃ 10
βεβιώκεσαν, ἰσχυροὶ δὲ ἔτι καὶ νέοι καὶ γενναῖοι τὰ σώματα.
τῶν δὲ μητέρων ἡ ἐμὴ περίεστιν.
21 Ὁ μὲν οὖν ἕτερος ἡμῶν οὐδεπώποτε εἰς πόλιν κατέβη,
πεντήκοντα ἔτη γεγονώς· ἐγὼ δὲ δὶς μόνον, ἅπαξ μὲν ἔτι
παῖς μετὰ τοῦ πατρὸς ὁπηνίκα τὴν ἀγέλην εἴχομεν, ὕστερον 15
δὲ ἧκέ τις ἀργύριον αἰτῶν, ὥσπερ ἔχοντάς τι, κελεύων
ἀκολουθεῖν εἰς τὴν πόλιν. ἡμῖν δὲ ἀργύριον μὲν οὐκ ἦν, ἀλλ'
22 ἀπωμοσάμην μὴ ἔχειν· εἰ δὲ μή, δεδωκέναι ἄν. ἐξενίσαμεν δὲ
αὐτὸν ὡς ἠδυνάμεθα κάλλιστα καὶ δύο ἐλάφεια δέρματα
ἐδώκαμεν· κἀγὼ ἠκολούθησα εἰς τὴν πόλιν. ἔφη γὰρ ἀνάγκη 20
εἶναι τὸν ἕτερον ἐλθεῖν καὶ διδάξαι περὶ τούτων.
    Εἶδον οὖν, οἷα καὶ πρότερον, οἰκίας πολλὰς καὶ μεγάλας
καὶ τεῖχος ἔξωθεν καρτερὸν καὶ οἰκήματά τινα ὑψηλὰ
καὶ τετράγωνα ἐν τῶι τείχει [τοὺς πύργους] καὶ πλοῖα
πολλὰ ὁρμοῦντα ὥσπερ ἐν λίμνηι [ἐν τῶι λιμένι] κατὰ 25
23 πολλὴν ἡσυχίαν. τοῦτο δὲ ἐνθάδε οὐκ ἔστιν οὐδαμοῦ ὅπου
κατηνέχθης· καὶ διὰ τοῦτο αἱ νῆες ἀπόλλυνται. ταῦτα
οὖν ἑώρων καὶ πολὺν ὄχλον ἐν ταὐτῶι συνειργμένον καὶ
θόρυβον ἀμήχανον καὶ κραυγήν, ὥστε ἐμοὶ ἐδόκουν πάντες
μάχεσθαι ἀλλήλοις. ἄγει οὖν με πρός τινας ἄρχοντας καὶ 30
εἶπε γελῶν, Οὗτός ἐστιν ἐφ' ὃν με ἐπέμψατε. ἔχει δὲ οὐδὲν εἰ

5–6 δ' ἔτι : δέ γε uel δέ τοι Emperius   10 λέγοντες Reiske : ἔλεγον   11 καὶ
νέοι secl. Dindorf   19 κάλλιστα Dindorf : μάλιστα   24 [τοὺς πύργους]
del. Geel   25 [ἐν τῶι λιμένι] del. Cobet   28 ταὐτῶι Reiske : τούτωι

34 ΔΙΩΝΟΣ

24 μή γε τὴν κόμην καὶ σκηνὴν μάλα ἰσχυρῶν ξύλων. οἱ δὲ
ἄρχοντες εἰς τὸ θέατρον ἐβάδιζον, κἀγὼ σὺν αὐτοῖς. τὸ δὲ
θέατρόν ἐστιν ὥσπερ φάραγξ κοῖλον, πλὴν οὐ μακρὸν
ἑκατέρωθεν, ἀλλὰ στρογγύλον ἐξ ἡμίσους, οὐκ αὐτόματον,
ἀλλ᾽ ᾠκοδομημένον λίθοις. ἴσως δέ μου καταγελᾶις ὅτι σοι 5
διηγοῦμαι σαφῶς εἰδότι ταῦτα.

Πρῶτον μὲν οὖν πολύν τινα χρόνον ἄλλα τινὰ ἔπραττεν
ὁ ὄχλος, καὶ ἐβόων ποτὲ μὲν πράιως καὶ ἱλαροὶ πάντες,
25 ἐπαινοῦντές τινας, ποτὲ δὲ σφόδρα καὶ ὀργίλως. ἦν δὲ τοῦτο
χαλεπὸν τὸ τῆς ὀργῆς αὐτῶν· καὶ τοὺς ἀνθρώπους εὐθὺς 1
ἐξέπληττον οἷς ἀνέκραγον, ὥστε οἱ μὲν αὐτῶν περιτρέχοντες
ἐδέοντο, οἱ δὲ τὰ ἱμάτια ἐρρίπτουν ὑπὸ τοῦ φόβου. ἐγὼ δὲ
καὶ αὐτὸς ἅπαξ ὀλίγου κατέπεσον ὑπὸ τῆς κραυγῆς, ὥσπερ
26 κλύδωνος ἐξαίφνης ἢ βροντῆς ἐπιρραγείσης. ἄλλοι δέ τινες
ἄνθρωποι παριόντες, οἱ δ᾽ ἐκ μέσων ἀνιστάμενοι, διελέγοντο
πρὸς τὸ πλῆθος, οἱ μὲν ὀλίγα ῥήματα, οἱ δὲ πολλοὺς λόγους.
καὶ τῶν μὲν ἤκουον πολύν τινα χρόνον, τοῖς δὲ ἐχαλέπαινον
εὐθὺς φθεγξαμένοις καὶ οὐδὲ γρύζειν ἐπέτρεπον.

Ἐπεὶ δὲ καθέστασάν ποτε καὶ ἡσυχία ἐγένετο,
27 παρήγαγον κἀμέ. καὶ εἶπέ τις, Οὗτός ἐστιν, ὦ ἄνδρες,
τῶν καρπουμένων τὴν δημοσίαν γῆν πολλὰ ἔτη οὐ μόνον
αὐτός, ἀλλὰ καὶ ὁ πατὴρ αὐτοῦ πρότερον, καὶ κατανέμουσι
τὰ ἡμέτερα ὄρη καὶ γεωργοῦσι καὶ θηρεύουσι καὶ οἰκίας
ἐνῳκοδομήκασι πολλὰς καὶ ἀμπέλους ἐμπεφυτεύκασι καὶ
ἄλλα πολλὰ ἔχουσιν ἀγαθὰ οὔτε τιμὴν καταβαλόντες οὐδενὶ
28 τῆς γῆς οὔτε δωρεὰν παρὰ τοῦ δήμου λαβόντες. ὑπὲρ τίνος
γὰρ ἂν καὶ ἔλαβον; ἔχοντες δὲ τὰ ἡμέτερα καὶ πλουτοῦντες
οὔτε λειτουργίαν πώποτε ἐλειτούργησαν οὐδεμίαν οὔτε
μοῖράν τινα ὑποτελοῦσι τῶν γιγνομένων, ἀλλ᾽ ἀτελεῖς καὶ
ἀλειτούργητοι διατελοῦσιν, ὥσπερ εὐεργέται τῆς πόλεως.
οἶμαι δέ, ἔφη, μηδὲ ἐληλυθέναι πώποτε αὐτοὺς ἐνθάδε.
29 κἀγὼ ἀνένευσα, ὁ δὲ ὄχλος ἐγέλασεν ὡς εἶδε. καὶ ὁ λέγων
ἐκεῖνος ὠργίσθη ἐπὶ τῶι γέλωτι καί μοι ἐλοιδορεῖτο.

23, 27 num τὰ ὑμέτερα?   24 πολλὰς post ἐμπεφυτεύκασι transp. von Arnim

ἔπειτα ἐπιστρέψας, Εἰ οὖν, ἔφη, δοκεῖ ταῦτα οὕτως, οὐκ ἂν
φθάνοιμεν ἅπαντες τὰ κοινὰ διαρπάσαντες, οἱ μὲν τὰ
χρήματα τῆς πόλεως, ὥσπερ ἀμέλει καὶ νῦν ποιοῦσί τινες,
οἱ δὲ τὴν χώραν κατανειμάμενοι μὴ πείσαντες ὑμᾶς, ἐὰν
ἐπιτρέψητε τοῖς θηρίοις τούτοις προῖκα ἔχειν πλέον ἢ χίλια 5
πλέθρα γῆς τῆς ἀρίστης, ὅθεν ὑμῖν ἔστι τρεῖς χοίνικας
Ἀττικὰς σίτου λαμβάνειν κατ' ἄνδρα.

30 Ἐγὼ δὲ ἀκούσας ἐγέλασα ὅσον ἐδυνάμην μέγιστον. τὸ δὲ
πλῆθος οὐκέτ' ἐγέλων, ὥσπερ πρότερον, ἀλλ' ἐθορύβουν.
ὁ δὲ ἄνθρωπος [ὁ ῥήτωρ] ἐχαλέπαινε καὶ δεινὸν ἐμβλέψας 10
εἰς ἐμὲ εἶπεν, Ὁρᾶτε τὴν εἰρωνείαν καὶ τὴν ὕβριν τοῦ
καθάρματος, ὡς καταγελᾶι πάνυ θρασέως; ὃν ἀπάγειν
ὀλίγου δέω καὶ τὸν κοινωνὸν αὐτοῦ – πυνθάνομαι γὰρ δύο
εἶναι τοὺς κορυφαίους τῶν κατειληφότων ἅπασαν σχεδὸν
31 τὴν ἐν τοῖς ὄρεσι χώραν – οἶμαι γὰρ αὐτοὺς μηδὲ τῶν 15
ναυαγίων ἀπέχεσθαι τῶν ἑκάστοτε ἐκπιπτόντων, ὑπὲρ
αὐτὰς σχεδόν τι τὰς Καφηρίδας οἰκοῦντας. πόθεν γὰρ οὕτως
πολυτελεῖς ἀγρούς, μᾶλλον δὲ ὅλας κώμας κατεσκευάσαντο
καὶ τοσοῦτον πλῆθος βοσκημάτων καὶ ζεύγη καὶ
32 ἀνδράποδα; καὶ ὑμεῖς δὲ ἴσως ὁρᾶτε αὐτοῦ τὴν ἐξωμίδα ὡς 20
φαύλη καὶ τὸ δέρμα ὃ ἐλήλυθε δεῦρο ἐναψάμενος τῆς ὑμετέρας
ἕνεκεν ἀπάτης, ὡς πτωχὸς δηλονότι καὶ οὐδὲν ἔχων. ἐγὼ
μὲν γάρ, ἔφη, βλέπων αὐτὸν μικροῦ δέδοικα, ὥσπερ οἶμαι
τὸν Ναύπλιον ὁρῶν ἀπὸ τοῦ Καφηρέως ἥκοντα. καὶ γὰρ
οἶμαι πυρσεύειν αὐτὸν ἀπὸ τῶν ἄκρων τοῖς πλέουσιν ὅπως 25
33 ἐκπίπτωσιν εἰς τὰς πέτρας. ταῦτα δὲ ἐκείνου λέγοντος καὶ
πολλὰ πρὸς τούτοις, ὁ μὲν ὄχλος ἡγριοῦτο· ἐγὼ δὲ ἠπόρουν
καὶ ἐδεδοίκειν μή τί με ἐργάσωνται κακόν.

Παρελθὼν δὲ ἄλλος τις, ὡς ἐφαίνετο, ἐπιεικὴς ἄνθρωπος
ἀπό τε τῶν λόγων οὓς εἶπε καὶ ἀπὸ τοῦ σχήματος, πρῶτον 30
μὲν ἠξίου σιωπῆσαι τὸ πλῆθος, καὶ ἐσιώπησαν· ἔπειτα εἶπε
τῆι φωνῆι πράιως ὅτι οὐδὲν ἀδικοῦσιν οἱ τὴν ἀργὴν τῆς
χώρας ἐργαζόμενοι καὶ κατασκευάζοντες, ἀλλὰ τοὐναντίον

10 [ὁ ῥήτωρ] del. Cobet

34 ἐπαίνου δικαίως ἂν τυγχάνοιεν· καὶ δεῖ μὴ τοῖς οἰκοδομοῦσι
καὶ φυτεύουσι τὴν δημοσίαν γῆν χαλεπῶς ἔχειν, ἀλλὰ τοῖς
καταφθείρουσιν. ἐπεὶ καὶ νῦν, ἔφη, ὦ ἄνδρες, σχεδόν τι τὰ
δύο μέρη τῆς χώρας ἡμῶν ἔρημά ἐστι δι᾽ ἀμέλειάν τε
καὶ ὀλιγανθρωπίαν. κἀγὼ πολλὰ κέκτημαι πλέθρα, ὥσπερ   5
οἶμαι καὶ ἄλλος τις, οὐ μόνον ἐν τοῖς ὄρεσιν, ἀλλὰ καὶ ἐν τοῖς
πεδινοῖς, ἃ εἴ τις ἐθέλοι γεωργεῖν, οὐ μόνον ἂν προῖκα δοίην,
35 ἀλλὰ καὶ ἀργύριον ἡδέως προστελέσαιμι. δῆλον γὰρ ὡς
ἐμοὶ πλέονος ἀξία γίγνεται, καὶ ἅμα ἡδὺ ὅραμα χώρα
οἰκουμένη καὶ ἐνεργός. ἡ δ᾽ ἔρημος οὐ μόνον ἀνωφελὲς κτῆμα   1(
τοῖς ἔχουσιν, ἀλλὰ καὶ σφόδρα ἐλεεινόν τε καὶ δυστυχίαν
36 τινὰ κατηγοροῦν τῶν δεσποτῶν. ὥστε μοι δοκεῖ μᾶλλον
ἑτέρους προτρέπειν, ὅσους ἂν δύνησθε τῶν πολιτῶν,
ἐργάζεσθαι τῆς δημοσίας γῆς ἀπολαβόντας, τοὺς μὲν
ἀφορμήν τινα ἔχοντας πλείω, τοὺς δὲ πένητας ὅσην ἂν   1
ἕκαστος ᾖ δυνατός, ἵνα ὑμῖν ἥ τε χώρα ἐνεργὸς ᾖ καὶ τῶν
πολιτῶν οἱ θέλοντες δύο τῶν μεγίστων ἀπηλλαγμένοι
37 κακῶν, ἀργίας καὶ πενίας. ἐπὶ δέκα μὲν οὖν ἔτη προῖκα
ἐχόντων· μετὰ δὲ τοῦτον τὸν χρόνον ταξάμενοι μοῖραν
ὀλίγην παρεχέτωσαν ἀπὸ τῶν καρπῶν, ἀπὸ δὲ τῶν   2(
βοσκημάτων μηδέν. ἐὰν δέ τις ξένος γεωργῇ, πέντε ἔτη
καὶ οὗτοι μηδὲν ὑποτελούντων, ὕστερον δὲ διπλάσιον ἢ
οἱ πολῖται. ὃς δὲ ἂν ἐξεργάσηται τῶν ξένων διακόσια
πλέθρα, πολίτην αὐτὸν εἶναι, ἵνα ὡς πλεῖστοι ὦσιν οἱ
προθυμούμενοι.   2

38 Ἐπεὶ νῦν γε καὶ τὰ πρὸ τῶν πυλῶν ἄγρια παντελῶς ἐστι
καὶ αἰσχρὰ δεινῶς, ὥσπερ ἐν ἐρημίαι τῆι βαθυτάτηι, οὐχ ὡς
προάστιον πόλεως· τὰ δέ γε ἐντὸς τείχους σπείρεται τὰ
πλεῖστα καὶ κατανέμεται. οὐκοῦν ἄξιον, ἔφη, θαυμάσαι τῶν
ῥητόρων, ὅτι τοὺς μὲν ἐπὶ τῶι Καφηρεῖ φιλεργοῦντας ἐν τοῖς   3(
ἐσχάτοις τῆς Εὐβοίας συκοφαντοῦσι, τοὺς δὲ τὸ γυμνάσιον
γεωργοῦντας καὶ τὴν ἀγορὰν κατανέμοντας οὐδὲν οἴονται
39 ποιεῖν δεινόν. βλέπετε γὰρ αὐτοὶ δήπουθεν ὅτι τὸ γυμνάσιον

4 ἔρημά Pflugk : ὀρεινά

ὑμῖν ἄρουραν πεποιήκασιν, ὥστε τὸν Ἡρακλέα καὶ ἄλλους
ἀνδριάντας συχνοὺς ὑπὸ τοῦ θέρους ἀποκεκρύφθαι, τοὺς μὲν
ἡρώων, τοὺς δὲ θεῶν· καὶ ὅτι καθ᾽ ἡμέραν τὰ τοῦ ῥήτορος
τούτου πρόβατα ἕωθεν εἰς τὴν ἀγορὰν ἐμβάλλει καὶ
κατανέμεται ⟨τὰ⟩ περὶ τὸ βουλευτήριον καὶ τὰ ἀρχεῖα· 5
ὥστε τοὺς πρῶτον ἐπιδημήσαντας ξένους τοὺς μὲν
καταγελᾶν τῆς πόλεως, τοὺς δὲ οἰκτείρειν αὐτήν. πάλιν οὖν
ταῦτα ἀκούσαντες ὠργίζοντο πρὸς ἐκεῖνον καὶ ἐθορύβουν.

40 Καὶ τοιαῦτα ποιῶν τοὺς ταλαιπώρους ἰδιώτας οἴεται δεῖν
ἀπαγαγεῖν, ἵνα δῆλον ὅτι μηδεὶς ἐργάζηται τὸ λοιπόν, ἀλλ᾽ 10
οἱ μὲν ἔξω λῃστεύωσιν, οἱ δ᾽ ἐν τῆι πόλει λωποδυτῶσιν.
ἐμοὶ δέ, ἔφη, δοκεῖ τούτους ἐᾶν ἐφ᾽ οἷς αὐτοὶ πεποιήκασιν,
ὑποτελοῦντας τὸ λοιπὸν ὅσον μέτριον, περὶ δὲ τῶν
ἔμπροσθεν προσόδων συγγνῶναι αὐτοῖς, ὅτι ἔρημον καὶ
ἀχρεῖον γεωργήσαντες τὴν γῆν κατελάβοντο. ἐὰν δὲ 15
τιμὴν θέλωσι καταβαλεῖν τοῦ χωρίου, ἀποδόσθαι αὐτοῖς
ἐλάττονος ἢ ἄλλοις.

41 Εἰπόντος δὲ αὐτοῦ τοιαῦτα, πάλιν ὁ ἐξ ἀρχῆς ἐκεῖνος
ἀντέλεγεν, καὶ ἐλοιδοροῦντο ἐπὶ πολύ. τέλος δὲ καὶ ἐμὲ
ἐκέλευον εἰπεῖν ὅτι βούλομαι.   20

Καὶ τί με, ἔφην, δεῖ λέγειν; Πρὸς τὰ εἰρημένα, εἶπέ τις τῶν
καθημένων. Οὐκοῦν λέγω, ἔφην, ὅτι οὐθὲν ἀληθές ἐστιν ὧν
42 εἴρηκεν. ἐγὼ μέν, ὦ ἄνδρες, ἐνύπνια ᾤμην, ἔφην, ὁρᾶν,
ἀγροὺς καὶ κώμας καὶ τοιαῦτα φλυαροῦντος. ἡμεῖς δὲ οὔτε
κώμην ἔχομεν οὔτε ἵππους οὔτε ὄνους οὔτε βοῦς. εἴθε γὰρ ἦν 25
ἔχειν ἡμᾶς ὅσα οὗτος ἔλεγεν ἀγαθά, ἵνα καὶ ὑμῖν ἐδώκαμεν
καὶ αὐτοὶ τῶν μακαρίων ἦμεν. καὶ τὰ νῦν δὲ ὄντα ἡμῖν ἱκανά
ἐστιν, ἐξ ὧν εἴ τι βούλεσθε λάβετε· κἂν πάντα ἐθέλητε, ἡμεῖς
ἕτερα κτησόμεθα. ἐπὶ τούτωι δὲ τῶι λόγωι ἐπήινεσαν.

43 Εἶτα ἐπηρώτα με ὁ ἄρχων τί δυνησόμεθα δοῦναι τῶι 30
δήμωι. κἀγώ, Τέσσαρα, ἔφην, ἐλάφεια δέρματα πάνυ καλά.
οἱ δὲ πολλοὶ αὐτῶν ἐγέλασαν. ὁ δὲ ἄρχων ἠγανάκτησε πρός

5 ⟨τὰ⟩ add. Reiske   6 πρῶτον Selden : πρώτους   15 γεωργήσοντες
Casaubon

με. Τὰ γὰρ ἄρκεια, ἔφην, σκληρά ἐστιν καὶ τὰ τράγεια οὐκ
ἄξια τούτων, ἄλλα δὲ παλαιά, τὰ δὲ μικρὰ αὐτῶν· εἰ δὲ
βούλεσθε, κἀκεῖνα λάβετε. πάλιν οὖν ἠγανάκτει καὶ ἔφη με
44 ἄγροικον εἶναι παντελῶς. κἀγώ, Πάλιν, εἶπον, αὖ καὶ σὺ
ἀγροὺς λέγεις; οὐκ ἀκούεις ὅτι ἀγροὺς οὐκ ἔχομεν;   5
ὁ δὲ ἠρώτα με εἰ τάλαντον ἑκάτερος Ἀττικὸν δοῦναι
θέλοιμεν. ἐγὼ δὲ εἶπον, Οὐχ ἵσταμεν τὰ κρέα ἡμεῖς· ἃ δ' ἂν
ᾖ, δίδομεν. ἔστι δὲ ὀλίγα ἐν ἁλσί, τἄλλα δ' ἐν τῶι καπνῶι
ξηρά, οὐ πολὺ ἐκείνων χείρω, σκελίδες ὑῶν καὶ ἐλάφειοι καὶ
45 ἄλλα γενναῖα κρέα. ἐνταῦθα δὴ ἐθορύβουν καὶ ψεύδεσθαί με   10
ἔφασαν. ὁ δὲ ἠρώτα με εἰ σῖτον ἔχομεν καὶ πόσον τινά. εἶπον
τὸν ὄντα ἀληθῶς· Δύο, ἔφην, μεδίμνους πυρῶν καὶ τέτταρας
κριθῶν καὶ τοσούτους κέγχρων, κυάμων δὲ ἡμίεκτον· οὐ γὰρ
ἐγένοντο τῆτες. τοὺς μὲν οὖν πυροὺς καὶ τὰς κριθάς, ἔφην,
ὑμεῖς λάβετε, τὰς δὲ κέγχρους ἡμῖν ἄφετε. εἰ δὲ κέγχρων   15
δεῖσθε, καὶ ταύτας λάβετε.
46 Οὐδὲ οἶνον ποιεῖτε; ἄλλος τις ἠρώτησεν. Ποιοῦμεν, εἶπον.
ἂν οὖν τις ὑμῶν ἀφίκηται, δώσομεν· ὅπως δὲ ἥξει φέρων
ἀσκόν τινα· ἡμεῖς γὰρ οὐκ ἔχομεν. Πόσαι γάρ τινές εἰσιν ὑμῖν
ἄμπελοι; Δύο μέν, ἔφην, αἱ πρὸ τῶν θυρῶν, ἔσω δὲ τῆς αὐλῆς 20
εἴκοσι· καὶ τοῦ ποταμοῦ πέραν ἃς ἔναγχος ἐφυτεύσαμεν,
ἕτεραι τοσαῦται· εἰσὶ δὲ γενναῖαι σφόδρα καὶ τοὺς βότρυς
φέρουσι μεγάλους, ὅταν οἱ παριόντες ἐπαφῶσιν αὐτούς.
47 ἵνα δὲ μὴ πράγματα ἔχητε καθ' ἕκαστον ἐρωτῶντες, ἐρῶ
καὶ τἄλλα ἅ ἐστιν ἡμῖν· αἶγες ὀκτὼ θήλειαι, βοῦς κολοβή,   25
μοσχάριον ἐξ αὐτῆς πάνυ καλόν, δρέπανα τέτταρα, δίκελλαι
τέτταρες, λόγχαι τρεῖς, μάχαιραν ἡμῶν ἑκάτερος κέκτηται
πρὸς τὰ θηρία. τὰ δὲ κεράμια σκεύη τί ἂν λέγοι τις; καὶ
γυναῖκες ἡμῖν εἰσι καὶ τούτων τέκνα· οἰκοῦμεν δὲ ἐν δυσὶ
σκηναῖς καλαῖς· καὶ τρίτην ἔχομεν οὗ κεῖται τὸ σιτάριον καὶ   30
τὰ δέρματα.
48 Νὴ Δία, εἶπεν ὁ ῥήτωρ, ὅπου καὶ τὸ ἀργύριον ἴσως
κατορύττετε. Οὐκοῦν, ἔφην, ἀνάσκαψον ἐλθών, ὦ μῶρε. τίς

2 ἄλλα : τἄλλα UB   30 καλαῖς : καλιαῖς Naber, del. σκηναῖς.

δὲ κατορύττει ἀργύριον; οὐ γὰρ δὴ φύεταί γε. ἐνταῦθα
πάντες ἐγέλων, ἐκείνου μοι δοκεῖν καταγελάσαντες.

Ταῦτα ἔστιν ἡμῖν· εἰ οὖν καὶ πάντα θέλετε, ἡμεῖς ἑκόντες
ὑμῖν χαριζόμεθα, καὶ οὐδὲν ὑμᾶς ἀφαιρεῖσθαι δεῖ πρὸς βίαν
49 ὥσπερ ἀλλοτρίων ἢ πονηρῶν· ἐπεί τοι καί πολῖται τῆς 5
πόλεώς ἐσμεν, ὡς ἐγὼ τοῦ πατρὸς ἤκουον. καί ποτε ἐκεῖνος
δεῦρο ἀφικόμενος, ἐπιτυχὼν ἀργυρίωι διδομένωι, καὶ αὐτὸς
ἔλαβεν ἐν τοῖς πολίταις. οὐκοῦν καὶ τρέφομεν ὑμετέρους
πολίτας τοὺς παῖδας. κἄν ποτε δέησθε, βοηθήσουσιν ὑμῖν
πρὸς λῃστὰς ἢ πρὸς πολεμίους. νῦν μὲν οὖν εἰρήνη ἐστίν· 10
ἐὰν δέ ποτε συμβῆι καιρὸς τοιοῦτος, εὔξεσθε τοὺς πολλοὺς
φανῆναι ὁμοίους ἡμῖν. μὴ γὰρ δὴ τοῦτόν γε τὸν ῥήτορα
νομίζετε μαχεῖσθαι τότε περὶ ὑμῶν, εἰ μή γε λοιδορούμενον
50 ὥσπερ τὰς γυναῖκας. τῶν μέντοι κρεῶν καὶ τῶν δερμάτων,
ὅταν γέ τοί ποτε ἔλωμεν θηρίον, μοῖραν δώσομεν· μόνον 15
πέμπετε τὸν ληψόμενον. ἐὰν δὲ κελεύσητε καθελεῖν τὰς
σκηνάς, εἴ τι βλάπτουσι, καθελοῦμεν. ἀλλ' ὅπως δώσετε ἡμῖν
ἐνθάδε οἰκίαν· ἢ πῶς ὑπενεγκεῖν δυνησόμεθα τοῦ χειμῶνος;
ἔστιν ὑμῖν οἰκήματα πολλὰ ἐντὸς τοῦ τείχους, ἐν οἷς οὐδεὶς
οἰκεῖ· τούτων ἡμῖν ἓν ἀρκέσει. εἰ δὲ οὐκ ἐνθάδε ζῶμεν οὐδὲ 20
πρὸς τῆι στενοχωρίαι τοσούτων ἀνθρώπων ἐν ταὐτῶι
διαγόντων καὶ ἡμεῖς ἐνοχλοῦμεν, οὐ δήπου διά γε τοῦτο
μετοικίζεσθαι ἄξιοί ἐσμεν.
51   Ὁ δὲ ἐτόλμησεν εἰπεῖν περὶ τῶν ναυαγίων πρᾶγμα οὕτως
ἀνόσιον καὶ πονηρόν – τοῦτο γὰρ μικροῦ ἐξελαθόμην εἰπεῖν, 25
ὃ πάντων πρῶτον ἔδει με εἰρηκέναι – τίς ἂν πιστεύσειέ ποτε
ὑμῶν; πρὸς γὰρ τῆι ἀσεβείαι καὶ ἀδύνατόν ἐστιν ἐκεῖθεν καὶ
ὁτιοῦν λαβεῖν, ὅπου καὶ τῶν ξύλων οὐδὲν πλέον ἔστιν ἰδεῖν
ἢ τὴν τέφραν· οὕτω πάνυ σμικρὰ ἐκπίπτει, καὶ ἔστιν ἐκείνη
52 μόνη ἡ ἀκτὴ ἁπασῶν ἀπρόσιτος. καὶ τοὺς †λάρους† ⟨οὓς⟩ 30
ἅπαξ εὑρόν ποτε ἐκβεβρασμένους, καὶ τούτους ἀνέπηξα εἰς
τὴν δρῦν τὴν ἱερὰν τὴν πλησίον τῆς θαλάττης. μὴ γὰρ εἴη

23 μετοικίζεσθαι : μισεῖσθαι M   30 †λάρους† : ταρρούς uel λάρκους Jacobs,
ταλάρους Pflugk   ⟨οὓς⟩ add. Reiske   31 ἀνέπηξα Emperius : ἐνέπηξα

ποτέ, ὦ Ζεῦ, λαβεῖν μηδὲ κερδᾶναι κέρδος τοιοῦτον ἀπὸ
ἀνθρώπων δυστυχίας. ἀλλὰ ὠφελήθην μὲν οὐδὲν πώποτε,
ἠλέησα δὲ πολλάκις ναυαγοὺς ἀφικομένους καὶ τῆι σκηνῆι
ὑπεδεξάμην καὶ φαγεῖν ἔδωκα καὶ πιεῖν καὶ εἴ τι ἄλλο
ἐδυνάμην ἐπεβοήθησα καὶ συνηκολούθησα μέχρι τῶν 5
53 οἰκουμένων. ἀλλὰ τίς ἂν ἐκείνων ἐμοὶ νῦν μαρτυρήσειεν;
οὐκοῦν οὐδὲ τοῦτο ἐποίουν μαρτυρίας ἕνεκεν ἢ χάριτος, ὅς
γε οὐδ᾿ ὁπόθεν ἦσαν ἠπιστάμην. μὴ γὰρ ὑμῶν γε μηδεὶς
περιπέσοι τοιούτωι πράγματι.

Ταῦτα δὲ ἐμοῦ λέγοντος ἀνίσταταί τις ἐκ μέσων· κἀγὼ 10
πρὸς ἐμαυτὸν ἐνεθυμήθην ὅτι ἄλλος τις τοιοῦτος τυχὸν ἐμοῦ
54 καταψευσόμενος. ὁ δὲ εἶπεν, Ἄνδρες, ἐγὼ πάλαι τοῦτον
ἀμφιγνοῶν ἠπίστουν ὅμως. ἐπεὶ δὲ σαφῶς αὐτὸν ἔγνωκα,
δεινόν μοι δοκεῖ, μᾶλλον δὲ ἀσεβές, μὴ εἰπεῖν ἃ συνεπίσταμαι
μηδ᾿ ἀποδοῦναι λόγωι χάριν, ἔργωι τὰ μέγιστα εὖ παθών. 15
55 εἰμὶ δέ, ἔφη, πολίτης, ὡς ἴστε, καὶ ὅδε, δείξας τὸν
παρακαθήμενον, καὶ ὃς ἐπανέστη· ἐτύχομεν δὲ πλέοντες ἐν
τῆι Σωκλέους νηὶ τρίτον ἔτος. καὶ διαφθαρείσης τῆς νεὼς
περὶ τὸν Καφηρέα παντελῶς ὀλίγοι τινὲς ἐσώθημεν ἀπὸ
πολλῶν. τοὺς μὲν οὖν πορφυρεῖς ἀνέλαβον· εἶχον γὰρ 20
αὐτῶν τινες ἀργύριον ἐν φασκωλίοις. ἡμεῖς δὲ γυμνοὶ
παντελῶς ἐκπεσόντες δι᾿ ἀτραποῦ τινος ἐβαδίζομεν,
ἐλπίζοντες εὑρήσειν σκέπην τινὰ ποιμένων ἢ βουκόλων,
56 κινδυνεύοντες ὑπὸ λιμοῦ τε καὶ δίψους διαφθαρῆναι. καὶ
μόλις ποτὲ ἤλθομεν ἐπὶ σκηνάς τινας καὶ στάντες ἐβοῶμεν. 25
προελθὼν δὲ οὗτος εἰσάγει τε ἡμᾶς ἔνδον καὶ ἀνέκαε πῦρ οὐκ
ἀθρόον, ἀλλὰ κατ᾿ ὀλίγον· καὶ τὸν μὲν ἡμῶν αὐτὸς ἀνέτριβε,
τὸν δὲ ἡ γυνὴ στέατι· οὐ γὰρ ἦν αὐτοῖς ἔλαιον· τέλος δὲ
57 ὕδωρ κατέχεον θερμόν, ἕως ἀνέλαβον ἀπεψυγμένους. ἔπειτα
κατακλίναντες καὶ περιβαλόντες οἷς εἶχον παρέθηκαν φαγεῖν 30
ἡμῖν ἄρτους πυρίνους, αὐτοὶ δὲ κέγχρον ἑφθὴν ἤσθιον.
ἔδωκαν δὲ καὶ οἶνον ἡμῖν πιεῖν, ὕδωρ αὐτοὶ πίνοντες, καὶ κρέα
ἐλάφεια ὀπτῶντες ἄφθονα, τὰ δὲ ἕψοντες· τῆι δ᾿ ὑστεραίαι
58 βουλομένους ἀπιέναι κατέσχον ἐπὶ τρεῖς ἡμέρας. ἔπειτα

7 τοῦτο : τότε Geel

προὔπεμψαν εἰς το πεδίον, καὶ ἀπιοῦσι κρέας ἔδωκαν καὶ
δέρμα ἑκατέρωι πάνυ καλόν. ἐμὲ δὲ ὁρῶν ἐκ τῆς κακοπαθείας
ἔτι πονηρῶς ἔχοντα ἐνέδυσε χιτώνιον, τῆς θυγατρὸς
ἀφελόμενος· ἐκείνη δὲ ἄλλο τι ῥάκος περιεζώσατο. τοῦτο
ἐπειδὴ ἐν τῆι κώμηι ἐγενόμην ἀπέδωκα. οὕτως ἡμεῖς γε ὑπὸ 5
τούτου μάλιστα ἐσώθημεν μετὰ τοὺς θεούς.

59   Ταῦτα δὲ ἐκείνου λέγοντος ὁ μὲν δῆμος ἤκουεν ἡδέως καὶ
ἐπήινουν με, ἐγὼ δὲ ἀναμνησθείς, Χαῖρε, ἔφην, Σωτάδη· καὶ
προσελθὼν ἐφίλουν αὐτὸν καὶ τὸν ἕτερον. ὁ δὲ δῆμος ἐγέλα
σφόδρα ὅτι ἐφίλουν αὐτούς. τότε ἔγνων ὅτι ἐν ταῖς πόλεσι 10
οὐ φιλοῦσιν ἀλλήλους.

60   Παρελθὼν δὲ ἐκεῖνος ὁ ἐπιεικὴς ὁ τὴν ἀρχὴν ὑπὲρ ἐμοῦ
λέγων, Ἐμοί, ὦ ἄνδρες, δοκεῖ καλέσαι τοῦτον εἰς τὸ
πρυτανεῖον ἐπὶ ξένια. οὐ γάρ, εἰ μὲν ἐν πολέμωι τινὰ ἔσωσε
τῶν πολιτῶν ὑπερασπίσας, πολλῶν ἂν καὶ μεγάλων 15
δωρεῶν ἔτυχε, νυνὶ δὲ δύο σώσας πολίτας, τυχὸν δὲ καὶ
61 ἄλλους οἳ οὐ πάρεισιν, οὐκ ἔστιν ἄξιος οὐδεμιᾶς τιμῆς. ἀντὶ
δὲ τοῦ χιτῶνος ὃν ἔδωκε τῶι πολίτηι κινδυνεύοντι, τὴν
θυγατέρα ἀποδύσας, ἐπιδοῦναι αὐτῶι τὴν πόλιν χιτῶνα
καὶ ἱμάτιον, ἵνα καὶ τοῖς ἄλλοις προτροπὴ γένηται δικαίοις 20
εἶναι καὶ ἐπαρκεῖν ἀλλήλοις, ψηφίσασθαι δὲ αὐτοῖς
καρποῦσθαι τὸ χωρίον καὶ αὐτοὺς καὶ τὰ τέκνα, καὶ μηδένα
αὐτοῖς ἐνοχλεῖν, δοῦναι δὲ αὐτῶι καὶ ἑκατὸν δραχμὰς εἰς
κατασκευήν· τὸ δὲ ἀργύριον τοῦτο ὑπὲρ τῆς πόλεως ἐγὼ
παρ' ἐμαυτοῦ δίδωμι. 25

62   Ἐπὶ τούτωι δὲ ἐπηινέθη, καὶ τἄλλα ἐγένετο ὡς εἶπεν.
καὶ ἐκομίσθη παραχρῆμα εἰς τὸ θέατρον τὰ ἱμάτια καὶ τὸ
ἀργύριον. ἐγὼ δὲ οὐκ ἐβουλόμην λαβεῖν, ἀλλ' εἶπον ὅτι οὐ
δύνασαι δειπνεῖν ἐν τῶι δέρματι. Οὐκοῦν, εἶπον, τὸ σήμερον
ἄδειπνος μενῶ. ὅμως δὲ ἐνέδυσάν με τὸν χιτῶνα καὶ 30
περιέβαλον τὸ ἱμάτιον. ἐγὼ δὲ ἄνωθεν βαλεῖν ἐβουλόμην τὸ
63 δέρμα, οἱ δὲ οὐκ εἴων. τὸ δὲ ἀργύριον οὐκ ἐδεξάμην οὐδένα
τρόπον, ἀλλ' ἀπωμοσάμην μὴ λήψεσθαι. Εἰ δὲ ζητεῖτε τίς
λάβηι, τῶι ῥήτορι, ἔφην, δότε, ὅπως κατορύξηι αὐτό·

14 ξένια Dindorf: ξενίαι   33 μὴ M corr.: om. cett.   λήψεσθαι secl. Wilamowitz

ἐπίσταται γὰρ δηλονότι. ἀπ' ἐκείνου δ' ἡμᾶς οὐδεὶς
ἠνώχλησε.

64 Σχεδὸν οὖν εἰρηκότος αὐτοῦ πρὸς ταῖς σκηναῖς ἦμεν. κἀγὼ
γελάσας εἶπον, Ἀλλ' ἕν τι ἀπεκρύψω τοὺς πολίτας, τὸ
κάλλιστον τῶν κτημάτων. Τί τοῦτο; εἶπεν. Τὸν κῆπον, ἔφην, 5
τοῦτον, πάνυ καλὸν καὶ λάχανα πολλὰ καὶ δένδρα ἔχοντα.
Οὐκ ἦν, ἔφη, τότε, ἀλλ' ὕστερον ἐποιήσαμεν.

65 Εἰσελθόντες οὖν εὐωχούμεθα τὸ λοιπὸν τῆς ἡμέρας, ἡμεῖς
μὲν κατακλιθέντες ἐπὶ φύλλων τε καὶ δερμάτων ἐπὶ στιβάδος
ὑψηλῆς, ἡ δὲ γυνὴ πλησίον παρὰ τὸν ἄνδρα καθημένη. 10
θυγάτηρ δὲ ὡραία γάμου διηκονεῖτο, καὶ ἐνέχει πιεῖν μέλανα
οἶνον ἡδύν. οἱ δὲ παῖδες τὰ κρέα παρεσκεύαζον, καὶ αὐτοὶ
ἅμα ἐδείπνουν παρατιθέντες, ὥστε ἐμὲ εὐδαιμονίζειν τοὺς
ἀνθρώπους ἐκείνους καὶ οἴεσθαι μακαρίως ζῆν πάντων

66 μάλιστα ὧν ἠπιστάμην. καίτοι πλουσίων μὲν οἰκίας τε 15
καὶ τραπέζας ἠπιστάμην, οὐ μόνον ἰδιωτῶν, ἀλλὰ καὶ
σατραπῶν καὶ βασιλέων, οἳ μάλιστα ἐδόκουν μοι τότε
ἄθλιοι, καὶ πρότερον δοκοῦντες, ἔτι μᾶλλον, ὁρῶντι τὴν ἐκεῖ
πενίαν τε καὶ ἐλευθερίαν, καὶ ὅτι οὐδὲν ἀπελείποντο οὐδὲ
τῆς περὶ τὸ φαγεῖν τε καὶ πιεῖν ἡδονῆς, ἀλλὰ καὶ τούτοις 20
ἐπλεονέκτουν σχεδόν τι.

67 Ἤδη δ' ἱκανῶς ἡμῶν ἐχόντων ἦλθε κἀκεῖνος ὁ ἕτερος,
συνηκολούθει δὲ υἱὸς αὐτῶι, μειράκιον οὐκ ἀγεννές, λαγὼν
φέρων. εἰσελθὼν δὲ οὗτος ἠρυθρίασεν· ἐν ὅσωι δὲ ὁ
πατὴρ αὐτοῦ ἠσπάζετο ἡμᾶς, αὐτὸς ἐφίλησε τὴν κόρην 25
καὶ τὸν λαγὼν ἐκείνηι ἔδωκεν. ἡ μὲν οὖν παῖς ἐπαύσατο
διακονουμένη καὶ παρὰ τὴν μητέρα ἐκαθέζετο, τὸ δὲ

68 μειράκιον ἀντ' ἐκείνης διηκονεῖτο. κἀγὼ τὸν ξένον ἠρώτησα,
Αὕτη, ἔφην, ἐστίν, ἧς τὸν χιτῶνα ἀποδύσας τῶι ναυαγῶι
ἔδωκας; καὶ ὃς γελάσας, Οὐκ, ἔφη, ἀλλ' ἐκείνη, εἶπε, πάλαι 30
πρὸς ἄνδρα ἐδόθη, καὶ τέκνα ἔχει μεγάλα ἤδη, πρὸς ἄνδρα
πλούσιον εἰς κώμην. Οὐκοῦν, ἔφην, ἐπαρκοῦσιν ὑμῖν ὅ τι ἂν

15-16 καίτοι ... ἠπιστάμην om. PH   16 ἰδιωτῶν secl. Wifstrand   30-
2 πάλαι πρὸς ἄνδρα πλούσιον εἰς κώμην ἐδόθη καὶ τέκνα ἔχει μεγάλα ἤδη
Herwerden

69 δέησθε; Οὐδέν, εἶπεν ἡ γυνή, δεόμεθα ἡμεῖς· ἐκεῖνοι δὲ
λαμβάνουσι καὶ ὁπηνίκα τι θηραθῆι καὶ ὀπώραν καὶ
λάχανα· οὐ γὰρ ἔστι κῆπος παρ' αὐτοῖς. ⟨πέρυσι δὲ⟩
πυροὺς ἐλάβομεν, σπέρμα ψιλόν, καὶ ἀπεδώκαμεν αὐτοῖς
εὐθὺς τῆς θερείας. Τί οὖν; ἔφην, καὶ ταύτην διανοεῖσθε διδόναι 5
πλουσίωι, ἵνα ὑμῖν καὶ αὐτὴ πυροὺς δανείσηι; ἐνταῦθα
μέντοι ἄμφω ἠρυθριασάτην, ἡ κόρη καὶ τὸ μειράκιον.

70 Ὁ δὲ πατὴρ αὐτῆς ἔφη, Πένητα ἄνδρα λήψεται, ὅμοιον
ἡμῖν κυνηγέτην· καὶ μειδιάσας ἔβλεψεν εἰς τὸν νεανίσκον.
κἀγώ, Τί οὖν οὐκ ἤδη δίδοτε; ἢ δεῖ ποθεν αὐτὸν ἐκ κώμης 10
ἀφικέσθαι; Δοκῶ μέν, εἶπεν, οὐ μακράν ἐστίν, ἀλλ' ἔνδον
ἐνθάδε. καὶ ποιήσομέν γε τοὺς γάμους ἡμέραν ἀγαθὴν
ἐπιλεξάμενοι. κἀγώ, Πῶς, ἔφην, κρίνετε τὴν ἀγαθὴν ἡμέραν;
καὶ ὅς, Ὅταν μὴ μικρὸν ἦι τὸ σελήνιον· δεῖ δὲ καὶ τὸν

71 ἀέρα εἶναι καθαρόν, αἰθρίαν λαμπράν. κἀγώ, Τί δέ; τῶι ὄντι 15
κυνηγέτης ἀγαθός ἐστιν; ἔφην. Ἔγωγε, εἶπεν ὁ νεανίσκος,
καὶ ἔλαφον καταπονῶ καὶ σῦν ὑφίσταμαι. ὄψει δὲ αὔριον ἂν
θέληις, ὦ ξένε. Καὶ τὸν λαγὼν τοῦτον σύ, ἔφην, ἔλαβες; Ἐγώ,
ἔφη γελάσας, τῶι λιναρίωι τῆς νυκτός· ἦν γὰρ αἰθρία πάνυ
καλὴ καὶ ἡ σελήνη τηλικαύτη τὸ μέγεθος ἡλίκη οὐδεπώποτε 20

72 ἐγένετο. ἐνταῦθα μέντοι ἐγέλασαν ἀμφότεροι, οὐ μόνον ὁ
τῆς κόρης πατήρ, ἀλλὰ καὶ ὁ ἐκείνου. ὁ δὲ ἠισχύνθη καὶ
ἐσιώπησε.

Λέγει οὖν ὁ τῆς κόρης πατήρ, Ἐγὼ μέν, ἔφη, ὦ παῖ, οὐδὲν
ὑπερβάλλομαι. ὁ δὲ πατήρ σου περιμένει, ἔστ' ἂν ἱερεῖον 25
πρίηται πορευθείς. δεῖ γὰρ θῦσαι τοῖς θεοῖς. εἶπεν οὖν ὁ
νεώτερος ἀδελφὸς τῆς κόρης, Ἀλλὰ ἱερεῖόν γε πάλαι οὗτος
παρεσκεύακε, καὶ ἔστιν ἔνδον τρεφόμενον ὄπισθεν τῆς

73 σκηνῆς, γενναῖον. ἠρώτων οὖν αὐτόν, Ἀληθῶς; ὁ δὲ ἔφη.
Καὶ πόθεν σοι; ἔφασαν. Ὅτε τὴν ὗν ἐλάβομεν τὴν τὰ τέκνα 30
ἔχουσαν, τὰ μὲν ἄλλα διέδρα· καὶ ἦν, ἔφη, ταχύτερα τοῦ
λαγώ· ἑνὸς δὲ ἐγὼ λίθωι ἔτυχον καὶ ἁλόντι τὸ δέρμα
ἐπέβαλον· τοῦτο ἠλλαξάμην ἐν τῆι κώμηι καὶ ἔλαβον ἀντ'

---

2 ὁπηνίκ' ἂν Dindorf   3 ⟨πέρυσι⟩ add. Casaubon : ⟨πέρυσι δὲ παρ' αὐτῶν⟩
Wilamowitz   32 ἁλόντι Geel : ἄλλοι τὸ

44   ΔΙΩΝΟΣ

74 αὐτοῦ χοῖρον καὶ ἔθρεψα ποιήσας ὄπισθεν συφεόν. Ταῦτα,
εἶπεν, ἄρα ἡ μήτηρ σου ἐγέλα, ὁπότε θαυμάζοιμι ἀκούων
γρυλιζούσης τῆς συός, καὶ τὰς κριθὰς οὕτως ἀνήλισκες.
Αἱ γὰρ εὐβοΐδες, εἶπεν, οὐχ ἱκαναὶ ἦσαν πιᾶναι, εἰ μή γε
βαλάνους ἤθελεν ἐσθίειν. ἀλλὰ εἰ βούλεσθε ἰδεῖν αὐτήν, ἄξω   5
πορευθείς. οἱ δὲ ἐκέλευον. ἀπήιεσαν οὖν ἐκεῖνός τε καὶ οἱ
75 παῖδες αὐτόθεν δρόμωι χαίροντες. ἐν δὲ τούτωι ἡ παρθένος
ἀναστᾶσα ἐξ ἑτέρας σκηνῆς ἐκόμισεν οὖα τετμημένα καὶ
μέσπιλα καὶ μῆλα χειμερινὰ καὶ τῆς γενναίας σταφυλῆς
βότρυς σφριγῶντας, καὶ ἔθηκεν ἐπὶ τὴν τράπεζαν,   10
καταψήσασα φύλλοις ἀπὸ τῶν κρεῶν, ὑποβαλοῦσα
καθαρὰν πτερίδα. ἧκον δὲ καὶ οἱ παῖδες τὴν ὗν ἄγοντες
76 μετὰ γέλωτος καὶ παιδιᾶς. συνηκολούθει δὲ ἡ μήτηρ τοῦ
νεανίσκου καὶ ἀδελφοὶ δύο παιδάρια· ἔφερον δὲ ἄρτους τε
καθαροὺς καὶ ὠὰ ἐφθὰ ἐν ξυλίνοις πίναξι καὶ ἐρεβίνθους   15
φρυκτούς.

Ἀσπασαμένη δὲ τὸν ἀδελφὸν ἡ γυνὴ καὶ τὴν θυγατέρα
[καὶ τὴν ἀδελφιδῆν] ἐκαθέζετο παρὰ τὸν αὑτῆς ἄνδρα καὶ
εἶπεν, Ἰδοὺ τὸ ἱερεῖον, ὃ οὗτος πάλαι ἔτρεφεν εἰς τοὺς γάμους,
καὶ τἆλλα τὰ παρ' ἡμῶν ἕτοιμά ἐστι, καὶ ἄλφιτα καὶ ἄλευρα   20
πεποίηται· μόνον ἴσως οἰναρίου προσδεησόμεθα· καὶ τοῦτο
77 οὐ χαλεπὸν ἐκ τῆς κώμης λαβεῖν. παρειστήκει δὲ αὐτῆι
πλησίον ὁ υἱὸς πρὸς τὸν κηδεστὴν ἀποβλέπων. καὶ ὃς
μειδιάσας εἶπεν. Οὗτος, ἔφη, ἐστὶν ὁ ἐπέχων· ἴσως γὰρ ἔτι
βούλεται πιᾶναι τὴν ὗν. καὶ τὸ μειράκιον, Αὕτη μέν, εἶπεν,   25
78 ὑπὸ τοῦ λίπους διαρραγήσεται. κἀγὼ βουλόμενος αὐτῶι
βοηθῆσαι, Ὅρα, ἔφην, μὴ ἕως πιαίνεται ἡ ὗς οὗτος ὑμῖν
λεπτὸς γένηται. ἡ δὲ μήτηρ, Ἀληθῶς, εἶπεν, ὁ ξένος λέγει,
ἐπεὶ καὶ νῦν λεπτότερος αὑτοῦ γέγονε· καὶ πρώιην ἠισθόμην
τῆς νυκτὸς αὐτὸν ἐγρηγορότα καὶ προελθόντα ἔξω τῆς   30
79 σκηνῆς. Οἱ κύνες, ἔφη, ὑλάκτουν καὶ ἐξῆλθον ὀψόμενος. Οὐ

4 εἰ μή γε : ἢ μηδὲ von Arnim : εἰ μόνας γε Cohoon   7 αὐτόθεν παῖδες codd.,
corr. Geel   18 [καὶ τὴν ἀδελφιδῆν] secl. Emperius, καὶ τὴν θυγατέρα secl.
Selden.   20 ἡμῶν Emperius : ἡμῖν   ἐστι secl. Schenkl   21 πεποίηται secl.
Schenkl   23 ὁ υἱὸς Emperius : οὗτος

σύ γε, εἶπεν, ἀλλὰ περιεπάτεις ἀλύων. μὴ οὖν πλείω χρόνον
ἐῶμεν ἀνιᾶσθαι αὐτόν. καὶ περιβαλοῦσα ἐφίλησε τὴν μητέρα
τῆς κόρης. ἡ δὲ πρὸς τὸν ἄνδρα τὸν ἑαυτῆς, Ποιῶμεν, εἶπεν,
ὡς θέλουσι. καὶ ἔδοξε ταῦτα, καὶ εἶπον, Εἰς τρίτην ποιῶμεν
τοὺς γάμους. παρεκάλουν δὲ κἀμὲ προσμεῖναι τὴν ἡμέραν.   5

80 κἀγὼ προσέμεινα οὐκ ἀηδῶς, ἐνθυμούμενος ἅμα τῶν
πλουσίων ὁποῖά ἐστι τά τε ἄλλα καὶ τὰ περὶ τοὺς γάμους,
προμνηστριῶν τε πέρι καὶ ἐξετάσεων οὐσιῶν τε καὶ
γένους, προικῶν τε καὶ ἕδνων καὶ ὑποσχέσεων καὶ ἀπατῶν,
ὁμολογιῶν τε καὶ συγγραφῶν, καὶ τελευταῖον πολλάκις ἐν   10
αὐτοῖς τοῖς γάμοις λοιδοριῶν καὶ ἀπεχθειῶν.

81   Ἅπαντα δὴ τοῦτον τὸν λόγον διῆλθον οὐκ ἄλλως οὐδ᾽ ὡς
τάχ᾽ ἂν δόξαιμί τισιν, ἀδολεσχεῖν βουλόμενος, ἀλλ᾽ οὗπερ
ἐξ ἀρχῆς ὑπεθέμην βίου καὶ τῆς τῶν πενήτων διαγωγῆς
παράδειγμα ἐκτιθείς, ὃ αὐτὸς ἠπιστάμην, τῶι βουλομένωι   15
θεάσασθαι λόγων τε καὶ ἔργων καὶ κοινωνιῶν τῶν πρὸς
ἀλλήλους, εἴ τι τῶν πλουσίων ἐλαττοῦνται διὰ τὴν πενίαν
πρὸς τὸ ζῆν εὐσχημόνως καὶ κατὰ φύσιν ἢ τῶι παντὶ πλέον

82 ἔχουσιν. καὶ δῆτα καὶ τὸ τοῦ Εὐριπίδου σκοπῶν, εἰ κατ᾽
ἀλήθειαν ἀπόρως αὐτοῖς ἔχει τὰ πρὸς τοὺς ξένους, ὡς   20
μήτε ὑποδέξασθαί ποτε δύνασθαι μήτε ἐπαρκέσαι δεομένωι
τινί, οὐδαμῆι τοιοῦτον εὑρίσκω τὸ τῆς ξενίας, ἀλλὰ καὶ
πῦρ ἐναύοντας προθυμότερον τῶν πλουσίων καὶ ὁδῶν
ἀπροφασίστους ἡγεμόνας – ἐπεί τοι τὰ τοιαῦτα καὶ
αἰσχύνοιντο ἄν – πολλάκις δὲ καὶ μεταδιδόντας ὧν ἔχουσιν   25
ἑτοιμότερον· οὐ γὰρ δὴ ναυαγῶι τις δώσει ἐκείνων οὔτε τὸ
τῆς γυναικὸς ἀλουργὲς ἢ τὸ τῆς θυγατρὸς οὐδὲ πολὺ ἧττον
τούτου φόρημα, τῶν χλαινῶν τινα ἢ χιτώνων, μυρία
ἔχοντες, ἀλλ᾽ οὐδὲ τῶν οἰκετῶν οὐδενὸς ἱμάτιον.

83   Δηλοῖ δὲ καὶ τοῦτο Ὅμηρος· τὸν μὲν γὰρ Εὔμαιον   30
πεποίηκε δοῦλον καὶ πένητα ὅμως τὸν Ὀδυσσέα καλῶς
ὑποδεχόμενον καὶ τροφῆι καὶ κοίτηι, τοὺς δὲ μνηστῆρας ὑπὸ
πλούτου καὶ ὕβρεως οὐ πάνυ ῥαιδίως αὐτῶι μεταδιδόντας

27 οὐδὲ : οὔτε von Arnim

46 ΔΙΩΝΟΣ

οὐδὲ τῶν ἀλλοτρίων, ὥς που καὶ αὐτὸς πεποίηται λέγων
πρὸς τὸν Ἀντίνουν, ὀνειδίζων τὴν ἀνελευθερίαν,

οὐ σύ γ' ἂν ἐξ οἴκου σῶι ἐπιστάτηι οὐδ' ἅλα δοίης,
ὃς νῦν ἀλλοτρίοισι παρήμενος οὔτι μοι ἔτλης
σίτου ἀπάρξασθαι, πολλῶν κατὰ οἶκον ἐόντων. 5

84 Καὶ τούτους μὲν ἔστω διὰ τὴν ἄλλην πονηρίαν εἶναι
τοιούτους· ἀλλ' οὐδὲ τὴν Πηνελόπην, καίτοι χρηστὴν
οὖσαν καὶ σφόδρα ἡδέως διαλεγομένην πρὸς αὐτὸν καὶ
περὶ τοῦ ἀνδρὸς πεπυσμένην, οὐδὲ ταύτην φησὶν ἱμάτιον
αὐτῶι δοῦναι γυμνῶι παρακαθημένωι, ἀλλ' ἢ μόνον 10
ἐπαγγέλλεσθαι, ἂν ἄρα φανῆι ἀληθεύων περὶ τοῦ
85 Ὀδυσσέως ὅτι ἐκείνου τοῦ μηνὸς ἥξοι, καὶ ὕστερον, ἐπειδὴ
τὸ τόξον ἤιτει, τῶν μνηστήρων, οὐ δυναμένων ἐντεῖναι,
χαλεπαινόντων ἐκείνωι ὅτι ἠξίου πρὸς αὐτοὺς ἁμιλλᾶσθαι
περὶ ἀρετῆς, ἀξιοῖ δοθῆναι αὐτῶι· οὐ γὰρ δὴ περὶ τοῦ 15
γάμου γε εἶναι κἀκείνωι τὸν λόγον, ἀλλ' ἐὰν τύχηι ἐπιτείνας
καὶ διαβαλὼν διὰ τῶν πελέκεων, ἐπαγγέλλεται αὐτῶι
86 δώσειν χιτῶνα καὶ ἱμάτιον καὶ ὑποδήματα· ὡς δέον αὐτὸν
τὸ Εὐρύτου τόξον ἐντεῖναι καὶ τοσούτοις νεανίσκοις ἐχθρὸν
γενέσθαι, τυχὸν δὲ καὶ ἀπολέσθαι παραχρῆμα ὑπ' αὐτῶν, 20
εἰ μέλλει τυγχάνειν ἐξωμίδος καὶ ὑποδημάτων, ἢ τὸν
Ὀδυσσέα, εἴκοσιν ἐτῶν οὐδαμοῦ πεφηνότα, ἥκοντα
ἀποδεῖξαι, καὶ ταῦτα ἐν ἡμέραις ῥηταῖς· εἰ δὲ μή, ἐν τοῖς
αὐτοῖς ἀπιέναι ῥάκεσι παρὰ τῆς σώφρονος καὶ ἀγαθῆς
Ἰκαρίου θυγατρὸς βασιλίδος. 25
87 Σχεδὸν δὲ καὶ ὁ Τηλέμαχος τοιαῦτα ἕτερα πρὸς τὸν
συβώτην λέγει περὶ αὐτοῦ, κελεύων αὐτὸν εἰς τὴν πόλιν
πέμπειν τὴν ταχίστην πτωχεύσοντα ἐκεῖ, καὶ μὴ πλείους
ἡμέρας τρέφειν ἐν τῶι σταθμῶι· καὶ γὰρ εἰ ξυνέκειτο αὐτοῖς
ταῦτα, ἀλλ' ὅ γε συβώτης οὐ θαυμάζει τὸ πρᾶγμα καὶ τὴν 30
88 ἀπανθρωπίαν, ὡς ἔθους δὴ ὄντος οὕτως ἀκριβῶς καὶ
ἀνελευθέρως πράττειν τὰ περὶ τοὺς ξένους τοὺς πένητας,

13 ἐντεῖναι Cobet : ἐπιτεῖναι

μόνους δὲ τοὺς πλουσίους ὑποδέχεσθαι φιλοφρόνως ξενίοις
καὶ δώροις, παρ' ὧν δῆλον ὅτι καὶ αὐτοὶ προσεδόκων
τῶν ἴσων ἂν τυχεῖν, ὁποῖα σχεδὸν καὶ τὰ τῶν νῦν ἐστι
89 φιλανθρωπίας τε πέρι καὶ προαιρέσεως. αἱ γὰρ δὴ δοκοῦσαι
φιλοφρονήσεις καὶ χάριτες, ἐὰν σκοπῆι τις ὀρθῶς, οὐδὲν 5
διαφέρουσιν ἐράνων καὶ δανείων, ἐπὶ τόκωι συχνῶι καὶ
ταῦτα ὡς τὸ πολὺ γιγνόμενα, εἰ μὴ νὴ Δί' ὑπερβάλλει τὰ
90 νῦν τὰ πρότερον, ὥσπερ ἐν τῆι ἄλληι ξυμπάσηι κακίαι. ἔχω
γε μὴν εἰπεῖν καὶ περὶ τῶν Φαιάκων καὶ τῆς ἐκείνων
φιλανθρωπίας, εἴ τωι δοκοῦσιν οὗτοι οὐκ ἀγεννῶς, οὐδ' 10
ἀναξίως τοῦ πλούτου προσενεχθῆναι τῶι Ὀδυσσεῖ, μεθ'
οἵας μάλιστα διανοίας καὶ δι' ἃς αἰτίας προὐτράπησαν
ἀφθόνως καὶ μεγαλοπρεπῶς χαρίζεσθαι. ἀλλὰ γὰρ πολὺ
πλείω τῶν ἱκανῶν καὶ τὰ νῦν ὑπὲρ τούτων εἰρημένα.
91 Δῆλόν γε μὴν ὡς ὁ πλοῦτος οὔτε πρὸς ξένους οὔτε ἄλλως 15
μέγα τι συμβάλλεται τοῖς κεκτημένοις, ἀλλὰ τοὐναντίον
γλίσχρους καὶ φειδωλοὺς ὡς τὸ πολὺ μᾶλλον τῆς πενίας
ἀποτελεῖν πέφυκεν. οὐδὲ γάρ, εἴ τις αὖ τῶν πλουσίων, εἷς
που τάχα ἐν μυρίοις, δαψιλὴς καὶ μεγαλόφρων τὸν τρόπον
εὑρεθείη, τοῦτο ἱκανῶς δείκνυσι τὸ μὴ οὐχὶ τοὺς πολλοὺς 20
92 χείρους περὶ ταῦτα γίγνεσθαι τῶν ἀπορωτέρων. ἀνδρὶ δὲ
πένητι μὴ φαύλωι τὴν φύσιν ἀρκεῖ τὰ παρόντα καὶ τὸ σῶμα
μετρίως ἀσθενήσαντι, τοιούτου ποτὲ νοσήματος ξυμβάντος,
οἷάπερ εἴωθε γίγνεσθαι τοῖς οὐκ ἀργοῖς οὐδ' ἑκάστοτε
ἐμπιμπλαμένοις, ἀνακτήσασθαι, καὶ ξένοις ἐλθοῦσι δοῦναι 25
προσφιλῆ ξένια χωρὶς ὑποψίας παρ' ἑκόντων διδόμενα
93 ἀλύπως, οὐκ ἴσως ἀργυροῦς κρατῆρας ἢ ποικίλους πέπλους ἢ
τέθριππον, [ἢ] τὰ Ἑλένης καὶ Μενέλεω Τηλεμάχωι δῶρα.
οὐδὲ γὰρ τοιούτους ὑποδέχοιντ' ἄν, ὡς εἰκός, ξένους,
σατράπας ἢ βασιλέας, εἰ μή γε πάνυ σώφρονας καὶ ἀγαθούς, 30
οἷς οὐδὲν ἐνδεὲς μετὰ φιλίας γιγνόμενον. ἀκολάστους δὲ
καὶ τυραννικοὺς οὔτ' ἂν οἶμαι δύναιντο θεραπεύειν ἱκανῶς
94 ξένους οὔτ' ἂν ἴσως προσδέοιντο τοιαύτης ξενίας. οὐδὲ γὰρ

24 οὐδ' U : om. cett.   28 [ἢ] secl. Geel

48   ΔΙΩΝΟΣ

τῶι Μενέλεωι δήπουθεν ἀπέβη πρὸς τὸ λῶιον, ὅτι ἐδύνατο
δέξασθαι τὸν πλουσιώτατον ἐκ τῆς Ἀσίας ξένον, ἄλλος δὲ
οὐδεὶς ἱκανὸς ἦν ἐν τῆι Σπάρτηι τὸν Πριάμου τοῦ βασιλέως
95 υἱὸν ὑποδέξασθαι. τοιγάρτοι ἐρημώσας αὐτοῦ τὴν οἰκίαν
καὶ πρὸς τοῖς χρήμασι τὴν γυναῖκα προσλαβών, τὴν δὲ 5
θυγατέρα ὀρφανὴν τῆς μητρὸς ἐάσας, ὤιχετο ἀποπλέων.
καὶ μετὰ ταῦτα ὁ Μενέλαος χρόνον μὲν πολὺν ἐφθείρετο
πανταχόσε τῆς Ἑλλάδος, ὀδυρόμενος τὰς αὐτοῦ συμφορὰς,
δεόμενος ἑκάστου τῶν βασιλέων ἐπαμῦναι. ἠναγκάσθη δὲ
ἱκετεῦσαι καὶ τὸν ἀδελφὸν ὅπως ἐπιδῶι τὴν θυγατέρα 10
96 σφαγησομένην ἐν Αὐλίδι. δέκα δὲ ἔτη καθῆστο πολεμῶν ἐν
Τροίαι, πάλιν ἐκεῖ κολακεύων τοὺς ἡγεμόνας τοῦ στρατοῦ
καὶ αὐτὸς καὶ ὁ ἀδελφός – εἰ δὲ μή, ὠργίζοντο καὶ ἠπείλουν
ἑκάστοτε ἀποπλεύσεσθαι – καὶ πολλοὺς πόνους καὶ
κινδύνους ἀμηχάνους ὑπομένων, ὕστερον δὲ ἠλᾶτο καὶ 15
οὐχ οἷός τ' ἦν δίχα μυρίων κακῶν οἴκαδ' ἀφικέσθαι.
97   Ἆρ' οὖν σφόδρα ἄξιον ἄγασθαι τοῦ πλούτου κατὰ τὸν
ποιητὴν καὶ τῶι ὄντι ζηλωτὸν ὑπολαβεῖν; ὅς φησιν αὐτοῦ
μέγιστον εἶναι ἀγαθὸν τὸ δοῦναι ξένοις, καὶ ἐάν ποτέ τινες
ἔλθωσι τρυφῶντες ἐπὶ τὴν οἰκίαν, μὴ ἀδύνατον γενέσθαι 20
παρασχεῖν κατάλυσιν καὶ προθεῖναι ξένια οἷς ἂν ἐκεῖνοι
98 μάλιστα ἥδοιντο; λέγομεν δὲ ταῦτα μεμνημένοι τῶν
ποιητῶν, οὐκ ἄλλως ἀντιπαρεξάγοντες ἐκείνοις οὐδὲ τῆς
δόξης ζηλοτυποῦντες ἣν ἀπὸ τῶν ποιημάτων ἐκτήσαντο
ἐπὶ σοφίαι, οὐ τούτων ἕνεκα φιλοτιμούμενοι ἐξελέγχειν 25
αὐτούς, ἀλλὰ παρ' ἐκείνοις μάλιστα εὑρήσειν ἡγούμενοι τὴν
τῶν πολλῶν διάνοιαν, ἃ δὴ καὶ τοῖς πολλοῖς ἐδόκει περί τε
πλούτου καὶ τῶν ἄλλων ἃ θαυμάζουσι, καὶ τί μέγιστον
οἴονταί σφισι γενέσθαι ἂν ἀφ' ἑκάστου τῶν τοιούτων.
99 δῆλον γὰρ ὅτι μὴ συμφωνοῦντος αὐτοῖς τοῦ ποιήματος 30
μηδὲ τὴν αὐτὴν γνώμην ἔχοντος οὐκ ἂν οὕτω σφόδρα

16 δίχα Emperius : διὰ   17 ἆρ' οὖν Geel : ἆρ' οὐ UBM : ἆρ' οὖν οὐ PH   ἆρ'
οὖν οὐ ... ἀνάξιον Capps   17 κατὰ Emperius : καὶ   18 ὅς : ὃ von Arnim
25 οὐ : num οὐδέ?   27 πολλοῖς : παλαίοις Geel   ἐδόκει : δοκεῖ Reiske   ἃ ...
ἐδόκει secl. Emperius   29 ἀφ' Selden : ἐφ'

ἐφίλουν οὐδὲ ἐπήινουν ὡς σοφούς τε καὶ ἀγαθοὺς †γενέσθαι†
100 καὶ τἀληθῆ λέγοντας. ἐπεὶ οὖν οὐκ ἔστιν ἕκαστον
ἀπολαμβάνοντα ἐλέγχειν τοῦ πλήθους, οὐδ' ἀνερωτᾶν
ἅπαντας ἐν μέρει, Τί γὰρ σύ, ὦ ἄνθρωπε, δέδοικας τὴν
πενίαν οὕτως πάνυ τὸν δὲ πλοῦτον ὑπερτιμᾶις, τί δ' αὖ 5
σὺ ἐλπίζεις κερδανεῖν μέγιστον ἂν τύχηις πλουτήσας ἢ νὴ
Δία ἔμπορος γενόμενος ἢ καὶ βασιλεύσας; ἀμήχανον γὰρ δὴ
101 τὸ τοιοῦτον καὶ οὐδαμῶς ἀνυστόν. οὕτως οὖν ἐπὶ τοὺς
προφήτας αὐτῶν καὶ συνηγόρους, τοὺς ποιητάς, ἐξ ἀνάγκης
ἴωμεν, ὡς ἐκεῖ φανερὰς καὶ μέτροις κατακεκλεισμένας 10
εὑρήσοντες τὰς τῶν πολλῶν δόξας· καὶ δῆτα οὐ πάνυ μοι
102 δοκοῦμεν ἀποτυγχάνειν. τοῦτο δὲ σύνηθες δήπου καὶ τοῖς
σοφωτέροις, ὃ νῦν ἡμεῖς ποιοῦμεν· ἐπεὶ καὶ αὐτοῖς τούτοις
τοῖς ἔπεσιν ἀντείρηκε τῶν πάνυ φιλοσόφων τις, ὃν οὐδείς,
ἐμοὶ δοκεῖν, φαίη ἂν ποτε φιλονεικοῦντα τούτοις τε 15
ἀντειρηκέναι καὶ τοῖς ὑπὸ Σοφοκλέους εἰς τὸν πλοῦτον
εἰρημένοις, ἐκείνοις μὲν ἐπ' ὀλίγον, τοῖς δὲ τοῦ Σοφοκλέους
ἐπὶ πλέον, οὐ μήν, ὥσπερ νῦν ἡμεῖς, διὰ μακρῶν, ἅτε οὐ
πρὸς τὸ ⟨παρα⟩χρῆμα κατὰ πολλὴν ἐξουσίαν διεξιὼν ἀλλ'
ἐν βίβλοις γράφων. 20
103 Γεωργικοῦ μὲν δὴ πέρι καὶ κυνηγετικοῦ τε καὶ ποιμενικοῦ
βίου τάδε, πλείω διατριβὴν ἴσως παρασχόντα τοῦ μετρίου,
λελέχθω, προθυμουμένων ἡμῶν ἀμηγέπηι δεῖξαι πενίαν ὡς
οὐκ ἄπορον χρῆμα βίου καὶ ζωῆς πρεπούσης ἀνδράσιν
ἐλευθέροις αὐτουργεῖν ἐθέλουσιν, ἀλλ' ἐπὶ κρείττω πολὺ καὶ 25
συμφορώτερα ἔργα καὶ πράξεις ἄγον καὶ μᾶλλον κατὰ φύσιν
104 ἢ ἐφ' οἷα ὁ πλοῦτος εἴωθε τοὺς πολλοὺς προτρέπειν. εἶεν δή,
περὶ τῶν ἐν ἄστει καὶ κατὰ πόλιν πενήτων σκεπτέον ἂν εἴη
τοῦ βίου καὶ τῶν ἐργασιῶν, πῶς ἂν μάλιστα διάγοντες καὶ
ποῖ' ἄττα μεταχειριζόμενοι δυνήσονται μὴ κακῶς ζῆν μηδὲ 30
φαυλότερον τῶν δανειζόντων ἐπὶ τόκοις συχνοῖς, εὖ μάλ'

---

1 †γενέσθαι† secl. Reiske : τελεστὰς Geel : ἀγαθοὺς ⟨δοκοῦντας ἐξηγητὰς⟩
γενέσθαι Wenkebach. num autem γενομένους?   19 πρὸς τὸ ⟨παρα⟩χρῆμα
scripsi : πρὸς τὸ χρῆμα codd. : παραχρῆμα von Arnim   20 ἐν βίβλοις susp.
Emperius : num ἐν ἰαμβείοις?   26 ἄγον καὶ Reiske : ἄγοντα

ἐπισταμένων τὸν ἡμερῶν τε καὶ μηνῶν ἀριθμόν, καὶ τῶν
συνοικίας τε μεγάλας καὶ ναῦς κεκτημένων καὶ ἀνδράποδα
πολλά.

105 Μήποτε σπάνια ἦι τὰ ἐν ταῖς πόλεσιν ἔργα τοῖς τοιούτοις,
ἀφορμῆς τε ἔξωθεν προσδεόμενα, ὅταν οἰκεῖν τε μισθοῦ δέηι 5
καὶ τἄλλ' ἔχειν ὠνουμένους, οὐ μόνον ἱμάτια καὶ σκεύη καὶ
σῖτον, ἀλλὰ καὶ ξύλα, τῆς γε καθ' ἡμέραν χρείας ἕνεκα [τοῦ
πυρός], κἂν φρυγάνων δέηι ποτὲ ἢ φύλλων ἢ ἄλλου ὁτουοῦν
106 τῶν πάνυ φαύλων, δίχα γε ὕδατος τὰ ἄλλα σύμπαντα
ἀναγκάζωνται λαμβάνειν τιμὴν κατατιθέντες, ἅτε πάντων 10
κατακλειομένων καὶ μηδενὸς ἐν μέσωι φαινομένου πλήν γε
οἶμαι τῶν ἐπὶ πράσει πολλῶν καὶ τιμίων. τάχα γὰρ ἂν
φανεῖται χαλεπὸν τοιούτωι βίωι διαρκεῖν μηδὲν ἄλλο κτῆμα
ἔξω τοῦ σώματος κεκτημένους, ἄλλως τε ὅταν μὴ τὸ τυχὸν
ἔργον μηδὲ πάνθ' ὁμοίως συμβουλεύωμεν αὐτοῖς ὅθεν ἔστι 15
107 κερδᾶναι· ὥστε ἴσως ἀναγκασθησόμεθα ἐκβαλεῖν ἐκ τῶν
πόλεων τῶι λόγωι τοὺς κομψοὺς πένητας, ἵνα παρέχωμεν
τῶι ὄντι καθ' Ὅμηρον τὰς πόλεις εὖ ναιεταώσας, ὑπὸ
μόνων τῶν μακαρίων οἰκουμένας, ἐντὸς δὲ τείχους οὐδένα
ἐάσομεν, ὡς ἔοικεν, ἐλεύθερον ἐργάτην. ἀλλὰ τοὺς τοιούτους 20
ἅπαντας τί δράσομεν; ἢ διασπείραντες ἐν τῆι χώραι
κατοικιοῦμεν, καθάπερ Ἀθηναίους φασὶ νέμεσθαι καθ' ὅλην
τὴν Ἀττικὴν τὸ παλαιὸν καὶ πάλιν ὕστερον τυραννήσαντος
108 Πεισιστράτου; οὐκοῦν οὐδὲ ἐκείνοις ἀξύμφορος ἡ τοιαύτη
δίαιτα ἐγένετο, οὐδὲ ἀγεννεῖς ἤνεγκε φύσεις πολιτῶν, 25
ἀλλὰ τῶι παντὶ βελτίους καὶ σωφρονεστέρους τῶν ἐν
ἄστει τρεφομένων ὕστερον ἐκκλησιαστῶν καὶ δικαστῶν καὶ
γραμματέων, ἀργῶν ἅμα καὶ βαναύσων. οὔκουν ὁ κίνδυνος
μέγας οὐδὲ χαλεπός, εἰ πάντες οὗτοι καὶ πάντα τρόπον
ἀγροῖκοι ἔσονται· οἶμαι δ' ὅμως αὐτοὺς οὐκ ἀπορήσειν οὐδὲ 30
ἐν ἄστει τροφῆς.

7–8 [τοῦ πυρός] secl. Naber   9 γε scripsi : δὲ   10 ἀναγκάζωνται Reiske:
ἀναγκάζονται   12 ἂν secl. Dindorf   24 οὔκουν Geel   28 ἀργῶν
Herwerden : ἀστῶν uel αὐτῶν   30 ἀγροῖκοι scripsi: ἄγροικοι

109 Ἀλλὰ ἴδωμεν πόσα καὶ ἅττα πράττοντες ἐπιεικῶς ἡμῖν
διάξουσιν, ἵνα μὴ πολλάκις ἀναγκασθῶσιν ἀργοὶ καθήμενοι
πρός τι τῶν φαύλων τραπῆναι. αἱ μὲν δὴ σύμπασαι κατὰ
πόλιν ἐργασίαι καὶ τέχναι πολλαὶ καὶ παντοδαπαί, σφόδρα
τε λυσιτελεῖς ἔνιαι τοῖς χρωμένοις, ἐάν τις τὸ λυσιτελὲς 5
110 σκοπῆι πρὸς ἀργύριον. ὀνομάσαι δὲ αὐτὰς πάσας κατὰ
μέρος οὐ ῥάιδιον διὰ τὸ πλῆθος καὶ τὴν ἀτοπίαν οὐχ ἧττον.
οὐκοῦν ὅδε εἰρήσθω περὶ αὐτῶν ἐν βραχεῖ ψόγος τε καὶ
ἔπαινος. ὅσαι μὲν σώματι βλαβεραὶ πρὸς ὑγίειαν ἢ πρὸς
ἰσχὺν τὴν ἱκανὴν δι' ἀργίαν τε καὶ ἑδραιότητα ἢ ψυχῆι 10
ἀσχημοσύνην τε καὶ ἀνελευθερίαν ἐντίκτουσι ἢ ἄλλως
ἀχρεῖοί καὶ πρὸς οὐδὲν ὄφελός εἰσιν, εὑρημέναι δι' ἀβελτερίαν
τε καὶ τρυφὴν τῶν πόλεων, ἅς γε τὴν ἀρχὴν μήτε τέχνας
μήτε ἐργασίας τό γε ὀρθὸν καλεῖν· οὐ γὰρ ἄν ποτε Ἡσίοδος
σοφὸς ὢν ἐπήινεσεν ὁμοίως πᾶν ἔργον, εἴ τι τῶν πονηρῶν 15
111 ἢ τῶν αἰσχρῶν ἠξίου ταύτης τῆς προσηγορίας· αἷς μὲν
ἄν τις προσῆι τούτων τῶν βλαβῶν καὶ ἡτισοῦν, μηδένα
ἅπτεσθαι τῶν ἐλευθέρων τε καὶ ἐπιεικῶν μηδὲ ἐπίστασθαι
μήτε αὐτὸν μήτε παῖδας τοὺς αὑτοῦ διδάσκειν, ὡς οὔτε
καθ' Ἡσίοδον οὔτε καθ' ἡμᾶς ἐργάτην ἐσόμενον ἄν 20
τι μεταχειρίζηται τοιοῦτον, ἀλλὰ ἀργίας τε ἅμα καὶ
αἰσχροκερδείας ἀνελεύθερον ἕξοντα ὄνειδος, βάναυσον καὶ
112 ἀχρεῖον καὶ πονηρὸν ἁπλῶς ὀνομαζόμενον. ὅσα δὲ αὖ μήτε
ἀπρεπῆ τοῖς μετιοῦσι μοχθηρίαν τε μηδεμίαν ἐμποιοῦντα
τῆι ψυχῆι μήτε νοσώδη τῶν τε ἄλλων νοσημάτων καὶ δῆτα 25
ἀσθενείας τε καὶ ὄκνου καὶ μαλακίας διὰ πολλὴν ἡσυχίαν
ἐγγιγνομένης ἐν τῶι σώματι, καὶ μὴν χρείαν γε ἱκανὴν
113 παρέχοντα πρὸς τὸν βίον, πάντα τὰ τοιαῦτα πράττοντες
προθύμως καὶ φιλοπόνως οὔποτ' ἂν ἐνδεεῖς ἔργου καὶ
βίου γίγνοιντο, οὐδ' ἂν ἀληθῆ τὴν ἐπίκλησιν παρέχοιεν 30
τοῖς πλουσίοις καλεῖν αὐτοὺς ἧιπερ εἰώθασιν, ἀπόρους

10 ψυχῆι Schenkl : ψυχῆς   11 ἐντίκτουσαι Wilamowitz   14 ⟨δεῖ⟩ καλεῖν
Reiske : ὀρθόν ⟨ἔστι⟩ Emperius   16 οὖν post μέν add. UB   24 ἀπρεπῆ
Reiske : ἀποτρέπει   27 χρείαν : χορηγίαν Pflugk

ὀνομάζοντας, τοὐναντίον μᾶλλον ἐκείνων ὄντες πορισταὶ καὶ μηδενὸς ἀποροῦντες ὡς ἔπος εἰπεῖν τῶν ἀναγκαίων καὶ χρησίμων.

114 Φέρε οὖν μνησθῶμεν ἀφ' ἑκατέρου τοῦ γένους, εἰ καὶ μὴ πάνυ ἀκριβῶς ἕκαστα φράζοντες ἀλλ' ὡς τύπωι γε 5 κατιδεῖν, τὰ ποῖ' ἄττα καὶ ὧν ἕνεκα οὐ προσιέμεθα, καὶ ποῖα θαρροῦντας ἐπιχειρεῖν κελεύομεν, μηδὲν φροντίζοντας τῶν ἄλλως τὰ τοιαῦτα προφερόντων, οἷον εἰώθασι λοιδορούμενοι προφέρειν πολλάκις οὐ μόνον τὰς αὐτῶν ἐργασίας, αἷς οὐδὲν ἄτοπον πρόσεστιν, ἀλλὰ καὶ τῶν 10 γονέων, ἄν τινος ἔριθος ἡ μήτηρ ἢ τρυγήτρια ἐξελθοῦσά ποτε ἢ μισθοῦ τιτθεύσηι παῖδα τῶν ὀρφανῶν ἢ πλουσίων ἢ ὁ πατὴρ διδάξηι γράμματα ἢ παιδαγωγήσηι· μηδὲν οὖν 115 τοιοῦτον αἰσχυνομένους ὁμόσε ἰέναι. οὐ γὰρ ἄλλως αὐτὰ ἐροῦσιν, ἄν λέγωσιν, ἢ ὡς σημεῖα πενίας, πενίαν αὐτὴν 15 λοιδοροῦντες δηλονότι καὶ προφέροντες ὡς κακὸν δή τι καὶ δυστυχές, οὐ τῶν ἔργων οὐδέν. ὥστε ἐπειδὴ οὔ φαμεν χεῖρον οὐδὲ δυστυχέστερον πλούτου πενίαν οὐδὲ πολλοῖς ἴσως ἀξυμφορώτερον, οὐδὲ τὸ ὄνειδος τοῦ ὀνείδους μᾶλλόν 116 τι βαρυντέον τοῦτ' ἐκείνου. εἰ γάρ τοι δέοι μὴ ὀνομάζοντας 20 τὸ πρᾶγμα ὃ ψέγουσι, τὰ καθ' ἡμέραν συμβαίνοντα δι' αὐτὸ βλασφημεῖν προφέροντας, πολὺ πλείω ἂν ἔχοιεν καὶ τῶι ὄντι αἰσχρὰ διὰ πλοῦτον γιγνόμενα, οὐχ ἥκιστα δὲ τὸ παρὰ τῶι Ἡσιόδωι κεκριμένον ἐπονείδιστον προφέρειν, τὸ τῆς ἀργίας, λέγοντες ὅτι σε, ὦ ἄνθρωπε, 25

οὔτε σκαπτῆρα θεοὶ θέσαν οὔτ' ἀροτῆρα,

καὶ ὅτι ἄλλως τὰς χεῖρας ἔχεις κατὰ τοὺς μνηστῆρας ἀτρίπτους καὶ ἀπαλάς.

117 Οὐκοῦν τόδε μὲν οἶμαι παντὶ τωι δῆλον καὶ πολλάκις λεγόμενον ἴσως, ὅτι βαφεῖς μὲν καὶ μυρεψοὺς [καὶ 30 βυρσοδέψας] σὺν κουρικῆι γυναικῶν τε καὶ ἀνδρῶν, οὐ

---

1 ὀνομάζοντες Casaubon   5 γε Reiske : τε   6 τὰ ποῖ' ἄττα Geel : τοιαῦτα
18–19 τοῖς δὲ πολλοῖς ἴσως καὶ ξυμφορώτερον von Arnim   20 δέοι Emperius :
δοκεῖ   21 καθ' ἡμέραν post ὀνομάζοντας codd., huc transp. Emperius
30–1 [καὶ βυρσοδέψας] secl. Pflugk

πολύ τι διαφερούσηι τὰ νῦν, καὶ ποικιλτικῆι πάσηι σχεδόν,
οὐκ ἐσθῆτος μόνον, ἀλλὰ καὶ τριχῶν καὶ χρωτός, ἐγχούσηι
καὶ ψιμυθίωι καὶ πᾶσι φαρμάκοις μηχανωμένηι ὥρας ψευδῆ
καὶ νόθα εἴδωλα, ἔτι δὲ ἐν οἰκιῶν ὀροφαῖς καὶ τοίχοις καὶ
ἐδάφει τὰ μὲν χρώμασι, τὰ δὲ λίθοις, τὰ δὲ χρυσῶι, τὰ δὲ 5
118 ἐλέφαντι ποικιλλόντων, τὰ δὲ αὐτῶν τοίχων γλυφαῖς, τὸ
μὲν ἄριστον μὴ παραδέχεσθαι καθόλου τὰς πόλεις, τὸ δὲ
⟨ἐφ'⟩ ἡμῖν ἐν τῶι παρόντι λόγωι διορίσαι μηδένα περὶ
τοιοῦτον γίγνεσθαι τῶν ἡμετέρων πενήτων· ὡς πρὸς τοὺς
πλουσίους ἡμεῖς ἀγωνιζόμεθα ὥσπερ χορῶι τὰ νῦν, οὐχ 10
ὑπὲρ εὐδαιμονίας, προκειμένου τοῦ ἀγῶνος – οὐ γὰρ πενίαι
τοῦτό γε πρόκειται τὸ ἆθλον οὐδὲ αὖ πλούτωι, μόνης δὲ
ἀρετῆς ἐστιν ἐξαίρετον – ἄλλως δὲ ὑπὲρ ἀγωγῆς τινος καὶ
μετριότητος βίου.
119 Καὶ τοίνυν οὐδ' ὑποκριτὰς τραγικοὺς ἢ κωμικοὺς ἤ 15
τινων μίμων ἀκράτου γέλωτος δημιουργοὺς οὐδὲ ὀρχηστὰς
οὐδὲ χορευτάς, πλήν γε τῶν ἱερῶν χορῶν, ἀλλ' ἐπί γε
τοῖς Νιόβης ἢ Θυέστου πάθεσιν ἄιδοντας ἢ ὀρχουμένους,
οὐδὲ κιθαρωιδοὺς οὐδὲ αὐλητὰς περὶ νίκης ἐν θεάτροις
ἀμιλλωμένους, εἰ καί τινες τῶν ἐνδόξων πόλεων ἐπὶ τούτοις 20
ἡμῖν δυσχερῶς ἕξουσι, Σμύρνα καὶ Χῖος, καὶ δῆτα σὺν
ταύταις καὶ τὸ Ἄργος, ὡς τὴν Ὁμήρου τε καὶ Ἀγαμέμνονος
120 δόξαν οὐκ ἐώντων αὔξεσθαι τὸ γοῦν ἐφ' ἡμῖν· τυχὸν δὲ
καὶ Ἀθηναῖοι χαλεπανοῦσιν, ἀτιμάζεσθαι νομίζοντες τοὺς
σφετέρους ποιητὰς τραγικοὺς καὶ κωμικούς, ὅταν τοὺς 25
ὑπηρέτας αὐτῶν ἀφαιρώμεθα, μηδὲν ἀγαθὸν φάσκοντες
ἐπιτηδεύειν· εἰκὸς δὲ ἀγανακτεῖν καὶ Θηβαίους, ὡς τῆς νίκης
αὐτῶν ὑβριζομένης ἣν προεκρίθησαν ὑπὸ τῆς Ἑλλάδος
121 νικᾶν ἐπ' αὐλητικῆι· ταύτην δὲ τὴν νίκην οὕτω σφόδρα
ἠγάπησαν ὥστε ἀναστάτου τῆς πόλεως αὐτοῖς γενομένης 30
καὶ ἔτι νῦν σχεδὸν οὐδὲ πλὴν μικροῦ μέρους, τῆς Καδμείας,

---

1 διαφερούσηι Morel : -αις uel -ας   2 ἐγχούσηι Casaubon : ἐπεγχούσηι uel
ἐπεχούσηι   3 ὥρας Emperius : ὡς ἄρα ψευδῆ P: ψευδεῖς   6 αὖ τῶν
Schenkl   8 ⟨ἐφ'⟩ Emperius : ⟨ἀρκοῦν⟩ Kayser : ⟨δεύτερον⟩ Capps   8 περὶ
scripsi : ἂν   15–16 ἢ ⟨διά⟩ τινων Reiske   17 ἀλλ' ⟨οὐκ⟩ ἐπί γε Reiske
28 ὑπὸ Reiske : ὑπὲρ   31 οὐδὲ scripsi : οὔσης

οἰκουμένης, τῶν μὲν ἄλλων οὐδενὸς ἐφρόντισαν τῶν
ἠφανισμένων ἀπὸ πολλῶν μὲν ἱερῶν, πολλῶν δὲ στηλῶν
καὶ ἐπιγραφῶν, τὸν δὲ Ἑρμῆν ἀναζητήσαντες πάλιν
ἀνώρθωσαν, ἐφ' ὧι ἦν τὸ ἐπίγραμμα τὸ περὶ τῆς αὐλητικῆς,

Ἑλλὰς μὲν Θήβας νικᾶν προέκρινεν ⟨ἐν⟩ αὐλοῖς·   5

Καὶ νῦν ἐπὶ μέσης τῆς ἀρχαίας ἀγορᾶς ἓν τοῦτο ἄγαλμα
122 ἕστηκεν ἐν τοῖς ἐρειπίοις· οὐ δὴ φοβηθέντες οὐδένα τούτων
οὐδὲ τοὺς ἐπιτιμήσοντας ἡμῖν, ὡς τὰ σπουδαιότατα παρὰ
τοῖς Ἕλλησι ψέγομεν, ἅπαντα τὰ τοιαῦτα οὐκ αἰδημόνων
οὐδὲ ἐλευθέρων ἀνθρώπων ἀποφαινόμενοι ἔργα, ὡς ἄλλα τε   1
πολλὰ δυσχερῆ πρόσεστιν αὐτοῖς καὶ δὴ μέγιστον τὸ τῆς
ἀναιδείας, τὸ μᾶλλον τοῦ δέοντος φρονεῖν τὸν ὄχλον, ὅπερ
[μέγιστον] θρασύνεσθαι καλεῖν ὀρθότερον.

123   Οὔκουν οὐδὲ κήρυκας ὠνίων οὐδὲ κλοπῶν ἢ δρασμῶν
μήνυτρα προτιθέντας, ἐν ὁδοῖς καὶ ἐν ἀγορᾶι φθεγγομένους   1
μετὰ πολλῆς ἐλευθερίας οὐδὲ συμβολαίων καὶ προκλήσεων
καὶ καθόλου τῶν περὶ δίκας καὶ ἐγκλήματα συγγραφεῖς,
προσποιουμένους νόμιμον ἐμπειρίαν, οὐδὲ αὖ τοὺς σοφούς
τε καὶ δεινοὺς δικορράφους τε καὶ συνηγόρους, μισθοῦ
πᾶσιν ὁμοίως ἐπαγγελλομένους βοηθήσειν καὶ ἀδικοῦσι   2
τὰ μέγιστα, καὶ ἀναισχυντήσειν ὑπὲρ τῶν ἀλλοτρίων
ἀδικημάτων καὶ σχετλιάσειν καὶ βοήσεσθαι καὶ ἱκετεύσειν
ὑπὲρ τῶν οὔτε φίλων οὔτε συγγενῶν σφίσιν ὄντων, σφόδρα
ἐντίμους καὶ λαμπροὺς ἐνίους εἶναι δοκοῦντας ἐν τῆι πόλει,
οὐδὲ τοιοῦτον οὐδένα ἀξιοῖμεν ἂν ἐκείνων γίγνεσθαι,   2
124 παραχωρεῖν δὲ ἑτέροις. χειροτέχνας μὲν γὰρ ἐξ αὐτῶν τινας
ἀνάγκη γενέσθαι, γλωσσοτέχνας δὲ καὶ δικοτέχνας οὐδεμία
ἀνάγκη.

Τούτων δὲ τῶν εἰρημένων τε καὶ ῥηθησομένων εἴ τινα

1 οἰκουμένης secl. Wilamowitz   5 ⟨ἐν⟩ add. Casaubon   8 ἐπιτιμήσοντας
Reiske : ἐπιτιμηθέντας   13 [μέγιστον] secl. Reiske : οἶμαί τινα Wenkebach
16 ἀνελευθερίας Herwerden, Cohoon συμβολαίων Emperius : συμβόλων
21–2 καὶ ἀναισχυντήσειν … ἀδικημάτων post ἐν τῆι πόλει (24) codd., huc
transp. Dindorf, Geelium secutus   29 εἴ τινα Emperius : ἔστιν ἃ

δοκεῖ χρήσιμα ταῖς πόλεσιν, ὥσπερ ταῖς νῦν οἰκουμέναις,
οἷον δὴ ἴσως τὸ περὶ τὴν τῶν δικῶν ἀναγραφὴν καὶ τῶν
συμβολαίων, τάχα δὲ καὶ κηρυγμάτων ἐνίων ὅπως ἂν ᾖ ὑφ'
ὧν γιγνόμενα ἥκιστα ἂν εἴη βλαβερά, οὐ νῦν καιρός ἐστι
125 διορίζειν. οὐ γὰρ πολιτείαν ἐν τῶι παρόντι διατάττομεν, 5
ὁποία τις ἂν ἢ ἀρίστη γένοιτο ἢ πολλῶν ἀμείνων, ἀλλὰ περὶ
πενίας προὐθέμεθα εἰπεῖν, ὡς οὐκ ἄπορα αὐτῆι τὰ πράγματά
ἐστιν, ἧιπερ δοκεῖ τοῖς πολλοῖς αὐτή τε εἶναι φευκτὸν καὶ
κακόν, ἀλλὰ μυρίας ἀφορμὰς πρὸς τὸ ζῆν παρέχει τοῖς
αὐτουργεῖν βουλομένοις οὔτε ἀσχήμονας οὔτε βλαβεράς. 10
126 ἀπὸ γὰρ αὐτῆς ἀρχῆς ταύτης τὰ περὶ γεωργίας καὶ θήρας
προὐτράπημεν προδιελθεῖν ἐπὶ πλέον πρότερον, καὶ νῦν
περὶ τῶν κατὰ ἄστυ ἐργασιῶν, τίνες αὐτῶν πρέπουσαι καὶ
ἀβλαβεῖς τοῖς μὴ κάκιστα βιωσομένοις καὶ τίνες χείρους ἂν
ἀποτελοῖεν τοὺς ἐπ' αὐτῶν. 15
127 Εἰ δὲ πολλὰ τῶν εἰρημένων καθόλου χρήσιμά ἐστι πρὸς
πολιτείαν καὶ τὴν τοῦ προσήκοντος αἵρεσιν, ταύτηι καὶ
δικαιότερον συγγνώμην ἔχειν τοῦ μήκους τῶν λόγων, ὅτι
οὐ μάτην ἄλλως οὐδὲ περὶ ἄχρηστα πλανωμένωι πλείονες
γεγόνασιν. ἡ γὰρ περὶ ἐργασιῶν καὶ τεχνῶν σκέψις καὶ 20
καθόλου περὶ βίου προσήκοντος ἢ μὴ τοῖς μετρίοις, καὶ καθ'
αὑτὴν ἀξία πέφηνεν πολλῆς καὶ πάνυ ἀκριβοῦς θεωρίας.
128 χρὴ οὖν τὰς ἐκτροπὰς τῶν λόγων, ἂν καὶ σφόδρα μακραὶ
δοκῶσι, μὴ μέντοι περί γε φαύλων μηδὲ ἀναξίων [λόγων]
μηδὲ οὐ προσηκόντων, μὴ δυσκόλως φέρειν, ὡς οὐκ αὐτὴν 25
λιπόντος τὴν τῶν ὅλων ὑπόθεσιν τοῦ λέγοντος ἕως ἂν
περὶ τῶν ἀναγκαίων καὶ προσηκόντων φιλοσοφίαι διεξίηι.
129 σχεδὸν γὰρ κατὰ τοῦτο μιμούμενοι τοὺς κυνηγέτας οὐκ ἂν
ἁμαρτάνοιμεν· οἵ γε ἐπειδὰν τὸ πρῶτον ἴχνος ἐκλαβόντες
κἀκείνωι ἑπόμενοι μεταξὺ ἐπιτύχωσιν ἑτέρωι φανερωτέρωι 30

---

1 [ταῖς] νῦν Wilamowitz : fortasse praestat [ταῖς] πόλεσιν   3 ἐνίων : ἔνια
Capps   3–4 ἢ ὑφ' ὧν Pflugk : ἧι ὑφ' ἡμῶν   15 ἀπ' αὐτῶν UBM
20 ἐργασιῶν Pflugk : γεωργιῶν   23 μακραὶ Reiske : μακροὶ   24 [λόγων]
secl. Casaubon : λόγου Reiske

καὶ μᾶλλον ἐγγύς, οὐκ ὤκνησαν τούτωι ξυνακολουθῆσαι,
130 καὶ ἑλόντες τὸ ἐμπεσὸν ὕστερον ἐπ' ἐκεῖνο μετῆλθον. ἴσως
οὖν οὐδὲ ἐκεῖνο μεμπτέον, ὅστις περὶ ἀνδρὸς δικαίου
καὶ δικαιοσύνης λέγειν ἀρξάμενος, μνησθεὶς πόλεως
παραδείγματος ἕνεκεν, πολλαπλάσιον λόγον ἀνάλωσεν 5
περὶ πολιτείας, καὶ οὐ πρότερον ἀπέκαμε πρὶν ἢ πάσας
μεταβολὰς καὶ ἅπαντα γένη πολιτειῶν διεξῆλθε, πάνυ
ἐναργῶς τε καὶ μεγαλοπρεπῶς τὰ ξυμβαίνοντα περὶ ἑκάστην
131 ἐπιδεικνύς, εἰ καὶ παρά τισιν αἰτίαν ἔχει περὶ τοῦ μήκους
τῶν λόγων καὶ τῆς διατριβῆς τῆς περὶ τὸ παράδειγμα 10
δήπουθεν· ἀλλ' ὡς οὐδὲν ὄντα πρὸς τὸ προκείμενον τὰ
εἰρημένα καὶ οὐδ' ὁπωστιοῦν σαφεστέρου δι' αὐτὰ τοῦ
ζητουμένου γεγονότος, οὗπερ ἕνεκεν ἐξ ἀρχῆς εἰς τὸν
λόγον παρελήφθη, διὰ ταῦτα, εἴπερ ἄρα, οὐ παντάπασιν
132 ἀδίκως εὐθύνεται. ἐὰν οὖν καὶ ἡμεῖς μὴ προσήκοντα μηδὲ 1
οἰκεῖα τῶι προκειμένωι φαινώμεθα διεξιόντες, μακρολογεῖν
εἰκότως ἂν λεγοίμεθα. καθ' αὑτὸ δὲ ἄλλως οὔτε μῆκος οὔτε
βραχύτητα ἐν λόγοις ἐπαινεῖν ἢ ψέγειν δίκαιον.

Περὶ δὲ τῶν λοιπῶν τῶν ἐν ταῖς πόλεσι πράξεων χρὴ
θαρροῦντας διαπερᾶναι, τῶν μὲν μιμνηισκομένους, τὰ δὲ καὶ 2
ἐῶντας ἄρρητά τε καὶ ἀμνημόνευτα.

133 Οὐ γὰρ δὴ περί γε πορνοβοσκῶν καὶ περὶ πορνοβοσκίας
ὡς ἀμφιβόλων ἀπαγορευτέον, ἀλλὰ καὶ πάνυ ἰσχυριστέον
τε καὶ ἀπορρητέον, λέγοντι μηδένα προσχρῆσθαι μήτε
οὖν πένητα μήτε πλούσιον ἐργασίαι τοιαύτηι, μισθὸν 2
ὕβρεως καὶ ἀκολασίας ὁμοίως παρὰ πᾶσιν ἐπονείδιστον
ἐκλέγοντας, ἀναφροδίτου μίξεως καὶ ἀνεράστων ἐρώτων
κέρδους ἕνεκα γιγνομένους συναγωγεῖς, αἰχμάλωτα σώματα
γυναικῶν ἢ παίδων ἢ ἄλλως ἀργυρώνητα ἐπ' αἰσχύνηι
προϊστάντας ἐπ' οἰκημάτων ῥυπαρῶν, πανταχοῦ τῆς 3

1 ξυνακολουθῆσαι Emperius : -ήσαντες, quo recepto possis in 2 μετελθεῖν coni-
cere   2 ἐπ' ἐκεῖνο μετῆλθον om. UBM, lac. ind. von Arnim   11 ἀλλ' ὡς
Casaubon : ἄλλως   17 λεγοίμεθα Wilamowitz : φαινώμεθα   27 ἀνεράστων
ἐρώτων Emperius : ἀνεράστου τῶν ἐρώντων   28 συναγωγεῖς Emperius :
συναγαγοῦσαι : συναγωγούς Pflugk

πόλεως ἀποδεδειγμένων, ἔν τε παρόδοις ἀρχόντων καὶ
134 ἀγοραῖς, πλησίον ἀρχείων τε καὶ ἱερῶν, μεταξὺ τῶν
ὁσιωτάτων, μήτ' οὖν βαρβαρικὰ σώματα μήτε Ἑλλήνων,
πρότερον μὲν οὐ πάνυ τὰ νῦν δὲ ἀφθόνωι τε καὶ πολλῆι
δουλείαι κεχρημένων, ἐπὶ τὴν τοιαύτην λώβην καὶ ἀνάγκην 5
ἄγοντας, ἱπποφορβῶν καὶ ὀνοφορβῶν πολὺ κάκιον καὶ
ἀκαθαρτότερον ἔργον ἐργαζομένους, οὐ κτήνεσι κτήνη δίχα
βίας ἑκόντα ἑκοῦσιν ἐπιβάλλοντας οὐδὲν αἰσχυνομένοις,
ἀλλὰ ἀνθρώποις αἰσχυνομένοις καὶ ἄκουσιν οἰστρῶντας καὶ
ἀκολάστους ἀνθρώπους ἐπ' ἀτελεῖ καὶ ἀκάρπωι συμπλοκῆι 10
σωμάτων φθορὰν μᾶλλον ἢ γένεσιν ἀποτελούσηι, οὐκ
135 αἰσχυνομένους οὐδένα ἀνθρώπων ἢ θεῶν, οὔτε Δία γενέθλιον
οὔτε Ἥραν γαμήλιον οὔτε Μοίρας τελεσφόρους ἢ λοχίαν
Ἄρτεμιν ἢ μητέρα Ῥέαν, οὐδὲ τὰς προεστώσας ἀνθρωπίνης
γενέσεως Εἰλειθυίας οὐδὲ Ἀφροδίτην ἐπώνυμον τῆς κατὰ 15
136 φύσιν πρὸς τὸ θῆλυ τοῦ ἄρρενος συνόδου τε καὶ ὁμιλίας· μὴ
δὴ ἐπιτρέπειν τὰ τοιαῦτα κέρδη μηδὲ νομοθετεῖν μήτε
ἄρχοντα μήτε νομοθέτην μήτ' ἐν ταῖς ἄκρως πρὸς ἀρετὴν
οἰκησομέναις πόλεσιν μήτ' ἐν ταῖς δευτέραις ἢ τρίταις ἢ
τετάρταις ἢ ὁποσταισοῦν, ἐὰν ἐπ' αὐτῶν τινι ἧι τὰ τοιαῦτα 20
137 κωλύειν. ἐὰν δ' ἄρα παλαιὰ ἔθη καὶ νοσήματα ἐσκιρωμένα
χρόνωι παραλάβηι, μήτοι γε παντελῶς ἐᾶν ἀθεράπευτα καὶ
ἀκόλαστα, ἀλλὰ σκοποῦντα τὸ δυνατὸν ἀμηιγέπηι στέλλειν
καὶ κολάζειν· ὡς οὔποτε φιλεῖ τὰ μοχθηρὰ μένειν ἐπὶ τοῖς
αὐτοῖς, ἀλλ' ἀεὶ κινεῖται καὶ πρόεισιν ἐπὶ τὸ ἀσελγέστερον, 25
μηδενὸς ἀναγκαίου μέτρου τυγχάνοντα.
138 Δεῖ δὴ ποιεῖσθαί τινα ἐπιμέλειαν, μὴ πάνυ τι πράιως μηδὲ
ῥαιθύμως φέροντας τὴν εἰς τὰ ἄτιμα καὶ δοῦλα σώματα
ὕβριν, οὐ ταύτηι μόνον ἧι κοινῆι τὸ ἀνθρώπινον γένος ἅπαν
ἔντιμον καὶ ὁμότιμον ὑπὸ τοῦ φύσαντος θεοῦ ταὐτὰ σημεῖα 30
καὶ σύμβολα ἔχον τοῦ τιμᾶσθαι δικαίως, καὶ λόγον καὶ

---

11 ἀποτελούσηι Reiske : ἀποτελούντων   οὐκ Emperius : οὔτε   20 ὁποσταισοῦν Naber : ὁποιαισοῦν   21 ἐνεσκιρρωμένα Cobet   23 συστέλλειν
Cobet

58   ΔΙΩΝΟΣ

ἐμπειρίαν καλῶν τε καὶ αἰσχρῶν, γέγονεν, ἀλλὰ κἀκεῖνο
ἐνθυμουμένους ὅτι χαλεπὸν ὕβρει τρεφομένηι δι' ἐξουσίαν
ὅρον τινὰ εὑρεῖν ὃν οὐκ ἂν ἔτι τολμήσαι διὰ φόβον
ὑπερβαίνειν, ἀλλ' ἀπὸ τῆς ἐν τοῖς ἐλάττοσι δοκοῦσι καὶ
ἐφειμένοις μελέτης καὶ συνηθείας ἀκάθεκτον τὴν ἰσχὺν καὶ   5
ῥώμην λαβοῦσα οὐδενὸς ἔτι φείδεται τῶν λοιπῶν.

139   Ἤδη οὖν χρὴ παντὸς μᾶλλον οἴεσθαι τὰς ἐν τῶι μέσωι
ταύτας φανερὰς καὶ ἀτίμους μοιχείας καὶ λίαν ἀναισχύντως
καὶ ἀνέδην γιγνομένας, ὅτι τῶν ἀδήλων καὶ ἀφανῶν εἴς
τε ἐντίμους γυναῖκας [τε] καὶ παῖδας ὕβρεων οὐχ ἥκιστα   1
παρέχουσι τὴν αἰτίαν τῶι πάνυ ῥαιδίως τὰ τοιαῦτα
τολμᾶσθαι, τῆς αἰσχύνης ἐν κοινῶι καταφρονουμένης, ἀλλ'
οὐχ, ὥσπερ οἴονταί τινες, ὑπὲρ ἀσφαλείας καὶ ἀποχῆς
ἐκείνων εὑρῆσθαι τῶν ἁμαρτημάτων.

140   Τάχ' οὖν λέγοι τις ἂν ἀγροικότερον οὕτω πως· Ὦ   1
σοφοὶ νομοθέται καὶ ἄρχοντες οἱ παραδεξάμενοι τὰ τοιαῦτα
ἀπ' ἀρχῆς, ὡς δή τι θαυμαστὸν εὑρηκότες ταῖς πόλεσιν
ὑμεῖς σωφροσύνης φάρμακον, ὅπως ὑμῖν μὴ τὰ φανερὰ
ταῦτα καὶ ἄκλειστα οἰκήματα τὰς κεκλεισμένας οἰκίας καὶ
τοὺς ἔνδοθεν θαλάμους ἀναπετάσηι καὶ τοὺς ἔξω καὶ φανερῶς   2
ἀσελγαίνοντας ἀπὸ μικρᾶς δαπάνης ἐπὶ τὰς ἐλευθέρας
καὶ σεμνὰς τρέψηι γυναῖκας μετὰ πολλῶν χρημάτων τε
καὶ δώρων, τὸ σφόδρα εὔωνον καὶ μετ' ἐξουσίας οὐκέτι
στέργοντας, ἀλλ' αὐτὸ δὴ τὸ κεκωλυμένον ἐν φόβωι τε καὶ
141   πολλοῖς ἀναλώμασι διώκοντας. ὄψεσθε δὲ αὐτὸ ἐμοὶ δοκεῖν   2
ἀκριβέστερον, ἐὰν σκοπῆτε· παρ' οἷς γὰρ καὶ τὰ τῶν
μοιχειῶν μεγαλοπρεπέστερόν πως παραπέμπεται, πολλῆς
καὶ σφόδρα φιλανθρώπου τῆς εὐγνωμοσύνης τυγχάνοντα,
τὰ μὲν πολλὰ ὑπὸ χρηστότητος οὐκ αἰσθανομένων τῶν
ἀνδρῶν, τὰ δέ τινα οὐχ ὁμολογούντων εἰδέναι, ξένους δὲ καὶ   3
φίλους καὶ ξυγγενεῖς τοὺς μοιχοὺς καλουμένους ἀνεχομένων,
καὶ αὐτῶν ἐνίοτε φιλοφρονουμένων καὶ παρακαλούντων ἐν

5 ἰσχὺν Reiske : αἰσχύνην   10 τε[1] secl. Reiske   τε[2] seclusi   11 τῶι
Selden : τοῦ   17 εὑρηκότες Jacobs : εὑρήκατε

ταῖς ἑορταῖς καὶ θυσίαις ἐπὶ τὰς ἑστιάσεις, ὡς ἂν οἶμαι τοὺς
142 οἰκειοτάτους, ἐπὶ δὲ τοῖς σφόδρα ἐκδήλοις καὶ φανεροῖς
μετρίας τὰς ὀργὰς ποιουμένων· παρ' οἷς, φημί, ταῦθ' οὕτως
ἐπιεικῶς ἐξενάγηται τὰ περὶ τὰς γυναῖκας, οὐδὲ περὶ τῶν
παρθένων ἐκεῖ θαρρῆσαι ῥάιδιον τῆς κορείας οὐδὲ τὸν 5
ὑμέναιον ὡς ἀληθῶς καὶ δικαίως ἀιδόμενον ἐν τοῖς παρθενικοῖς
143 γάμοις πιστεῦσαί ποτε. ἢ οὐκ ἀνάγκη πολλὰ ἐοικότα
ξυμβαίνειν αὐτόθι τοῖς παλαιοῖς μύθοις, δίχα γε τῆς τῶν
πατέρων ὀργῆς καὶ πολυπραγμοσύνης, †ἀλλὰ† πολλῶν
μιμουμένων τοὺς λεγομένους τῶν θεῶν ἔρωτας χρυσοῦ τε 10
πολλοῦ διαρρέοντος διὰ τῶν ὀρόφων καὶ πάνυ ῥαιδίως, ἄτε
144 οὐ χαλκῶν ὄντων οὐδὲ λιθίνων τῶν οἰκημάτων, καὶ νὴ Δία
ἀργύρου στάζοντος οὐ κατ' ὀλίγον οὐδ' εἰς τοὺς τῶν
παρθένων κόλπους μόνον, ἀλλ' εἴς τε μητέρων καὶ τροφῶν
καὶ παιδαγωγῶν, καὶ ἄλλων πολλῶν καὶ καλῶν δώρων 15
τῶν μὲν κρύφα εἰσιόντων διὰ τῶν στεγῶν, ἔστι δ' ὧν
145 φανερῶς κατ' αὐτάς που τὰς κλισιάδας; τί δ'; ἐν ποταμοῖς
καὶ ἐπὶ κρηνῶν οὐκ εἰκὸς ὅμοια πολλὰ γενέσθαι τοῖς
πρότερον λεγομένοις ὑπὸ τῶν ποιητῶν; πλὴν ἴσως γε οὐ
δημόσια γιγνόμενα οὐδ' ἐν τῶι φανερῶι, κατ' οἰκίας δὲ 20
οὕτως εὐδαίμονας, κήπων τε καὶ προαστείων πολυτελεῖς
ἐπαύλεις, ἔν τισι νυμφῶσι κατεσκευασμένοις καὶ θαυμαστοῖς
ἄλσεσιν, ἄτε οὐ ⟨περὶ⟩ πενιχρὰς οὐδὲ πενήτων βασιλέων
οἵας ὑδροφορεῖν τε καὶ παίζειν παρὰ τοῖς ποταμοῖς,
ψυχρὰ λουτρὰ λουομένας καὶ ἐν αἰγιαλοῖς ἀναπεπταμένοις, 25
ἀλλὰ μακαρίας καὶ μακαρίων γονέων, ἐν βασιλικαῖς
καταγωγαῖς ἴδια πάντα ταῦτα ἐχούσαις πολὺ κρείττονα
καὶ μεγαλοπρεπέστερα τῶν κοινῶν.
146 Ἀλλ' ἴσως γε οὐδὲν ἧττον ἔμελλον ἐν ἐκείνηι τῆι
πόλει παῖδας προσδοκᾶν ἐσομένους, οἷον Ὅμηρος εἴρηκεν 30

4 ἐξενάγηται scripsi : ἐξάγεται : ξεναγεῖται Geel   5 κορείας Jacobs : χορείας
7 οὐκ Pflugk : οὖν   9 †ἀλλὰ† secl. von Arnim : ἅμα Pflugk : expectes τἆλλα
uel τἆλλα γε   17 κλισιάδας Gasda : κλισίας   20 δημόσια von Arnim :
δημοσίαι   21 οὕτως : ὄντως Geel   22—3 κατεσκιασμένους θαυμαστοῖς
ἄλσεσιν Geel   23 ⟨περὶ⟩ suppl. Reiske   25 αἰγιαλοῖς Pflugk : ἄλεσιν

Εὔδωρον, υἱὸν Ἑρμοῦ καὶ Πολυδώρας, ὑποκοριζόμενος αὐτὸν οἶμαι κατὰ τὴν γένεσιν,

παρθένιος, τὸν ἔτικτε χορῶι καλὴ Πολυδώρη.

147 σχεδὸν δὲ καὶ παρὰ Λακεδαιμονίοις ἔτυχόν τινες ταύτης τῆς ἐπωνυμίας τῶν οὕτως γενομένων, Παρθενίαι κληθέντες 5 συχνοί· ὥστ', εἰ μὴ διεφθείροντο οἱ πλείους τῶν ἐν ταῖς οὕτως τρυφώσαις πόλεσι γιγνομένων, ἅτε οὐδαμῶς οἶμαι δαιμονίου τυγχάνοντες ἐπιμελείας, οὐδὲν ἂν ἐκώλυε πάντα 148 μεστὰ ἡρώων εἶναι. νῦν δὲ οἱ μὲν ἀπόλλυνται παραχρῆμα· ὅσοι δ' ἂν καὶ τραφῶσι, κρύφα ἐν δούλου σχήματι μένουσιν ιο ἄχρι γήρως, ἅτε οὐδὲν αὐτοὺς δυναμένων τῶν σπειράντων προσωφελεῖν.

Εἶεν δή, παρ' οἷς ἂν καὶ τὰ περὶ τὰς κόρας οὕτως ἀμελῶς 149 ἔχηι, τί χρὴ προσδοκᾶν τοὺς κόρους, ποίας τινὸς παιδείας καὶ ἀγωγῆς τυγχάνειν; ἔσθ' ὅπως ἂν ἀπόσχοιτο τῆς τῶν ι5 ἀρρένων λώβης καὶ φθορᾶς τό γε ἀκόλαστον γένος, τοῦτον ἱκανὸν καὶ σαφῆ ποιησάμενον ὅρον τὸν τῆς φύσεως, ἀλλ' οὐκ ἂν ἐμπιμπλάμενον πάντα τρόπον τῆς περὶ γυναῖκας ἀκρασίας, διακορὲς γενόμενον τῆς ἡδονῆς ταύτης, ζητοίη 150 ἑτέραν μείζω καὶ παρανομωτέραν ὕβριν; ὡς τά γε γυναικῶν, 2ο αὐτῶν σχεδόν τι τῶν ἐλευθέρων καὶ παρθένων, ἐφάνη ῥάιδια, καὶ οὐδεὶς πόνος θηρῶντι μετὰ πλούτου τὴν τοιάνδε θήραν· οὐδὲ ἐπὶ τὰς πάνυ σεμνὰς καὶ σεμνῶν τῶι ὄντι γυναῖκας καὶ θυγατέρας ὅστις ἂν ἴηι σὺν τῆι τοῦ Διὸς μηχανῆι, χρυσὸν 151 μετὰ χεῖρας φέρων, οὐ μήποτε ἀποτυγχάνηι. ἀλλ' αὐτά που 2 τὰ λοιπὰ δῆλα παρὰ πολλοῖς γιγνόμενα· ὅ γε ἄπληστος τῶν τοιούτων ἐπιθυμιῶν, ὅταν μηδὲν εὑρίσκηι σπάνιον μηδὲ ἀντιτεῖνον ἐν ἐκείνωι τῶι γένει, καταφρονήσας τοῦ ῥαιδίου καὶ ἀτιμάσας τὴν ἐν ταῖς γυναιξὶν Ἀφροδίτην, ὡς ἕτοιμον δή τινα καὶ τῶι ὄντι θῆλυν παντελῶς, ἐπὶ τὴν ἀνδρωνῖτιν 3ο

μεταβήσεται, τοὺς ἄρξοντας αὐτίκα μάλα καὶ δικάσοντας καὶ
152 στρατηγήσοντας ἐπιθυμῶν καταισχύνειν, ὡς ἐνθάδε που τὸ
χαλεπὸν καὶ δυσπόριστον εὑρήσων τῶν ἡδονῶν εἶδος, τοῖς
ἄγαν φιλοπόταις καὶ οἰνόφλυξι ταὐτὸ πεπονθὼς πάθος,
οἳ πολλάκις μετὰ πολλὴν ἀκρατοποσίαν καὶ συνεχῆ οὐκ 5
ἐθέλοντες πιεῖν αὐχμὸν ἐξεπίτηδες μηχανῶνται διά τε
ἱδρώτων καὶ σιτίων ἁλμυρῶν καὶ δριμέων προσφορᾶς.

ΟΛΥΜΠΙΚΟΣ Η ΠΕΡΙ ΤΗΣ ΠΡΩΤΗΣ
ΤΟΥ ΘΕΟΥ ΕΝΝΟΙΑΣ

1 Ἀλλ' ἢ τὸ λεγόμενον, ὦ ἄνδρες, ἐγὼ καὶ παρ' ὑμῖν καὶ
παρ' ἑτέροις πλείοσι πέπονθα τὸ τῆς γλαυκὸς ἄτοπον καὶ
παράδοξον πάθος; ἐκείνην γὰρ οὐδὲν σοφωτέραν αὐτῶν
οὖσαν οὐδὲ βελτίω τὸ εἶδος, ἀλλὰ τοιαύτην ὁποίαν ἴσμεν,
ὅταν δήποτε φθέγξηται λυπηρὸν καὶ οὐδαμῶς ἡδύ, 5
περιέπουσι τὰ ἄλλα ὄρνεα, καὶ ὅταν γε ἴδηι μόνον, τὰ μὲν
καθιζόμενα ἐγγύς, τὰ δὲ κύκλωι περιπετόμενα, ὡς μὲν ἐμοὶ
δοκεῖ, καταφρονοῦντα τῆς φαυλότητος καὶ τῆς ἀσθενείας· οἱ
δὲ ἄνθρωποί φασιν ὅτι θαυμάζει τὴν γλαῦκα τὰ ὄρνεα.

2 Πῶς δὲ οὐ τὸν ταῶ μᾶλλον ὁρῶντα θαυμάζει, καλὸν οὕτω 10
καὶ ποικίλον, ἔτι δ' αὐτὸν ἐπαιρόμενον καὶ ἐπιδεικνύντα τὸ
κάλλος τῶν πτερῶν, ὅταν ἁβρύνηται πρὸς τὴν θήλειαν,
ἀνακλάσας τὴν οὐρὰν καὶ περιστήσας αὐτῶι πανταχόθεν
ὥσπερ εὐειδὲς θέατρον ἤ τινα γραφῆι μιμηθέντα οὐρανὸν
ποικίλον ἄστροις, σύν τε τῶι λοιπῶι σώματι θαυμαστόν, 15
ἐγγύτατα χρυσοῦ κυάνωι κεκραμένου, καὶ δὴ ἐν ἄκροις τοῖς
πτεροῖς οἷον ὀφθαλμῶν ἐνόντων ἤ τινων δακτυλίων τό τε
3 σχῆμα καὶ κατὰ τὴν ἄλλην ὁμοιότητα; εἰ δ' αὖ τις ἐθέλοι
σκοπεῖν τῆς πτερώσεως τὸ κοῦφον, ὡς μὴ χαλεπόν ἐστι
μηδὲ δύσφορον διὰ τὸ μῆκος, ἐν μέσωι μάλα ἥσυχον καὶ 20
ἀτρεμοῦντα παρέχει θεάσασθαι ἑαυτόν, ὥσπερ ἐν πομπῆι
περιστρεφόμενος· ὅταν δὲ βουληθῆι ἐκπλῆξαι, σείων τὰ
πτερὰ καί τινα ἦχον οὐκ ἀηδῆ ποιῶν, οἷον ἀνέμου κινήσαντος
οὐ πολλοῦ πυκνήν τινα ὕλην.

Ἀλλ' οὔτε τὸν ταῶ πάντα ταῦτα καλλωπιζόμενον τὰ 25
ὄρνεα βούλεται ὁρᾶν οὔτε τῆς ἀηδόνος ἀκούοντα τῆς φωνῆς
4 ἕωθεν ἐπορθρευομένης οὐδὲν πάσχει πρὸς αὐτήν, ἀλλ' οὐδὲ
τὸν κύκνον ἀσπάζεται διὰ τὴν μουσικήν, οὐδὲ ὅταν ὑμνῆι τὴν

3 σοφωτέραν : σεμνοτέραν Stich : εὐφωνοτέραν Geel, Wenkebach   αὐτῶν : τὴν
αὐδὴν Wenkebach   5 δήποτε : γε ποτε Wenkebach   14 θέατρον : ἄντρον
Μ   15 τε scripsi : γε   σώματι : χρώματι coni. von Arnim   17 δακτυλίων :
ἀκτίνων UBP   19 ἐστι Reiske : εἶναι

ὑστάτην ᾠδὴν ἅτε εὐγήρως, ὑπὸ ἡδονῆς τε καὶ λήθης τῶν
ἐν τῶι βίωι χαλεπῶν εὐφημῶν ἅμα καὶ προπέμπων ἀλύπως
αὐτόν, ὡς ἔοικε, πρὸς ἄλυπον τὸν θάνατον – οὔκουν οὐδὲ τότε
ἀθροίζεται κηλούμενα τοῖς μέλεσι πρὸς ὄχθην ποταμοῦ τινος
ἢ λειμῶνα πλατὺν ἢ καθαρὰν ἠϊόνα λίμνης ἤ τινα σμικρὰν 5
εὐθαλῆ ποταμίαν νησῖδα.

5   Ὡς δὲ καὶ ὑμεῖς τοσαῦτα μὲν θεάματα ἔχοντες τερπνά,
τοσαῦτα δὲ ἀκούσματα, τοῦτο μὲν ῥήτορας δεινούς, τοῦτο δὲ
ξυγγραφέας ἡδίστους ἐμμέτρων καὶ ἀμέτρων λόγων, τοῦτο
δὲ πολλοὺς σοφιστὰς ὡς ταῶς ποικίλους δόξηι καὶ μαθηταῖς 10
ἐπαιρομένους οἷον πτεροῖς, ὑμεῖς δὲ ἐμοὶ πρόσιτε καὶ βούλεσθε
ἀκούειν, τοῦ μηδὲν εἰδότος μηδὲ φάσκοντος εἰδέναι, ἆρ᾽ οὐκ
ὀρθῶς ἀπεικάζω τὴν σπουδὴν ὑμῶν τῶι περὶ τὴν γλαῦκα
γιγνομένωι σχεδὸν οὐκ ἄνευ δαιμονίας τινὸς βουλήσεως ⟨καὶ⟩
6   τύχης; καὶ τῆι Ἀθηνᾶι λέγεται προσφιλὲς εἶναι τὸ ὄρνεον, 15
τῆι καλλίστηι τῶν θεῶν καὶ σοφωτάτηι, καὶ τῆς γε Φειδίου
τέχνης παρὰ Ἀθηναίοις ἔτυχεν, οὐκ ἀπαξιώσαντος αὐτὴν
συγκαθιδρῦσαι τῆι θεῶι, συνδοκοῦν τῶι δήμωι. Περικλέα δὲ
καὶ αὐτὸν λαθὼν ἐποίησεν, ὥς φασιν, ἐπὶ τῆς ἀσπίδος.

    Οὐ μέντοι ταῦτά γε εὐτυχήματα νομίζειν ἔπεισί μοι τῆς 20
7   γλαυκός, εἰ μή τινα φρόνησιν ἄρα κέκτηται πλείω. ὅθεν,
οἶμαι, καὶ τὸν μῦθον Αἴσωπος ξυνέστησεν ὅτι σοφὴ οὖσα
ξυνεβούλευε τοῖς ὀρνέοις τῆς δρυὸς ἐν ἀρχῆι φυομένης μὴ
ἐᾶσαι, ἀλλ᾽ ἀνελεῖν πάντα τρόπον· ἔσεσθαι γὰρ φάρμακον
ἀπ᾽ αὐτῆς ἄφυκτον, ὑφ᾽ οὗ ἁλώσονται, τὸν ἰξόν. πάλιν δὲ τὸ 25
λίνον τῶν ἀνθρώπων σπειρόντων, ἐκέλευε καὶ τοῦτο ἐκλέγειν
8   τὸ σπέρμα· μὴ γὰρ ἐπ᾽ ἀγαθῶι φυήσεσθαι. τρίτον δὲ ἰδοῦσα
τοξευτήν τινα ἄνδρα προέλεγεν ὅτι Οὗτος ὁ ἀνήρ φθάσει ὑμᾶς
τοῖς ὑμετέροις πτεροῖς, πεζὸς ὢν αὐτὸς πτηνὰ ἐπιπέμπων
βέλη. τὰ δὲ ἠπίστει τοῖς λόγοις καὶ ἀνόητον αὐτὴν ἡγοῦντο 30
καὶ μαίνεσθαι ἔφασκον· ὕστερον δὲ πειρώμενα ἐθαύμαζε καὶ

---

1 εὐγήρως : εὔγηρυς P   9–10 ita Reiske : τοῦτο δὲ ταῶς ποικίλους τοῦτο δὲ
ὡς πολλοὺς σοφιστάς codd.   ταῶς ... ὡς secl. Emperius   14 lacuna ante
σχεδὸν fortasse ponenda   14–15 ⟨καὶ⟩ τύχης scripsi (cf. 1.57) : ὑφ᾽ ἧς
16 γε Reiske : τε   19 αὐτὸν Jacobs : αὐτὸν   25 τὸν ἰξόν secl. Naber

τῶι ὄντι σοφωτάτην ἐνόμιζεν. καὶ διὰ τοῦτο, ἐπὰν φανῆι, πρόσεισιν ὡς [πρὸς] ἅπαντα ἐπισταμένην· ἡ δὲ συμβουλεύει μὲν αὐτοῖς οὐδὲν ἔτι, ὀδύρεται δὲ μόνον.

9 Ἴσως οὖν παρειλήφατε ὑμεῖς λόγον τινὰ ἀληθῆ καὶ ξυμβουλὴν συμφέρουσαν, ἥντινα ξυνεβούλευσε φιλοσοφία 5 τοῖς πρότερον Ἕλλησιν, ἣν οἱ τότε μὲν ἠγνόησαν καὶ ἠτίμασαν, οἱ δὲ νῦν ὑπομιμνήσκονται καί μοι προσίασι διὰ τὸ σχῆμα, φιλοσοφίαν τιμῶντες ὥσπερ τὴν γλαῦκα, ἄφωνον τό γε ἀληθὲς καὶ ἀπαρρησίαστον οὖσαν. ἐγὼ μὲν γὰρ οὐδὲν αὐτῶι ξύνοιδα οὔτε πρότερον εἰπόντι σπουδῆς ἄξιον οὔτε 10 νῦν ἐπισταμένωι πλέον ὑμῶν· ἀλλὰ εἰσὶν ἕτεροι σοφοὶ καὶ μακάριοι παντελῶς ἄνδρες, οὓς ὑμῖν ἐγώ, εἰ βούλεσθε, μηνύσω, ἕκαστον ὀνομαστὶ δεικνύμενος. καὶ γὰρ νὴ Δία τοῦτο μόνον οἶμαι χρήσιμον ἔχειν, τὸ γιγνώσκειν τοὺς σοφούς τε καὶ δεινοὺς καὶ πάντα ἐπισταμένους· οἷς ἐὰν ὑμεῖς 1 ἐθέλητε ξυνεῖναι τἄλλα ἐάσαντες, καὶ γονεῖς καὶ πατρίδας καὶ θεῶν ἱερὰ καὶ προγόνων τάφους, ἐκείνοις ξυνακολουθοῦντες ἔνθα ἂν ἄγωσιν ἢ καὶ μένοντές που καθιδρυθῶσιν, εἴτε εἰς τὴν Βαβυλῶνα τὴν Νίνου καὶ Σεμιράμιδος εἴτε ἐν Βάκτροις ἢ Σούσοις ἢ Παλιβόθροις ἢ ἄλληι τινὶ πόλει τῶν ἐνδόξων καὶ 2 πλουσίων, χρήματα διδόντες ἢ καὶ ἄλλωι τρόπωι πείθοντες,

11 εὐδαιμονέστεροι ἔσεσθε αὐτῆς τῆς εὐδαιμονίας· εἰ δ' αὐτοὶ μὴ βούλεσθε, καταμεμφόμενοι τὴν αὐτῶν φύσιν ἢ πενίαν ἢ γῆρας ἢ ἀσθένειαν, ἀλλὰ τοῖς γε υἱέσι μὴ φθονοῦντες μηδὲ ἀφαιρούμενοι τῶν μεγίστων ἀγαθῶν, ἑκοῦσί τε ἐπιτρέποντες 2 καὶ ἄκοντας πείθοντες ἢ βιαζόμενοι πάντα τρόπον, ὡς ἂν παιδευθέντες ἱκανῶς καὶ γενόμενοι σοφοὶ παρὰ πᾶσιν Ἕλλησι καὶ βαρβάροις ὀνομαστοὶ ὦσι τὸ λοιπόν, διαφέροντες ἀρετῆι καὶ δόξηι καὶ πλούτωι καὶ δυνάμει τῆι πάσηι σχεδόν. οὐ γὰρ μόνον πλούτωι, φασίν, ἀρετὴ καὶ κῦδος ὀπηδεῖ, ἀλλὰ καὶ 3 πλοῦτος ἀρετῆι συνέπεται ἐξ ἀνάγκης.

2 [πρὸς] seclusi   18 ἄγωσιν Emperius : ἀπῶσιν   18 καθιδρύωσιν Wilamowitz   18–19 εἰς τὴν Βαβυλῶνα secl. Wilamowitz   19 ἐν τῆι Νίνου Wilamowitz   20 Παλιβόθροις Geel : Παλιμβάθροις uel sim. codd.   30 ἀρετὴ Geel : ἀρετὴν ὀπηδεῖ M : ὀπηδεῖν   31 πλοῦτος von Arnim : λόγος   λόγοις ἀρετὴ Reiske

12 Ταῦτα δὲ ὑμῖν ἐναντίον τοῦδε τοῦ θεοῦ προλέγω καὶ ξυμβουλεύω δι᾽ εὔνοιαν καὶ φιλίαν προαγόμενος. οἶμαι δὲ ἐμαυτὸν ⟨ἂν⟩ πρῶτον πείθειν καὶ παρακαλεῖν εἴ μοι τὰ τοῦ σώματος καὶ τὰ τῆς ἡλικίας ἐπεδέχετο· ἀλλ᾽ ἀγαπᾶν ἀνάγκη διὰ τὸ κακοπαθεῖν, εἴ πού τι δυνησόμεθα, εὑρέσθαι παρὰ τῶν 5 παλαιῶν ἀνδρῶν ὥσπερ ἀπερριμμένον ἤδη καὶ ἕωλον σοφίας λείψανον χήτει τῶν κρειττόνων τε καὶ ζώντων διδασκάλων. Ἐρῶ δὲ ὑμῖν καὶ ἄλλο ὃ πέπονθα τῆι γλαυκὶ παραπλήσιον, 13 ἐὰν καὶ βούλησθε καταγελᾶν τῶν λόγων. ὥσπερ γὰρ ἐκείνη αὐτὴ μὲν οὐδὲν χρῆται τοῖς προσπετομένοις, ἀνδρὶ δὲ 10 ὀρνιθοθήραι πάντων λυσιτελέστατον κτημάτων – οὐδὲν γὰρ δεῖ οὔτε τροφὴν προβάλλειν οὔτε φωνὴν μιμεῖσθαι, μόνον δ᾽ ἐπιδεικνύντα τὴν γλαῦκα πολὺ πλῆθος ἔχειν ὀρνέων – οὕτω κἀμοὶ τῆς σπουδῆς τῶν πολλῶν οὐδὲν ὄφελος. οὐ γὰρ λαμβάνω μαθητάς, εἰδὼς ὅτι οὐδὲν ἂν ἔχοιμι διδάσκειν, 15 ἅτε οὐδ᾽ αὐτὸς ἐπιστάμενος· ὡς δὲ ψεύδεσθαι καὶ ἐξαπατᾶν ὑπισχνούμενος, οὐκ ἔχω ταύτην τὴν ἀνδρείαν· σοφιστῆι δὲ ἀνδρὶ ξυνὼν μεγάλα ἂν ὠφέλουν ὄχλον πολὺν ἀθροίζων πρὸς αὐτόν, ἔπειτα ἐκείνωι παρέχων ὅπως βούλεται διαθέσθαι τὴν ἄγραν. ἀλλ᾽ οὐκ οἶδα ὅπως, οὐδείς με ἀναλαμβάνει τῶν 20 σοφιστῶν οὐδὲ ἥδονται ὁρῶντες.

14 Σχεδὸν μὲν οὖν ἐπίσταμαι ὅτι πιστεύετέ μοι λέγοντι ὑπὲρ τῆς ἀπειρίας τε κἀνεπιστημοσύνης τῆς ἐμαυτοῦ, δῆλον ὡς διὰ τὴν αὐτῶν ἐπιστήμην καὶ φρόνησιν, καὶ τοῦτο οὐκ ἐμοὶ μόνον, ἀλλὰ καὶ Σωκράτει δοκεῖτέ μοι πιστεύειν ἄν, ταὐτὰ ὑπὲρ 25 αὐτοῦ προβαλλομένωι πρὸς ἅπαντας ὡς οὐδὲν ἤιδει· τὸν δὲ Ἱππίαν καὶ τὸν Πῶλον καὶ τὸν Γοργίαν, ὧν ἕκαστος αὐτὸν μάλιστα ἐθαύμαζε καὶ ἐξεπλήττετο, σοφοὺς ἂν ἡγεῖσθαι 15 καὶ μακαρίους· ὅμως δὲ προλέγω ὑμῖν ὅτι ἐσπουδάκατε ἀνδρὸς ἀκοῦσαι τοσοῦτον πλῆθος ὄντες οὔτε καλοῦ τὸ εἶδος 30 οὔτε ἰσχυροῦ, τῆι τε ἡλικίαι παρηκμακότος ἤδη, μαθητὴν

---

3 ⟨ἂν⟩ add. Emperius   4 ἀλλ᾽ ἀγαπᾶν Geel : ἀλλὰ γὰρ   6 ἕωλον Reiske :
βῶλον   7 χήτει Reiske : δή τι   12 προβάλλειν Morel : προσβάλλειν
15 οὐδὲν ἂν Jacobs : οὐδένα   16 ὡς δὲ Pflugk : ὥστε

δὲ οὐδένα ἔχοντος, τέχνην δὲ ἢ ἐπιστήμην οὐδεμίαν
ὑπισχνουμένου σχεδὸν οὔτε τῶν σεμνῶν οὔτε τῶν
ἐλαττόνων, οὔτε μαντικὴν οὔτε σοφιστικήν, ἀλλ᾽ οὐδὲ
ῥητορικήν τινα ἢ κολακευτικὴν δύναμιν, οὐδὲ δεινοῦ
ξυγγράφειν, οὐδὲ ἔργον τι ἔχοντος ἄξιον ἐπαίνου καὶ 5
σπουδῆς, ἀλλ᾽ ἢ μόνον κομῶντος·

εἰ δ᾽ ὑμῖν δοκέει τόδε λωίτερον καὶ ἄμεινον,

δραστέον τοῦτο καὶ πειρατέον ὅπως ἂν ἦι δυνατὸν ἡμῖν.
16 οὐ μέντοι λόγων ἀκούσεσθε ὁποίων ἄλλου τινὸς τῶν νῦν,
ἀλλὰ πολὺ φαυλοτέρων καὶ ἀτοπωτέρων ὁποίους δὴ καὶ 1〈
ὁρᾶτε. χρὴ δὲ ἐὰν ὑμᾶς ἔμβραχυ, ὅ τι ἂν ἐπίηι μοι, τούτωι
ἕπεσθαι, καὶ μὴ ἀγανακτεῖν ἐὰν φαίνωμαι πλανώμενος ἐν τοῖς
λόγοις, ὥσπερ ἀμέλει καὶ τὸν ἄλλον χρόνον ἔζηκα ἀλώμενος,
ἀλλὰ συγγνώμην ἔχειν, ἅτε ἀκούοντας ἀνδρὸς ἰδιώτου καὶ
ἀδολέσχου.   1

Καὶ γὰρ δὴ τυγχάνω μακράν τινα ὁδὸν τὰ νῦν πεπορευμέ-
νος, εὐθὺ τοῦ Ἴστρου καὶ τῆς Γετῶν χώρας ἢ Μυσῶν, ὡς
17 φησιν Ὅμηρος κατὰ τὴν νῦν ἐπίκλησιν τοῦ ἔθνους. ἦλθον
δὲ οὐ χρημάτων ἔμπορος οὐδὲ τῶν πρὸς ὑπηρεσίαν τοῦ
στρατοπέδου σκευοφόρων ἢ βοηλατῶν, οὐδὲ πρεσβείαν 2
ἐπρέσβευον συμμαχικὴν ἤ τινα εὔφημον, τῶν ἀπὸ γλώττης
μόνον συνευχομένων ⟨ἀλλὰ⟩

γυμνὸς ἄτερ κόρυθός τε καὶ ἀσπίδος, οὐδ᾽ ἔχον ἔγχος,

18 οὐ μὴν οὐδὲ ἄλλο ὅπλον οὐθέν, ὥστε ἐθαύμαζον ὅπως με
ἠνείχοντο ὁρῶντες. οὔτε ⟨γὰρ⟩ ἱππεύειν ἐπιστάμενος οὔτε 2
τοξότης ἱκανὸς ὢν οὔθ᾽ ὁπλίτης, ἀλλ᾽ οὐδὲ [τῶν κούφων
καὶ ἀνόπλων τὴν βαρεῖαν ὅπλισιν στρατιωτῶν οὐδ᾽]
ἀκοντιστὴς ἢ λιθοβόλος, οὐδ᾽ αὖ τεμεῖν ὕλην ἢ τάφρον

---

10 ἀκοπωτέρων Cohoon   ὁποῖον Schwartz   11 ἔμβραχυ Geel : ἐν βραχεῖ
13 ἔζηκα Reiske : ἐξῆκα   22 ⟨ἀλλὰ⟩ addidi. Post συνευχομένων inueniuntur
in codd. ἄλλο δὲ οὐδὲν ... ἀοίδιμον, quae in §26 transposui   25 ⟨γὰρ⟩ add.
Wilamowitz   26-7 [τῶν κούφων ... οὐδὲ] seclusi; τὴν βαρεῖαν ... οὐδὲ
secl. Reiske

ὀρύττειν δυνατὸς οὐδὲ ἀμῆσαι χιλὸν ἐκ πολεμίου λειμῶνος
πυκνὰ μεταστρεφόμενος, οὐδὲ ἐγεῖραι σκηνὴν ἢ χάρακα,
ὥσπερ ἀμέλει ξυνέπονται τοῖς στρατοπέδοις πολεμικοί τινες
19 ὑπηρέται – πρὸς ἄπαντα δὴ ταῦτα ἀμηχάνως ἔχων ἀφικόμην
εἰς ἄνδρας οὐ νωθροὺς οὐδὲ σχολὴν ἄγοντας ἀκροᾶσθαι 5
λόγων, ἀλλὰ μετεώρους καὶ ἀγωνιῶντας καθάπερ ἵππους
ἀγωνιστὰς ἐπὶ τῶν ὑσπλήγων, οὐκ ἀνεχομένους τὸν χρόνον,
ὑπὸ σπουδῆς δὲ καὶ προθυμίας κόπτοντας τὸ ἔδαφος ταῖς
ὁπλαῖς· ἔνθα γε ἦν ὁρᾶν πανταχοῦ μὲν ξίφη, πανταχοῦ δὲ
θώρακας, πανταχοῦ δὲ δόρατα, πάντα δὲ ἵππων, πάντα δὲ 10
ὅπλων, πάντα δὲ ὡπλισμένων ἀνδρῶν μεστά. μόνος δὴ ἐν
τοσούτοις φαινόμενος ῥᾴθυμος ἀτεχνῶς σφόδρα τε εἰρηνικὸς
πολέμου θεατής, τὸ μὲν σῶμα ἐνδεής, τὴν δὲ ἡλικίαν προήκων,
20 οὐ χρυσοῦν σκῆπτρον φέρων οὐδὲ στέμματα ἱερὰ θεοῦ τινος
ἐπὶ λύσει θυγατρὸς ἥκων εἰς τὸ στρατόπεδον ἀναγκαίαν 15
ὁδόν, ἀλλ᾽ ἐπιθυμῶν ἰδεῖν ἄνδρας ἀγωνιζομένους ὑπὲρ ἀρχῆς
καὶ δυνάμεως, τοὺς δὲ ὑπὲρ ἐλευθερίας τε καὶ πατρίδος· ἔπειτα
οὐ τὸν κίνδυνον ἀποκνήσας, μὴ τοῦτο ἡγησάσθω μηδείς,
ἀλλ᾽ εὐχῆς τινος μνησθεὶς παλαιᾶς δεῦρο ἀπετράπην πρὸς
ὑμᾶς, ἀεὶ τὰ θεῖα κρείττω καὶ προύργιαίτερα νομίζων τῶν 20
ἀνθρωπίνων, ἡλίκα ἂν ᾖ.
21   Πότερον οὖν ἥδιον ὑμῖν καὶ μᾶλλον ἐν καιρῶι περὶ τῶν ἐκεῖ
διηγήσασθαι, τοῦ τε ποταμοῦ τὸ μέγεθος καὶ τῆς χώρας τὴν
φύσιν ἢ ὡρῶν ὡς ἔχουσι κράσεως καὶ τῶν ἀνθρώπων ⟨περὶ⟩
τοῦ γένους, ἔτι δέ, οἶμαι, τοῦ πλήθους καὶ τῆς παρασκευῆς, ἢ 25
μᾶλλον ἅψασθαι τῆς πρεσβυτέρας τε καὶ μείζονος ἱστορίας
22 περὶ τοῦδε τοῦ θεοῦ, παρ᾽ ὧι νῦν ἐσμεν – οὗτος γὰρ δὴ κοινὸς
ἀνθρώπων καὶ θεῶν βασιλεύς τε καὶ ἄρχων καὶ πρύτανις καὶ
πατήρ, ἔτι δὲ εἰρήνης καὶ πολέμου ταμίας, ὡς τοῖς πρότερον
ἐμπείροις καὶ σοφοῖς ποιηταῖς ἔδοξεν – ἐάν πως ἱκανοὶ 30
γενώμεθα τήν τε φύσιν αὐτοῦ καὶ τὴν δύναμιν ὑμνῆσαι

6 μετεώρους Jacobs : ὑμετέρους : δριμυτέρους Geel   10–11 πάντα δὲ ὅπλων
secl. Dindorf   24 ⟨περὶ⟩ add. Reiske

λόγωι βραχεῖ καὶ ἀποδέοντι τῆς ἀξίας, αὐτά που ταῦτα
λέγοντες;

23   Ἆρ' οὖν κατὰ Ἡσίοδον ἄνδρα ἀγαθὸν καὶ Μούσαις φίλον
ἀρκτέον, ὡς ἐκεῖνος μάλα ἐμφρόνως οὐκ αὐτὸς ἐτόλμησεν
ἄρξασθαι παρ' αὐτοῦ διανοηθείς, ἀλλὰ τὰς Μούσας παρακαλεῖ 5
διηγήσασθαι περὶ τοῦ σφετέρου πατρός; τῶι παντὶ γὰρ
μᾶλλον πρέπον τόδε τὸ ἆισμα ταῖς θεαῖς ἢ τοὺς ἐπὶ Ἴλιον
ἐλθόντας ἀριθμεῖν, αὐτούς τε καὶ τὰ σέλματα τῶν νεῶν ἐφεξῆς,
ὧν οἱ πολλοὶ ἀνόητοι ἦσαν· καὶ ποιητὴς σοφώτερός τε καὶ
ἀμείνων ὁ παρακαλῶν ἐπὶ τοῦτο τὸ ἔργον ὧδέ πως·   1

24   Μοῦσαι Πιερίηθεν ἀοιδῆισι κλείουσαι,
       δεῦτε Δί' ἐννέπετε σφέτερον πατέρ' ὑμνείουσαι,
       ὅν τε διὰ βροτοὶ ἄνδρες ὁμῶς ἄφατοί τε φατοί τε
       ῥητοί τ' ἄρρητοί τε, Διὸς μεγάλοιο ἕκητι·
       ῥέα μὲν γὰρ βριάει, ῥέα δὲ βριάοντα χαλέπτει,   1
       ῥεῖα δ' ἀρίζηλον μινύθει καὶ ἄδηλον ἀέξει,
       ῥεῖα δέ τ' ἰθύνει σκολιὸν καὶ ἀγήνορα κάρφει
       Ζεὺς ὑψιβρεμέτης, ὃς ὑπέρτατα δώματα ναίει.

25 ὑπολαβόντες οὖν εἴπατε πότερον ἁρμόζων ὁ λόγος οὗτος καὶ
τὸ ἆισμα τῆι συνόδωι γένοιτ' ἄν, ὦ παῖδες Ἠλείων – ὑμεῖς 2
γὰρ ἄρχοντες καὶ ἡγεμόνες τῆσδε τῆς πανηγύρεως, ἔφοροί τε
καὶ ἐπίσκοποι τῶν ἐνθάδε ἔργων καὶ λόγων – ἢ δεῖ θεατὰς
εἶναι μόνον τοὺς ἐνθάδε ἥκοντας τῶν τε ἄλλων δηλονότι
παγκάλων καὶ σφόδρα ἐνδόξων θεαμάτων καὶ δὴ μάλιστα τῆς
τοῦ θεοῦ θείας καὶ τῶι ὄντι μακαρίας εἰκόνος, ἣν ὑμῶν οἱ 2
πρόγονοι δαπάνης τε ὑπερβολῆι καὶ τέχνης ἐπιτυχόντες τῆς
ἄκρας εἰργάσαντο καὶ ἀνέθεσαν, πάντων ὅσα ἐστὶν ἐπὶ γῆς
ἀγάλματα κάλλιστον καὶ θεοφιλέστατον, πρὸς τὴν Ὁμηρικὴν
ποίησιν, ὥς φασι, Φειδίου παραβαλλομένου, τοῦ κινήσαντος
26 ὀλίγωι νεύματι τῶν ὀφρύων τὸν ξύμπαντα Ὄλυμπον, ὡς 3
ἐκεῖνος μάλιστα ἐναργῶς καὶ πεποιθότως ἐν τοῖς ἔπεσιν
εἴρηκεν·

1-2 αὐτά που τὰ μέγιστα (uel κράτιστα) Reiske   5 ἄρξασθαι Reiske :
εὔξασθαι   25 θείας scripsi : θρησκείας codd. : θεσπεσίας Kayser : σεβασμίας
Wenkebach   29 κινήσαντος Herwerden (cf. §79) : δινήσαντος

ἢ καὶ κυανέηισιν ἐπ' ὀφρύσι νεῦσε Κρονίων,
ἀμβρόσιαι δ' ἄρα χαῖται ἐπερρώσαντο ἄνακτος
κρατὸς ἀπ' ἀθανάτοιο, μέγαν δ' ἐλέλιξεν Ὄλυμπον,

ἢ καὶ περὶ αὐτῶν τούτων σκεπτέον ἡμῖν ἐπιμελέστερον, τῶν τε
ποιημάτων καὶ ἀναθημάτων καὶ ἀτεχνῶς εἴ τι τοιουτότροπόν   5
ἐστι τὴν ἀνθρωπίνην περὶ τοῦ δαιμονίου δόξαν ἀμηιγέπηι
πλάττον καὶ ἀνατυποῦν, ἅτε ἐν φιλοσόφου διατριβῆι τὰ νῦν,
ἄλλο δὲ οὐδὲν χρὴ πολυπραγμονεῖν οὐδὲ ἀκούειν οὐδενὸς ἀλλ'
ἢ μόνον σάλπιγγος ἱερᾶς καὶ τῶν μακαρίων κηρυγμάτων, ὡς
ὅδε μὲν νικᾶι πάλην παίδων, ὅδε δὲ ἀνδρῶν, ὅδε δὲ πυγμήν,   10
ὅδε δὲ παγκράτιον, ὅδε δὲ πένταθλον, ὅδε δὲ στάδιον, ἐνὶ
βήματι σχεδὸν εὐδαίμων γενόμενος, αὐτόν τε καὶ τὴν πατρίδα
καὶ τὸ σύμπαν ἀποφήνας γένος ἀοίδιμον;

27   Περὶ δὴ θεῶν τῆς τε καθόλου φύσεως καὶ μάλιστα τοῦ
πάντων ἡγεμόνος πρῶτον μὲν καὶ ἐν πρώτοις δόξα καὶ   15
ἐπίνοια κοινὴ τοῦ ξύμπαντος ἀνθρωπίνου γένους, ὁμοίως
μὲν Ἑλλήνων, ὁμοίως δὲ βαρβάρων, ἀναγκαία καὶ ἔμφυτος
ἐν παντὶ τῶι λογικῶι γινομένη κατὰ φύσιν ἄνευ θνητοῦ
διδασκάλου καὶ μυσταγωγοῦ χωρὶς ἀπάτης κεκράτηκε, διά
τε τὴν ξυγγένειαν τὴν πρὸς αὐτοὺς καὶ πολλὰ μαρτύρια   20
τἀληθοῦς οὐκ ἐῶντα κατανυστάξαι καὶ ἀμελῆσαι τοὺς
28   πρεσβυτάτους καὶ παλαιοτάτους· ἅτε γὰρ οὐ μακρὰν οὐδ'
ἔξω τοῦ θείου διοικισμένοι καθ' αὑτούς, ἀλλὰ ἐν αὐτῶι μέσωι
πεφυκότες, μᾶλλον δὲ συμπεφυκότες ἐκείνωι καὶ προσεχόμενοι
πάντα τρόπον, οὐκ ἐδύναντο μέχρι πλείονος ἀξύνετοι μένειν,   25
ἄλλως τε [σύνεσιν καὶ λόγον εἰληφότες περὶ αὐτου, ἅτε δὴ]
περιλαμπόμενοι πάντοθεν θείοις καὶ μεγάλοις φάσμασιν
οὐρανοῦ τε καὶ ἄστρων, ἔτι δὲ ἡλίου καὶ σελήνης, νυκτός

---

7 ⟨οὖσιν⟩ post τὰ νῦν add. Reiske; uide ad 43   8–13 ἄλλο ... ἀοίδιμον; uide
ad §17. Huc transposui, post Ὄλυμπον (3) Emperius, post ἥκοντας (68, 23)
Reiske, post λόγων (68, 22) Kayser : secl. Valesius   12 αὐτόν Capps :
αὑτόν   14 δὴ Reiske : δὲ   19 κεκράτηκε scripsi (κεχώρηκεν Sauppe) : καὶ
χαρᾶς codd. (sed χωρεῖ P) : καὶ ταραχῆς Reiske : καὶ φθορᾶς Emperius : γλισχρᾶς
Theiler   19 διά : ἐδήλου Capps   23 θείου : num θεοῦ?   24 προσεχόμενοι :
περιεχόμενοι Reiske   26 [σύνεσιν ... ἅτε δὴ] om. UPY   περὶ : παρ' Reiske

τε καὶ ἡμέρας ἐντυγχάνοντες ποικίλοις καὶ ἀνομοίοις
εἴδεσιν, ὄψεις τε ἀμηχάνους ὁρῶντες καὶ φωνὰς ἀκούοντες
παντοδαπὰς ἀνέμων τε καὶ ὕλης καὶ ποταμῶν καὶ θαλάττης,
ἔτι δὲ ζῴων ἡμέρων καὶ ἀγρίων, αὐτοί τε φθόγγον ἥδιστον
καὶ σαφέστατον ἱέντες καὶ ἀγαπῶντες τῆς ἀνθρωπίνης φωνῆς 5
τὸ γαῦρον καὶ ἐπιστῆμον, ἐπιθέμενοι σύμβολα τοῖς εἰς
αἴσθησιν ἀφικνουμένοις, ὡς πᾶν τὸ νοηθὲν ὀνομάζειν καὶ
δηλοῦν, εὐμαρῶς ἀπείρων πραγμάτων [καὶ] μνήμας καὶ
29 ἐπινοίας παραλαμβάνοντες. πῶς οὖν ἀγνῶτες εἶναι ἔμελλον
καὶ μηδεμίαν ἕξειν ὑπόνοιαν τοῦ σπείραντος καὶ φυτεύσαντος 10
καὶ σῴζοντος καὶ τρέφοντος, πανταχόθεν ἐμπιμπλάμενοι
τῆς θείας φύσεως διά τε ὄψεως καὶ ἀκοῆς συμπάσης τε
ἀτεχνῶς αἰσθήσεως, νεμόμενοι μὲν ἐπὶ γῆς, ὁρῶντες δ' ἐξ
οὐρανοῦ φῶς, τροφὰς δὲ ἀφθόνους ἔχοντες, εὐπορήσαντος καὶ
30 προπαρασκευάσαντος τοῦ προπάτορος θεοῦ, πρώτην μὲν 15
οἱ πρῶτοι καὶ αὐτόχθονες τὴν γεώδη, μαλακῆς ἔτι καὶ πίονος
τῆς ἰλύος τότε οὔσης, ὥσπερ ἀπὸ μητρὸς τῆς γῆς λιχμώμενοι,
καθάπερ τὰ φυτὰ νῦν ἕλκουσι τὴν ἐξ αὐτῆς ἰκμάδα, δευτέραν
δὲ τὰ ἤδη προϊόντα καρπῶν τε αὐτομάτων καὶ πόας οὐ
σκληρᾶς, ἅμα δρόσωι γλυκείαι καὶ 20

νάμασι νυμφῶν ποτίμοις,

καὶ δὴ καὶ τοῦ περιέχοντος ἠρτημένοι καὶ τρεφόμενοι τῆι
διηνεκεῖ τοῦ πνεύματος ἐπιρροῆι, ἀέρα ὑγρὸν ἕλκοντες, ὥσπερ
νήπιοι παῖδες οὔποτε ἐπιλείποντος γάλακτος ἀεί σφισι θηλῆς
31 ἐγκειμένης; σχεδὸν γὰρ ἂν ταύτην δικαιότερον λέγοιμεν 25
πρώτην τροφὴν τοῖς τε πρότερον καὶ τοῖς ὕστερον ἁπλῶς·
ἐπειδὰν γὰρ ἐκπέσηι τῆς γαστρὸς νωθρὸν ἔτι καὶ ἀδρανὲς
τὸ βρέφος, δέχεται μὲν ἡ γῆ, ἡ τῶι ὄντι μήτηρ, ὁ δὲ ἀὴρ
εἰσπνεύσας τε καὶ περιψύξας εὐθὺς ἤγειρεν ὑγροτέραι τροφῆι

6 γαῦρον : γλαφυρὸν Selden   8 [καὶ] om. M   16–17 τοῖς πρώτοις καὶ
αὐτόχθοσι ... λιχμωμένοις ⟨καὶ⟩ Wilamowitz   19 τὰ ἤδη προϊόντα scripsi :
τοῖς ἤδη προϊοῦσι   22 ἠρτημένοι : πειρώμενοι Wenkebach   23 ὥσπερ
Emperius : ὥστε   24 θηλῆς Morel : λήθης   25 γὰρ ἂν Reiske : γὰρ οὖν
29 περιψύξας Sonny : εἰσψύξας

γάλακτος καὶ φθέγξασθαι παρέσχεν. ταύτην εἰκότως πρώτην
32 λέγοιτ' ἂν τοῖς γεννωμένοις ἡ φύσις ἐπισχεῖν θηλήν. ἃ δὴ
πάσχοντες, πρὸς δὲ αὖ τούτοις αἰσθανόμενοι τῶν ὡρῶν, ὅτι
τῆς ἡμετέρας ἕνεκα γίγνονται σωτηρίας πάνυ ἀκριβῶς καὶ
πεφεισμένως ἑκατέρας τῆς ὑπερβολῆς, ἔτι δὲ καὶ τόδε ἐξαίρετον 5
ἔχοντες ἐκ τῶν θεῶν πρὸς τὰ ἄλλα ζῶια, λογίζεσθαί τε
καὶ διανοεῖσθαι περὶ αὐτῶν, ἐπινοοῦντες οὐκ ἐδύναντο μὴ
33 θαυμάζειν καὶ ἀγαπᾶν τὸ δαιμόνιον. σχεδὸν οὖν ὅμοιον
ὥσπερ εἴ τις ἄνδρα Ἕλληνα ἢ βάρβαρον μυεῖσθαι παραδοὺς
εἰς μυστικόν τινα μυχὸν ⟨εἰσάγοι⟩ ὑπερφυῆ κάλλει καὶ 10
μεγέθει, πολλὰ μὲν ὁρῶντα μυστικὰ θεάματα, πολλῶν δὲ
ἀκούοντα τοιούτων φωνῶν, σκότους τε καὶ φωτὸς ἐναλλὰξ
αὐτῶι φαινομένων, ἄλλων τε μυρίων γιγνομένων, ἔτι δὲ εἰ
καθάπερ εἰώθασιν ἐν τῶι καλουμένωι θρονισμῶι καθίσαντες
τοὺς μυουμένους οἱ τελοῦντες κύκλωι περιχορεύοιεν· ἆρά 15
γε τὸν ἄνδρα τοῦτον μηδὲν παθεῖν εἰκὸς τῆι ψυχῆι μηδ'
ὑπονοῆσαι τὰ γιγνόμενα, ὡς μετὰ γνώμης καὶ παρασκευῆς
πράττεται σοφωτέρας, εἰ καὶ πάνυ τις εἴη τῶν μακρόθεν καὶ
ἀνωνύμων βαρβάρων, μηδενὸς ἐξηγητοῦ μηδὲ ἑρμηνέως
34 παρόντος, ἀνθρωπίνην ψυχὴν ἔχων; ἢ τοῦτο μὲν οὐκ 20
ἀνυστόν, κοινῆι δὲ ξύμπαν τὸ τῶν ἀνθρώπων γένος τὴν
ὁλόκληρον καὶ τῶι ὄντι τελείαν τελετὴν μυούμενον, οὐκ ἐν
οἰκήματι μικρῶι παρασκευασθέντι πρὸς ὑποδοχὴν ὄχλου
βραχέος ὑπὸ Ἀθηναίων, ἀλλὰ ἐν τῶιδε τῶι κόσμωι,
ποικίλωι καὶ σοφῶι δημιουργήματι, μυρίων ἑκάστοτε 25
θαυμαστῶν φαινομένων, ἔτι δὲ οὐκ ἀνθρώπων ὁμοίων
τοῖς τελουμένοις, ἀλλὰ θεῶν ἀθανάτων θνητοὺς τελούντων,
νυκτί τε καὶ ἡμέραι καὶ φωτὶ καὶ ἄστροις, εἰ θέμις εἰπεῖν,
ἀτεχνῶς περιχορευόντων ἀεί, τούτων ξυμπάντων μηδεμίαν
αἴσθησιν μηδὲ ὑποψίαν λαβεῖν, μάλιστα δὲ τοῦ κορυφαίου 30

7–8 ἐπινοοῦντες . . . τὸ δαιμόνιον : post πάσχοντες (3) codd., huc transtuli. : post
τῆς ὑπερβολῆς (5) posuit von Arnim   9 παραδοὺς : παραδοίη Casaubon
10 μυχὸν Selden : μῦθον UBM : οἶκον P   ⟨εἰσάγοι⟩ addidi, Reiskium secutus
15 περιχορεύοιεν Theiler (— ευσαίεν iam Selden) : περιχορεύειν   26 θαυμαστῶν :
θαυμάτων Reiske   30 μάλιστα secl. von Arnim

72   ΔΙΩΝΟΣ

⟨τοῦ⟩ προεστῶτος τῶν ὅλων καὶ κατευθύνοντος τὸν ἅπαντα
οὐρανὸν καὶ κόσμον, οἷον σοφοῦ κυβερνήτου νεὼς ἄρχοντος
πάνυ καλῶς τε καὶ ἀνενδεῶς παρεσκευασμένης;
35   Οὐ γὰρ ἐπὶ τῶν ἀνθρώπων τὸ τοιοῦτον γιγνόμενον
θαυμάσαι τις ἄν, πολὺ δὲ μᾶλλον ὅπως καὶ μέχρι τῶν   5
θηρίων διικνεῖται τῶν ἀφρόνων καὶ ἀλόγων, ὡς καὶ ταῦτα
γιγνώσκειν καὶ τιμᾶν τὸν θεὸν καὶ προθυμεῖσθαι ζῆν κατὰ τὸν
ἐκείνου θεσμόν· ἔτι δὲ μᾶλλον ἀπεοικότως τὰ φυτά, οἷς μηδεμία
μηδενὸς ἔννοια, ἀλλὰ ἄψυχα καὶ ἄφωνα ἁπλῇ τινι φύσει
διοικούμενα, ὡς δὴ καὶ ταῦτα ἑκουσίως καὶ βουλόμενα καρπὸν   10
ἐκφέρει τὸν προσήκοντα ἑκάστωι· οὕτω πάνυ ἐναργὴς καὶ
36   πρόδηλος ἡ τοῦδε τοῦ θεοῦ γνώμη καὶ δύναμις. ἀλλ᾽
ἦπου σφόδρα γελοῖοι καὶ ἀρχαῖοι δόξομεν ἐπὶ τοῖς λόγοις,
ἐγγυτέρω φάσκοντες εἶναι τὴν τοιαύτην ξύνεσιν τοῖς θηρίοις
καὶ τοῖς δένδροις ἤπερ ἡμῖν τὴν ἀπειρίαν τε καὶ ἄγνοιαν;   15
ὁπότε ἄνθρωποί τινες σοφώτεροι γενόμενοι τῆς ἁπάσης
σοφίας, οὐ κηρὸν ἐγχέαντες τοῖς ὠσίν, ὥσπερ, οἶμαί, φασι
τοὺς Ἰθακησίους ναύτας ὑπὲρ τοῦ μὴ κατακοῦσαι τῆς τῶν
Σειρήνων ὡιδῆς, ἀλλὰ μολύβδου τινὸς μαλθακὴν ὁμοῦ καὶ
ἄτρωτον ὑπὸ φωνῆς φύσιν, ἔτι δέ, οἶμαι, πρὸ τῶν ὀφθαλμῶν   20
σκότος πολὺ προβαλόμενοι καὶ ἀχλύν, ὑφ᾽ ἧς Ὅμηρός
φησι κωλύεσθαι τὸν καταληφθέντα διαγιγνώσκειν θεόν,
ὑπερφρονοῦσι τὰ θεῖα, καὶ μίαν ἱδρυσάμενοι δαίμονα πονηρὰν
καὶ †ἄλυπον† τρυφήν τινα ἢ ῥαιθυμίαν πολλὴν καὶ ἀνειμένην
ὕβριν, Ἡδονὴν ἐπονομάζοντες, γυναικείαν τῶι ὄντι θεόν,   25
προτιμῶσι καὶ θεραπεύουσι κυμβάλοις τισὶν ὑποψοφοῦσι καὶ
37   αὐλοῖς ὑπὸ σκότος αὐλουμένοις, ἧς εὐωχίας οὐδεὶς ἐκείνοις
φθόνος, εἰ μέχρι τοῦ ἅιδειν αὐτοῖς τὸ σοφὸν ἦν ἀλλὰ μὴ τοὺς
θεοὺς ἡμῶν ἀφηιροῦντο καὶ ἀπώικιζον, ἐξελαύνοντες ἐκ τῆς
αὐτῶν πόλεώς τε καὶ ἀρχῆς [ἐκ] τοῦδε τοῦ κόσμου παντὸς   30
εἴς τινας χώρας ἀτόπους, καθάπερ ἀνθρώπους δυστυχεῖς εἴς

1 ⟨τοῦ⟩ suppl. Geel   10 ὡς δὴ καὶ ταῦτα : ὅμως δὲ καὶ αὐτὰ von Arnim
15 τὴν ... ἄγνοιαν secl. Geel   24 †ἄλυπον† : ἄτοπον Hertlein : num ἀνόσιον?
26 ὑποψοφοῦσι Capps : ἢ ψόφοις : ἐπιψόφοις Reiske   30 [ἐκ] seclusi, auctore
Geelio

τινας νήσους ἐρήμους, τάδε δὲ τὰ ξύμπαντα φάσκοντες
ἀγνώμονα καὶ ἄφρονα καὶ ἀδέσποτα καὶ μηδένα ἔχοντα
ἄρχοντα μηδὲ ταμίαν μηδὲ ἐπιστάτην πλανᾶσθαι εἰκῆι καὶ
φέρεσθαι, μηδενὸς μήτε νῦν προνοοῦντος μήτε πρότερον
ἐργασαμένου τὸ πᾶν, μηδὲ ὥσπερ οἱ παῖδες τοὺς τροχοὺς 5
αὐτοὶ κινήσαντες εἶτα ἐῶσιν ἀφ' αὑτῶν φέρεσθαι.

38   Ταῦτα μὲν οὖν ἐπεξῆλθεν ὁ λόγος καθ' αὑτὸν ἐκβάς·
τυχὸν γὰρ οὐ ῥάιδιον τὸν τοῦ φιλοσόφου νοῦν καὶ λόγον
ἐπισχεῖν, ἔνθα ἂν ὁρμήσηι, τοῦ ξυναντῶντος ἀεὶ φαινομένου
ξυμφέροντος καὶ ἀναγκαίου τοῖς ἀκροωμένοις, οὐ μελετηθέντα 10
πρὸς ὕδωρ καὶ δικανικὴν ἀνάγκην, ὥσπερ οὖν ἔφη τις, ἀλλὰ
μετὰ πολλῆς ἐξουσίας καὶ ἀδείας. οὐκοῦν τό γε ἀναδραμεῖν οὐ
χαλεπόν, ὥσπερ ἐν πλῶι τοῖς ἱκανοῖς κυβερνήταις οὐ πολὺ
παραλλάξασι.

39   Τῆς γὰρ περὶ τὸ θεῖον δόξης καὶ ὑπολήψεως πρώτην μὲν 15
ἀτεχνῶς πηγὴν ἐλέγομεν τὴν ἔμφυτον ἅπασιν ἀνθρώποις
ἐπίνοιαν, ἐξ αὐτῶν γιγνομένην τῶν ἔργων καὶ τἀληθοῦς, οὐ
κατὰ πλάνην συστᾶσαν οὐδὲ ὡς ἔτυχεν, ἀλλὰ πάνυ ἰσχυρὰν
καὶ ἀέναον ἐκ τοῦ παντὸς χρόνου καὶ παρὰ πᾶσι τοῖς ἔθνεσιν
ἀρξαμένην καὶ διαμένουσαν, σχεδόν τι κοινὴν καὶ δημοσίαν 20
τοῦ λογικοῦ γένους.

Δευτέραν δὲ λέγομεν τὴν ἐπίκτητον καὶ δι' ἑτέρων
ἐγγιγνομένην ταῖς ψυχαῖς [ἢ] λόγοις τε καὶ μύθοις καὶ ἔθεσι,
τοῖς μὲν ἀδεσπότοις τε καὶ ἀγράφοις, τοῖς δὲ ἐγγράφοις καὶ
40   σφόδρα γνωρίμους ἔχουσι τοὺς κυρίους. τῆς δὲ τοιαύτης 25
ὑπολήψεως τὴν μέν τινα ἑκουσίαν καὶ παραμυθητικὴν φῶμεν,
τὴν δὲ ἀναγκαίαν καὶ προστακτικήν. λέγω δὲ τοῦ μὲν
ἑκουσίου καὶ παραμυθίας ἐχομένην τὴν τῶν ποιητῶν, τοῦ δὲ
ἀναγκαίου καὶ προστάξεως τὴν τῶν νομοθετῶν· τούτων γὰρ
οὐδετέραν ἰσχῦσαι δυνατὸν μὴ πρώτης ἐκείνης ὑπούσης, δι' 30
ἣν βουλομένοις ἐγίγνοντο καὶ τρόπον τινὰ προειδόσιν αὐτοῖς

17–18 οὐ κατὰ πλάνην : οὐκέτι πολλὴν UBM   22 λέγομεν τὴν Reiske :
λεγομένην   22 δι' ἑτέρων Reiske : δι' οὐδετέρων   23 [ἢ] om. M   καὶ δὴ
οὐχ ἑτέρως ... ἢ Capps   31 ⟨ἐν⟩εγίγνοντο Capps

αἵ τε προστάξεις καὶ παραμυθίαι, τὰ μὲν ὀρθῶς καὶ ξυμφώνως
ἐξηγουμένων ποιητῶν καὶ νομοθετῶν τῆι τε ἀληθείαι καὶ ταῖς
41 ἐννοίαις, τῶν δὲ ἀποπλανωμένων ἔν τισιν. ἀμφοῖν δὲ τοῖν
λεγομένοιν ποτέραν πρεσβυτέραν φῶμεν τῶι χρόνωι παρά
γε ἡμῖν τοῖς Ἕλλησι ποίησιν ἢ νομοθεσίαν, οὐκ ἂν ἔχοιμι 5
διατεινόμενος εἰπεῖν τῶι παρόντι. πρέπει δὲ ἴσως τὸ ἀζήμιον
καὶ παραμυθητικὸν ἀρχαιότερον εἶναι τοῦ μετὰ ζημίας καὶ
42 προστάξεως. σχεδὸν οὖν μέχρι τοῦδε ὁμοίως πρόεισι τοῖς
ἀνθρώποις τὰ περὶ τοῦ πρώτου καὶ ἀθανάτου γονέως, ὃν καὶ
πατρῷον Δία καλοῦμεν οἱ τῆς Ἑλλάδος κοινωνοῦντες, καὶ τὰ 10
περὶ τῶν θνητῶν καὶ ἀνθρωπίνων γονέων. καὶ γὰρ δὴ ἡ πρὸς
ἐκείνους εὔνοια καὶ θεραπεία τοῖς ἐκγόνοις πρώτη μὲν ἀπὸ τῆς
φύσεως καὶ τῆς εὐεργεσίας ἀδίδακτος ὑπάρχει, τὸ γεννῆσαν
καὶ τρέφον καὶ στέργον τοῦ γεννηθέντος εὐθὺς ἀντιφιλοῦντος
43 καὶ ἀντιθεραπεύοντος ὅπως ἂν ἦι δυνατόν, δευτέρα δὲ καὶ 15
τρίτη, ποιητῶν καὶ νομοθετῶν, τῶν μὲν παραινούντων μὴ
ἀποστερεῖν χάριν τὸ πρεσβύτερον καὶ ξυγγενές, ἔτι δὲ αἴτιον
ζωῆς καὶ τοῦ εἶναι, τῶν δὲ ἐπαναγκαζόντων καὶ ἀπειλούντων
κόλασιν τοῖς οὐ πειθομένοις, ἄνευ τοῦ διασαφεῖν καὶ δηλοῦν
ὁποῖοί τινές εἰσιν οἱ γονεῖς καὶ τίνων εὐεργεσιῶν χρέος 20
ὀφειλόμενον κελεύουσι μὴ ἀνέκτιτον ἐᾶν. †ἐν τοῖς περὶ τῶν
θεῶν λόγοις καὶ μύθοις μᾶλλον δὲ τοῦτο ἰδεῖν ἔστιν ἐπ'
ἀμφοτέρων γιγνόμενον.†

Ὁρῶ μὲν οὖν ἔγωγε τοῖς πολλοῖς πανταχοῦ τὴν ἀκρίβειαν
κοπῶδες καὶ τὴν περὶ τοὺς λόγους οὐδὲν ἧττον, οἷς μέλει 25
πλήθους μόνον, οὐδὲν δὲ προειπόντες οὐδὲ διαστειλάμενοι
περὶ τοῦ πράγματος οὐδὲ ἀπό τινος ἀρχῆς ἀρχόμενοι τῶν
λόγων ἀλλ' αὐτό γε, ὥς φασιν, ἁπλύτοις ποσὶ διεξίασι τὰ
φανερώτατα καὶ γυμνότατα. καὶ ποδῶν μὲν ἁπλύτων οὐ

1 τὰ scripsi : τῶν   7 παραμυθητικὸν scripsi : ποιητικὸν : πειστικὸν Koehler
20 εὐεργεσιῶν Emperius : εὐεργετῶν   21 ἀνέκτιτον Morel : ἀνέκτιστον
21–3 †ἐν τοῖς ... γιγνόμενον† : nondum sanata. ἐν δὲ τοῖς ... μᾶλλον ἔτι τοῦτο
Wilamowitz. malim equidem τοῦτο ... γιγνόμενον, μᾶλλον δὲ ἐν τοῖς ... μύθοις
24–75, 6 ὁρῶ ... λόγους post ἐν φιλοσόφου διατριβῆι τὰ νῦν (69, 7) transp.
Emperius   25 τὴν Capps : τὰ   28 αὐτό γε : αὐτόθεν Wilamowitz
29 γυμνότατα : ἑτοιμότατα Sonny

μεγάλη βλάβη διά τε πηλοῦ καὶ πολλῶν καθαρμάτων ἰόντων,
γλώττης δὲ ἀνεπιστήμονος οὐ μικρὰ ζημία γίγνεται τοῖς
ἀκροωμένοις. ἀλλὰ γὰρ εἰκὸς τοὺς πεπαιδευμένους, ὧν λόγον
τινὰ ἔχειν ἄξιον, συνεξανύειν καὶ συνεκπονεῖν, μέχρις ἂν ὡς ἐκ
καμπῆς τινος καὶ δυσχωρίας καταστήσωμεν εἰς εὐθεῖαν τοὺς 5
λόγους.

44   Τριῶν δὴ προκειμένων γενέσεων τῆς ⟨τοῦ⟩ δαιμονίου
παρ' ἀνθρώποις ὑπολήψεως, ἐμφύτου, ποιητικῆς, νομικῆς,
τετάρτην φῶμεν τὴν πλαστικήν τε καὶ δημιουργικὴν τῶν
περὶ τὰ θεῖα ἀγάλματα καὶ τὰς εἰκόνας, λέγω δὲ γραφέων 10
τε καὶ ἀνδριαντοποιῶν καὶ λιθοξόων καὶ παντὸς ἁπλῶς
τοῦ καταξιώσαντος αὑτὸν ἀποφῆναι μιμητὴν διὰ τέχνης
τῆς δαιμονίας φύσεως, εἴτε σκιαγραφίαι μάλα ἀσθενεῖ καὶ
ἀπατηλῆι πρὸς ὄψιν, ⟨εἴτε⟩ χρωμάτων μίξει καὶ γραμμῆς
ὅρωι σχεδὸν τὸ ἀκριβέστατον περιλαμβανούσης, εἴτε λίθων 15
γλυφαῖς εἴτε ξοάνων ἐργασίαις, κατ' ὀλίγον τῆς τέχνης
ἀφαιρούσης τὸ περιττόν, ἕως ἂν καταλίπηι αὐτὸ τὸ
φαινόμενον εἶδος, εἴτε χωνείαι χαλκοῦ καὶ τῶν ὁμοίων ὅσα
τίμια διὰ πυρὸς ἐλαθέντων ἢ ῥυέντων ἐπί τινας τύπους, εἴτε
κηροῦ πλάσει ῥᾶιστα ξυνακολουθοῦντος τῆι τέχνηι καὶ 20
45   πλεῖστον ἐπιδεχομένου τὸ τῆς μετανοίας· οἷος ἦν Φειδίας τε
καὶ Ἀλκαμένης καὶ Πολύκλειτος, ἔτι δὲ Ἀγλαοφῶν καὶ
Πολύγνωτος καὶ Ζεῦξις καὶ πρότερος αὐτῶν ὁ Δαίδαλος. οὐ
γὰρ ἀπέχρη τούτοις περὶ τἆλλα ἐπιδείκνυσθαι τὴν αὑτῶν
δεινότητα καὶ σοφίαν, ἀλλὰ καὶ θεῶν εἰκόνας καὶ διαθέσεις 25
παντοδαπὰς ἐπιδεικνύντες, ἰδίαι τε καὶ δημοσίαι χορηγοὺς
τὰς πόλεις λαμβάνοντες, πολλῆς ἐνέπλησαν ὑπονοίας καὶ
ποικίλης περὶ τοῦ δαιμονίου, οὐ παντελῶς διαφερόμενοι
τοῖς ποιηταῖς καὶ νομοθέταις, τὸ μὲν ὅπως μὴ δοκῶσι
παράνομοι καὶ ταῖς ἐπικειμέναις ἐνέχωνται ζημίαις, τὸ δὲ 30
ὁρῶντες προκατειλημμένους αὐτοὺς ὑπὸ τῶν ποιητῶν καὶ
46   πρεσβυτέραν οὖσαν τὴν ἐκείνων εἰδωλοποιΐαν. οὔκουν
ἐβούλοντο φαίνεσθαι τοῖς πολλοῖς ἀπίθανοι καὶ ἀηδεῖς

καινοποιοῦντες. τὰ μὲν οὖν πολλὰ τοῖς μύθοις ἑπόμενοι καὶ
συνηγοροῦντες ἔπλαττον, τὰ δὲ καὶ παρ' αὐτῶν εἰσέφερον,
ἀντίτεχνοι καὶ ὁμότεχνοι τρόπον τινὰ γιγνόμενοι τοῖς
ποιηταῖς, ὡς ἐκεῖνοι δι' ἀκοῆς ἐπιδεικνύντες, ἀτεχνῶς καὶ
αὐτοὶ δι' ὄψεως ἐξηγούμενοι τὰ θεῖα τοῖς πλείοσι καὶ 5
ἀπειροτέροις θεαταῖς. πάντα δὲ ταῦτα τὴν ἰσχὺν ἔσχεν ἀπὸ
τῆς πρώτης ἀρχῆς ἐκείνης, ὡς ἐπὶ τιμῆι καὶ χάριτι ποιούμενα
τοῦ δαιμονίου.

47   Καὶ μὴν δίχα γε τῆς ἁπλῆς καὶ πρεσβυτάτης ἐννοίας
περὶ θεῶν καὶ ξυγγενῶς πᾶσιν ἀνθρώποις ἅμα τῶι λόγωι 10
φυομένης, πρὸς τοῖς τρισὶ τούτοις ἑρμηνεῦσι καὶ διδασκάλοις
[ποιητικῆς καὶ νομοθετικῆς καὶ δημιουργικῆς], τέταρτον
ἀνάγκη παραλαβεῖν, οὐδαμῆι ῥάιθυμον οὐδὲ ἀπείρως
ἡγούμενον ἔχειν ὑπὲρ αὐτῶν, λέγω δὲ τὸν φιλόσοφον ἄνδρα,
†ἢ λόγων† ἐξηγητὴν καὶ προφήτην τῆς ἀθανάτου φύσεως 15
ἀληθέστατον ἴσως καὶ τελειότατον.

48   Τὸν μὲν οὖν νομοθέτην ἐάσωμεν τὰ νῦν εἰς εὐθύνας ἄγειν,
ἄνδρα αὐστηρὸν καὶ τοὺς ἄλλους αὐτὸν εὐθύνοντα· δέοι
γὰρ ἂν αὐτὸν αὐτοῦ φείδεσθαι καὶ τῆς ὑμετέρας ἀσχολίας.
ὑπὲρ δὲ τῶν λοιπῶν ἑκάστου γένους προχειρισάμενοι τὸν 20
ἄκρον σκοπῶμεν, εἴ τινα ὠφέλειαν ἢ καὶ βλάβην φανήσονται
πεποιηκότες πρὸς εὐσέβειαν τοῖς αὐτῶν ἔργοις ἢ λόγοις,
ὅπως τε ἔχουσιν ὁμολογίας ἢ τοῦ διαφέρεσθαι ἀλλήλοις,
καὶ τίς αὐτῶν ξυνέπεται τῶι ἀληθεῖ μάλιστα, τῆι πρώτηι
καὶ ἀδόλωι γνώμηι σύμφωνος ὤν. πάντες †τοιγαροῦν† 25
οὗτοι ξυνάιδουσιν, ὥσπερ ἑνὸς ἴχνους λαβόμενοι, καὶ τοῦτο
σώιζοντες, οἱ μὲν σαφῶς, οἱ δὲ ἀδηλότερον. οὐ γὰρ ἂν ἴσως
δέοιτο παραμυθίας ⟨ὁ⟩ τῆι ἀληθείαι φιλόσοφος, εἰ πρὸς
σύγκρισιν ἄγοιτο ποιηταῖς ἀγαλμάτων ἢ μέτρων, καὶ ταῦτα
ἐν ὄχλωι πανηγύρεως ἐκείνοις φίλων δικαστῶν.   30

9 δίχα γε secl. von Arnim   12 [ποιητικῆς ... δημιουργικῆς] secl. von Arnim
14 num ⟨τῶν⟩ ὑπὲρ αὐτῶν ⟨λόγων⟩, omisso ἢ λόγων (15)?   15 †ἢ λόγων† :
λόγωι von Arnim : τὸν λόγωι Jacobs : διὰ λόγων Geel. num delendum?
21 ἢ Wilamowitz : τε   25 †τοιγαροῦν† corruptum : πάντες ... ἀδηλότερον
secl. Emperius, fortasse recte   27 οὐ γὰρ : καὶ γὰρ Reiske : fortasse ⟨ἀλλ'⟩
οὐ γὰρ   28 ⟨ὁ⟩ add. Reiske   εἰ ⟨μὴ⟩ von Arnim

49 Εἰ γάρ τις Φειδίαν πρῶτον ἐν τοῖς Ἕλλησιν εὐθύνοι,
τὸν σοφὸν τοῦτον καὶ δαιμόνιον ἐργάτην τοῦ σεμνοῦ
καὶ παγκάλου δημιουργήματος, καθίσας δικαστὰς τοὺς
βραβεύοντας τῶι θεῶι τὸν ἀγῶνα, μᾶλλον δὲ κοινὸν
δικαστήριον ξυμπάντων Πελοποννησίων, ἔτι δὲ Βοιωτῶν 5
καὶ Ἰώνων καὶ τῶν ἄλλων Ἑλλήνων τῶν πανταχοῦ κατὰ
τὴν Εὐρώπην καὶ τὴν Ἀσίαν, οὐ τῶν χρημάτων λόγον
ἀπαιτῶν οὐδὲ τῆς περὶ τὸ ἄγαλμα δαπάνης, ὁπόσων χρυσὸς
ὠνήθη ταλάντων καὶ ἐλέφας, ἔτι δὲ κυπάριττος καὶ θύον,
πρὸς τὴν ἐντὸς ἐργασίαν μόνιμος ὕλη καὶ ἀδιάφθορος, τροφῆς 10
τε καὶ μισθῶν ἀναλώματος τοῖς ἐργασαμένοις οὐκ ὀλίγοις
οὐδὲ ὀλίγον χρόνον ἄλλοις τε οὐ φαύλοις δημιουργοῖς καὶ
τῶι πλεῖστον καὶ τελεώτατον μισθὸν ⟨ἀπολαβόντι⟩ ὑπὲρ
τῆς τέχνης Φειδίαι· ταῦτα μὲν γὰρ Ἠλείοις προσήκοντα
λογίσασθαι τοῖς ἀναλώσασιν ἀφθόνως καὶ μεγαλοπρεπῶς, 15
50 ἡμεῖς δὲ ὑπὲρ ἄλλου φήσομεν τῶι Φειδίαι προκεῖσθαι τὸν
ἀγῶνα· εἰ οὖν δὴ λέγοι τις πρὸς αὐτόν·

Ὦ βέλτιστε καὶ ἄριστε τῶν δημιουργῶν, ὡς μὲν οὐχ ἡδὺ
καὶ προσφιλὲς ὅραμα καὶ τέρψιν ἀμήχανον θέας εἰργάσω
πᾶσιν Ἕλλησι καὶ βαρβάροις, ὅσοι ποτὲ δεῦρο ἀφίκοντο 20
51 πολλοὶ πολλάκις, οὐδεὶς ἀντερεῖ. τῶι γὰρ ὄντι καὶ τὴν
ἄλογον ἂν ἐκπλήξειε τοῦτό γε τῶν ζώιων φύσιν, εἰ δύναιντο
προσιδεῖν μόνον, ταύρων τε τῶν ἀεὶ πρὸς τόνδε τὸν βωμὸν
ἀγομένων, ὡς ἑκόντας ὑπέχειν τοῖς καταρχομένοις, εἴ τινα
παρέξουσι τῶι θεῶι χάριν, ἔτι δὲ ἀετῶν τε καὶ ἰκτίνων καὶ 25
λεόντων, ὡς τὸ ἀνήμερον καὶ ἄγριον σβέσαντας τοῦ θυμοῦ
πολλὴν ἡσυχίαν ἄγειν, τερφθέντας ὑπὸ τῆς θέας· ἀνθρώπων
δέ, ὃς ἂν ἦι παντελῶς ἐπίπονος τὴν ψυχήν, πολλὰς
ἀναντλήσας συμφορὰς καὶ λύπας ἐν τῶι βίωι μηδὲ ὕπνον
ἡδὺν ἐπιβαλλόμενος, καὶ ὃς δοκεῖ μοι κατ' ἐναντίον στὰς 30

---

10 πρὸς ... ἀδιάφθορος von Arnim : πρὸς τὴν ἐν τῆι ἐργασίαι μόνιμον
ὕλην καὶ ἀδιάφθορον 11 ἀναλώματος Geel : ἀνάλωμα 13 τῶι ...
⟨ἀπολαβόντι⟩ von Arnim (sed omisso καὶ τελεώτατον) : τοῦ πλείστου καὶ
τελεωτάτου μισθοῦ Geel 18 οὐχ scripsi : οὖν codd.; om. edd. 25 ἰκτίνων
Jacobs : ἵππων 27 τερφθέντας Geel : -τα 29 ἀναντλήσας Dindorf : ἀπ-

τῆσδε τῆς εἰκόνος ἐκλαθέσθαι πάντων ὅσα ἐν ἀνθρωπίνωι
52 βίωι δεινὰ καὶ χαλεπὰ γίγνεται παθεῖν. οὕτως σύγε ἀνεῦρες
καὶ ἐμηχανήσω θέαμα, ἀτεχνῶς

νηπενθές τ᾽ ἄχολόν τε, κακῶν ἐπίληθες ἁπάντων·

τοσοῦτον φῶς καὶ τοσαύτη χάρις ἔπεστιν ἀπὸ τῆς τέχνης. 5
οὐδὲ γὰρ ἂν αὐτὸν τὸν Ἥφαιστον εἰκὸς ἐγκαλέσαι τῶιδε τῶι
ἔργωι, κρίνοντα πρὸς ἡδονὴν καὶ τέρψιν ἀνθρωπίνης ὄψεως.
Εἰ δ᾽ αὖ τὸ πρέπον εἶδος καὶ τὴν ἀξίαν μορφὴν τῆς θεοῦ
φύσεως ἐδημιούργησας ὕληι τε ἐπιτερπεῖ χρησάμενος ἀνδρός
τε μορφὴν ὑπερφυῆ τὸ κάλλος καὶ τὸ μέγεθος δείξας, πλὴν 10
ἀνδρός, καὶ τἄλλα ποιήσας ὡς ἐποίησας, σκοπῶμεν τὰ νῦν·
ὑπὲρ ὧν ἀπολογησάμενος ἱκανῶς ἐν τοῖς παροῦσι καὶ πείσας
ὅτι τὸ οἰκεῖον καὶ τὸ πρέπον ἐξεῦρες σχήματός τε καὶ
μορφῆς τῶι πρώτωι καὶ μεγίστωι θεῶι, μισθὸν ἕτερον τοῦ
53 παρ᾽ Ἠλείων προσλάβοις ⟨ἂν⟩ μείζω καὶ τελειότερον. ὁρᾶις 15
γὰρ ὅτι οὐ μικρὸς ἀγὼν οὐδ᾽ ὁ κίνδυνος ἡμῖν. πρότερον μὲν
γάρ, ἅτε οὐδὲν σαφὲς εἰδότες, ἄλλην ἄλλος ἀνεπλάττομεν
ἰδέαν πᾶν τὸ θνητόν, κατὰ τὴν ἑαυτοῦ δύναμιν καὶ φύσιν
ἕκαστος ἰνδαλλόμενοι καὶ ὀνειρώττοντες, εἴ τέ πού τινα μικρὰ
καὶ ἄσημα συλλέγομεν τῶν ἔμπροσθεν εἰκάσματα τεχνιτῶν, 20
οὐ πάνυ τούτοις οὔτε πιστεύοντες οὔτε προσέχοντες τὸν
νοῦν. σὺ δέ γε ἰσχύϊ τέχνης ἐνίκησας καὶ ξυνέλεξας τὴν
Ἑλλάδα πρῶτον, ἔπειτα τοὺς ἄλλους, τῶιδε τῶι φάσματι,
θεσπέσιον καὶ λαμπρὸν ἀποδείξας, ὡς μηδένα τῶν ἰδόντων
54 δόξαν ἑτέραν ἔτι λαβεῖν ῥαιδίως. ἆρ᾽ οὖν οἴει τὸν Ἴφιτον 25
καὶ τὸν Λυκοῦργον καὶ τοὺς τότε Ἠλείους διὰ χρημάτων
ἀπορίαν τὸν μὲν ἀγῶνα καὶ τὴν θυσίαν ποιῆσαι τῶι Διὶ
πρέπουσαν, ἄγαλμα δὲ μηδὲν ἐξευρεῖν ἐπ᾽ ὀνόματι καὶ
σχήματι τοῦ θεοῦ, σχεδόν τι προέχοντας δυνάμει τῶν
ὑστέρων, ἢ μᾶλλον φοβηθέντας μήποτε οὐ δύναιντο ἱκανῶς 30

1 ἐκλαθέσθαι ⟨ἂν⟩ Geel.   6 ἂν om. UBM   10 ἐποίεις post ἀνδρός τε UBM :
ποιήσας Reiske   15 ⟨ἂν⟩ add. Geel   18 θνητόν : θεῖον Capps. πᾶν τὸ
θνητὸν del. von Arnim. περὶ τὸ ἀθάνατον Wenkebach   19 εἴ τέ : num
εἰ δέ?   22 ξυνήλλαξας Emperius, fortasse recte   30 δύναιντο Schwartz :
ἐδύναντο

ἀπομιμήσασθαι διὰ θνητῆς τέχνης τὴν ἄκραν καὶ τελειοτάτην
φύσιν;
55 Πρὸς δὴ ταῦτα τυχὸν εἴποι ἂν Φειδίας, ἅτε ἀνὴρ οὐκ
ἄγλωττος οὐδὲ ἀγλώττου πόλεως, ἔτι δὲ συνήθης καὶ ἑταῖρος
Περικλέους·   5
Ἄνδρες Ἕλληνες, ὁ μὲν ἀγὼν τῶν πώποτε μέγιστος· οὐ
γὰρ περὶ ἀρχῆς οὐδὲ περὶ στρατηγίας μιᾶς πόλεως οὐδὲ περὶ
νεῶν πλήθους ἢ πεζοῦ στρατοπέδου, πότερον ὀρθῶς ἢ μὴ
διώικηται, τὰ νῦν ὑπέχω λόγον, ἀλλὰ περὶ τοῦ πάντων
κρατοῦντος θεοῦ καὶ τῆς πρὸς ἐκεῖνον ὁμοιότητος, εἴτε 10
εὐσχημόνως καὶ προσεοικότως γέγονεν, οὐδὲν ἐλλείπουσα
τῆς δυνατῆς πρὸς τὸ δαιμόνιον ἀνθρώποις ἀπεικασίας, εἴτε
ἀναξία καὶ ἀπρεπής.
56 Ἐνθυμεῖσθε δὲ ὅτι οὐκ ἐγὼ πρῶτος ὑμῖν ἐγενόμην ἐξηγητὴς
καὶ διδάσκαλος τῆς ἀληθείας. οὐδὲ γὰρ ἔφυν ἔτι κατ' ἀρχὰς 15
τῆς Ἑλλάδος οὐδέπω σαφῆ καὶ ἀραρότα δόγματα ἐχούσης
περὶ τούτων, ἀλλὰ πρεσβυτέρας τρόπον τινὰ καὶ ⟨τὰ⟩ περὶ
τοὺς θεοὺς ἤδη πεπεισμένης καὶ νομιζούσης ἰσχυρῶς. καὶ ὅσα
μὲν λιθοξόων ἔργα ἢ γραφέων ἀρχαιότερα τῆς ἐμῆς τέχνης
σύμφωνα ἦσαν, πλὴν ὅσον κατὰ τὴν ἀκρίβειαν τῆς ποιήσεως, 20
57 ἐῶ λέγειν· δόξας δὲ ὑμετέρας κατέλαβον παλαιὰς ἀκινήτους,
αἷς οὐκ ἦν ἐναντιοῦσθαι δυνατόν, καὶ δημιουργοὺς ἄλλους
περὶ τὰ θεῖα, πρεσβυτέρους ἡμῶν καὶ πολὺ σοφωτέρους
ἀξιοῦντας εἶναι, τοὺς ποιητάς, ἐκείνων μὲν δυναμένων εἰς
πᾶσαν ἐπίνοιαν ἄγειν διὰ τῆς ποιήσεως, τῶν δὲ ἡμετέρων 25
58 αὐτουργημάτων μόνην ταύτην ἱκανὴν ἐχόντων εἰκασίαν· τὰ
γὰρ θεῖα φάσματα, λέγω δὲ ἡλίου καὶ σελήνης καὶ σύμπαντος
οὐρανοῦ καὶ ἄστρων, αὐτὰ μὲν καθ' αὑτὰ φαινόμενα
θαυμαστὰ πάντως, ἡ δὲ μίμησις αὐτῶν ἁπλῆ καὶ ἄτεχνος, εἴ
τις ἐθέλοι τὰ σελήνης σχήματα ἀφομοιοῦν ἢ τὸν ἡλίου 30
κύκλον· ἔτι δὲ ἤθους καὶ διανοίας αὐτὰ μὲν ἐκεῖνα μεστὰ
πάντως, ἐν δὲ τοῖς εἰκάσμασιν οὐδὲν ἐνδεικνύμενα τοιοῦτον.
59 ὅθεν ἴσως καὶ τὸ ἐξ ἀρχῆς οὕτως ἐνομίσθη τοῖς Ἕλλησι. νοῦν

---

17 ⟨τὰ⟩ add. Schwartz   21 num ⟨τὰς⟩ παλαιάς, uel ⟨καὶ⟩ ἀκινήτους?
32 πάντως Reiske : πάντων   33 ὅθεν Selden : οἶον   οὕτως : οὔπω Capps

γὰρ καὶ φρόνησιν αὐτὴν μὲν καθ' αὑτὴν οὔτε τις πλάστης
οὔτε τις γραφεὺς εἰκάσαι δυνατὸς ἔσται· ἀθέατοι γὰρ τῶν
τοιούτων καὶ ἀνιστόρητοι παντελῶς πάντες. τὸ δὲ ἐν ὧι
τοῦτο γιγνόμενόν ἐστιν οὐχ ὑπονοοῦντες ἀλλ' εἰδότες
ἐπ' αὐτὸ καταφεύγομεν, ἀνθρώπινον σῶμα ὡς ἀγγεῖον 5
φρονήσεως καὶ λόγου θεῶι προσάπτοντες, ἐνδείαι καὶ ἀπορίαι
παραδείγματος τῶι φανερῶι τε καὶ εἰκαστῶι τὸ ἀνείκαστον
καὶ ἀφανὲς ἐνδείκνυσθαι ζητοῦντες, συμβόλου δυνάμει
χρώμενοι, κρεῖττον ἤ φασι τῶν βαρβάρων τινὰς ζώιοις
τὸ θεῖον ἀφομοιοῦν κατὰ σμικρὰς καὶ ἀτόπους ἀφορμάς. ι•
ὁ δὲ πλεῖστον ὑπερβαλὼν κάλλει καὶ σεμνότητι καὶ
μεγαλοπρεπείαι, σχεδὸν οὗτος πολὺ κράτιστος δημιουργὸς
⟨τύπος⟩ τῶν περὶ τὰ θεῖα ἀγαλμάτων.

60   Οὐδὲ γὰρ ὡς βέλτιον ὑπῆρχεν ἂν μηδὲν ἵδρυμα μηδὲ
εἰκόνα θεῶν ἀποδεδεῖχθαι παρ' ἀνθρώποις φαίη τις ἄν, ὡς ι
πρὸς μόνα ὁρᾶν δέον τὰ οὐράνια. ταῦτα μὲν γὰρ ξύμπαντα
ὅ γε νοῦν ἔχων σέβει, θεοὺς ἡγούμενος μακαρίους μακρόθεν
ὁρῶν· διὰ δὲ τὴν πρὸς τὸ δαιμόνιον ὁρμὴν ἰσχυρὸς ἔρως
πᾶσιν ἀνθρώποις ἐγγύθεν τιμᾶν καὶ θεραπεύειν τὸ θεῖον,
προσιόντας καὶ ἁπτομένους μετὰ πειθοῦς, θύοντας καὶ 2•
61   στεφανοῦντας. ἀτεχνῶς γὰρ ὥσπερ νήπιοι παῖδες πατρὸς
ἢ μητρὸς ἀπεσπασμένοι δεινὸν ἵμερον ἔχοντες καὶ πόθον
ὀρέγουσι χεῖρας οὐ παροῦσι πολλάκις ὀνειρώττοντες, οὕτω
καὶ θεοῖς ἄνθρωποι ἀγαπῶντες δικαίως διά τε εὐεργεσίαν
καὶ συγγένειαν, προθυμούμενοι πάντα τρόπον συνεῖναί τε 2•
καὶ ὁμιλεῖν· ὥστε καὶ πολλοὶ τῶν βαρβάρων πενίαι τε καὶ
ἀπορίαι τέχνης ὄρη θεοὺς ἐπονομάζουσι καὶ δένδρα ἀργὰ καὶ
ἀσήμους λίθους, οὐδαμῆι οὐδαμῶς οἰκειότερα τὴν μορφήν.

62   Εἰ δ' ὑμῖν ἐπαίτιός εἰμι τοῦ σχήματος, οὐκ ἂν φθάνοιτε
Ὁμήρωι πρότερον χαλεπῶς ἔχοντες· ἐκεῖνος γὰρ οὐ μόνον 3•
μορφὴν ἐγγύτατα τῆς δημιουργίας ἐμιμήσατο, χαίτας τε

12–13 δημιουργοῖς ⟨τύπος⟩ Schwartz : δημιουργὸς   18 ὁρμὴν Wilamowitz :
γνώμην   24 θεοῖς Reiske : θεοὺς   28 τὴν μορφήν Cohoon : τῆς μορφῆς   τῆς
⟨ἀνθρωπίνης⟩ μορφῆς Geel

ὀνομάζων τοῦ θεοῦ, ἔτι δὲ ἀνθερεῶνα εὐθὺς ἐν ἀρχῆι τῆς
ποιήσεως, ὅτε φησὶν ἱκετεύειν τὴν Θέτιν ὑπὲρ τιμῆς τοῦ
παιδός· πρὸς δὲ τούτοις ὁμιλίας τε καὶ βουλεύσεις καὶ
δημηγορίας ⟨ἔνεμε⟩ τοῖς θεοῖς, ἔτι δὲ ἐξ Ἴδης ἀφίξεις πρὸς
οὐρανὸν καὶ Ὄλυμπον, ὕπνους τε καὶ συμπόσια καὶ μίξεις,   5
μάλα μὲν ὑψηλῶς σύμπαντα κοσμῶν τοῖς ἔπεσιν, ὅμως δὲ
ἐχόμενα θνητῆς ὁμοιότητος, καὶ δή γε καὶ ὁπότε ἐτόλμησεν
Ἀγαμέμνονα προσεικάσαι τοῦ θεοῦ τοῖς κυριωτάτοις μέρεσιν,
εἰπών

    ὄμματα καὶ κεφαλὴν ἴκελος Διὶ τερπικεραύνωι.   10

63 τὸ δέ γε τῆς ἐμῆς ἐργασίας οὐκ ἄν τις οὐδὲ μανεὶς [τινι]
ἀφομοιώσειεν οὐδενὶ θνητῶι, πρὸς κάλλος ἢ μέγεθος [θεοῦ]
συνεξεταζόμενον, ἀφ' οὗ γε εἰ μὴ Ὁμήρου πολὺ φανῶ
κρείττων καὶ σοφώτερος ποιητής, τοῦ δόξαντος ὑμῖν ἰσοθέου
τὴν σοφίαν, ἣν βούλεσθε ζημίαν ἕτοιμος ὑπέχειν ἐγώ. λέγω   15
64 δὲ πρὸς τὸ δυνατὸν τῆς ἐμαυτοῦ τέχνης· δαψιλὲς γὰρ χρῆμα
ποίησις καὶ πάντα τρόπον εὔπορον καὶ αὐτόνομον, καὶ
χορηγίαι γλώττης καὶ πλήθει ῥημάτων ἱκανὸν ἐξ αὐτοῦ
πάντα δηλῶσαι τὰ τῆς ψυχῆς βουλήματα, κἂν ὁποιονοῦν
διανοηθῆι σχῆμα ἢ ἔργον ἢ πάθος ἢ μέγεθος οὐκ ἂν   20
ἀπορήσειεν, ἀγγέλου φωνῆς πάνυ ἐναργῶς σημαινούσης
ἕκαστα·

    στρεπτὴ γὰρ γλῶσσ' ἐστὶ βροτῶν, πολέες δ' ἔνι μῦθοι,

φησὶν Ὅμηρος αὐτός,

    παντοῖοι, ἐπέων δὲ πολὺς νομὸς ἔνθα καὶ ἔνθα.   25

65 κινδυνεύει γὰρ οὖν τὸ ἀνθρώπινον γένος ἁπάντων ἐνδεὲς
γενέσθαι μᾶλλον ἢ φωνῆς καὶ λέξεως· τούτου δὲ μόνου
κέκτηται θαυμαστόν τινα πλοῦτον. οὐδὲν γοῦν παραλέλοιπεν

3-4 βουλήσεις καὶ δημιουργίας codd., corr. Reiske   4 ⟨ἔνεμε⟩ add. Capps
11 [τινι] om. M m.pr.   12 οὐδενὶ P : οὐδὲ UBM, secl. Wilamowitz   θνητῶι :
ἀνδρὶ (Reiske) γνωστῶι Wenkebach   12 [θεοῦ] secl. Emperius   13 ἀφ'
οὗ : ὅπου Capps   14 σοφώτερος Wenkebach : σωφρονέστερος

ἄφθεγκτον οὐδὲ ἄσημον τῶν πρὸς αἴσθησιν ἀφικνουμένων, ἀλλ' εὐθὺς ἐπιβάλλει τῶι νοηθέντι σαφῆ σφραγῖδα ὀνόματος, πολλάκις δὲ καὶ πλείους φωνὰς ἑνὸς πράγματος, ὧν ὁπόταν φθέγξηταί τινα, παρέσχε δόξαν οὐ πολὺ ἀσθενεστέραν τἀληθοῦς. πλείστη μὲν οὖν ἐξουσία καὶ δύναμις ἀνθρώπωι 5
66 περὶ λόγον ἐνδείξασθαι τὸ παραστάν. ἡ δὲ τῶν ποιητῶν τέχνη μάλα αὐθάδης καὶ ἀνεπίληπτος, ἄλλως τε Ὁμήρου, τοῦ πλείστην ἄγοντος παρρησίαν, ὃς οὐχ ἕνα εἵλετο χαρακτῆρα λέξεως, ἀλλὰ πᾶσαν τὴν Ἑλληνικὴν γλῶτταν διῃρημένην τέως ἀνέμιξε, Δωριέων τε καὶ Ἰώνων, ἔτι δὲ 1
τὴν Ἀθηναίων, εἰς ταὐτὸ κεράσας πολλῶι μᾶλλον ἢ τὰ χρώματα οἱ βαφεῖς, οὐ μόνον τῶν καθ' αὑτὸν ἀλλὰ καὶ τῶν πρότερον, εἴ πού τι ῥῆμα ἐκλελοιπός, καὶ τοῦτο ἀναλαβὼν ὥσπερ νόμισμα ἀρχαῖον ἐκ θησαυροῦ ποθεν ἀδεσπότου
67 διὰ φιλορρηματίαν, πολλὰ δὲ καὶ βαρβάρων ὀνόματα, 1
φειδόμενος οὐδενὸς ὅ τι μόνον ἡδονὴν ἢ σφοδρότητα ἔδοξεν αὐτῶι ῥῆμα ἔχειν· πρὸς δὲ τούτοις μεταφέρων οὐ τὰ γειτνιῶντα μόνον οὐδὲ ἀπὸ τῶν ἐγγύθεν, ἀλλὰ τὰ πλεῖστον ἀπέχοντα, ὅπως κηλήσῃ τὸν ἀκροατὴν μετ' ἐκπλήξεως καταγοητεύσας, καὶ οὐδὲ ταῦτα κατὰ χώραν ἐῶν, ἀλλὰ τὰ 2
μὲν μηκύνων, τὰ δὲ συναιρῶν τὰ δὲ ἄλλως παρατρέπων.
68 Τελευτῶν δὲ αὐτὸν ἀπέφαινεν οὐ μόνον μέτρων ποιητήν, ἀλλὰ καὶ ῥημάτων, παρ' αὑτοῦ φθεγγόμενος, τὰ μὲν ἁπλῶς τιθέμενος ὀνόματα τοῖς πράγμασι, τὰ δ' ἐπὶ τοῖς κυρίοις ἐπονομάζων, οἷον σφραγῖδα σφραγῖδι ἐπιβάλλων ἐναργῆ 2
καὶ μᾶλλον εὔδηλον, οὐδενὸς φθόγγου ἀπεχόμενος ἀλλὰ ἔμβραχυ ποταμῶν τε μιμούμενος φωνὰς καὶ ὕλης καὶ ἀνέμων καὶ πυρὸς καὶ θαλάττης, ἔτι δὲ χαλκοῦ καὶ λίθου καὶ ξυμπάντων ἁπλῶς ζώιων καὶ ὀργάνων, τοῦτο μὲν θηρίων, τοῦτο δὲ ὀρνίθων, τοῦτο δὲ αὐλῶν τε καὶ συρίγγων· καναχάς 3
τε καὶ βόμβους καὶ κτύπον καὶ δοῦπον καὶ ἄραβον πρῶτος

---

11 ⟨καὶ Αἰολέων⟩ post Ἀθηναίων add. Reiske   15 φιλορρηματίαν Geel : φιλοχρηματίαν   17 ῥῆμα secl. von Arnim   26 καὶ μᾶλλον : μᾶλλον καὶ von Arnim

ἐξευρὼν καὶ ὀνομάσας ποταμούς τε μορμύροντας καὶ βέλη
κλάζοντα καὶ βοῶντα κύματα καὶ χαλεπαίνοντας ἀνέμους
καὶ ἄλλα τοιαῦτα δεινὰ καὶ ἄτοπα ⟨καὶ⟩ τῶι ὄντι θαύματα,
69 πολλὴν ἐμβάλλοντα τῆι γνώμηι ταραχὴν καὶ θόρυβον· ὥστε
οὐκ ἦν αὐτῶι ἀπορία φοβερῶν ὀνομάτων καὶ ἡδέων, ἔτι δὲ 5
λείων καὶ τραχέων καὶ μυρίας ἄλλας ἐχόντων διαφορὰς ἔν τε
τοῖς ἤχοις καὶ τοῖς διανοήμασιν. ὑφ' ἧς ἐποποιΐας δυνατὸς
ἦν ὁποῖον ἐβούλετο ἐμποιῆσαι τῆι ψυχῆι πάθος.

Τὸ δὲ ἡμέτερον αὖ γένος, τὸ χειρωνακτικὸν καὶ
δημιουργικόν, οὐδαμῆι ἐφικνεῖται τῆς τοιαύτης ἐλευθερίας, 10
ἀλλὰ πρῶτον μὲν ὕλης προσδεόμεθα, ἀσφαλοῦς μὲν ὥστε
διαμεῖναι, οὐ πολὺν δὲ ἐχούσης κάματον, πορισθῆναί τε οὐ
70 ῥαιδίας, ἔτι δὲ οὐκ ὀλίγων συνεργῶν. πρὸς δὲ αὖ τούτοις
ἓν σχῆμα ἑκάστης εἰκόνος ἀνάγκη ἐργάσασθαι καὶ τοῦτο
ἀκίνητον καὶ μένον, ὥστε τὴν πᾶσαν ἐν αὐτῶι τοῦ θεοῦ 15
ξυλλαβεῖν φύσιν καὶ δύναμιν. τοῖς δὲ ποιηταῖς πολλάς τινας
μορφὰς καὶ παντοδαπὰ εἴδη περιλαβεῖν τῆι ποιήσει ῥάιδιον,
κινήσεις τε καὶ ἡσυχίας προστιθέντας αὐτοῖς, ὅπως ἂν
ἑκάστοτε πρέπειν ἡγῶνται καὶ ἔργα καὶ λόγους, καὶ προσέτι
οἶμαι, τὸ τῆς δαπάνης καὶ τὸ τοῦ χρόνου. μιᾶι γὰρ ἐπιπνοίαι 20
καὶ ὁρμῆι τῆς ψυχῆς ἐνεχθεὶς ὁ ποιητὴς πολύ τι πλῆθος ἐπῶν
ἤρυσεν, ὥσπερ ἐκ πηγῆς ὕδατος ὑπερβλύσαντος, πρὶν
ἐπιλιπεῖν αὐτὸν καὶ διαρρυῆναι τὸ φάντασμα καὶ τὴν ἐπίνοιαν
ἣν ἔλαβε. τὸ δέ γε ἡμέτερον τῆς τέχνης ἐπίπονον καὶ βραδύ,
μόλις καὶ ⟨κατ'⟩ ὀλίγον προβαῖνον, ἅτε, οἶμαι, πετρώδει καὶ 25
στερεᾶι κάμνον ὕληι.
71 Τὸ δὲ πάντων χαλεπώτατον, ἀνάγκη παραμένειν τῶι
δημιουργῶι τὴν εἰκόνα ἐν τῆι ψυχῆι τὴν αὐτὴν ἀεί, μέχρις ἂν
ἐκτελέσηι τὸ ἔργον, πολλάκις καὶ πολλοῖς ἔτεσι. καὶ δὴ τὸ

---

3 ⟨καὶ⟩ addidi   5 φοβερῶν Reiske : φανερῶν   7 ἐποποιΐας : num
ὀνοματοποιΐας?   14 ἐργάσασθαι Wilamowitz : εἰργάσθαι   17 παντοδαπὰ
εἴδη Casaubon : παντοδαπᾶς ἐπειδὴ : παντοδαπὰ προσώπων εἴδη Wenkebach
19 προσέστιν P   20 δαπάνης Geel : ἀπάτης : χαλεπότητος Capps, alii alia
20 ἐπιπνοίαι Selden : ἐπινοίαι   21–2 ἐπῶν ἤρυσεν Selden : ἐπήρυσεν : ἐπῶν
ἐπήρυσεν Reiske   25 ⟨κατ'⟩ add. Reiske

λεγόμενον, ὡς ἔστιν ἀκοῆς πιστότερα ὄμματα, ἀληθὲς ἴσως·
πολύ γε μὴν δυσπειστότερα καὶ πλείονος δεόμενα ἐναργείας.
ἡ μὲν γὰρ ὄψις αὐτοῖς τοῖς ὁρωμένοις συμβάλλει, τὴν δὲ ἀκοὴν
οὐκ ἀδύνατον ἀναπτερῶσαι καὶ παραλογίσασθαι, ῥήματα
72 εἰσπέμποντα γεγοητευμένα μέτροις καὶ ἤχοις. καὶ μὴν τά γε 5
ἡμέτερα τῆς τέχνης ἀναγκαῖα μέτρα πλήθους τε πέρι καὶ
μεγέθους, τοῖς δὲ ποιηταῖς ἔξεστι καὶ ταῦτα ἐφ' ὁποσονοῦν
αὐξῆσαι. τοιγαροῦν Ὁμήρωι μὲν ῥάιδιον ἐγένετο εἰπεῖν τὸ
μέγεθος τῆς Ἔριδος ὅτι

   οὐρανῶι ἐστήριξε κάρη καὶ ἐπὶ χθονὶ βαίνει,   1

ἐμοὶ δὲ ἀγαπητὸν δήπουθεν πληρῶσαι τὸν ὑπὸ Ἠλείων ἢ
Ἀθηναίων ἀποδειχθέντα τόπον.
73 Σὺ μὲν οὖν φήσεις, ὦ σοφώτατε τῶν ποιητῶν Ὅμηρε,
πολὺ τῆι τε δυνάμει τῆς ποιήσεως καὶ τῶι χρόνωι προέχων·
σχεδὸν γὰρ πρῶτος ἐπέδειξας τοῖς Ἕλλησι τῶν τε ἄλλων 1
ἁπάντων θεῶν καὶ δὴ τοῦ μεγίστου θεῶν πολλὰς καὶ
καλὰς εἰκόνας, τὰς μέν τινας ἡμέρους, τὰς δὲ φοβερὰς καὶ
74 δεινάς. ὁ δὲ ἡμέτερος εἰρηνικὸς καὶ πανταχοῦ πρᾶιος, οἷος
ἀστασιάστου καὶ ὁμονοούσης τῆς Ἑλλάδος ἐπίσκοπος· ὃν
ἐγὼ μετὰ τῆς ἐμαυτοῦ τέχνης καὶ τῆς Ἠλείων πόλεως σοφῆς 2
καὶ ἀγαθῆς βουλευσάμενος ἱδρυσάμην, ἥμερον καὶ σεμνὸν ἐν
ἀλύπωι σχήματι, τὸν βίου καὶ ζωῆς καὶ ξυμπάντων δοτῆρα
τῶν ἀγαθῶν, κοινὸν ἀνθρώπων καὶ πατέρα καὶ σωτῆρα καὶ
φύλακα, ὡς δυνατὸν ἦν θνητῶι διανοηθέντι μιμήσασθαι τὴν
θείαν καὶ ἀμήχανον φύσιν.   2
75 Σκόπει δέ, εἰ μὴ πάσαις ταῖς ἐπωνυμίαις ταῖς τοῦ θεοῦ
πρεπούσαν εὑρήσεις τὴν εἰκόνα· Ζεὺς γὰρ μόνος θεῶν
πατὴρ καὶ βασιλεὺς ἐπονομάζεται, Πολιεύς τε καὶ Φίλιος
καὶ Ἑταιρεῖος, πρὸς δὲ τούτοις Ἱκέσιός τε καὶ Ξένιος καὶ

---

2 δυσπειστότερα Jacobs : δυσπιστ-   ἐναργείας Reiske : ἐνεργείας   4 ῥήματα :
μὴ ῥήματα M : μιμήματα Wilamowitz : ληρήματα Geel   15 γὰρ om.
M   ἐπιδείξας Rouse, ἐπιδεῖξαι Geel (uterque omisso γὰρ)   22 τὸν Emperius :
τοῦ   28–9 Πολιεύς τε ⟨καὶ Ὁμόγνιος⟩.... Ἱκέσιός τε ⟨καὶ Φύξιος⟩ καὶ Ξένιος
⟨καὶ Κτήσιος⟩ Reiske, cf. Or. 1.39 sqq.

Ἐπικάρπιος καὶ μυρίας ἄλλας ἐπικλήσεις ἔχων πάσας ἀγαθάς,
βασιλεὺς μὲν κατὰ τὴν ἀρχὴν καὶ δύναμιν ὠνομασμένος,
πατὴρ δέ, οἶμαι, διά τε κηδεμονίαν καὶ τὸ πρᾶιον, Πολιεὺς
δὲ κατὰ τὸν νόμον καὶ τὸ κοινὸν ὄφελος, Ὁμόγνιος δὲ διὰ
76 τὴν τοῦ γένους κοινωνίαν θεοῖς καὶ ἀνθρώποις, Φίλιος δὲ καὶ 5
Ἑταιρεῖος, ὅτι πάντας ἀνθρώπους ξυνάγει καὶ βούλεται
φίλους εἶναι ἀλλήλοις, ἐχθρὸν δὲ ἢ πολέμιον οὐδένα οὐδενός,
Ἱκέσιος δέ, ὡς ἂν ἐπήκοός τε καὶ ἵλεως τοῖς δεομένοις, Φύξιος
δὲ διὰ τὴν τῶν κακῶν ἀπόφυξιν, Ξένιος δέ, ὅτι δεῖ μηδὲ τῶν
ξένων ἀμελεῖν μηδὲ ἀλλότριον ἡγεῖσθαι ἀνθρώπων μηδένα, 10
Κτήσιος δὲ καὶ Ἐπικάρπιος, ἅτε τῶν καρπῶν αἴτιος καὶ
δοτὴρ πλούτου καὶ δυνάμεως.
77 Ὅτου δὲ ἦν ἐπιδεῖξαι ταῦτα μὴ φθεγγόμενον, ἆρα οὐχ
ἱκανῶς ἔχει κατὰ τὴν τέχνην; τὴν μὲν γὰρ ἀρχὴν καὶ τὸν
βασιλέα βούλεται δηλοῦν τὸ ἰσχυρὸν τοῦ εἴδους καὶ τὸ 15
μεγαλοπρεπές· τὸν δὲ πατέρα καὶ τὴν κηδεμονίαν τὸ πρᾶιον
καὶ προσφιλές· τὸν δὲ Πολιέα καὶ Νόμιμον ἥ τε σεμνότης
καὶ τὸ αὐστηρόν· τὴν δὲ ἀνθρώπων καὶ θεῶν ξυγγένειαν
αὐτό που τὸ τῆς μορφῆς ὅμοιον ἐν εἴδει συμβόλου· τὸν δὲ
Φίλιον καὶ Ἱκέσιον καὶ Ξένιον καὶ Φύξιον καὶ πάντα τὰ 20
τοιαῦτα ἁπλῶς ⟨ἡ⟩ φιλανθρωπία καὶ τὸ πρᾶιον καὶ τὸ
χρηστὸν ἐμφαινόμενον. προσομοιοῖ δὲ τὸν Κτήσιον καὶ τὸν
Ἐπικάρπιον ἥ τε ἁπλότης καὶ ἡ μεγαλοφροσύνη δηλουμένη
διὰ τῆς μορφῆς· ἀτεχνῶς γὰρ διδόντι καὶ χαριζομένωι
μάλιστα προσέοικε τἀγαθά. 25
78 Ταῦτα μὲν οὖν ὡς οἷόν τε ἦν ἐμιμησάμην, ἅτε οὐκ ἔχων
ὀνομάσαι· συνεχῶς δὲ ἀστράπτοντα ἐπὶ πολέμωι καὶ φθορᾶι
πλήθους ἢ ὄμβρων ὑπερβολὴν ⟨τεύχοντα⟩ ἢ χαλάζης ἢ
χιόνος, ἢ τανύοντα κυανῆν Ἶριν, τοῦ πολέμου ξύμβολον, ἢ
ἀστέρα πέμποντα ξυνεχεῖς σπινθῆρας ἀποβάλλοντα, δεινὸν 30

---

13 Ὅτου Reiske : ὅσου   19 ἐν εἴδει συμβόλου suspecta et fortasse delenda :
αἰνίττεται διὰ συμβόλου von Arnim   ὃν ἤδη σύμβολον Capps   21 ⟨ἡ⟩ add.
Jacobs   καὶ τὸ πρᾶιον secl. von Arnim   22 ἐμφαινόμενα προσομοιοῖ· τὸν δὲ
von Arnim   28 ὑπερβολῆι P   ⟨τεύχοντα⟩ addidi : ⟨ἐφιέντα⟩ Reiske :
⟨καταχέοντα⟩ Schwartz

τέρας ναύταις ἢ στρατιώταις ἢ ἐπιπέμποντα ἔριν ἀργαλέαν
Ἕλλησι καὶ βαρβάροις, ⟨ὥστε⟩ ἔρωτα ἐμβάλλειν πολέμου
καὶ μάχης ἄπαυστον κάμνουσιν ἀνθρώποις καὶ ἀπειρηκόσιν,
οὐκ ἦν διὰ τῆς τέχνης μιμεῖσθαι, οὐδέ γε ἱστάντα ἐπὶ
πλάστιγγος ἀνθρώπων ἡμιθέων κῆρας ἢ στρατοπέδων
ὅλων, αὐτομάτωι ῥοπῆι κρινομένας· οὐ μὴν οὐδὲ παρὸν
79 ἠθέλησά γ᾽ ἄν ποτε. βροντῆς γὰρ εἴδωλον ἄφθογγον ἢ
ἀστραπῆς ἢ κεραυνοῦ εἴκασμα ἀλαμπὲς ἐκ τῶν τῆιδέ γε
[ἐπιγείων] μεταλλευμάτων ποῖον ἄν τι καὶ γένοιτο; ἔτι δὲ γῆν
σειομένην καὶ κινούμενον Ὄλυμπον ὑπὸ νεύματι βραχεῖ τῶν
ὀφρύων ἤ τινα νέφους περὶ τῆι κεφαλῆι στέφανον Ὁμήρωι μὲν
εἰπεῖν εὐμαρὲς καὶ πολλὴ πρὸς τὰ τοιαῦτα ἅπαντα ἐλευθερία,
τῆι δέ γε ἡμετέραι τέχνηι παντελῶς ἄπορον, ἐγγύθεν ἐχούσηι
καὶ σαφῆ τὸν ἔλεγχον τῆς ὄψεως.

80 Εἰ δ᾽ αὖ τὸ τῆς ὕλης ἀσημότερον ἡγεῖταί τις ἢ κατὰ τὴν
ἀξίαν τοῦ θεοῦ, τοῦτο μὲν ἀληθές τε καὶ ὀρθόν· ἀλλ᾽ οὔτε
τοὺς δόντας οὔτε τὸν ἑλόμενον καὶ δοκιμάσαντα ἐν δίκηι
μέμφοιτ᾽ ἄν. οὐ γὰρ ἦν ἑτέρα φύσις ἀμείνων οὐδὲ λαμπροτέρα
πρὸς ὄψιν, ἣν δυνατὸν εἰς χεῖρας ἀνθρώπων ἀφικέσθαι καὶ
81 μεταλαβεῖν δημιουργίας. ἀέρα γὰρ καὶ πῦρ ἐργάσασθαι ἢ
τὴν ἄφθονον πηγὴν ὕδατος [ἔν τισι θνητοῖς ὀργάνοις] ὅσον
τε ἐν ἅπασι τούτοις στερεὸν ἕρμα – λέγω δὲ οὐ χρυσοῦ καὶ
λίθου, ταῦτα μὲν γὰρ σμικρὰ καὶ φαῦλα, ἀλλὰ τὴν πᾶσαν
ἰσχυρὰν καὶ βαρεῖαν οὐσίαν – ἰδίαι τε ἕκαστον διακρίνοντα
καὶ συμπλέκοντα εἰς [ταὐτὸ] γένεσιν ζώιων καὶ φυτῶν, οὐδὲ
θεοῖς πᾶσι δυνατὸν ἢ μόνωι τούτωι σχεδὸν ὂν πάνυ καλῶς
ποιητὴς προσεῖπεν ἕτερος,

Δωδωναῖε μεγασθενὲς ἀριστοτέχνα πάτερ.

1 στρατιώταις ἢ Geel : στρατιώτηι   2 ⟨ὥστε⟩ ... ἐμβάλλειν von Arnim :
ἐμβάλλει   4 οὐκ ... μιμεῖσθαι : haec post κρινομένας (6) habent codd., huc
transtulit von Arnim   7–8 ἢ ἀστραπῆς sec. von Arnim   9 [ἐπιγείων]
seclusi : ὑπογείων Capps   16 οὔτε τὸν Dindorf : οὐδὲ τὸν   20 γὰρ
Reiske : γε   21 [ἔν ... ὀργάνοις] secl. Emperius   22 ἕρμα Morel :
ἔρυμα   24 ἰδέαν γε ἑκάστην Capps   25 συμπλέκοντα von Arnim :
ἐμπλέκοντα : συστῆσαι Capps (εἰς ταὐτὸ ⟨ἕκαστον συστῆσαι⟩ γένος)   [ταὐτὸ]
secl. von Arnim   γένεσιν von Arnim : γένος   26 ⟨ἀλλ᾽⟩ ἢ Capps

82 οὗτος γὰρ δὴ πρῶτος καὶ τελειότατος δημιουργός, χορηγὸν
λαβὼν τῆς αὑτοῦ τέχνης οὐ τὴν Ἠλείων πόλιν ἀλλὰ τὴν
πᾶσαν τοῦ παντὸς ὕλην. Φειδίαν δὲ ἢ Πολύκλειτον οὐκ
ἂν εἰκότως ἀπαιτοῖτε πλέον οὐδέν, ἀλλὰ καὶ ταῦτα μείζω
83 καὶ σεμνότερα τῆς ἡμετέρας χειρωναξίας. οὐδὲ γὰρ τὸν 5
Ἥφαιστον Ὅμηρος ἐν ἄλλοις πεποίηκεν ἐπιδεικνύμενον τὴν
ἐμπειρίαν, ἀλλὰ τεχνίτην μὲν θεὸν εὐπόρησεν ἐπὶ τὸ τῆς
ἀσπίδος ἔργον, ὕλην δὲ ἑτέραν οὐκ ἐφίκετο εὑρεῖν. φησὶ γὰρ
οὕτω·

χαλκὸν δ᾽ ἐν πυρὶ βάλλεν ἀτειρέα κασσίτερόν τε 10
καὶ χρυσὸν τιμῆντα καὶ ἄργυρον.

ἀνθρώπων μὲν οὖν ἔγωγε οὐδενὶ παραχωρήσαιμ᾽ ⟨ἂν⟩
κρείττονα ἐμοῦ ποτε γενέσθαι περὶ τὴν τέχνην, αὑτῶι δὲ τῶι
Διί, δημιουργοῦντι τὸν ἅπαντα κόσμον, οὐ χρὴ ξυμβάλλειν
οὐδένα θνητόν. 15
84 Ταῦτ᾽ οὖν εἰπόντα καὶ ἀπολογησάμενον τὸν Φειδίαν
εἰκότως ἐμοὶ δοκοῦσιν οἱ Ἕλληνες στεφανῶσαι ἄν.

Ἴσως δὲ τοὺς πολλοὺς λέληθεν ὁ λόγος ὑπὲρ ὧν γέγονε,
καὶ μάλα, ἐμοὶ δοκεῖν, φιλοσόφοις τε ἁρμόττων καὶ πλήθει
ἀκοῦσαι, περί τε ἀγαλμάτων ἱδρύσεως, ὅπως δεῖ ἱδρῦσθαι, 20
καὶ περὶ ποιητῶν, ὅπως ἄμεινον ἢ χεῖρον διανοοῦνται περὶ
τῶν θείων, ἔτι δὲ περὶ τῆς πρώτης ἐπινοίας θεοῦ, ποία τις
καὶ τίνα τρόπον ἐν τοῖς ἀνθρώποις ἐγένετο. πολλὰ δέ, οἶμαι,
καὶ περὶ τῆς δυνάμεως ἐρρήθη τοῦ Διὸς κατὰ τὰς ἐπωνυμίας.
εἰ δὲ μετ᾽ εὐφημίας τοῦ τε ἀγάλματος καὶ τῶν ἱδρυσαμένων, 25
85 πολὺ ἄμεινον. τῶι γὰρ ὄντι τοιοῦτος ἡμῖν προσορᾶν ἔοικε,
πάνυ εὔνους καὶ κηδόμενος, ὥστ᾽ ἔμοιγε μικροῦ φθέγγεσθαι
δοκεῖ.

Τάδε μὲν οὕτως, †ʼΗλεῖοι δὲ καὶ† ἡ σύμπασα Ἑλλάς,
καλῶς καὶ προσηκόντως ἐπιτελεῖ, θυσίας τε θύουσα ἐκ τῶν 30
παρόντων μεγαλοπρεπεῖς καὶ δὴ καὶ τὸν εὐκλεέστατον

12 ⟨ἂν⟩ add. Pflugk   18–26 ἴσως ... ἄμεινον secl. von Arnim   22 τῆς
Reiske : τε   24 κατὰ τὰς : καὶ τῆς Capps   29 sqq. [ʼΗλεῖοι δὲ καὶ] ὦ σύμπασα
Ἑλλάς ... ἐπιτελεῖς (30) ... διαφυλάττεις (88, 2) ... αὐτήν σ᾽ (88, 4) von Arnim

ἀγῶνα τιθεῖσα ⟨ὡς⟩ ἀπ' ἀρχῆς εὐεξίας καὶ ῥώμης καὶ τάχους,
ὅσα τε ἑορτῶν καὶ μυστηρίων ἔθη λαβοῦσα διαφυλάττει.
ἀλλὰ ἐκεῖνο φροντίζων σκοπῶ, ὅτι

αὐτήν γ' οὐκ ἀγαθὴ κομιδὴ ἔχει, ἀλλ' ἅμα γῆρας
λυγρὸν ἔχεις αὐχμεῖς τε κακῶς καὶ ἀεικέα ἔσσαι.

5

1 ⟨ὡς⟩ add. Wilamowitz   4 γ' : σ' Homerus (ω 249)

ΒΟΡΥΣΘΕΝΙΤΙΚΟΣ ΟΝ ΑΝΕΓΝΩ ΕΝ ΤΗΙ ΠΑΤΡΙΔΙ

1 Ἐτύγχανον μὲν ἐπιδημῶν ἐν Βορυσθένει τὸ θέρος, ὡς
τότε εἰσέπλευσα [μετὰ τὴν φυγήν], βουλόμενος ἐλθεῖν,
ἐὰν δύνωμαι, διὰ Σκυθῶν εἰς Γέτας, ὅπως θεάσωμαι τἀκεῖ
πράγματα ὁποῖά ἐστι. καὶ δὴ καὶ περιεπάτουν περὶ
πλήθουσαν ἀγορὰν παρὰ τὸν Ὕπανιν. ἡ γὰρ πόλις τὸ μὲν 5
ὄνομα εἴληφεν ἀπὸ τοῦ Βορυσθένους διὰ τὸ κάλλος καὶ τὸ
μέγεθος τοῦ ποταμοῦ, κεῖται δὲ πρὸς τῶι Ὑπάνιδι, ἥ τε
νῦν καὶ ἡ πρότερον οὕτως ὠικεῖτο, οὐ πολὺ ἄνωθεν τῆς
2 Ἱππολάου καλουμένης ἄκρας ἐν τῶι κατ' ἀντικρύ. τοῦτο δέ
ἐστι τῆς χώρας ὀξὺ καὶ στερεὸν ὥσπερ ἔμβολον, περὶ ὃ 10
συμπίπτουσιν οἱ ποταμοί. τὸ δὲ ἐντεῦθεν ἤδη λιμνάζουσι
μέχρι θαλάττης ἐπὶ σταδίους σχεδόν τι διακοσίους· καὶ τὸ
εὖρος οὐχ ἧττον ταύτηι τῶν ποταμῶν. ἔστι δὲ αὐτοῦ τὸ μὲν
πλέον τέναγος καὶ γαλήνη ταῖς εὐδίαις ὥσπερ ἐν λίμνηι
γίγνεται σταθερά. ἐν δὲ τοῖς δεξιοῖς φαίνεται ποταμός, καὶ 15
τεκμαίρονται οἱ εἰσπλέοντες ἀπὸ τοῦ ῥεύματος τὸ βάθος.
ὅθενπερ καὶ ἐξίησι, διὰ τὴν ἰσχὺν τοῦ ῥοῦ· εἰ δὲ μή, ῥαιδίως
3 ἂν ἐφράττετο τοῦ νότου πολλοῦ κατὰ στόμα εἰσπνέοντος. τὸ
δὲ λοιπὸν ἠιών ἐστιν ὑλώδης καὶ δασεῖα καλάμωι καὶ δένδροις.
φαίνεται δὲ τῶν δένδρων πολλὰ καὶ ἐν μέσηι τῆι λίμνηι, 20
ὡς ἱστοῖς προσεοικέναι, καὶ ἤδη τινὲς τῶν ἀπειροτέρων
διήμαρτον, ὡς ἐπὶ πλοῖα ἐπέχοντες. ταύτηι δὲ καὶ τῶν ἁλῶν
ἐστι τὸ πλῆθος, ὅθεν οἱ πλείους τῶν βαρβάρων λαμβάνουσιν
ὠνούμενοι τοὺς ἅλας καὶ τῶν Ἑλλήνων καὶ Σκυθῶν οἱ
Χερρόνησον οἰκοῦντες τὴν Ταυρικήν. ἐκδιδόασι δὲ οἱ ποταμοὶ 25
εἰς θάλασσαν παρὰ φρούριον Ἀλέκτορος, ὃ λέγεται τῆς
γυναικὸς εἶναι τοῦ Σαυροματῶν βασιλέως.
4 Ἡ δὲ πόλις ἡ τῶν Βορυσθενιτῶν τὸ μέγεθός ἐστιν οὐ
πρὸς τὴν παλαιὰν δόξαν διὰ τὰς συνεχεῖς ἁλώσεις καὶ

1–2 ὡς τότε : ὁπότε Geel   2 [μετὰ τὴν φυγήν] secl. Emperius   15 σταθερᾶι
Reiske   18 ἂν ἐφράττετο von Arnim : ἀνεφράττετο : ἂν ἐνεφράττετο Reiske
19 ὑλώδης : ἑλώδης Emperius

τοὺς πολέμους. ἅτε γὰρ ἐν μέσοις οἰκοῦσα τοῖς βαρβάροις
τοσοῦτον ἤδη χρόνον, καὶ τούτοις σχεδόν τι τοῖς
πολεμικωτάτοις, ἀεὶ μὲν πολεμεῖται, πολλάκις δὲ καὶ ἑάλωκεν·
⟨ἑάλω δὲ⟩ τὴν τελευταίαν καὶ μεγίστην ἅλωσιν οὐ πρὸ
πλειόνων ἢ πεντήκοντα καὶ ἑκατὸν ἐτῶν. εἶλον δὲ καὶ ταύτην 5
Γέται καὶ τὰς ἄλλας τὰς ἐν τοῖς ἀριστεροῖς τοῦ Πόντου
5 πόλεις μέχρι Ἀπολλωνίας. ὅθεν δὴ καὶ σφόδρα ταπεινὰ τὰ
πράγματα κατέστη τῶν ταύτηι Ἑλλήνων, τῶν μὲν οὐκέτι
συνοικισθεισῶν πόλεων, τῶν δὲ φαύλως, καὶ τῶν πλείστων
βαρβάρων εἰς αὐτὰς συρρυέντων. πολλαὶ γὰρ δή τινες ἁλώσεις 1
κατὰ πολλὰ μέρη γεγόνασι τῆς Ἑλλάδος, ἅτε ἐν πολλοῖς
τόποις διεσπαρμένης. ἁλόντες δὲ τότε οἱ Βορυσθενῖται πάλιν
συνώικησαν, ἐθελόντων ἐμοὶ δοκεῖν τῶν Σκυθῶν διὰ τὸ δεῖσθαι
τῆς ἐμπορίας καὶ τοῦ κατάπλου τῶν Ἑλλήνων. ἐπαύσαντο
γὰρ εἰσπλέοντες ἀναστάτου τῆς πόλεως γενομένης, ἅτε 1
οὐκ ἔχοντες ὁμοφώνους τοὺς ὑποδεχομένους οὐδὲ αὐτῶν
Σκυθῶν ἀξιούντων οὐδὲ ἐπισταμένων ἐμπόριον αὐτῶν
κατασκευάσασθαι τὸν Ἑλληνικὸν τρόπον.
6 Σημεῖον δὲ τῆς ἀναστάσεως ἥ τε φαυλότης τῶν
οἰκοδομημάτων καὶ τὸ συνεστάλθαι τὴν πόλιν ἐς βραχύ. 2
μέρει γὰρ τινι προσωικοδόμηται τοῦ παλαιοῦ περιβόλου,
καθ' ὃ πύργοι τινὲς οὐ πολλοὶ διαμένουσιν οὐ πρὸς τὸ μέγεθος
οὐδὲ πρὸς τὴν ἰσχὺν τῆς πόλεως. τὸ δὲ μεταξὺ συμπέφρακται
κατ' ἐκεῖνο ταῖς οἰκίαις οὐκ ἐχούσαις ὁποῖα διαλείπει. τειχίον
δὲ παραβέβληται πάνυ ταπεινὸν καὶ ἀσθενές. τῶν δὲ πύργων 2
εἰσί τινες πολὺ ἀφεστῶτες τοῦ νῦν οἰκουμένου, ὥστε μηδ'
εἰκάσαι ὅτι μιᾶς ἦσαν πόλεως. ταῦτά τε δὴ οὖν σημεῖα ἐναργῆ
τῆς ἁλώσεως καὶ τὸ μηδὲν τῶν ἀγαλμάτων διαμένειν ὑγιὲς
τῶν ἐν τοῖς ἱεροῖς, ἀλλὰ ξύμπαντα λελωβημένα εἶναι, ὥσπερ
τὰ ἐπὶ τῶν μνημάτων. 3
7 Ὅπερ οὖν ἔφην, ἔτυχον περιπατῶν πρὸ τῆς πόλεως, καί
τινες ἐξῄεσαν ἔνδοθεν τῶν Βορυσθενιτῶν πρὸς ἐμέ, ὥσπερ

---

4 ⟨ἑάλω δὲ⟩ suppleui   9 καὶ τῶν suspectum   24 συνεχούσαις ὅπου τι
διαλείπει Casaubon, fortasse recte   25 περιβέβληται T (= Marcianus 421)

εἰώθεσαν· ἔπειτα Καλλίστρατος ἐφ᾽ ἵππου τὸ μὲν πρῶτον
παρίππευσεν ἡμᾶς ἔξωθεν προσελαύνων, παρελθὼν δὲ ὀλίγον
κατέβη, καὶ τὸν ἵππον τῶι ἀκολούθωι παραδοὺς αὐτὸς
πάνυ κοσμίως προσῆλθεν ὑπὸ τὸ ἱμάτιον τὴν χεῖρα
ὑποστείλας. παρέζωστο δὲ μάχαιραν μεγάλην τῶν ἱππικῶν 5
καὶ ἀναξυρίδας εἶχε καὶ τὴν ἄλλην στολὴν Σκυθικήν, ἄνωθεν
δὲ τῶν ὤμων ἱμάτιον μικρὸν μέλαν, λεπτόν, ὥσπερ εἰώθασιν
οἱ Βορυσθενῖται. χρῶνται δὲ καὶ τῆι ἄλληι ἐσθῆτι μελαίνηι ὡς
τὸ πολὺ ἀπὸ γένους τινὸς Σκυθῶν τῶν Μελαγχλαίνων, ὡς
ἐμοὶ δοκοῦσι, κατὰ τοῦτο ὀνομασθέντων ὑπὸ τῶν Ἑλλήνων. 10
8   Ἦν δὲ ὡς ὀκτωκαίδεκα ἐτῶν ὁ Καλλίστρατος, πάνυ καλὸς
καὶ μέγας, πολὺ ἔχων Ἰωνικὸν τοῦ εἴδους. ἐλέγετο δὲ καὶ τὰ
πρὸς τὸν πόλεμον ἀνδρεῖος εἶναι, καὶ πολλοὺς Σαυροματῶν
τοὺς μὲν ἀνηιρηκέναι, τοὺς δὲ αἰχμαλώτους εἰληφέναι.
ἐσπουδάκει δὲ καὶ περὶ λόγους καὶ φιλοσοφίαν, ὥστε καὶ 15
ἐκπλεῦσαι σὺν ἐμοὶ ἐπεθύμει. διὰ πάντα δὴ ταῦτα εὐδοκίμει
παρὰ τοῖς πολίταις, οὐχ ἥκιστα δὲ ἀπὸ τοῦ κάλλους, καὶ εἶχε
πολλοὺς ἐραστάς. πάνυ γὰρ δὴ τοῦτο ἐμμεμένηκεν αὐτοῖς
ἀπὸ τῆς μητροπόλεως, τὸ περὶ τοὺς ἔρωτας τοὺς τῶν
ἀρρένων· ὥστε κινδυνεύουσιν ἀναπείθειν καὶ τῶν βαρβάρων 20
ἐνίους οὐκ ἐπ᾽ ἀγαθῶι σχεδόν, ἀλλ᾽ ὡς ἂν ἐκεῖνοι τὸ τοιοῦτον
ἀποδέξαιντο, βαρβαρικῶς καὶ οὐκ ἄνευ ὕβρεως.
9   Εἰδὼς οὖν αὐτὸν φιλόμηρον ὄντα περὶ τούτου εὐθὺς
ἐπυνθανόμην. σχεδὸν δὲ καὶ πάντες οἱ Βορυσθενῖται περὶ τὸν
ποιητὴν ἐσπουδάκασιν ἴσως διὰ τὸ πολεμικοὶ εἶναι ἔτι νῦν, 25
εἰ μὴ ἄρα καὶ ⟨διὰ⟩ τὴν πρὸς τὸν Ἀχιλλέα εὔνοιαν· τοῦτον
μὲν γὰρ ὑπερφυῶς τιμῶσι, καὶ νεὼν τὸν μὲν ἐν τῆι νήσωι τῆι
Ἀχιλλέως καλουμένηι ἵδρυνται, τὸν δὲ ἐν τῆι πόλει· ὥστε
οὐδὲ ἀκούειν ὑπὲρ οὐδενὸς ἄλλου θέλουσιν ἢ Ὁμήρου. καὶ
τἆλλα οὐκέτι σαφῶς ἑλληνίζοντες διὰ τὸ ἐν μέσοις οἰκεῖν τοῖς 30
βαρβάροις, ὅμως τήν γε Ἰλιάδα ὀλίγου πάντες ἴσασιν ἀπὸ
στόματος.
10   Εἶπον οὖν προσπαίζων πρὸς αὐτόν, Πότερόν σοι δοκεῖ, ὦ

26 ⟨διὰ⟩ add. von Arnim

Καλλίστρατε, ἀμείνων ποιητὴς Ὅμηρος ἢ Φωκυλίδης; καὶ ὃς γελάσας ἔφη, Ἀλλ' οὐδὲ ἐπίσταμαι ἔγωγε τοῦ ἑτέρου ποιητοῦ τὸ ὄνομα, οἶμαι δὲ μηδὲ τούτων μηδένα. οὐδὲ γὰρ ἡγούμεθα ἡμεῖς ἄλλον τινὰ ποιητὴν ἢ Ὅμηρον. τοῦτον δὲ σχεδόν τι οὐδὲ ἄλλος οὐδεὶς ἀγνοεῖ. μόνου γὰρ Ὁμήρου 5 μνημονεύουσιν οἱ ποιηταὶ αὐτῶν ἐν τοῖς ποιήμασιν, καὶ ἄλλως μὲν εἰώθασι λέγειν, ἀεὶ δὲ ὁπόταν μέλλουσι μάχεσθαι παρακελεύωνται τοῖς αὐτῶν [ὥσπερ τὰ Τυρταίου ἐν Λακεδαίμονι ἐλέγετο]. εἰσὶ δὲ πάντες οὗτοι τυφλοὶ καὶ οὐχ ἡγοῦνται δυνατὸν εἶναι ἄλλως τινὰ ποιητὴν γενέσθαι. 1⟨0⟩

11 Τοῦτο μέν, ἔφην, ἀπολελαύκασιν [οἱ ποιηταὶ αὐτῶν] ἀπὸ Ὁμήρου ὥσπερ ἀπὸ ὀφθαλμίας. τὸν δὲ Φωκυλίδην ὑμεῖς μὲν οὐκ ἐπίστασθε, ὡς λέγεις· πάνυ δὲ τῶν ἐνδόξων γέγονε ποιητῶν. ὥσπερ οὖν ἐπειδάν τις τῶν ἐμπόρων καταπλεύσηι πρὸς ὑμᾶς οὐ πρότερον ⟨παρα⟩γεγονώς, οὐκ εὐθὺς 1⟨5⟩ ἠτιμάσατε αὐτόν, ἀλλὰ πρότερον γευσάμενοι τοῦ οἴνου, κἂν ἄλλο τι φορτίον ἄγηι δεῖγμα λαβόντες, ἐὰν μὲν ἀρέσηι ὑμᾶς, ὠνεῖσθε, εἰ δὲ μή, ἐᾶτε· οὕτως, ἔφην, καὶ τῆς τοῦ Φωκυλίδου 12 ποιήσεως ἔξεστί σοι λαβεῖν δεῖγμα ἐν βραχεῖ. καὶ γάρ ἐστιν οὐ τῶν μακράν τινα καὶ συνεχῆ ποίησιν εἰρόντων, 2⟨0⟩ ὥσπερ ὁ ὑμέτερος μίαν ἑξῆς διέξεισι μάχην ἐν πλείοσιν ἢ πεντακισχιλίοις ἔπεσιν, ἀλλὰ κατὰ δύο καὶ τρία ἔπη αὐτῶι καὶ ἀρχὴν ἡ ποίησις καὶ πέρας λαμβάνει. ὥστε καὶ προστίθησι τὸ ὄνομα αὐτοῦ καθ' ἕκαστον διανόημα, ἅτε σπουδαῖον καὶ πολλοῦ ἄξιον ἡγούμενος, οὐχ ὥσπερ Ὅμηρος οὐδαμοῦ τῆς 2⟨5⟩ 13 ποιήσεως ὠνόμασεν αὐτόν. ἢ οὐ δοκεῖ σοι εἰκότως προσθεῖναι Φωκυλίδης τῆι τοιαύτηι γνώμηι καὶ ἀποφάσει,

καὶ τόδε Φωκυλίδου· πόλις ἐν σκοπέλωι κατὰ κόσμον οἰκεῦσα σμικρὴ κρέσσων Νίνου ἀφραινούσης,

5 μόνου Casaubon : μόνοι   6 αὐτῶν scripsi : αὐτῶν   7–8 μέλλουσι ... παρακελεύωνται Emperius : μέλλωσι ... παρακελεύονται   8–9 [ὥσπερ ... ἐλέγετο] secl. Emperius   (παρακ. ... ἐλέγετο secl. Cobet)   11 [οἱ ποιηταὶ αὐτῶν] secl. Jacobs   15 ⟨παρα⟩γεγονώς Emperius : γεγονώς

ἀλλ' οὐ πρὸς ὅλην Ἰλιάδα καὶ Ὀδύσσειαν ταῦτα τὰ ἔπη
ἐστὶ τοῖς μὴ παρέργως ἀκροωμένοις; ἢ μᾶλλον ὑμῖν ἀκούειν
συνέφερε περὶ τῶν τοῦ Ἀχιλλέως πηδήσεών τε καὶ ὀρούσεων
καὶ τῆς φωνῆς, ὅτι μόνον φθεγξάμενος ἔτρεπε τοὺς Τρῶας;
ταῦτα μᾶλλον ὠφελεῖ ὑμᾶς ἐκμανθάνοντας ἢ ἐκεῖνο, ὅτι ἡ   5
σμικρὰ πόλις ἐν τραχεῖ σκοπέλωι κειμένη κρείττων ἐστὶ καὶ
εὐτυχεστέρα κατὰ κόσμον οἰκοῦσα ἢ μεγάλη ἐν λείωι καὶ
πλατεῖ πεδίωι, ἐάνπερ ἀκόσμως καὶ ἀνόμως ὑπὸ ἀνθρώπων
ἀφρόνων οἰκῆται;

14   Καὶ ὃς οὐ μάλα ἡδέως ἀποδεξάμενος, ῏Ω ξένε, εἶπεν, ὅτι ἡμεῖς 10
σε ἀγαπῶμεν καὶ σφόδρα αἰδούμεθα· ὡς ἄλλως γε οὐδεὶς
ἂν ἠνέσχετο Βορυσθενιτῶν εἰς Ὅμηρον καὶ Ἀχιλλέα τοιαῦτα
εἰπόντος. ὁ μὲν γὰρ θεὸς ἡμῶν ἐστιν, ὡς ὁρᾶις, ὁ δὲ καὶ σχεδόν
τι μετὰ τοὺς θεοὺς τιμᾶται. κἀγὼ πραῧναι βουλόμενος αὐτόν,
ἅμα δὲ ἐπί τι χρήσιμον ἀγαγεῖν, Παραιτοῦμαί σε, εἶπον, καθ' 15
Ὅμηρον συγγνώμην ἔχειν μοι,

                              εἴ τι κακὸν νῦν
εἴρηται.

αὖθις γάρ ποτε ἐπαινεσόμεθα Ἀχιλλέα τε καὶ Ὅμηρον ὅσα
15 δοκεῖ ἡμῖν ὀρθῶς λέγειν. τὸ δὲ παρὸν σκεπτέον ἂν εἴη τὸ   20
τοῦ Φωκυλίδου, ὡς ἐμοὶ δοκεῖ σφόδρα καλῶς λέγειν ὑπὲρ
τῆς πόλεως. Σκόπει, ἔφη, ἐπεὶ καὶ τούσδε ὁρᾶις πάντας
ἐπιθυμοῦντας ἀκοῦσαί σου καὶ διὰ τοῦτο συνερρυηκότας
δεῦρο πρὸς τὸν ποταμόν, καίτοι οὐ σφόδρα ἀθορύβως
ἔχοντας. οἶσθα γὰρ δήπου ὅτι χθὲς οἱ Σκύθαι προσελάσαντες 25
μεσημβρίας τοὺς μέν τινας ἀπέκτειναν τῶν σκοπῶν οὐ
προσέχοντας, τοὺς δὲ ἐζωγρήκασιν ἴσως· οὐ γάρ πω
ἐπιστάμεθα διὰ τὸ μακροτέραν αὐτοῖς γενέσθαι τὴν φυγήν,
ἅτε οὐ πρὸς τὴν πόλιν φεύγουσιν.

16   ῏Ην δὲ τῶι ὄντι ταῦτα οὕτως, καὶ αἵ τε πύλαι συγκέκλειντο 30
καὶ τὸ σημεῖον ἦρτο ἐπὶ τοῦ τείχους τὸ πολεμικόν. ἀλλ' ὅμως

10 fortasse ⟨οἶσθ'⟩ ὅτι Innes   11 ἄλλως Casaubon : ἄλλος

οὕτως ἦσαν φιλήκοοι καὶ τῶι τρόπωι Ἕλληνες, ὥστε μικροῦ δεῖν ἅπαντες παρῆσαν ἐν τοῖς ὅπλοις, βουλόμενοι ἀκούειν. κἀγὼ ἀγάμενος αὐτῶν τὴν προθυμίαν, Βούλεσθε, ἔφην, καθιζώμεθα ἰόντες ποι τῆς πόλεως; τυχὸν γὰρ νῦν οὐ πάντες ὁμοίως ἀκούουσιν ἐν τῶι βαδίζειν, ἀλλ' οἱ ὄπισθεν πράγματα 5 ἔχουσι καὶ παρέχουσι τοῖς πρὸ αὐτῶν, σπεύδοντες ἐγγυτέρω 17 προσελθεῖν. ὡς δὲ τοῦτο εἶπον, εὐθὺς ὥρμησαν ἅπαντες εἰς τὸ τοῦ Διὸς ἱερόν, οὗπερ εἰώθασι βουλεύεσθαι. καὶ οἱ μὲν πρεσβύτατοι καὶ οἱ γνωριμώτατοι καὶ οἱ ἐν ταῖς ἀρχαῖς κύκλωι καθίζοντο ἐπὶ βάθρων· τὸ δὲ λοιπὸν πλῆθος 1 ἐφεστήκεσαν. ἦν γὰρ εὐρυχωρία πολλὴ πρὸ τοῦ νεώ. πάνυ οὖν ἄν τις ἥσθη τῆι ὄψει φιλόσοφος ἀνήρ, ὅτι ἅπαντες ἦσαν τὸν ἀρχαῖον τρόπον, ὥς φησιν Ὅμηρος τοὺς Ἕλληνας, κομῶντες καὶ τὰ γένεια ἀφεικότες, εἷς δὲ ἐν αὐτοῖς μόνος ἐξυρημένος, καὶ τοῦτον ἐλοιδόρουν τε καὶ ἐμίσουν ἅπαντες. 1 ἐλέγετο δὲ οὐκ ἄλλως τοῦτο ἐπιτηδεύειν, ἀλλὰ κολακεύων Ῥωμαίους καὶ τὴν πρὸς αὐτοὺς φιλίαν ἐπιδεικνύμενος· ὥστε εἶδεν ἄν τις ἐπ' ἐκείνου τὸ αἰσχρὸν τοῦ πράγματος καὶ οὐδαμῆι πρέπον ἀνδράσιν.

18 Ἐπεὶ δὲ ἡσυχία ἐγένετο, εἶπον ὅτι δοκοῦσί μοι ὀρθῶς 2 ποιεῖν, πόλιν οἰκοῦντες ἀρχαίαν καὶ Ἑλληνίδα, βουλόμενοι ἀκοῦσαι περὶ πόλεως, καὶ πρῶτόν γε, ἔφην, ὅ τι ἐστὶν αὐτὸ τοῦτο ὑπὲρ οὗ ὁ λόγος γνῶναι σαφῶς· οὕτω γὰρ ἂν εἴητε ἅμα ἠισθημένοι καὶ ὁποῖόν τί ἐστιν. οἱ γὰρ πολλοί, ἔφην, ἄνθρωποι τὸ ὄνομα αὐτὸ ἴσασι καὶ φθέγγονται τοῦ 2 19 πράγματος ἑκάστου, τὸ δὲ πρᾶγμα ἀγνοοῦσιν. οἱ δὲ πεπαιδευμένοι τοῦτο φροντίζουσιν, ὅπως καὶ τὴν δύναμιν εἴσονται ἑκάστου οὗ λέγουσιν· οἷον τὸ τοῦ ἀνθρώπου ὄνομα πάντες οὕτω λέγουσιν οἱ ἑλληνίζοντες, ἐὰν δὲ πύθηι τινὸς αὐτῶν ὅ τι ἐστὶ τοῦτό, λέγω δὲ ὁποῖόν τι καὶ καθ' ὃ μηδενὶ τῶν ἄλλων ταὐτόν, οὐκ ἂν ἔχοι εἰπεῖν ἀλλ' ἢ δεῖξαι μόνον αὐτὸν ἢ ἄλλον, ὥσπερ οἱ βάρβαροι. ὁ δὲ ἔμπειρος τῶι πυνθανομένωι τί ἐστιν ἄνθρωπος ἀποκρίνεται ὅτι ζῶιον

23 num ⟨δεῖ⟩ γνῶναι uel γνωστέον?

λογικὸν θνητόν. τὸ γὰρ τοῦτο εἶναι μόνωι ἀνθρώπωι
20 συμβέβηκε καὶ οὐδενὶ ἄλλωι. οὕτως οὖν καὶ τὴν πόλιν φασὶν
εἶναι πλῆθος ἀνθρώπων ἐν ταὐτῶι κατοικούντων ὑπὸ νόμου
διοικούμενον. ἤδη οὖν δῆλον ὅτι τῆς προσηγορίας ταύτης
οὐδεμιᾶι προσήκει τῶν καλουμένων πόλεων τῶν ἀφρόνων καὶ 5
ἀνόμων. οὔκουν οὐδὲ περὶ Νίνου εἴη ἂν ὁ ποιητὴς ὡς περὶ
πόλεως εἰρηκώς, ἀφραινούσης γε αὐτῆς. ὥσπερ γὰρ οὐδὲ
ἄνθρωπος ἐκεῖνός ἐστιν ὧι μὴ πρόσεστι τὸ λογικόν, οὕτως
οὐδὲ πόλις, ἧι μὴ συμβέβηκε νομίμωι εἶναι. νόμιμος δὲ οὐκ ἂν
εἴη ποτὲ ἄφρων καὶ ἄκοσμος οὖσα. 10
21 Ἴσως οὖν ζητῆσαι ἄν τις, εἰ ἐπειδὰν οἱ ἄρχοντες καὶ
προεστῶτες ὦσι φρόνιμοι καὶ σοφοί, τὸ δὲ λοιπὸν πλῆθος
διοικῆται κατὰ τὴν τούτων γνώμην νομίμως καὶ σωφρόνως,
τὴν τοιαύτην χρὴ καλεῖν σώφρονα καὶ νόμιμον καὶ τῶι ὄντι
πόλιν ἀπὸ τῶν διοικούντων· ὥσπερ χορὸν ἴσως φαίημεν ἂν 15
μουσικόν, τοῦ κορυφαίου μουσικοῦ ὄντος, τῶν δὲ ἄλλων
ἐκείνωι συνεπομένων καὶ μηδὲν παρὰ μέλος φθεγγομένων ἢ
22 σμικρὰ καὶ ἀδήλως. ἀγαθὴν μὲν γὰρ ἐξ ἀπάντων ἀγαθῶν
πόλιν οὔτε τις γενομένην πρότερον οἶδε θνητὴν οὔτε ποτὲ
ὡς ἐσομένην ὕστερον ἄξιον διανοηθῆναι, πλὴν εἰ μὴ θεῶν 20
μακάρων κατ' οὐρανόν, οὐδαμῶς ἀκίνητον οὐδὲ ἀργήν, ἀλλὰ
σφοδρὰν οὖσαν καὶ πορευομένην, τῶν μὲν ἡγουμένων τε καὶ
πρώτων θεῶν ⟨τῶν δὲ δευτέρων τε καὶ ἑπομένων⟩ χωρὶς
ἔριδος καὶ ἥττης· οὔτε γὰρ ἐρίζειν θεοὺς οὔτε ἡττᾶσθαι θέμις
οὔτε ὑπ' ἀλλήλων ἅτε φίλων οὔτε ὑπὸ ἄλλων κρειττόνων, 25
ἀλλὰ πράττειν ἀκωλύτως τὰ σφέτερα ἔργα μετὰ πάσης φιλίας
ἀεὶ πάντων κοινῆς, τῶν μὲν φανερωτάτων πορευομένων
ἑκάστου καθ' ἑαυτόν, οὐ πλανωμένων ἄλλως ἀνόητον πλάνην
ἀλλὰ χορείαν εὐδαίμονα χορευόντων μετά τε νοῦ καὶ
φρονήσεως τῆς ἄκρας, τοῦ δὲ λοιποῦ πλήθους ὑπὸ τῆς κοινῆς 30
φορᾶς ἀγομένου μιᾶι γνώμηι καὶ ὁρμῆι τοῦ ξύμπαντος
οὐρανοῦ.

13 διοικῆται Reiske : διοικεῖται   18 ἀγαθῶν suspectum   19 θνητὴν secl.
von Arnim   23 ⟨τῶν ... ἑπομένων⟩ post Arnimium supplevi

23 Μίαν γὰρ δὴ ταύτην καθαρῶς εὐδαίμονα πολιτείαν εἴτε
καὶ πόλιν χρὴ καλεῖν τὴν θεῶν πρὸς ἀλλήλους κοινωνίαν,
ἐάν τε καὶ ξύμπαν τὸ λογικὸν περιλάβηι τις, ἀνθρώπων
σὺν θεοῖς ἀριθμουμένων, ὡς παῖδες σὺν ἀνδράσι λέγονται
μετέχειν πόλεως, φύσει πολῖται ὄντες οὐ τῶι φρονεῖν τε καὶ 5
πράττειν τὰ τῶν πολιτῶν οὐδὲ τῶι κοινωνεῖν τοῦ νόμου,
ἀξύνετοι ὄντες αὐτοῦ. ἐκ δὲ τῶν ἄλλων πανταχοῦ πασῶν
σχεδὸν ἁπλῶς ἡμαρτημένων τε καὶ φαύλων πρὸς τὴν ἄκραν
εὐθύτητα τοῦ θείου καὶ μακαρίου νόμου καὶ τῆς ὀρθῆς
διοικήσεως, ὅμως δὲ πρὸς τὸ παρὸν εὐπορήσομεν παράδειγμα 1
τῆς ἐπιεικέστερον ἐχούσης πρὸς τὴν παντελῶς διεφθαρμένην,
ὡς ἐν πᾶσι νοσοῦσι τόν γ᾽ ἐλαφρότατα διάγοντα τῶι κάκιστα
διακειμένωι παραβάλλοντες.

24 Ἐγὼ μὲν οὖν πρός τι τοιοῦτον ὥρμων τῶι λόγωι. μεταξὺ
δὲ τῶν παρόντων εἷς ἐφθέγξατο εἰς τὸ μέσον, ὅσπερ ἦν 1
πρεσβύτατος αὐτῶν καὶ μέγιστον ἀξίωμα ἔχων, εἶπε δὲ πάνυ
εὐλαβούμενος, Μηδαμῶς, ὦ ξένε, ἄγροικον μηδὲ βαρβαρικὸν
ἡγήσηι τὸ τοιοῦτον, ὅτι μεταξὺ λέγοντί σοι ἐμποδὼν
ἐγενόμην. παρ᾽ ὑμῖν μὲν γὰρ οὐκ ἔθος ἐστὶ τὸ τοιοῦτο διὰ τὸ
πολλὴν ἀφθονίαν εἶναι τῶν ⟨ἐκ⟩ φιλοσοφίας λόγων καὶ περὶ 2
παντὸς ὅτου ἂν ἐπιθυμῆι τις ἐξεῖναι παρὰ πολλῶν ἀκοῦσαι·
παρ᾽ ἡμῖν δὲ ὥσπερ τέρας τι τοῦτο πέφηνε τὸ σὲ ἡμῖν
25 ἀφικέσθαι. τὸ δὲ λοιπὸν σχεδόν τι δεῦρο ἀφικνοῦνται ὀνόματι
Ἕλληνες, τῆι δὲ ἀληθείαι βαρβαρώτεροι ἡμῶν, ἔμποροι καὶ
ἀγοραῖοι, ῥάκη φαῦλα καὶ οἶνον πονηρὸν εἰσκομίζοντες καὶ
τά γε παρ᾽ ἡμῶν οὐδὲν βελτίω τούτων ἐξαγόμενοι. σὲ δὲ
αὐτὸς ἡμῖν ὁ Ἀχιλλεὺς ἔοικε δεῦρο ἀπὸ τῆς νήσου διαπέμψαι,
καί σε πάνυ μὲν ἡδέως ὁρῶμεν, πάνυ δὲ ἡδέως ἀκούομεν ὅ
τι ἂν λέγηις. οὐ μέντοι πολύν τινα χρόνον ἡγούμεθα ἔσεσθαι
τοῦτον οὐδὲ βουλόμεθα, ἀλλά σε εὖ πράξαντα οἴκαδε
26 κατελθεῖν τὴν ταχίστην. νῦν οὖν ἐπεὶ ἧψω τῶι λόγωι τῆς

---

3 ξύμπαν τὸ Casaubon : ξύμπαντα   10 εὐπορήσομεν Reiske : -σωμεν
παράδειγμα von Arnim : παραδειγμάτων : παράδειγμα τὸ Emperius   12 γ᾽
Emperius : δ᾽   20 ⟨ἐκ⟩ add. Emperius   29 λέγηις Emperius : λέγηι
τις

θείας διοικήσεως, αὐτός τε ἀνεπτέρωμαι δαιμονίως καὶ τούσδε
ὁρῶ πάντας ὀργῶντας πρὸς ἐκεῖνον τὸν λόγον· καὶ γὰρ ἡμῖν
ἔδοξας μεγαλοπρεπῶς καὶ τοῦ πράγματος οὐκ ἀναξίως ὅσα
εἶπες εἰρηκέναι καὶ ὡς ἂν μάλιστα ἡμεῖς βουλοίμεθα ἀκοῦσαι.
τῆς μὲν γὰρ ἀκριβεστέρας ταύτης φιλοσοφίας ἄπειροί ἐσμεν, 5
Ὁμήρου δέ, ὡς οἶσθα, ἐρασταὶ καί τινες οὐ πολλοὶ Πλάτωνος·
ὧν δὴ κἀμὲ ὁρᾷς ὄντα, ἀεί ποτε ἐντυγχάνοντα τοῖς ἐκείνου
ὅπως ἂν δύνωμαι· καίτοι ἴσως ἄτοπον βαρβαρίζοντα τῶν
ποιητῶν μάλιστα τῶι ἑλληνικωτάτωι καὶ σοφωτάτωι χαίρειν
καὶ ξυνεῖναι, καθάπερ εἴ τις μικροῦ τυφλὸς τὸ μὲν ἄλλο φῶς 10
ἀποστρέφοιτο, πρὸς αὐτὸν δὲ τὸν ἥλιον ἀναβλέποι.
27   Ἔχει μὲν δὴ τὰ ἡμέτερα οὕτως. σὺ δὲ εἰ θέλεις πᾶσιν ἡμῖν
χαρίσασθαι, τὸν μὲν ὑπὲρ τῆς θνητῆς πόλεως ἀναβαλοῦ
λόγον, ἐὰν ἄρα σχολὴν ἡμῖν οἱ γείτονες παράσχωσιν εἰς
αὔριον καὶ μὴ δέηι προσγυμνάζεσθαι αὐτοῖς, ὥσπερ ἔθος ἡμῖν 15
τὸ πολύ· περὶ δὲ τῆς θείας εἴτε πόλεως εἴτε διακοσμήσεως
φίλον σοι καλεῖν, εἰπὲ ὅπηι τε καὶ ὅπως ἔχει, ὡς δύνασαι
ἐγγύτατα τείνων τῆς τοῦ Πλάτωνος ἐλευθερίας περὶ τὴν
φράσιν, οἷον δὴ καὶ ἄρτι ποιεῖν ἡμῖν ἔδοξας. εἰ γὰρ μηδενὸς
ἄλλου, τῆς γε φωνῆς ξυνίεμεν ὑπὸ συνηθείας ὅτι οὐ σμικρὸν 20
οὐδὲ πόρρω τοῦ Ὁμήρου φθέγγεται.
28   Κἀγὼ σφόδρα γε ἥσθην τῆι ἁπλότητι τοῦ πρεσβύτου,
καὶ γελάσας εἶπον, Ὦ φίλε Ἱεροσῶν, εἴ με ἐκέλευες χθὲς
εἰσβεβληκότων ὑμῖν τῶν πολεμίων λαβόντα ὅπλα ὥσπερ
τὸν Ἀχιλλέα μάχεσθαι, τὸ μὲν ἕτερον ἐπείσθην ἄν, πειρώμενος 25
ἀμύνεσθαι ὑπὲρ ἀνδρῶν φίλων, τὸ δὲ ἕτερον οὐκ ἄν, οἶμαι,
ἐδυνάμην, καίτοι σφόδρα βουλόμενος, ὁμοίως τῶι Ἀχιλλεῖ
ἀγωνίζεσθαι. καὶ νῦν ὧν κελεύεις ποιήσω τὸ ἕτερον,
προθυμήσομαι εἰπεῖν τὸν λόγον, ὡς ἂν ἐγὼ δύνωμαι κατ'
ἐμαυτόν·   30

    ἀνδράσι δὲ προτέροισιν ἐριζέμεν οὐκ ἐθελήσω,

9 ποιητῶν Heinze : πολιτῶν   23 Ἱεροσῶν Boeckh : ροσῶν uel ρόσων
εἴ με Selden : εἰ μὲν

98 ΔΙΩΝΟΣ

οὔτε Πλάτωνι οὔτε ʽΟμήρωι. οὐ γάρ τοι οὐδὲ τῶι Εὐρύτωι
φησὶ συνενεγκεῖν ὁ ποιητής, ὅτι ἤριζε πρὸς τοὺς κρείττονας.
29 οὐ μέντοι σπουδῆς γε, ἔφην, οὐδὲν ἀπολείψομεν. ταῦτα δὲ
εἰπὼν πρὸς ἐκεῖνον οὐδὲν ἧττον ὑπεκίνουν καὶ ἀνεφερόμην
τρόπον τινὰ ἀναμνησθεὶς Πλάτωνός τε καὶ ʽΟμήρου.   5
Τὸ μὲν δὴ τῆς πόλεως οὕτως, ἔφην, δεῖ ἀκούειν ὡς οὐκ
ἄντικρυς τῶν ἡμετέρων [ζῶιον] τὸν κόσμον ἀποφαινομένων
[ἢ] πόλιν· ἐναντίον γὰρ ⟨ἂν⟩ ὑπῆρχε τοῦτο τῶι λόγωι τῶι
περὶ τῆς πόλεως, ⟨ἦν⟩, ὥσπερ οὖν εἶπον, σύστημα ἀνθρώπων
ὡρίσαντο· ἅμα τε οὐκ ἦν ἴσως πρέπον οὐδὲ πιθανὸν κυρίως   1
εἰπόντας εἶναι τὸν κόσμον ζῶιον ἔπειτα φάσκειν ὡς ἔστι πόλις·
30 τὸ γὰρ αὐτὸ πόλιν τε καὶ ζῶιον οὐκ ἄν, οἶμαι, ῥαιδίως
ὑπομένοι τις ὑπολαβεῖν. ἀλλὰ τὴν νῦν διακόσμησιν, ὁπηνίκα
διήιρηται καὶ μεμέρισται τὸ πᾶν εἰς πολλάς τινας μορφὰς
φυτῶν τε καὶ ζώιων θνητῶν καὶ ἀθανάτων, ἔτι δὲ ἀέρος καὶ   1
γῆς καὶ ὕδατος καὶ πυρός, ἐν οὐδὲν ἧττον πεφυκὸς ἐν ἅπασι
τούτοις καὶ μιᾶι ψυχῆι καὶ δυνάμει διεπόμενον, ἀμηιγέπηι
πόλει προσεικάζουσι διὰ τὸ πλῆθος τῶν ἐν αὐτῆι γιγνομένων
τε καὶ ἀπογιγνομένων, ἔτι δὲ τὴν τάξιν καὶ τὴν εὐκοσμίαν τῆς
διοικήσεως.   2
31 ʽΟ δὲ λόγος οὗτος ἔμβραχυ ἐσπούδακε ξυναρμόσαι τῶι
θείωι τὸ ἀνθρώπειον γένος καὶ ἑνὶ λόγωι περιλαβεῖν πᾶν τὸ
λογικόν, κοινωνίας ἀρχὴν καὶ δικαιοσύνης μόνην ταύτην
ἰσχυρὰν καὶ ἄλυτον εὑρίσκων. πόλις μὲν γὰρ δὴ κατὰ
τοῦτο ἂν εἴη λεγομένη μὰ Δί᾿ οὐ φαύλων οὐδὲ μικρῶν   2
τυχοῦσα ἡγεμόνων οὐδὲ ὑπὸ τυράννων τε καὶ δήμων καὶ
δεκαρχιῶν δὴ καὶ ὀλιγαρχιῶν καί τινων ἄλλων τοιούτων
ἀρρωστημάτων διαφορουμένη καὶ στασιάζουσα τὸν ἅπαντα
χρόνον, ἀλλὰ τῆι σωφρονεστάτηι καὶ ἀρίστηι βασιλείαι

4 ὑπεκίνουν Cobet : ὑπ᾿ ἐκείνων   6 δεῖ Reiske : δεῖν UB : δὴ M   7 τῶν
ἡμετέρων Emperius : τῶν ἡμερῶν M : τῶν ἥμερον UB [ζῶιον] om. M
8 [ἢ] om. M ⟨ἂν⟩ add. Emperius τοῦτο Selden : τούτωι   9 ⟨ἦν⟩
add. Emperius   16 ἕν von Arnim : ἐν οὐδὲν M : οὐδενὶ   17 διεπόμενον
Emperius : -μένων ἀμηιγέπηι Emperius : ἃ μήτε τῆι   22 θείωι Geel : θεῶι
23 δικαιοσύνης Reiske : -ην   27 δεκαδαρχιῶν M

κεκοσμημένη, τῷ ὄντι βασιλευομένη κατὰ νόμον μετὰ πάσης
32 φιλίας καὶ ὁμονοίας· ὅπερ δὴ ὁ σοφώτατος καὶ [ὁ]
πρεσβύτατος ἄρχων καὶ νομοθέτης ἅπασι προστάττει
θνητοῖς καὶ ἀθανάτοις, ὁ τοῦ ξύμπαντος ἡγεμὼν οὐρανοῦ καὶ
τῆς ὅλης δεσπότης οὐσίας, αὐτὸς οὕτως ἐξηγούμενος καὶ 5
παράδειγμα παρέχων τὴν αὑτοῦ διοίκησιν τῆς εὐδαίμονος καὶ
μακαρίας καταστάσεως· ὃν οἱ θεῖοι ποιηταὶ μαθόντες ἐκ
Μουσῶν ὑμνοῦσιν ἅμα καὶ ὀνομάζουσι πατέρα θεῶν καὶ
ἀνθρώπων.

33 Κινδυνεύει γὰρ οὖν δὴ τὸ ποιητικὸν γένος οὐ πάνυ 10
ἄστοχον εἶναι τῶν ἱερῶν λόγων οὐδὲ ἀπὸ στόχου φθέγγεσθαι
τὰ τοιαῦτα πολλάκις, οὐ μέντοι οὐδὲ μεμυῆσθαι καθαρῶς
κατὰ θεσμὸν καὶ νόμον τῶν μυουμένων οὐδὲ εἰδέναι τοῦ
ξύμπαντος πέρι τῆς ἀληθείας σαφὲς οὐδὲν ὡς ἔπος εἰπεῖν·
ἀτεχνῶς δὲ ἔοικεν ὅμοιον εἶναι τοῖς ἔξω περὶ θύρας ὑπηρέταις 15
τῶν τελετῶν, πρόθυρα κοσμοῦσι καὶ βωμοὺς τοὺς ἐν τῶι
φανερῶι καὶ τὰ ἄλλα τὰ τοιαῦτα παρασκευάζουσιν, οὐδέ
ποτ᾽ ἔνδον παριοῦσιν. ὅθεν δὴ καὶ θεράποντας Μουσῶν
αὐτοὺς ὀνομάζουσιν, οὐ μύστας οὐδὲ ἄλλο σεμνὸν ὄνομα.

34 οὐκοῦν, ὡς ἔφην, τοὺς πλησίον ἀναστρεφομένους τελετῆς τινος 20
πρὸς ταῖς εἰσόδοις εἰκὸς τό γε τοσοῦτον ἔνδοθεν αἰσθάνεσθαί
τινος, ἤτοι ῥήματος ἐκβοηθέντος ἑνὸς μυστικοῦ ἢ πυρὸς
ὑπερφανέντος, καὶ τοῖς ποιηταῖς ἐνίοτε, λέγω δὲ τοῖς πάνυ
ἀρχαίοις, φωνή τις ἐκ Μουσῶν ἀφίκετο βραχεῖα καί πού τις
ἐπίπνοια θείας φύσεώς τε καὶ ἀληθείας, καθάπερ αὐγὴ πυρὸς 25
ἐξ ἀφανοῦς λάμψαντος· ἃ ἔπασχον ἐκ Μουσῶν καὶ κατείχοντο
35 Ὅμηρός τε καὶ Ἡσίοδος. οἱ δὲ μετ᾽ ἐκείνους ὕστερον ἐπὶ
σκηνὰς καὶ θέατρα τὴν αὑτῶν σοφίαν ἀγαγόντες ἀμύητοι
ἀμυήτοις πολλάκις ἐξέφερον ἀτελῆ παραδείγματα ὀργίων·
θαυμαζόμενοι δὲ ὑπὸ τῶν πολλῶν ἐπεχείρουν αὐτοὶ τελεῖν 30
τὸν ὄχλον, τῶι ὄντι βακχείων τινὰς σκηνὰς ἀκαλύπτους
πηξάμενοι ἔν τισι τραγικαῖς τριόδοις.

2 [ὁ] secl. Wilamowitz   6 τὴν ... διοίκησιν Emperius : τῆς ... διοικήσεως
12 μέντοι Emperius : τοίνυν   26–7 ἃ ... Ἡσίοδος susp. von Arnim

Οὗτοι δ᾽ οὖν πάντες οἱ ποιηταὶ κατὰ ταὐτὰ τὸν πρῶτον
καὶ μέγιστον θεὸν πατέρα καλοῦσι συλλήβδην ἅπαντος τοῦ
36 λογικοῦ γένους καὶ δὴ καὶ βασιλέα. οἷς πειθόμενοι οἱ
ἄνθρωποι Διὸς βασιλέως ἱδρύονται βωμούς, καὶ δὴ καὶ
πατέρα αὐτὸν οὐκ ὀκνοῦσι προσαγορεύειν τινὲς ἐν ταῖς 5
εὐχαῖς, ὡς τοιαύτης τινὸς ἀρχῆς καὶ συστάσεως οὔσης τοῦ
παντός. ὥστε ταύτηι γε οὐδὲ οἶκον δοκοῦσί μοι ὀκνῆσαι ἂν
ἀποφήνασθαι τοῦ Διὸς τὸν ἅπαντα κόσμον, εἴπερ ἐστὶ πατὴρ
τῶν ἐν αὐτῶι, καὶ νὴ Δία πόλιν, ὥσπερ ἡμεῖς προσεικάζομεν
37 κατὰ τὴν μείζονα ἀρχήν. βασιλεία γὰρ πόλει μᾶλλον ἢ οἴκῳ 1
πρεπόντως ἂν λέγοιτο. οὐ γὰρ δὴ βασιλέα εἰπόντες τὸν ἐπὶ
τῶν ὅλων οὐκ ἂν βασιλεύεσθαι τὸ ὅλον ὁμολογοῖεν οὐδὲ
βασιλεύεσθαι φήσαντες οὐκ ἂν πολιτεύεσθαι φαῖεν οὐδὲ
εἶναι πολιτείαν [βασιλικὴν] τοῦ παντός. πολιτείαν δ᾽ αὖ
συγχωροῦντες πόλιν οὐκ ἂν ἀποτρέποιντο ὁμολογεῖν ἤ τι 1
τούτῳ παραπλήσιον τὸ πολιτευόμενον.
38   Ὅδε μὲν οὖν ὁ τῶν φιλοσόφων λόγος, ἀγαθὴν καὶ
φιλάνθρωπον ἀποδεικνὺς κοινωνίαν δαιμόνων καὶ ἀνθρώπων,
μεταδιδοὺς νόμου καὶ πολιτείας οὐ τοῖς τυχοῦσι τῶν ζώιων,
ἀλλ᾽ ὅσοις μέτεστι λόγου καὶ φρονήσεως, πολὺ κρείττω καὶ 2
δικαιοτέραν τῆς Λακωνικῆς νομοθεσίαν εἰσηγούμενος, καθ᾽ ἣν
οὐδὲ ὑπάρχει τοῖς Εἵλωσι γενέσθαι Σπαρτιάταις, ὅθεν δὴ καὶ
διατελοῦσιν ἐπιβουλεύοντες τῆι Σπάρτηι.
39   Ἕτερος δὲ μῦθος ἐν ἀπορρήτοις τελεταῖς ὑπὸ μάγων
ἀνδρῶν ἄιδεται θαυμαζόμενος, οἳ τὸν θεὸν τοῦτον ὑμνοῦσιν 2
ὡς τέλειόν τε καὶ πρῶτον ἡνίοχον τοῦ τελειοτάτου ἅρματος.
τὸ γὰρ Ἡλίου ἅρμα νεώτερόν φασιν εἶναι πρὸς ἐκεῖνο
κρινόμενον, φανερὸν δὲ τοῖς πολλοῖς, ἅτε προδήλου
γιγνομένης τῆς φορᾶς. ὅθεν κοινῆς φήμης τυγχάνειν, ὡς
ἔοικεν ἀπὸ πρώτων σχεδόν τι τῶν ποιητῶν ἀνατολὰς καὶ 3
δύσεις ἑκάστοτε λεγόντων κατὰ ταὐτὰ πάντων ἐξηγουμένων

1 ταὐτὰ Selden : ταῦτα   9 τῶν Jacobs : αὐτῶν   14 [βασιλικὴν] secl. von
Arnim   21 νομοθεσίαν Reiske : -ίας   29 κοινῆς φήμης Reiske : κοιναῖς
φήμαις   30 ἀπὸ Emperius : ὑπὸ   31 καὶ post λεγόντων UB   ταὐτὰ
Reiske : ταῦτα

ζευγνυμένους τε τοὺς ἵππους καὶ τὸν "Ηλιον αὐτὸν
ἐπιβαίνοντα τοῦ δίφρου.

40 Τὸ δὲ ἰσχυρὸν καὶ τέλειον ἅρμα τὸ Διὸς οὐδεὶς ἄρα
ὕμνησεν ἀξίως τῶν τῇδε οὔτε "Ομηρος οὔτε 'Ησίοδος,
ἀλλὰ Ζωροάστρης καὶ μάγων παῖδες ᾄδουσι παρ' ἐκείνου 5
μαθόντες· ὃν Πέρσαι λέγουσιν ἔρωτι σοφίας καὶ δικαιοσύνης
ἀποχωρήσαντα τῶν ἀνθρώπων καθ' αὐτὸν ἐν ὄρει τινὶ
ζῆν· ἔπειτα ἀφθῆναι τὸ ὄρος πυρὸς ἄνωθεν πολλοῦ
κατασκήψαντος συνεχῶς τε κάεσθαι. τὸν οὖν βασιλέα σὺν τοῖς
ἐλλογιμωτάτοις Περσῶν ἀφικνεῖσθαι πλησίον, βουλόμενον 10
εὔξασθαι τῶι θεῶι· καὶ τὸν ἄνδρα ἐξελθεῖν ἐκ τοῦ πυρὸς
ἀπαθῆ, φανέντα δὲ αὐτοῖς ἵλεων θαρρεῖν κελεῦσαι καὶ
θῦσαι θυσίας τινάς, ὡς ἥκοντος εἰς τὸν τόπον τοῦ θεοῦ.

41 συγγίγνεσθαί τε μετὰ ταῦτα οὐχ ἅπασιν, ἀλλὰ τοῖς ἄριστα
πρὸς ἀλήθειαν πεφυκόσι καὶ θεοῦ ξυνιέναι δυναμένοις, 15
οὓς Πέρσαι μάγους ἐκάλεσαν, ἐπισταμένους θεραπεύειν τὸ
δαιμόνιον, οὐχ ὡς "Ελληνες ἀγνοίᾳ τοῦ ὀνόματος οὕτως
ὀνομάζουσιν ἀνθρώπους γόητας. ἐκεῖνοι δὲ τά τε ἄλλα δρῶσι
κατὰ λόγους ἱερούς καὶ δὴ τῷ Διὶ τρέφουσιν ἅρμα Νισαίων
ἵππων· οἱ δέ εἰσι κάλλιστοι καὶ μέγιστοι τῶν κατὰ τὴν 'Ασίαν· 20
τῶι δέ γε 'Ηλίωι ἕνα ἵππον.

42 'Εξηγοῦνται δὲ τὸν μῦθον οὐχ ὥσπερ οἱ παρ' ἡμῖν
προφῆται τῶν Μουσῶν ἕκαστα φράζουσι μετὰ πολλῆς
πειθοῦς, ἀλλὰ μάλα αὐθαδῶς. εἶναι γὰρ δὴ τοῦ ξύμπαντος
μίαν ἀγωγήν τε καὶ ἡνιόχησιν ὑπὸ τῆς ἄκρας ἐμπειρίας τε καὶ 25
ῥώμης γιγνομένην ἀεί, καὶ ταύτην ἄπαυστον ἐν ἀπαύστοις
αἰῶνος περιόδοις. τοὺς δὲ 'Ηλίου καὶ Σελήνης δρόμους,
καθάπερ εἶπον, μερῶν εἶναι κινήσεις, ὅθεν ὑπ' ἀνθρώπων
ὁρᾶσθαι σαφέστερον. τῆς δὲ τοῦ ξύμπαντος κινήσεως καὶ
φορᾶς μὴ ξυνιέναι τοὺς πολλούς, ἀλλ' ἀγνοεῖν τὸ μέγεθος 30
τοῦδε τοῦ ἀγῶνος.

43 Τὸ δὴ μετὰ τοῦτο αἰσχύνομαι φράζειν τῶν ἵππων πέρι

7 ἀνθρώπων Bidez–Cumont (1938) 11 29 : ἄλλων   28 ἀνθρώπων von
Arnim : αὐτῶν   30 ξυνιέναι Reiske : ξυνεῖναι

102 ΔΙΩΝΟΣ

καὶ τῆς ἡνιοχήσεως, ὅπως ἐξηγούμενοι λέγουσιν, οὐ πάνυ
τι φροντίζοντες ὅμοιόν σφισι γίγνεσθαι πανταχῆι τὸ τῆς
εἰκόνος. ἴσως γὰρ ἂν φαινοίμην ἄτοπος παρὰ Ἑλληνικά τε
καὶ χαρίεντα ἄισματα βαρβαρικὸν ἄισμα ἐπάιδων· ὅμως δὲ
τολμητέον.   5

Φασὶ τῶν ἵππων τὸν πρῶτον ἄνωθεν ἀπείρωι διαφέρειν
κάλλει τε καὶ μεγέθει καὶ ταχυτῆτι, ἅτε ἔξωθεν περιτρέχοντα
τὸ μήκιστον τοῦ δρόμου, αὐτοῦ Ζηνὸς ἱερόν· πτηνὸν δὲ εἶναι,
τὴν δὲ χρόαν λαμπρόν, αὐγῆς τῆς καθαρωτάτης· τὸν δὲ Ἥλιον
ἐν αὐτῶι καὶ τὴν Σελήνην σημεῖα προφανῆ ὁρᾶσθαι, ὥσπερ   1•
οἶμαι καὶ τῶνδε τῶν ἵππων ἐστὶ σημεῖα, τὰ μὲν μηνοειδῆ,
44 τὰ δὲ ἀλλοῖα. ταῦτα δὲ ὑφ' ἡμῶν ὁρᾶσθαι συνεστραμμένα,
καθάπερ ⟨ἐν⟩ αὐγῆι λαμπρᾶι φλογὸς σπινθῆρας ἰσχυροὺς
διαθέοντας, ἰδίαν δὲ κίνησιν ἔχειν καθ' αὑτά. καὶ τἆλλα ἄστρα
δι' ἐκείνου φαινόμενα καὶ ξύμπαντα ἐκείνου πεφυκότα μέρη   1
τὰ μὲν περιφέρεσθαι σὺν αὐτῶι μίαν ταύτην ἔχοντα κίνησιν,
τὰ δὲ ἄλλους θεῖν δρόμους. τυγχάνειν δὲ παρὰ τοῖς ἀνθρώποις
ταῦτα μὲν ἰδίου ἕκαστον ὀνόματος, τὰ δὲ ἄλλα κατὰ πλῆθος
ἀθρόα, διανενεμημένα εἴς τινα σχήματα καὶ μορφάς.
45   Ὁ μὲν δὴ λαμπρότατος ἵππος καὶ ποικιλώτατος αὐτῶι τε   2•
Διὶ προσφιλέστατος, ὧδέ πως ὑμνούμενος ὑπ' αὐτῶν, θυσίας
τε καὶ τιμὰς ἅτε πρῶτος εἰκότως πρώτας ἔλαχεν· δεύτερος
δὲ μετ' ἐκεῖνον ἁπτόμενος αὐτοῦ καὶ πλησιώτατος Ἥρας
ἐπώνυμος, εὐήνιος καὶ μαλακός, πολὺ δὲ ἥττων κατά τε ῥώμην
καὶ τάχος. χροιὰν δὲ τῆι μὲν αὐτοῦ φύσει μέλας, φαιδρύνεται   2
δὲ ἀεὶ τὸ καταλαμπόμενον Ἡλίωι, τὸ δὲ σκιασθὲν ἐν τῆι
46 περιφορᾶι τὴν αὐτοῦ μεταλαμβάνει τῆς χρόας ἰδέαν. τρίτος
Ποσειδῶνος ἱερός, τοῦ δευτέρου βραδύτερος. τούτου δὲ
μυθολογοῦσιν εἴδωλον οἱ ποιηταὶ γενέσθαι παρ' ἀνθρώποις,
ἐμοὶ δοκεῖν, ὅντινα ὀνομάζουσι Πήγασον, καί φασιν ἀνεῖναι   3•
κρήνην ἐν Κορίνθωι χαράξαντα τῆι ὁπλῆι. ὁ δὲ δὴ τέταρτος

4 ἐπάιδων Emperius : παίδων   7 ἅτε Emperius : τά τε   11 ἵππων : ἄστρων
Bruns   12 συνεστραμμένα : fortasse συστρεφόμενα, nisi ταῦτα ... διαθέοντας
(12–14) post μορφάς (19) transponere malis   13 ⟨ἐν⟩ add. Emperius

εἰκάσαι πάντων ἀτοπώτατος, στερεός τε καὶ ἀκίνητος,
οὐχ ὅπως πτερωτός, ἐπώνυμος Ἑστίας. ὅμως δὲ οὐκ
ἀποτρέπονται τῆς εἰκόνος, ἀλλὰ ἐνεζεῦχθαί φασι καὶ τοῦτον
τῶι ἅρματι, μένειν δὲ κατὰ χώραν χαλινὸν ἀδάμαντος
47 ἐνδακόντα. συνερείδειν δὲ πανταχόθεν αὐτῶι τοῖς μέρεσι, καὶ 5
τὼ δύο τὼ πλησίον ὁμοίως πρὸς αὐτὸν ἐγκλίνειν, ἀτεχνῶς
ἐπιπίπτοντε καὶ ὠθουμένω· τὸν δὲ ἐξωτάτω [πρῶτον] ἀεὶ
περὶ τὸν ἑστῶτα ὡς νύσσαν φέρεσθαι.
Τὸ μὲν οὖν πολὺ μετ᾽ εἰρήνης καὶ φιλίας διατελοῦσιν
ἀβλαβεῖς ὑπ᾽ ἀλλήλων. ἤδη δέ ποτε ἐν μήκει χρόνου καὶ 10
πολλαῖς περιόδοις ἰσχυρὸν ἆσθμα τοῦ πρώτου προσπεσὸν
ἄνωθεν, οἷα δὴ θυμοειδοῦς, ἐθέρμηνε τοὺς ἄλλους, σφοδρότερόν
γε μὴν τὸν τελευταῖον· τήν τε δὴ χαίτην περιέφλεξεν αὐτοῦ,
48 ἧι μάλιστα ἠγάλλετο, καὶ τὸν ἅπαντα κόσμον. τοῦτο δὲ
τὸ πάθος ἅπαξ Ἕλληνας μνημονεύοντάς φασι Φαέθοντι 15
προσάπτειν, οὐ δυναμένους μέμφεσθαι τὴν Διὸς ἡνιόχησιν,
τούς τε Ἡλίου δρόμους οὐκ ἐθέλοντας ψέγειν. διό φασι
νεώτερον ἡνίοχον, Ἡλίου παῖδα θνητόν, ἐπιθυμήσαντα
χαλεπῆς καὶ ἀξυμφόρου πᾶσι τοῖς θνητοῖς παιδιᾶς,
αἰτησάμενον παρὰ τοῦ πατρὸς ἐπιστῆναι τῶι δίφρωι, 20
φερόμενόν τε ἀτάκτως πάντα καταφλέξαι ζῶια καὶ φυτά, καὶ
τέλος αὐτὸν διαφθαρῆναι πληγέντα ὑπὸ κρείττονος πυρός.
49 Πάλιν δὲ ὅταν διὰ πλειόνων ἐτῶν ὁ Νυμφῶν καὶ Ποσειδῶνος
ἱερὸς πῶλος ἐπαναστῇ, παρὰ τὸ σύνηθες ἀγωνιάσας καὶ
ταραχθείς, ἱδρῶτι πολλῶι κατέκλυσε τὸν αὐτὸν τοῦτον ἅτε 25
ὁμόζυγα· πειρᾶται δὴ τῆς ἐναντίας τῆι πρότερον φθορᾶι,
ὕδατι πολλῶι χειμαζόμενος. καὶ τοιοῦτον ἕνα χειμῶνα
διηγεῖσθαι τοὺς Ἕλληνας ὑπὸ νεότητός τε καὶ μνήμης
ἀσθενοῦς, καὶ .[λέγουσι] Δευκαλίωνα βασιλεύοντα τότε
σφίσιν ἀρκέσαι πρὸ τῆς παντελοῦς φθορᾶς. 30
50 Ταῦτα δὲ σπανίως ξυμβαίνοντα δοκεῖν μὲν ἀνθρώποις διὰ

5 αὐτῶι von Arnim : αὐτῶι   7 [πρῶτον] secl. von Arnim   13 τε
Emperius : δὲ   27 τοιοῦτον Emperius : τοῦτον   29 [λέγουσι] secl.
Reiske   31 δοκεῖν Geel : δοκεῖ

τὸν αὐτῶν ὄλεθρον γίγνεσθαι μὴ κατὰ λόγον μηδὲ μετέχειν
τῆς τοῦ παντὸς τάξεως, λανθάνειν δὲ αὐτοὺς ὀρθῶς γιγνόμενα
καὶ κατὰ γνώμην τοῦ σώιζοντος καὶ κυβερνῶντος τὸ πᾶν.
εἶναι γὰρ ὅμοιον ὥσπερ ὅταν ἅρματος ἡνίοχος τῶν ἵππων
τινὰ κολάζηι χαλινῶι σπάσας ἢ κέντρωι ἁψάμενος, ὁ δ'   5
ἐσκίρτησε καὶ ἐταράχθη, παραχρῆμα εἰς δέον καθιστάμενος.
Μίαν μὲν οὖν ⟨λέγουσι⟩ ταύτην ἡνιόχησιν ἰσχυράν,
51 οὐχ ὅλου φθειρομένου τοῦ παντός, πάλιν δὲ ἑτέραν τῆς
τῶν τεττάρων κινήσεως καὶ μεταβολῆς ἐν ἀλλήλοις
μεταβαλλομένων καὶ διαλλαττόντων τὰ εἴδη μέχρις ἂν εἰς μίαν   1c
ἅπαντα συνέλθηι φύσιν ἡττηθέντα τοῦ κρείττονος. ὅμως δὲ
καὶ ταύτην τὴν κίνησιν ἡνιοχήσει προσεικάζειν τολμῶσιν
ἐλάσει τε ἅρματος, ἀτοπωτέρας δεόμενοι τῆς εἰκόνος· οἷον εἴ
τις θαυματοποιὸς ἐκ κηροῦ πλάσας ἵππους, ἔπειτα ἀφαιρῶν
καὶ περιξύων ἀφ' ἑκάστου προστιθεὶς ἄλλοτε ἄλλωι, τέλος   1ε
δὲ ἅπαντας εἰς ἕνα τῶν τεττάρων ἀναλώσας μίαν μορφὴν
52 ἐξ ἁπάσης τῆς ὕλης ἐργάζοιτο. εἶναί γε μὴν τὸ τοιοῦτο
μὴ καθάπερ ἀψύχων πλασμάτων ἔξωθεν τοῦ δημιουργοῦ
πραγματευομένου καὶ μεθιστάντος τὴν ὕλην, αὐτῶν δὲ
ἐκείνων γίγνεσθαι τὸ πάθος, ὥσπερ ἐν ἀγῶνι μεγάλωι τε καὶ   2ε
ἀληθινῶι περὶ νίκης ἐριζόντων· γίγνεσθαι δὲ τὴν νίκην καὶ τὸν
στέφανον ἐξ ἀνάγκης τοῦ πρώτου καὶ κρατίστου τάχει τε καὶ
ἀλκῆι καὶ τῆι ξυμπάσηι ἀρετῆι, ὃν εἴπομεν ἐν ἀρχῆι τῶν
53 λόγων ἐξαίρετον εἶναι Διός. τοῦτον γάρ, ἅτε πάντων
ἀλκιμώτατον καὶ φύσει διάπυρον, ταχὺ ἀναλώσαντα τοὺς   2
ἄλλους, καθάπερ, οἶμαι, τῶι ὄντι κηρίνους, ἐν οὐ πολλῶι
τινι χρόνωι, δοκοῦντι δὲ ἡμῖν ἀπείρωι πρὸς τὸν ἡμέτερον
αὐτῶν λογισμόν, καὶ τὴν οὐσίαν πάντων πᾶσαν εἰς αὑτὸν
ἀναλαβόντα, πολὺ κρείττω καὶ λαμπρότερον ὀφθῆναι τοῦ
πρότερον, ὑπ' οὐδενὸς ἄλλου θνητῶν οὐδὲ ἀθανάτων ἀλλ'   3
αὐτὸν ὑφ' αὑτοῦ νικηφόρον γενόμενον τοῦ μεγίστου ἀγῶνος.
στάντα δὲ ὑψηλὸν καὶ γαῦρον, χαρέντα τῆι νίκηι, τόπον τε

7 ⟨λέγουσι⟩ add. Reiske   14 num ⟨τέτταρας⟩ πλάσας?   17 ἐργάζοιτο von
Arnim : ἐργάσοιτο

ὡς πλεῖστον καταλαβεῖν καὶ μείζονος χώρας δεηθῆναι τότε
ὑπὸ ῥώμης καὶ μένους.

54 Κατὰ τοῦτο δὴ γενόμενοι τοῦ λόγου δυσωποῦνται τὴν
αὐτὴν ἐπονομάζειν τοῦ ζῴου φύσιν. εἶναι γὰρ αὐτὸν ἤδη
τηνικάδε ἁπλῶς τὴν τοῦ ἡνιόχου καὶ δεσπότου ψυχήν, 5
μᾶλλον δὲ αὐτὸ τὸ φρονοῦν καὶ τὸ ἡγούμενον αὐτῆς. [οὕτως
δὴ λέγομεν καὶ ἡμεῖς τιμῶντες καὶ σεβόμενοι τὸν μέγιστον
55 θεὸν ἔργοις τε ἀγαθοῖς καὶ ῥήμασιν εὐφήμοις.] λειφθεὶς γὰρ
δὴ μόνος ὁ νοῦς καὶ τόπον ἀμήχανον ἐμπλήσας αὑτοῦ,
ἅτε γ᾽ ἐπ᾽ ἴσης πανταχῇ κεχυμένος, οὐδενὸς ἐν αὑτῶι 10
πυκνοῦ λειφθέντος, ἀλλὰ πάσης ἐπικρατούσης μανότητος,
ὅτε κάλλιστος γίγνεται τὴν καθαρωτάτην λαβὼν αὐγῆς
ἀκηράτου φύσιν, εὐθὺς ἐπόθησε τὸν ἐξ ἀρχῆς βίον. ἔρωτα δὴ
λαβὼν τῆς ἡνιοχήσεως ἐκείνης καὶ ἀρχῆς καὶ ὁμονοίας τῆς
τε τῶν τριῶν φύσεων καὶ ἡλίου καὶ σελήνης καὶ τῶν ἄλλων 15
ἄστρων ἁπάντων τε ἁπλῶς ζῴων καὶ φυτῶν, ὥρμησεν ἐπὶ
τὸ γεννᾶν καὶ διανέμειν ἕκαστα καὶ δημιουργεῖν τὸν ὄντα
νῦν κόσμον ἐξ ἀρχῆς πολὺ κρείττω καὶ λαμπρότερον ἅτε
56 νεώτερον. ἀστράψας δὲ ὅλος οὐκ ἄτακτον οὐδὲ ῥυπαρὰν
ἀστραπήν, οἵα χειμέριος ἐλαυνομένων βιαιότερον πολλάκις 20
τῶν νεφῶν διῇξεν, ἀλλὰ καθαρὸν καὶ ἀμιγῆ παντὸς
σκοτεινοῦ, μετέβαλε ῥαιδίως ἅμα τῇ νοήσει. μνησθεὶς δὲ
Ἀφροδίτης καὶ γενέσεως ἐπράϋνε καὶ ἀνῆκεν αὑτόν, καὶ πολὺ
τοῦ φωτὸς ἀποσβέσας εἰς ἀέρα πυρώδη τρέπεται πυρὸς
ἠπίου. μιχθεὶς δὲ τότε Ἥραι καὶ μεταλαβὼν τοῦ τελειοτάτου 25
λέχους, ἀναπαυσάμενος ἀφίησι τὴν πᾶσαν αὖ τοῦ παντὸς
γονήν. τοῦτον ὑμνοῦσι παῖδες σοφῶν ἐν ἀρρήτοις τελεταῖς
57 Ἥρας καὶ Διὸς εὐδαίμονα γάμον. ὑγρὰν δὲ ποιήσας τὴν ὅλην
οὐσίαν, ἓν σπέρμα τοῦ παντός, αὐτὸς ἐν τούτωι διαθέων,
καθάπερ ἐν γονῇι πνεῦμα τὸ πλάττον καὶ δημιουργοῦν, τότε 30
δὴ μάλιστα προσεοικὼς τῇ τῶν ἄλλων συστάσει ζῴων, καθ᾽

6–8 [οὕτως ... εὐφήμοις] secl. Casaubon   9–10 αὑτοῦ ἅτε γ᾽ ἐπ᾽ ἴσης von der
Muehll (ἅτ᾽ ἐπ᾽ ἴσης iam Wilamowitz) : αὐτοῦ γε πίθως uel sim. codd.
12 αὐγῆς Emperius : αὐτὸς   19 ὅλος von Arnim : ὅλον   20 οἷα Casaubon
(sed ἐν χειμερίοις) : οἶαν

ὅσον ἐκ ψυχῆς καὶ σώματος συνεστάναι λέγοιτ᾿ ἂν οὐκ ἀπὸ
τρόπου, τὰ λοιπὰ ἤδη ῥαιδίως πλάττει καὶ τυποῖ, λείαν καὶ
μαλακὴν αὐτῶι περιχέας τὴν οὐσίαν καὶ πᾶσαν εἴκουσαν
εὐπετῶς.

58   Ἐργασάμενος δὲ καὶ τελεώσας ἀπέδειξεν ἐξ ἀρχῆς τὸν ὄντα 5
κόσμον εὐειδῆ καὶ καλὸν ἀμηχάνως, πολὺ δὴ λαμπρότερον
ἢ οἷος ὁρᾶται νῦν. πάντα γάρ που καὶ τἄλλα ἔργα
τῶν δημιουργῶν καινὰ ἀπὸ τῆς τέχνης καὶ τῶν χειρῶν
παραχρῆμα τοῦ ποιήσαντος κρείττω καὶ στιλπνότερα, καὶ
τῶν φυτῶν τὰ νεώτερα εὐθαλέστερα τῶν παλαιῶν ὅλα τε 10
βλαστοῖς ἐοικότα. καὶ μὴν τά γε ζῶια εὐχάριτα καὶ προσηνῆ
ἰδεῖν μετὰ τὴν γένεσιν, οὐ μόνον τὰ κάλλιστα αὐτῶν, πῶλοί
τε καὶ μόσχοι καὶ σκύλακες, ἀλλὰ καὶ θηρίων σκύμνοι τῶν
59 ἀγριωτάτων. ἡ μὲν γὰρ ἀνθρώπου φύσις νηπία τε καὶ
ὑδαρὴς ὁμοία Δήμητρος ἀτελεῖ χλόῃ, προελθοῦσα δὲ εἰς τὸ 15
μέτρον ὥρας καὶ νεότητος παντὸς ἀτεχνῶς φυτοῦ κρεῖττον
καὶ ἐπιφανέστερον βλάστημα· ὁ δὲ ξύμπας οὐρανός τε
καὶ κόσμος, ὅτε πρῶτον συνετελέσθη, κοσμηθεὶς ὑπὸ τῆς
σοφωτάτης τε καὶ ἀρίστης τέχνης, ἄρτι τῶν τοῦ δημιουργοῦ
χειρῶν ἀπηλλαγμένος, λαμπρὸς καὶ διαυγὴς καὶ πᾶσι τοῖς 20
μέρεσι παμφαίνων, νήπιος μὲν οὐδένα χρόνον ἐγένετο οὐδὲ
ἀσθενὴς κατὰ τὴν ἀνθρωπίνην τε καὶ θνητὴν τῆς φύσεως
60 ἀσθένειαν, νέος δὲ καὶ ἀκμάζων εὐθὺς ἀπὸ τῆς ἀρχῆς. ὅτε
δὴ καὶ ὁ δημιουργὸς αὐτοῦ καὶ πατὴρ ἰδὼν ἤσθη μὲν οὐδαμῶς
– ταπεινὸν γὰρ ἐν ταπεινοῖς πάθος – ἐχάρη δὲ καὶ ἐτέρφθη 25
διαφερόντως

  ἥμενος Οὐλύμπωι, ἐγέλασσε δέ οἱ φίλον ἦτορ
  γηθοσύνηι, ὅθ᾿ ὁρᾶτο θεοὺς

τοὺς ἅπαντας ἤδη γεγονότας καὶ παρόντας.

  Τὴν δὲ τότε μορφὴν τοῦ κόσμου, λέγω δὲ τήν τε ὥραν 30
καὶ τὸ κάλλος ἀεὶ καλοῦ ὄντος ἀμηχάνως, οὐδεὶς δύναιτ᾿ ἂν
ἀνθρώπων διανοηθῆναι καὶ εἰπεῖν ἀξίως οὔτε τῶν νῦν οὔτε

8 καινὰ Reiske : καὶ τὰ   17 δὲ von Arnim : δὴ

τῶν πρότερον, εἰ μὴ Μοῦσαί τε καὶ Ἀπόλλων ἐν θείωι ῥυθμῶι
61 τῆς εἰλικρινοῦς τε καὶ ἄκρας ἁρμονίας. ὅθεν δὴ καὶ ἡμεῖς
ἐάσωμεν τὰ νῦν, ὅσον ἡμῖν δυνατὸν ἐπᾶραι τὸν λόγον οὐκ
ὀκνήσαντες. εἰ δὲ ἀτεχνῶς ὑψηλόν τε καὶ ἐξίτηλον ἀπέβη τὸ
τοῦ λόγου σχῆμα, ὥσπερ οἱ δεινοὶ περὶ τοὺς ὄρνιθάς φασι τὸν 5
σφόδρα ἄνω χωρήσαντα καὶ τοῖς νέφεσιν ἐγκρύψαντα αὑτὸν
ἀτελῆ τὴν μαντείαν ποιεῖν, οὐκ ἐμὲ ἄξιον αἰτιᾶσθαι, τὴν δὲ
Βορυσθενιτῶν ἀξίωσιν, ὡς τότε ἐκεῖνοι λέγειν προσέταξαν.

COMMENTARY

7 Euboicus

Title

Philostratus (*VS* 487) and Synesius (*Dio* 2) know it as Εὐβοεύς, a title appropriate to §§1–80; but Synesius at least knows the whole (Introd. p. 12). Photius calls it Εὐβοϊκὸς ἢ κυνηγετικός. *Euboicus* is not inappropriate, since the main episode takes place in Euboea, though the speech was of course not delivered in Euboea (neither was *Borystheniticus* delivered at Olbia).

1 'I am going to relate a personal experience from my wanderings; not only old men, but also vagrants, are inclined to be garrulous. My story is about something that happened to me in the heart of Greece.' **Τόδε μὴν ... διηγήσομαι:** the forward-looking τόδε and adversative μήν suggest that D. has just related something *not* within his own experience. The conditions would be met if there was a *prolalia* (cf. *Ol.* 1–10) about a remote or mythical people living in simple innocence. This beginning supports von Arnim's view (Introd. p. 12) that the speech is incomplete; and there are other reasons for thinking this also (see on 81, 125). But the abrupt beginning may be just a device, a way of plunging *in medias res*, leaving the reader to infer the purpose of what is said: cf. *Or.* 15.1 (ἀλλὰ μήν), Xenophon's *Conv.*, *Oecon.*, *Apol.*, *Lac. resp.*, and Aristides' advice (2.534.13 Spengel) on beginning with a particle like καίτοι in order to produce ἀφέλεια, 'simplicity' (Schmid (1887) 181; Bompaire (1958) 312). **ἰδών, οὐ παρ' ἑτέρων ἀκούσας:** the eyewitness is more reliable (Heraclitus fr. 101a, Hdt. 1.8, Plaut. *Truc.* 490: a proverbial thought), and this way of assuring us of the reliability of a narrative is standard: e.g. Eur. *IT* 901 τάδ' εἶδον αὐτή, κοὐ κλύουσ' ἀπαγγελῶ (cf. *Suppl.* 684, *Tro.* 482; Soph. *Tr.* 747). **οὐ μόνον πρεσβυτικὸν ... ἀλητικόν:** it is a familiar idea that old men are talkative (Demetrius, Περὶ ἑρμηνείας 7 οἱ γέροντες μακρολόγοι διὰ τὴν ἀσθένειαν; [Longinus] 9.11, with Bühler (1964) 51). D. here seems to apologize for a fault he has not yet committed – unless indeed this is not the real beginning. Jones (1978) 135 and Brunt (1973) 9 think that he implies that he is old; von Arnim (1898) 455 argues that he thinks of his exile as far behind him. These inferences are false: D. means only that the experiences of the vagrant, like those of the old, are agreeable to recall and tempting to retell: *forsan et haec olim meminisse iuuabit.*   **τὸ μηδένα διωθεῖσθαι ... λόγων** 'finding it difficult to reject any topic that comes one's way'. Cf. 102ff., 124ff., 12.38. D.'s insistence on his lack of relevance, apparently apologetic, is also an assertion of his 'philosophical' stance, and implies disparagement of the rhetoricians' constraints of scale and order. He may have in mind, e.g., Pl. *Rep.* 394D: οὐ γάρ ... πω οἶδα, ἀλλ' ὅπηι ἂν ὁ λόγος ὥσπερ πνεῦμα φέρηι, ταύτηι ἰτέον. It also suits him as a 'vagrant': cf. 1.56, where the characters of ἀδολέσχης and πλάνης go together, and you should not be afraid to tell a story to a powerful person, even if he despises you ὡς ἀδολέσχου καὶ πλάνητος.   **ἀλητικόν:** see 13.11, where D. describes the reactions of people to him during his exile: some called him ἀλήτης, some πτωχός, some φιλόσοφος. Cf. also 1.50ff., and Introd. p. 5.   **οἵοις ἀνδράσι ... ζῶσι:** like Odysseus (*Od.* 1.3), D. studies the people he meets on his travels, and wants to talk about them.   **ἐν μέσηι σχεδόν τι τῆι Ἑλλάδι** 'virtually in the heart of Greece'. D. is extremely fond of σχεδόν or σχεδόν τι, which soften the assurance of a statement: 39 occurrences in these three speeches alone. It is perhaps characteristic of his informal stance.

2-4 'Crossing from Chios, I was wrecked in Euboea. The crew joined some purple-fishers, and I was left alone, but fell in with a hunter. I had seen the deer he was chasing lying on the beach.'

2 Ἐτύγχανον μὲν ... : for this way of beginning, cf. 36.1. μέν arouses expectations, here answered by χειμῶνος δὲ γενομένου. But inceptive or preparatory μέν need not be answered: Denniston (1954) 382–4.

D. is crossing from Chios to mainland Greece, very likely to Athens. This suits the circumstances of his *relegatio*, which debarred him from Italy and from Bithynia: Jones (1978) 46. It was late in the season (for ἔξω implying 'after', cf. Xen. *Cyr.* 4.4.1), the boat is small, and there is a storm. Travellers were advised not to put to sea between mid-November and mid-March; but shipwreck was a hazard at any time: *haud ulla carina | consenuit* (Prop. 3.7.35–6).   **ἀκατίωι:** a light boat of some kind: undecked, and perhaps with each rower manning two oars.   **τὰ Κοῖλα τῆς Εὐβοίας:** cf. §7 and §31. It is clear from §31 that

D. means an area at the south end of Euboea – either on the outer coast (between Caphereus and Cyme: cf. Ptol. *Geogr.* 3.15.25) or between Caphereus and Geraistos. Ancient evidence (beginning with Hdt. 8.13) is confusing: Strabo (10.445C) identifies τὰ Κοῖλα with the coast on the inner side of the island, between Aulis and Geraistos. This at least cannot be what D. means. For differing views, see W. K. Pritchett, *Studies in ancient topography* II (1965) 19–23, and H. A. Mason in *Hesperia* 41 (1952) 136–40. The outer, harbourless coast fits the story best (note πρὸς τὸ πέλαγος, §7), and we can hardly be more precise than this.   **πορφυρεῖς:** fishers for *murex*, the source of the purple dye much prized for clothing, and found in many areas (Euboea, Laconia, Phocis, Thessaly and Gyarus are all mentioned in literary sources of the Roman period). The fishermen travelled far, and took on passengers (see below §55). The Stoic Zeno (Diog. Laert. 7.2) was travelling in the purple trade between Phoenicia and Piraeus when he was shipwrecked.

3 συχνόν 'a considerable distance'. Cf. e.g. Xen. *Anab.* 1.8.10, *Cyr.* 6.3.12.   **ἑώρων, ἐπιτυγχάνω:** the imperfect describes a situation, the historic present the event that interrupted it. See [Longinus] 25, with Russell's note: also WS §1893.   **τὴν ῥαχίαν** 'the beach', as in Thuc. 4.10 παρ' αὐτὴν τὴν ῥαχίαν.

4 ἠπορημένους 'at a loss'. The middle is not uncommon (LSJ s.v. 1; Dio 9.10 ἠποροῦντο), and the perfect indicates the state of bafflement.   **ἀποβιασθέν** 'forced back', and so driven to leap over the cliff.   **κυνηγέτην ... στολῆς:** hunters and shepherds, who work in lonely places, are likely people for shipwrecked sailors to encounter: cf. Virg. *Aen.* 1.305ff., where Venus in the guise of a huntress meets Aeneas in the *inculta* of Libya. The deer and the dogs can have left D. in little doubt; but the στολή must have been fairly distinctive – tunic, short cloak, cudgel perhaps (Pollux 5.17–18). It is something of a common-place that occupations can be detected from appearance: sailors, farm-ers, shopkeepers (Dio 72.1); goatherd (Theocr. 7.13).   **τὰ γένεια ὑγιῆ** 'healthily bearded'. ὑγιῆ is masc. acc. sing.   **κομῶντα ... ἐκόμων:** the allusion is to *Il.* 2.542 τῶι δ' ἅμ' Ἄβαντες ἕποντο θοοί, ὄπιθεν κομόωντες. In 2.12, D. makes Alexander say that Homer shamed the Euboeans by describing them as having a hair-style now associated with effeminate boys. This interpretation is perhaps his own. His views on beards and hair are often given: he took the 'philosophical' line (see esp. Musonius 114–16 Hense) that shaving was unnatural, wrote an 'encomium of hair' (lost, but known to Synesius), and thought a hand-some head of hair and a good beard a mark of a philosopher (72.1) and a king (47.25 κομῶ καὶ γένεια ἔχω; τοῦτο δ' ἴσως οὐ τυραννικόν ἐστιν ἀλλὰ βασιλικόν). Note also 36.17, where the citizen who shaves is supposed to do so in order to flatter Roman manners. (Romans did not wear beards much in the second half of the first century, but Hadrian's example then encouraged a change of fashion which was already under way.) See in general *RAC* s.v. Haar (B. Költing).

5-9 'I helped the hunter skin and cut up the deer, and accepted his invitation to his home, which was about five miles away.'

5 ὦ ξένε: the paradosis varies between ξένε and ξεῖνε. Wilamowitz' idea that 'the old form survived in the remote mountains' (*Griechisches Lesebuch* II 1.10) is shown to be fantasy by 36.4, where an 'Ionian'-looking person says ὦ ξένε, and by §10 below, where there is no dispute about the text.   **κάμοῦ ξυλλαμβάνοντος** 'with me *too* helping'.   τὰ ὀπίσθια 'the back legs'. The hunter is an ordinary mortal, not like Odysseus (*Od.* 10.161ff.) or Aeneas (Virg. *Aen.* 1.187ff.), who can take the whole animal home.

6 οὐκ ἔστι πλόϊμα 'it's not sailing weather'. Cf. Dion. Hal. *AR* 1.63 πλωΐμων δὲ γενομένων. The use of the plural adj. is perhaps felt as an Atticism: Schmid (1887) 120.   **καὶ μὴ ... φοβηθῆις**: of what is he 'not to be afraid'? Most obviously, the bad weather. This is why von Arnim at first proposed to transpose the phrase to follow ὁρᾶις; later, he preferred to place it after τὴν οἴκησιν, thereby making it a reassur-ance about the distance to be walked by an obviously unfit person (§8). The text is best left as it is; the speaker is not expected to be absolutely orderly. He repeats his reassurance below: ἀλλ' ἴθι καὶ μηδὲν δείσηις (§7).   **εἶπεν**: it is worth considering the small change to εἰπεῖν: 'it is not easy to say [sc. when the storm will stop]'.   **ὅταν ... τῆς Εὐβοίας**: clouds on hills are notoriously a sign of rain: Theophrastus, *De signis* 3.8 quotes Archilochus (fr. 56 Diehl = fr. 105 West):

> Γλαῦχ' ὅρα· βαθὺς γὰρ ἤδη κύμασιν ταράσσεται
> πόντος, ἀμφὶ δ' ἄκρα Γυρέων ὀρθὸν ἵσταται νέφος,
> σῆμα χειμῶνος.

So in Worcestershire:

> When Bredon Hill puts on his hat,
> Ye men of the vale, beware of that!

καὶ ἅμα ἠρώτα: in keeping with traditional hospitality, the hunter has offered help before asking questions. So Alcinous entertains Odysseus before asking who he is and whence he comes (*Od.* 7.238).   **ὑπὸ σπουδῆς τινος**: he does not tell us what his business was. Contrast 12.19, 36.1, where he represents himself as motivated by curiosity to see human behaviour or strange countries (in the tradition of Odysseus, Solon, Herodotus, and Plato).

7 ἐλαφροὶ παντελῶς πλέοντες 'sailing with a very light cargo'. They were unable to take much baggage on the tiny ἀκάτιον.   **ἀνακτήσηι σαυτόν** 'you shall revive yourself'. Cf. Longus 2.18.1 τὸ μάλιστα ἀνακτησάμενον αὐτόν – what most revived Daphnis was a kiss from Chloe.   **ἐπιμελησόμεθα ὅπως σωθῆις**: for the subjunctive in object clauses of this kind, see WS §2214.   **ἐπειδή σε . . . ἅπαξ** 'now that we have once come to know you'.

8 τῶν ἀστικῶν: cf. §49 for the countryman's contempt for the townsman's weakness. In Menander's *Dyskolos*, the young man from the city tries to prove himself to the old farmer whose daughter he loves by digging, hoeing, and working hard: 367ff., 766ff. (τρυφερὸς ὢν δίκελλαν ἔλαβες).   **πολλήν**: Geel, Mazon, and Avezzù defend ἄλλην, and if this is right, the hunter diagnoses some special debility in his guest, over and above what a 'townee' might be expected to have. D. does in fact often complain of ill health: 45.1, 47.23, 48.8, 52.1.   **οὐ γὰρ ἐπιβουλευθῆναί ποτε ἔδεισα**: it is a commonplace that the poor need not fear robbers: Juv. 10.22 *cantabit uacuus coram latrone uiator*. D.'s ἱμάτιον is a poor one, not valuable enough to tempt a thief.

9 ἐν ἄληι συνεχεῖ: this clearly refers to the exile (Intro. p. 4ff.), cf. esp. 19.1 διὰ τὴν ἄλην καὶ τὴν μεταβολὴν τοῦ βίου καὶ τὴν δοκοῦσαν . . . τοῦ σώματος ταλαιπωρίαν.   **ἀτὰρ οὖν δή**: a conspicuous Atticism, cf. Pl. *Rep.* 367E. Denniston (1954) 51 remarks that ἀτάρ was thought colloquial, not used by orators. ἀτὰρ οὖν occurs again in D., 77/78.2.   **πενία χρῆμα . . . ἱερὸν καὶ ἄσυλον**: in 6.60–2, D. makes Diogenes speak in terms appropriate to himself (cf. von Arnim (1898) 260), and very like this passage: 'I go where I wish, by night or alone by day; I feel safe, if it is necessary, walking through an army camp with no herald's staff (ἄνευ κηρυκείου) or even among robbers . . .'

10–63 'While we were walking the hunter told me his story: first (§§10–20) the history of the family, how the two shepherds stayed on when the owner's estates were confiscated by the emperor, and how they and their sons – himself and his partner – had lived by working a little land, but mainly by hunting; and then (§§21–63) the story of his one visit, as an adult, to the neighbouring city, following a demand for rent; this included his report of the speeches made in the assembly against him, by him, and by an old acquaintance in his defence.'

10 Ἡμεῖς γάρ: γάρ presupposes preceding words of the hunter (e.g. 'I live with my family') or a question from D.

11 οὔτε ... ἐκτησάμεθα: there is a slight inconcinnity here, since the first οὔτε-phrase is simply an adjective, while the second has a finite verb. Ros (1938) 428 cites some Thucydidean parallels: e.g. 8.21 τοῖς γεωμόροις μετεδίδοσαν οὔτε ἄλλου οὐδενός, οὔτε ἐκδοῦναι ... ἐξῆν. ἐλεύθεροι ... μισθοῦ βουκόλοι: these were free, hired herdsmen, not slaves: later (§49) it appears they were citizens of the neighbouring city. ἀνδρὸς μακαρίου 'a rich man'; cf. §107, §145. μακάριος, like Lat. *beatus*, often means 'rich'. Wilamowitz says it is 'aus der vulgären Sprache', but there is no evidence for this, and it is clearly classical: Pl. *Meno* 71A, Aristot. *EN* 1157b21.   πολλοὺς δὲ καὶ καλούς: Dindorf's correction is necessary, for πολύς always precedes καλός when they are combined (WS §2879).

12 ὑπὸ τοῦ βασιλέως: the great local magnate attracted the emperor's cupidity and suffered death and the confiscation of his property. Highet (1973) 35–40 and Jones (1978) 57 thought Nero; Cohoon prefers Domitian. Internal chronology favours Nero. The two sons, whose fathers were the original 'squatters', now have children of marriageable age, though they themselves did not marry till after the confiscation (§20). So, assuming that the dramatic date is during D.'s exile, which seems almost certain, the events here described must have taken place at least 20 years before 96; Vespasian is thus the latest emperor to be considered, and his predecessors seem more likely.   τὰ ἡμέτερα ἄττα βοΐδια 'our few poor little cattle'. Cf. Liban. *Decl.* 27.19 τὰ μὲν βοΐδια καὶ οἱ κύνες ζῶσι τὸν ἐμὸν βίον.

13 When the herds were confiscated, they were at the summer pasture in the mountains, where the herdsmen had made some shelter, not in the winter pasture on lower ground. For seasonal movement of cattle in ancient times, see Stella Georgoudi, 'La transhumance dans la Grèce ancienne', *R.E.G.* 87 (1974) 155–85. Varro, *De re rustica* 2.2.9–12 gives a picturesque account; Theocr. 7.111 reverses the experience to devise an ingenious curse against Pan – that he shall keep his flocks in Thrace in winter and Ethiopia in summer.   ὡς ἂν: WS §1766. οἶμαι is parenthetical.

14–15 The ecphrasis of the site is skilful: it stresses both the pleasantness and the practical convenience of the place (the woods are 'soft', and they are also free of flies and other pests); and it is constructed mainly of simple sentences, or lists of features. Cf. Horace's description of his farm, *Epist.* 1.16.5ff. *continui montes, ni dissocientur opaca | ualle … | fons etiam riuo dare nomen idoneus.* We may recall that D. wrote a famous ecphrasis (lost) on the hackneyed theme of Tempe (Synesius, *Dio* 3), which we see also in Aelian, *VH* 3.1: the hunters' place too is a *locus amoenus*, with a breeze to temper the summer heat, beautiful meadows, tall trees, and green grass all the year round. But there is a difficult detail: ἀπόρρυτον ἑκατέρωθεν ought to mean 'well drained at both ends' (cf. Xen. *Eq.* 4.3), but this is a strange thing to say of a deep ravine, and at a point in the description where the water-supply has not been mentioned. Von der Mühll's ἀπόρρηκτον, 'sheer', 'steep', is attractive, and is close to the original reading in M, ἀπόρρητον. The proximity of κατάρρυτοι (below) adds to the grounds for suspecting ἀπόρρυτον.

14 ἐποιοῦντο: sc. the fathers, whose activities are the subject of §§14–20.   οἶστρον 'gadfly', a well-known scourge of cattle: see M. Davies and J. Kathirithamby, *Greek insects* (1986) 162–4.

15 εὐθαλοῦς: cf. 12.4.   μέχρι ἂν εὕρωσι: 'until they should find'. They said to themselves 'we shall stay until we find': WS §2420.

16 ὑπέστρεψαν 'turned back' – perfectly natural behaviour in the dogs: a similar story in Varro, *De re rustica* 2.9.6: *e desiderio hominum diebus paucis postea canes sua sponte, cum dierum multorum uia interesset, sibi ex agris cibaria praebuerunt atque in Vmbriam ad pastores redierunt.*

17 τῶν ἄρκτων: Schwartz was right, for τῶν ἀνθρώπων makes no sense, and τῶν ἄλλων or τῶν τοιούτων would be too vague. The animal meant is a serious threat; the dogs 'join forces' to oppose it. To attack a bear on its hind legs would be something like attacking a man, as is said; and the detail that it appears 'early and late' is also appropriate to the bear. Bears were common in many mountainous areas of Europe until recent times, and D. certainly thinks of them as present in his Euboea, since the hunter has bearskins (§43). There is no reason to think this unrealistic. (O. Keller, *Die antike Tierwelt* 1 175ff. rejected Pausanias' evidence for bears in Greece in Roman times, but this was merely because the great huntsman Xenophon does not mention them: *contra*, J. M. C. Toynbee, *Animals in Roman life and art* 93ff.)   ὀψὲ μεταμανθάνοντες … πεινῶντες 'learning late in life to enjoy flesh rather than mash, because they could have a good meal of whatever was caught, whereas they went hungry if there was nothing'. [σίτου] is presumably a misplaced gloss on μάζης: cf. Grattius, *Cyn.* 307 for milk and *maza* as food for puppies, Arrian, *Cyn.* 8.1 for mash as food for hounds. Herd-dogs are safer if not allowed meat (cf. Varro 2.9.10); anyway, the herdsmen themselves would be living on bread, milk, and cheese rather than on meat most of the time.　**ἀμηιγέπηι**: cf. 7.103, 137; 12.26. This word – 'somehow or other' – is a conspicuous Atticism, recommended by Moeris (p. 50 Pierson) and ridiculed as affected by Lucian (*Lexiphanes* 21, *Rhet. praec.* 16).　**ὀψιμαθεῖς καὶ βραδύτεροι θηρευταί**: what is learned late is not learned so well, and the 'late learner' is a figure of fun: Isocr. 10.2, Pl. *Soph.* 251B, *Rep.* 409B, Theophr. *Char.* 27. It is only bad things that are best learned late, if at all: Iambl. *VP* 31.209 makes the point with reference to sex.

18 ἦν πεφηνός 'had come into view', equivalent to plpf. ἐπεφήνει. **οὔτε . . . τινά**: the implication is that they sought work in the town (cf. §21) or in a village (cf. §68, §73).　**τῆς θήρας ἡ χειμερινή** 'the winter part of the hunting'. This usage is commonest with πολύς (τῆς γῆς τὴν πολλήν, Thuc. 2.56) and ἥμισυς (ἐπὶ τῆι ἡμισείαι τῆς γῆς, Thuc. 5.31), but is sometimes found with other adjectives: so τὴν ἀργὴν τῆς χώρας, below §33. See WS §1313.

19 ὡς ἂν . . . σημαινόμενα 'because the ground on which they show is wet'.　**τηλαυγῆ** 'conspicuous', 'visible at a distance': an elevated word, but occurring in late prose: Strabo p. 807c ἀφορῶνται δ' ἐνθένδε τηλαυγῶς αἱ πυραμίδες.　**πράγματα ἔχειν** 'to have trouble'.　**ἔτι** 'also', unless there is a hyperbaton and it is to be taken with ἐν ταῖς εὐναῖς, 'still in their forms'.

20 καὶ νέοι: Dindorf's deletion (as a dittography of καὶ γενναῖοι) may be right, but Cohoon retains the words, νέοι meaning 'youthful': cf. 35.21 ζῶσι δὲ πλεῖον τετρακοσίων ἐτῶν, πάντα τὸν χρόνον τοῦτον ὡραῖοι καὶ νέοι.

21 Cf. §18: the fathers had been to the town in search of work, and the speaker, as a child, at an earlier time, before the crash. The city is never named: Carystus would fit (Jones (1978) 58), but D. is deliberately vague.　**ὥσπερ ἔχοντάς τι . . . δεδωκέναι ἄν**: the hunters' treatment of the official is in character – naïve, hospitable, anxious to please. It appears (§28) that they have farmed public land without making any payment or performing any public service. But the situation is hardly clear. If the land had belonged to the rich man whose property had been confiscated, it would presumably have gone to the *fiscus* or *patrimonium Caesaris*. How did the city have a claim on it? δεδωκέναι ἄν represents ἐδεδώκειν or ἐδεδώκεμεν ἄν, an alternative for ἔδωκα ἄν: WS §§2306–10.

22 Εἶδον οὖν: the countryman's culture-shock at seeing the city is something of a commonplace: Liban. *Decl.* 26.6, 27.6; but also Virgil, *Ecl.* 1.19, and Calp. Sic. *Ecl.* 7.   **οἰκήματα . . . τείχει**: the huntsman has never seen towers before, so he describes them in terms of what he knows, cf. §24. [τοὺς πύργους] is a gloss: it spoils the ἦθος.   **ὥσπερ ἐν λίμνηι**: nor has he ever seen a protected harbour, but thinks of a pond as the only possible place of calm water: so [ἐν τῶι λιμένι] is also out of character.

23 ἄγει οὖν 'Well then, he takes me ...' This 'almost purely temporal' use of οὖν is common in simple narratives: Denniston (1954) 425.   **τὴν κόμην** 'his hair', cf. §4. The official finds it absurd that he has to present this shaggy figure to the magistrates.

24 ἐκατέρωθεν 'at the two ends', cf. §14. The theatre is like his own valley, but blocked at one end by the rounded auditorium. The description is again in character: so Calpurnius Siculus (*Ecl.* 7.30–4) makes his rustic Corydon describe an amphitheatre as like the valley he knows: *qualiter haec patulum concedit uallis in orbem | ... | sic ibi planitiem curuae sinus ambit harenae*. Theatres were often places of assembly: with this scene cf. Acts 19.29–32 (Ephesus) ὥρμησάν τε ὁμοθυμαδὸν εἰς τὸ θέατρον ... ἄλλοι μὲν οὖν ἄλλο τι ἔκραζον· ἦν γὰρ ἡ ἐκκλησία συγκεχυμένη. **ἐπαινοῦντές τινας**: because much of the business would be the recognition of εὐεργεσίαι, acts of generosity or other services, by honorific decrees.

25 τὰ ἱμάτια ἐρρίπτουν: they 'threw off their cloaks' to run faster.

26 παριόντες 'coming forward' to the platform, as distinct from speaking ἐκ μέσων, 'from the floor'.   **οὐδὲ γρύζειν ἐπέτρεπον** 'they wouldn't let them so much as squeak'. Cf. Isaeus 8.27 οὐκ ἐτόλμησε γρύξαι τὸ παράπαν οὐδέν, and the phrase οὐδὲ γρῦ (e.g. Aristoph. *Plutus* 17, Demosth. 19.39).

27–32 The speech for the prosecution – which the hunter does not report in full (§33) – is given a comic colour by the hunter's interruptions and the exaggerated charges which the orator brings.

27 τὰ ἡμέτερα ὄρη: cf. τὰ ἡμέτερα, §28. In both places, the orator seems to miss a point; it would be more telling to speak of 'your' moun-

tains (ὑμέτερα), to engage the *demos*'s interests more closely.   **καὶ**
οἰκίας . . . ἐμπεφυτεύκασι: von Arnim objected to the exaggeration
in 'many houses' and moved πολλάς to go with ἀμπέλους. But this is to
miss the caricature: cf. §31, where he says they built 'whole villages'.
δωρεάν 'free of charge', LSJ s.v. II.

28 οἶμαι δέ . . . μηδὲ ἐληλυθέναι: cf. §31 οἶμαι . . . μηδὲ . . .
ἀπέχεσθαι. μή as the negative of infinitives in indirect speech is common
in D. as in most late authors: μή in fact increasingly displaces οὐ in all
kinds of subordinate constructions, and with all verbs that are not in
the indicative: Blass–Debrunner §§426–32, C. F. D. Moule, *Idiom-Book
of N.T. Greek*² (1959) 155–7. This is one of the areas in which even
Atticizing writers like D. diverge most obviously from classical norms.

29 ἐπιστρέψας 'turning back' to the audience, having finished his
abuse (ἐλοιδορεῖτο) of the hunter.   **οὐκ ἂν φθάνοιμεν** 'we couldn't
be too quick', cf. 12.62 for this classical idiom (LSJ s.v. IV.2).   **τοῖς**
θηρίοις τούτοις 'these animals'. Again a classical term of invective (e.g.
Demosth. 21.185).   **χίλια πλέθρα**: something under 100 hectares or
250 acres.   **τρεῖς χοίνικας Ἀττικάς**: about 3 litres. The number of
citizens eligible for the distribution is of course not stated; but it is clear
that this is a quite absurd prediction of yield.

30 τὸ δὲ πλῆθος οὐκέτ' ἐγέλων . . . ἀλλ' ἐθορύβουν: for this
common *constructio ad sensum* (recommended as Attic by Moeris (p. 2
Pierson)), cf. 7.59, 36.17, 4.83, 77/78.2; WS §950.   **τὴν εἰρωνείαν**
καὶ τὴν ὕβριν 'mockery and insolence'. εἰρωνεία has a variety of nuances
– pretended ignorance (Socratic 'irony'), mock-modesty, deceitfulness
(Theophr. *Char.* 1), frivolity (Demosth. *Phil.* 1.37); here the addition
of ὕβρις suggests it means simply 'mockery' (cf. Pl. *Symp.* 218D); but
the orator may be anticipating the suggestion he makes below that
the hunter is deliberately concealing his prosperity by appearing in
wretched clothing (§32).   **καθάρματος** 'outcast', another stock term
of classical invective, common in comedy and oratory.   **ἀπάγειν**
'arrest', 'take off to prison'.   **τοὺς κορυφαίους** 'the ringleaders' –
strictly chorus leaders (cf. 12.34, 36.21), but commonly used for the
'head' persons in any enterprise: e.g. Hdt. 3.82, Pl. *Tht.* 173C.

31 μηδὲ τῶν ναυαγίων ἀπέχεσθαι 'not even keep their hands off the
wrecks'. Caphereus (τὰς Καφηρίδας, sc. πέτρας), modern Cabo D'Oro,
is the traditional site of many wrecks. It was here that Nauplius lit the
fires to wreck the Greek fleet returning from Troy, in revenge for the

execution of his son Palamedes. Roman law took the threat of wreckers seriously, and Ulpian (*Digest* 47.9.10) regards it as a governor's duty to take precautions *ne piscatores nocte lumine ostenso fallant nauigantes, quasi in portum aliquem delaturi, eoque modo in periculum naues et qui in eis sunt deducant sibique exsecrandam praedam parent.* Cf. also Sen. *Contr.* 8.6, where prejudice against a rich defendant is heightened by accusing him of wrecking: *erat in summis montium iugis ardua diuitis specula: illic iste naufragiorum reliquias computabat, illic uectigal infelix et quantum sibi iratum redderet mare.* L. Friedlaender, *Roman life and manners*[7] (1908–13) I 282–3.

32 τὴν ἐξωμίδα 'his tunic', a one-sleeved garment leaving one shoulder bare, worn by slaves and poor men (cf. §86 for the implication that it is cheap): in Crates, *Epist.* 7, ἐξωμίδας Μεγαρικάς are essential clothing, just as beans, sprats, and water are essential nourishment, for one who wants no luxury. The orator's ruse is transparent: he has to explain the discrepancy between his account of the hunter's riches and his impoverished appearance, and so he says it is all a trick to win sympathy. He then ends by heightening *indignatio* (as a prosecutor's peroration should) with another reference to the wrecker Nauplius.   **ὡς πτωχὸς δηλονότι καὶ οὐδὲν ἔχων:** cf. Aristoph. *Plutus* 552–3 πτωχοῦ μὲν γὰρ βίος, ὃν σὺ λέγεις, ζῆν ἐστιν μηδὲν ἔχοντα, | τοῦ δὲ πένητος ζῆν φειδόμενον καὶ τοῖς ἔργοις προσέχοντα. The hunter is of course πένης but not πτωχός: the two terms are mutually exclusive (Vischer (1965) 30–1).

33–40 We are next given the speech of a moderate man, who argues that the hunter has done the city some service; in view of the decay of the territory, it would be sensible to encourage the poor to cultivate public land by giving them use of it rent-free. The speaker also makes a personal attack on the previous speaker, who lets his own sheep graze in the deserted agora.

33 ἐπιεικής 'decent'. The word generally connotes a willingness to forgo one's strict rights, and in general to act moderately: Dover, *Greek popular morality* (1974) 191. Strict Stoics were not sure that it was a quality of the truly 'good' man, because it involved pleading against due punishment for the wicked: 'the ἐπιεικής thinks the penalties imposed by the law on wrongdoers too harsh' (*SVF* III 640). In D., however, it is regularly praise: the good ruler needs ἐπιείκεια (1.5) to complement his θάρσος, and it roughly corresponds to *clementia*.   **ἠξίου σιωπῆσαι ... καὶ ἐσιώπησαν:** a gentle request is all

that is needed, for the speaker's known character ensures silence.
τὴν ἀργὴν τῆς χώρας: see on §18.

34 ὀλιγανθρωπίαν: see also on 7.121, 12.85, 36.6. The complaint
that Greece is depopulated is a common one at this period: Plu. *De
defectu oraculorum* 413F τῆς κοινῆς ὀλιγανδρίας [i.e. the universal depopulation of the provinces by στάσεις and wars] ... πλεῖστον μέρος ἡ Ἑλλὰς
μετέσχηκε. D. has similar complaints elsewhere: 7.121 on Thebes; 12.85
on Greece in general; 36.6 on Olbia; 33.25 on Thessaly and Arcadia;
31.158 (of the ancient powers of Greece, only Rhodes retains importance). So also Strabo: 7.7.10 (Dodona and Epirus generally); 8.4.11
(only 30 villages left in Laconia); 8.8.1 (Arcadia ruined by wars; pasture
of horses and asses has displaced population); 9.2.5 (Thebes 'not even
a decent village', though Tanagra and Thespiae survive). It is difficult
to evaluate these statements. There is doubtless some exaggeration, due
to the sense of contrast with classical greatness, as inferred from classical
authors and surviving monuments, and the *topos* of decline is such a
persistent feature of ancient literature that all its manifestations must
be suspect to the historian; none the less, the first century B.C. had been
quite disastrous (Mithridatic wars, Roman civil wars) and mainland
Greece no longer had much economic importance: cf. Rostovtzeff,
Economic and social history of the Roman Empire[2] (1957) 254, Bowersock
(1965) 85-100.

35 ἐνεργός 'at work', so 'cultivated': *SIG* 685.72.

36 ἀργίας: not 'unemployment' as a social evil, but rather 'idleness',
leading to the vices detected, e.g., by Plato in the Athenian democracy
(*Gorg.* 515E, with Dodds (1959) 356-7).

37 'Let them hold it free of charge for ten years; after this period let
them be assessed and give a small proportion of the crops, but nothing
from the animals.' These arrangements grant a right of *emphyteusis* (cf.
§27 ἐμπεφυτεύκασι), a term familiar in Roman law. Larsen (in *Economic
survey of ancient Rome* IV 477) cites a relevant parallel from Thisbe in
Boeotia (*SIG*[3] 884), where land was leased in small plots for planting,
rent-free for the first five years, and heritable. Similar is the scheme laid
down in the *Lex Manciana* from Tunisia (*CIL* VIII 25902), where a period
of free cultivation is allowed before rent becomes due. Herodian (2.4.6)
seems to say that Pertinax proposed a more ambitious scheme of the
same kind, with ten years' immunity, for all public land 'in Italy and
the provinces'. The plan reported in our passage is at least in accord

with the spirit of the times: Nerva and his successors aimed at a similar revival of rural life (and increase of population) by the arrangements of the *alimenta*, a set of schemes by which loans were offered to land-owners at low rates, and the interest paid for the support of children in the district. (On this see *CAH* xi 210ff., Duncan-Jones (1982) 288–322.)   **διακόσια πλέθρα**: some 20 hectares or 50 acres.   **ἵνα . . . προθυμούμενοι**: cf. note on §61 for the 'hortative' element in proposals for reward. Here the speaker assumes that citizen-status is a very attractive offer; his audience of citizens will agree.

38 καὶ . . . πυλῶν 'even the area in front of the gates' – i.e. the nearest cultivable land is not cultivated, whereas the area within the walls, which ought to be built up, is planted or grazed (**κατανέμεται**). **δεινῶς** 'terribly', here a simple intensifier; Thesleff (1954) 185 con-jectures it is Ionic rather than classical Attic: D. has it only four times.   **τῶν ῥητόρων**: for the genitive, see LSJ s.v. θαυμάζω 3. Here and below (§39) the word is used in the classical sense of 'speaker in the assembly', 'politician', not as 'teacher of rhetoric'.   **τὸ γυμνάσιον**: Eretria had a gymnasium, the evidence about Carystus is not clear. Heracles and Hermes are the most usual divine patrons of gymnasia.

39 δήπουθεν: cf. §94, §131. Recommended by Moeris (p. 130 Pierson) as an Attic equivalent of δηλονότι (which D. uses §40), and ridiculed by Lucian (see on ἀμηιγέπηι, §17), this word is not confined to strict Atticists, since Strabo and Plutarch use it. D.'s use is odd: 16 of his 25 examples are in *Or.* 31 (*To the Rhodians*), which Jones and others regard as an early work.   **ὑπὸ τοῦ θέρους** 'by the harvest', LSJ s.v. ii.

40 Καὶ τοιαῦτα . . . λωποδυτῶσιν 'and, though he does this sort of thing, he wants to haul off unfortunate private citizens to prison – presumably in order that no one should work in future, but those outside the town turn to brigandage, and those inside to mugging'. δηλονότι makes it clear that the ἵνα-clause expresses the assumed purpose, not (as it grammatically might, in Greek of this period) the expected consequence, of the politician's actions. The λωποδύτης is strictly a robber who steals his victim's clothes; but the word has a somewhat wider sense here.   **ἔρημον . . . κατελάβοντο** 'they farmed the land when it was barren and useless and thus took possession of it'.

41–63 The hunter next relates how he was invited to speak. After some interchange with his opponent and with others, he settled to a denial of the accusation of wrecking (§§51–3). His story was confirmed

(§§53–9) by a man whom he rescued two years ago; gifts and reward followed (§§60–3).

41 ἀντέλεγεν ... ἐλοιδοροῦντο ... ἐκέλευον: the rest of the debate is not given. For the use of the imperfect with verbs of saying and the like, see WS §1891; so also (e.g.) ἐπηρώτα (§43), ἠρώτα (§44).   **τῶν καθημένων:** they are sitting in the theatre.   **οὐθέν:** see LSJ s.v. οὐθείς. The form is not common in Dio's text, but we cannot say how consistent he was in this matter.

42 οὔτε ἵππους ... οὔτε βοῦς: an answer to §31. He does not deny the slaves (ἀνδράποδα) there mentioned, though it is plain that he has none.   **ἐδώκαμεν ... ἦμεν:** indicatives denote a purpose not fulfilled because dependent on an unrealized condition: WS §2185c. He would have liked to be generous and one of the rich (τῶν μακαρίων) himself.

43 Τὰ γὰρ ἄρκεια ... αὐτῶν 'Well, the bearskins are hard, and the goatskins not equal in value to these [i.e. the deerskins he offers], but some old and others small.' With UB's τἆλλα, the old and small skins would be of some other kind, not previously mentioned. Cf. §57 ὀπτῶντες ... τὰ δὲ ἕψοντες, with K–G ii 265 n. 4.   **ἄγροικον ... ἀγρούς:** the play on words is difficult to reproduce. Grammarians (Ammonius, *De diff. voc.* 6 Nickau) distinguish ἄγροικος 'boorish', which is what the orator means, from ἀγροῖκος 'living in the country', which is how the hunter understands what was said to him; so he replies 'There you are, talking about farms again.' In §108, D. himself seems to use the word literally, and it should perhaps be written ἀγροῖκοι there.

44 τάλαντον ... Ἀττικόν: a (silver) talent represents a large sum, several thousand pounds of today's money. The hunter again misunderstands; he takes it as a measure of weight (ἵσταμεν, 'we weigh'), and supposes they want the rent in kind. A 'talent' in this sense is about 20 kg.   **δίδομεν** 'we offer'.

45 Δύο ... μεδίμνους: i.e. 96 χοίνικες, about 105 litres: they have less wheat than barley or millet, easier crops on poor ground.   **κέγχρων** 'millet', *Panicum miliareum*, still used for human as well as animal food in the Mediterranean countries: not so nice as wheat, cf. §57, where the hunter's family eat millet but give their guests wheaten bread.   **ἡμίεκτον:** 4 χοίνικες, a little over 4 litres.   **τῆτες** 'this year', a word known from Old Comedy (e.g. Aristoph. *Ach.* 400), and probably used by D. here to lend archaic colour. He does not use it elsewhere.

46 ὅπως δὲ ἥξει 'but make sure he comes …' WS §2213: the third person is uncommon in this construction, but cf. Lys. 1.21 ὅπως … μηδεὶς ἀνθρώπων πεύσεται. **Πόσαι γὰρ … ἄμπελοι;** 'Oh, how many vines have you?' γάρ presents the question as raised by the hunter's remark that they do not have any wine-skins. Denniston (1954) 81ff. **ἐπαφῶσιν** 'leave them for us', 'let them grow': from ἐπαφίημι. An odd use: ἀφίημι (LSJ s.v. III) would be more natural. (Schmid (150) and Koolmeister–Tallmeister, s.v., take it from ἐπαφάω, 'touch lightly'; but this does not make sense.)

47 βοῦς κολοβή: a cow without horns or with the horns sawn off. κολοβός is used also of damaged clothing (Artemid. 2.3) and broken teeth (Artemid. 1.31). The following list, in its detail and *naïveté* (μοσχάριον … πάνυ καλόν), is in character. δρέπανα are billhooks (in Pollux 5.19, a list of tools and weapons) and are for cutting wood; δίκελλαι are two-pronged mattocks; the λόγχαι must be wide and sharp (Pollux, *ibid.*); and each man has his own μάχαιρα ('knife', 'dagger') to cut up the meat (everything else is common property).   **σκηναῖς καλαῖς** 'beautiful huts'; again the *naïveté* of praising one's own property. Naber (*Mnem.* 38 (1910) 73) was suspicious of this banal phrase, and proposed καλιαῖς, 'huts', deleting σκηναῖς as a gloss on this. He could be right.   **τὸ σιτάριον** 'our little stock of corn'.

48 ὅπου … κατορύττετε: the suggestion that money may be buried seems absurd to the hunter, who thinks it makes sense to bury only what will grow in the ground. The orator, however, is alluding to a common practice. Misers – and many people in times of danger – hoarded money in this way, as Plutus himself says in Aristophanes (*Plut.* 23–4): ἦν μὲν γὰρ ὡς φειδωλὸν εἰσελθὼν τύχω, | εὐθὺς κατώρυξέν με κατὰ τῆς γῆς κάτω.

49 πολῖται τῆς πόλεως ἐσμεν: his father had told him that they were citizens of the city, and had once actually shared in a distribution of money. Such largesses were common: they might be from the emperor or a governor, but more often from the expected, and morally compulsory, generosity of wealthy citizens. Rural populations were normally accepted as citizens: Ulpian (*Digest* 50.1.30) states the principle: *qui ex uico ortus est, eam patriam intellegitur habere, cui reipublicae uicus ille respondet.* Distributions, however, might be restricted to urban residents, and the hunter's father was perhaps lucky: see on this passage R. Duncan-Jones, *The economy of the Roman Empire*² (1982) 259.   **τρέφομεν ὑμετέρους**

πολίτας: countrymen make good soldiers (Roman armies were largely recruited from rural populations) and hunting was believed to be a particularly good preparation for military life. See, e.g., Hor. *Odes* 3.6.37–8 (*rusticorum mascula militum | proles*), Xen. *Cyneg.* 1, Philostr. *Heroicus* 37 (52 Lannoy), Max. Tyr. *Or.* 24 Hobein.   πρὸς λήιστας ἢ πρὸς πολεμίους: piracy on sea and brigandage by land (λήιστας covers both) were common in all periods; open warfare in which the city's forces are engaged is hardly possible under Roman rule, and there is thus a touch of unreality about the reference to πολεμίους. The 'peace' which prevails is the *pax Romana*.   μὴ γὰρ . . . τὰς γυναῖκας: the hunter no doubt takes an unfavourable view of the orator's physical condition: cf. §8 on the weakness of townsmen.

50 καθελοῦμεν: a late form of the future of καθαιρέω.   ὑπενεγκεῖν . . . τοῦ χειμῶνος: the genitive is odd (D. has ὑπενεγκεῖν τὸ θέρος, 3.80, the normal usage), but cf. the use with ἀνέχεσθαι, 'endure' (LSJ s.v. ἀνέχω 3; K–G ɪ 388).   εἰ δὲ οὐκ ἐνθάδε ζῶμεν: εἰ here 'approaches the sense of ἐπεί' (WS §2698d), and so οὐ is properly used rather than μή. So: 'But if we do not live here [sc. 'as is the case'] and are not causing extra inconvenience over and above the crowding of so many people inhabiting the same space, we don't therefore deserve to be moved.' Heavily ironical: it is not a crime to live out of town. Wilamowitz preferred M's μισεῖσθαι, on the ground that the speaker would contradict himself if he first asked to be housed within the walls, and then argued against it. But the point is more forceful as it is.

51 περὶ τῶν ναυαγίων: cf. §31.   μικροῦ ἐξελαθόμην: this technique of 'nearly forgetting' is recommended by Hermogenes (359 Rabe) as a device of ἀλήθεια, 'sincerity'.   καὶ ἀδύνατόν ἐστιν . . . λαβεῖν: a naïve remark, and so in character. The speaker does not seem to see that he may be giving the impression that he might wreck a ship if there was anything to be got from it.   τὴν τέφραν 'wood dust', 'splinters' (?). The word usually denotes 'ash' produced by burning, but this is not appropriate here.   μόνη . . . ἀπρόσιτος: this shore is 'the only one of them all that is inaccessible' (by sea). μόνη 'stresses the pre-eminence of the quality' (Thesleff (1954) 160); it is a means of intensification, and should not be pressed literally.

52 †λάρους†: there are several possible corrections available, none wholly convincing: ταλάρους 'baskets', λάρκους 'baskets' (such as charcoal-burners use: Aristoph. *Ach.* 333), ταρρούς 'oar-blades'. None

of these things is a likely source of profit, and the baskets at least seem unlikely objects to fasten to the Sacred Oak. ⟨οὓς⟩ must anyway be added:
καὶ τούτους, 'even these', picks up the object.   ἐκβεβρασμένους
'washed up', cf. Hdt. 7.188ff., esp. 190 πολλὰ μὲν χρύσεα ποτήρια
ὑστέρωι χρόνωι ἐκβρασσόμενα ἀνείλετο. Ulpian, *Digest* 47.9.6: *qui eiecta
naue quid rapuit, hoc edicto tenetur.* '*eiecta*' hoc est quod *Graeci aiunt* ἐξεβράσθη.
εἰς τὴν δρῦν τὴν ἱεράν: the oak is especially associated with Zeus (so
the appeal ὦ Ζεῦ is apt); so in Homer, who has a Sacred Oak by the
Scaean Gates (*Il.* 5.693 etc.), and evidence for this form of cult is
common from Hellenistic and later times (O. Kern, *RE* s.v. Baumkultus
162ff., Nilsson (1941) I 194). The verb ἀνέπηξα is appropriate: the
ἐν- compound would imply that the object was stuck *into* the tree.
κερδᾶναι κέρδος: the cognate accusative (WS §1564) lends some
solemnity to his declaration.   **μέχρι τῶν οἰκουμένων** 'as far as the
inhabited parts'.

53 μὴ ... πράγματι 'I hope none of you has such an accident.'
Despite Denniston (1954) 94, γάρ seems here to have no force other
than to introduce a wish, as in εἰ γάρ. The orator ends by cap-
turing his audience's good will by wishing them well.   **ἄλλος ...
καταψευσόμενος** 'here's another of the same sort, I dare say, going to
tell lies against me'. τυχόν, 'maybe', is common in D., but less so than
the classical synonym ἴσως.

54 πάλαι ... ὅμως 'doubtful about (or 'half recognizing') him for
a long time I yet couldn't believe it'.

55 Σωκλέους: here and below (§59 Σωτάδη) D. chooses common names, also appropriate to voyages and rescues, since they are
related to σώιζω, 'save'.   **τρίτον ἔτος** 'two years ago', WS §1585.
πορφυρεῖς: see on §2.   **ἐν φασκωλίοις** 'in bags'.   **σκέπην** 'hut',
'shelter': σκέπη is usually less concrete – 'shelter', 'protection' – but the
meaning here seems clear.

56 ἐβοῶμεν ... εἰσάγει: the tenses are carefully chosen, the historic
present indicating the event that put an end to their standing there and
calling out.   **στέατι** 'lard', hard animal fat, a cheap substitute for
olive oil; the detail is doubtless realistic, but there is a literary precedent
in *Od.* 21.178, where Antinous tells the goatherd Melanthius to bring
out a round cake made of στέαρ so that the suitors can anoint themselves
before trying out the bow. D.'s rustics preserve Homeric ways.

57 περιβαλόντες οἷς εἶχον 'dressing us in what they had'.   **ἄρτους**

πυρίνους . . . κέγχρον ἐφθήν: cf. §45. The 'boiled millet' will be a sort of porridge. Hospitality continues in the same vein, the hosts eating less well.

58 προὔπεμψαν 'escorted', 'accompanied'.   **ἐνέδυσε:** the subject is now singular, i.e. the man he has now recognized.   **ἄλλο τι ῥάκος** 'some rag instead', WS §1272. There is of course no implication that the tunic is a 'rag'; that would be very impolite.   **μετὰ τοὺς θεούς:** cf. 36.14.

59 ἤκουεν . . . καὶ ἐπήινουν: see on §30.   **ὁ δὲ δῆμος . . . οὐ φιλοῦσιν ἀλλήλους:** the hunter kisses his old friends. As Wilamowitz says, the crowd laughs at the sight of the leather-clad rustic kissing these elegant gentlemen; but a moral point is made by the double sense of φιλεῖν, since the hunter then says what D. means us to interpret 'they do not love one another in cities'. On kissing as a common gesture of friendship (on hands and face or forehead), see Kroll, *RE* Suppl. v 511ff. It is common in Homer: e.g. *Il.* 6.474, 8.371, *Od.* 21.224 (where Odysseus reveals himself to Eumaeus and Philoetius).

60 εἰς τὸ πρυτανεῖον ἐπὶ ξένια: a standard form of reward, cf. e.g. *IG* ii² 6.15 καλέσαι δὲ καὶ ἐπὶ ξένια Εὐρύπυλον ἐς τὸ πρυτανεῖον ἐς αὔριον (403 b.c. or later).   **οὐ γὰρ . . . τιμῆς:** a characteristically rhetorical period, sharply contrasting with the hunter's narrative style. 'It is inconceivable that, whereas he would have won many great rewards if he had protected a citizen with his shield in war and saved his life, he should not be worthy of any reward now, when he has saved two citizens and maybe others who are not here now.' No question-mark is needed at τιμῆς. See Lysias 10.8 with Jebb's note (*Attic orators*² (1888) 273), Lysias 31.28, Pl. *Gorg.* 512A, with Dodds *ad loc.*

61 ἵνα . . . ἀλλήλοις: this 'hortative' element is regular in honorific decrees: e.g. *IG* xii 9.906 (*SIG* 898: Chalcis, third century) καλῶς ποιεῖτε ἀμειβόμενοι τοὺς ἀγαθοὺς ἄνδρας . . . μόνως γὰρ οὕτως καὶ τοὺς ἄλλους ἐπὶ πολλοῖς προτρέπομεν; *IG* xii 7.388 (Amorgos, third century) ὅπως οὖν καὶ ὁ δῆμος ὁ ἡμέτερος φαίνηται τοὺς καλοὺς καὶ ἀγαθοὺς τῶν ἀνδρῶν τιμῶν καταξίως τῶν εἰς ἑαυτὸν εὐεργεσιῶν καὶ πολλοὶ προτρέπωνται ἐπὶ τὸ εὐεργετεῖν τὸν δῆμον. Jones (1978) 61. For ἐπαρκεῖν, 'help out', cf. §68, §82.   **ἐγὼ παρ' ἐμαυτοῦ δίδωμι:** the speaker's generosity makes him also a benefactor, and so gives him prestige. Cf. Pliny's offer (*Epist.* 4.13.5) to pay a third of the cost of the schoolmaster at Comum.

62 εἶπον ὅτι οὐ δύνασαι: for ὅτι 'with the value of quotation marks' see WS §2590a.   **ἐν τῶι δέρματι** 'in your leather'.   **ἄνωθεν** 'on top'. He would be a ridiculous figure in goatskin *and* himation; and perhaps it is suggested that he doesn't want to risk losing the goatskin.

63 ⟨μὴ⟩ λήψεσθαι: cf. §28.   **τίς λάβηι:** indirect deliberative question, 'who is to get it': WS §1805. The point in ὅπως κατορύξηι refers to §48.   **ἀπ' ἐκείνου . . . ἠνώχλησε** 'thenceforth, no one troubled us'.

64 The main narrative resumes (from §10). 'We were now at the huts, and I had to say that he must have failed to declare his lovely garden to the authorities; but he told me he had been quite truthful, because the garden wasn't made till later.'   **γελάσας:** WS §1873c2. Cf. μειδιάσας §70, §77, etc.

65–6 'We went in and had a simple meal, waited on by the daughter of the house. I thought how much happier all this was than the houses of the rich and powerful.'

65 κατακλιθέντες . . . ὑψηλῆς: they rest on beds of leaves and skins, like the inhabitants of Plato's 'first city' – ὑῶν πόλις as Glaucon calls it (*Rep.* 372B) – who κατακλινέντες ἐπὶ στιβάδων ἐστρωμένων μίλακί τε καὶ μυρρίναις εὐωχήσονται. This must be in D.'s mind: cf. below §§129–32 for his concern with *Rep.* But this is also a pastoral scene: cf. Longus 2.3.1 ἐκ φυλλάδος στιβάδας ὑποστορέσας.   **ὡραία γάμου** 'ripe for marriage', WS §1418.   **ἐνέχει** 'poured': for the form, see W. G. Rutherford, *The new Phrynichus* (1881) 300. D. writes correct Attic. In Longus too (3.8.2) the daughter (Chloe) pours the wine.   **μέλανα οἶνον ἡδύν** 'good red wine', as opposed to white (οἶνος λευκός, Longus 1.16.4); it is 'sweet' because it is mature enough, and ἡδύς is more a general mark of approval than a description of a specifically 'sweet' taste. Cf. *Od.* 2.349–50.

66 καίτοι . . . ἠπιστάμην was omitted in PH by accident (the scribe's eye jumped from the preceding ἠπιστάμην). Wifstrand (*Eikota* 16) argued that ἰδιωτῶν was an interpolation resulting from an attempt to make sense of the resulting text. He deletes it and reads οὐ μόνον ἀλλὰ καὶ σατραπῶν, 'and indeed governors as well'. For this elliptical use of οὐ μόνον ἀλλὰ καί cf. 43.10 καὶ τοὺς νέους ἐκώλυε διαφθείρεσθαι, οὐ μόνον ἀλλὰ καὶ τοὺς πρεσβυτέρους.   **σατραπῶν:** i.e. provincial governors (cf. §93). Greek literary writers liked to avoid technical terms of Roman administration; it helped to make the writing more classical. This use of σατράπης occurs several times in D. (47.9, 49.6, 50.6, 66.12, 77/78.28), usually (as here) in an enumeration of high offices. **μάλιστα . . . ἄθλιοι** 'extremely miserable'. ἔτι μᾶλλον seems to go with τότε: 'even more (did they seem miserable) then, when I observed the poverty and liberty in that place ...' For D.'s Stoic moralizing interpretation of 'freedom', see esp. *Or.* 14 and 15. **καὶ τούτοις**: i.e. in the pleasures of eating and drinking. 'Better is a dinner of herbs where love is, than a stalled ox and hatred therewith' (Proverbs 15.16). The superiority of plain fare is a commonplace: J. E. B. Mayor, *Thirteen Satires of Juvenal* (1889) I xxvi–xxxv applies ancient castigation to nineteenth-century luxury, and the passage makes good reading.

67–9 'When we had finished, the other hunter came in with his son, who was bringing a hare as a present for the girl. I asked about the family, and the wife explained that they had one daughter well married; the younger girl and the boy blushed when I asked if she was to be married too.'

67 οὐκ ἀγεννές 'handsome', a common type of litotes: WS §2694. **λαγὼν φέρων**: a hare is a common courting gift and is specially appropriate to the hunter. It is certainly alive, to be kept as a pet. (See Dover (1978) 4 n. 5 for its use in homosexual contexts; *Anth. Pal.* 7.207 (Meleager = *Hellenistic Epigrams*, ed. Gow and Page, 4320–6) for an epitaph on a hare that dies of over-feeding while in the possession of a beautiful girl.)

68 πρὸς ἄνδρα ἐδόθη . . . εἰς κώμην: an odd sentence, the second πρὸς ἄνδρα taking up and defining the first: 'she was given to a husband long ago, and she's got big children now – to a rich husband in the village'. διδόναι πρός τινα, 'to give in marriage to ...', is unusual (we expect the dative); but for the addition of the place (εἰς κώμην) cf. *Od.* 15.367 τὴν μὲν ... Σάμηνδε δόσαν. Herwerden (*Mnem.* N.S. 22 (1894) 125ff.) would recast: πάλαι πρὸς ἄνδρα πλούσιον εἰς κώμην ἐδόθη καὶ τέκνα κ.τ.λ. Something like this may well be right.

69 ὁπηνίκα 'when'. Dindorf need not be right to add ἄν, since late authors are not consistent in following the Attic prose rule requiring it with subjunctives in general conditional, relative or temporal clauses: Schmid (1887) I 244 (Lucian). This passage is used by Garnsey (1988) 56–7 to illustrate an exchange economy, where neighbours and family groups co-operate to be self-sufficient. D. seems to make a point of this. **⟨πέρυσι δὲ⟩**: Casaubon's excellent πέρυσι, 'last year', is right, since we need a date. It fell out before πυρούς (haplography); Wilamowitz' παρ' αὐτῶν is unnecessary.   εὐθὺς τῆς θερείας 'as soon as we had harvested'.   ἠρυθριασάτην 'blushed'. Like other classicizing authors, D. sometimes affects the dual: Schmid (1887) 1 87 cites some 20 instances, as against about 80 in Lucian (II 35). It had disappeared from the spoken language.

70–80 'The girl's father made the situation clear. I asked how they chose the day for the marriage, and after some banter about the full moon and the availability of a pig for sacrifice, it was decided to have it the day after tomorrow; I was asked to stay, and gladly did so. How much better than the formalities of rich weddings!'

70 Δοκῶ μέν 'in my opinion': for μέν *solitarium* see WS §2896, Denniston (1954) 380.   ἔνδον ἐνθάδε 'here in the house'.   "Οταν μὴ μικρὸν ἦι τὸ σελήνιον 'When the moon isn't small.' The effect of the diminutive is perhaps to give a touch of common speech (so Wilamowitz: cf. λινάριον §71, οἰνάριον §76, βοΐδια §12) rather than to mean 'the little moon' (as LSJ take it). For full moon as a lucky day for weddings, cf. Eur. *IA* 716–17 τίνι δ' ἐν ἡμέραι γαμεῖ; | ὅταν σελήνης εὐτυχὴς ἔλθηι κύκλος, Pind. *Isthm.* 8.43 ἐν διχομηνίδεσσιν δὲ ἑσπέραις ἐρατὸν λύοι κεν χαλινόν (Thetis). But Hesiod (*WD* 800) recommends the fourth of the month, and the new moon is often advised (Plu. fr. 105 Sandbach).   αἰθρίαν λαμπράν 'bright, clear weather'.

71 καταπονῶ 'exhaust', 'run down'.   ὑφίσταμαι 'stand up to'. Cf. Philostr. *Heroicus* 190 (52.15 Lannoy) τὸ δὲ ὑφίστασθαι μυκωμένους καὶ θαρσεῖν τὰς αἰχμὰς τῶν κεράτων, 'to stand up to them when they bellow and not be afraid of the points of their horns'. Xen. *Cyneg.* 10.12 gives a vivid (and alarming) account of how to face a wild boar, looking into his eye and watching the movements of the head.   τῶι λιναρίωι 'net', 'snare'.

72 Λέγει . . . ἔφη: such repetitions are common in Xenophon (e.g. *Oecon.* 10.1, *Symp.* 1.15, *Mem.* 1.2.52) from whom D. (cf. §77) adopts it. It makes the story seem more fluently told: 'So he says, "Well, boy", he says . . .'   ἔστ' ἂν . . . πορευθείς 'until he has gone and bought a victim'. Only domestic animals were offered in sacrifice, game would not do ('Wild wird nicht geopfert', Wilamowitz (1902) *ad loc*). The origins of sacrificial rites in the practice of hunting (Burkert (1985) 58) are remote and do not override this principle.

73 ἠρώτων . . . ἔφη '"Is that true?" they asked him; and he said

that it was.'   **καὶ πόθεν σοι;** 'How come?' Cf. LSJ s.v. πόθεν
1 4.   **ἀλόντι:** he throws the skin he is wearing over his capture (so
Geel).   **ἠλλαξάμην:** whereas his father had thought of going to buy
one, the boy gets his porker by exchange.   **χοῖρον:** a young pig, so
a cheap sacrifice; it needed to be fattened up.   **συφεόν** 'pigsty'.

74 Ταῦτα . . . ἄρα . . . 'So that's why . . .' Denniston (1954) 37: the
idiom is common in Aristophanes.   **γρυλιζούσης** 'grunting', also an
Aristophanic word (*Ach.* 746, *Plutus* 307).   **ἀνήλισκες:** this also goes
with ταῦτα . . . ἄρα: 'so that's why you used up the barley as you did'.
εὐβοΐδες 'chestnuts'. Athenaeus (54B) tells us that Εὐβοϊκὰ κάρυα or
κάστανα are hard to digest and produce wind, but are fattening if you
can take them. It seems that they are not as fattening to pigs as barley
or acorns.   **εἰ μή γε . . . ἐσθίειν** 'seeing that she wouldn't eat acorns'.
Cohoon's εἰ μόνας γε . . . means 'if she was only willing to eat nuts' –
he thus takes βαλάνους generically, including the chestnuts; so also
Avezzù.   **αὐτόθεν** 'then and there', 'at once'.

75 οὖα τετμημένα 'sliced sorb-apples'. The fruits of *Sorbus domestica*
can be sliced, sun-dried and stored; they can be softened by boiling in
water for winter use. Cf. Palladius 2.15.4.   **μέσπιλα** 'medlars'. As
the season is late autumn (§2), these may be fresh from the tree; but
again, they can be preserved (Palladius 4.10.22).   **μῆλα χειμερινά**
'winter apples'. According to Artemidorus 1.73, this is a very tart fruit,
also called μῆλα κυδώνια ('quinces'); but it is unclear what precise
species D. means.   **τῆς γενναίας σταφυλῆς:** cf. §46 εἰσὶ δὲ γενναῖαι
σφόδρα. The phrase recalls Pl. *Laws* 844E ὃς δ' ἂν τὴν γενναίαν νῦν
λεγομένην σταφυλὴν ἢ τὰ γενναῖα σῦκα ἐπονομαζόμενα ὀπωρίζειν
βούληται, where these kinds are distinguished from ἄγροικος ὀπώρα,
which was stored in bulk or used for wine. So these are 'choice grapes',
for eating, fresh and juicy (σφριγῶντας).

All this is still like Plato's 'first city' (*Rep.* II 372), but also like the
Cynic asceticism of Diogenes: in D. *Or.* 6.62 Diogenes is content with
μῆλα καὶ κέγχροι καὶ κριθαὶ καὶ ὄροβοι καὶ τὰ εὐτελέστατα τῶν ὀσπρίων
καὶ φηγὸς ὑπὸ τῆι τέφραι καὶ ὁ τῆς κρανείας καρπός.   **καταψήσασα
. . . πτερίδα:** she 'wiped it down with leaves after the meat, and put
down fresh fern'.

76 ἄρτους . . . καθαρούς 'white loaves'.   **ἐρεβίνθους φρυκτούς**
'roasted chickpeas'.   **τὸν ἀδελφόν** 'her brother'.   **[καὶ τὴν
ἀδελφιδῆν]:** Emperius was right to delete this phrase rather than καὶ

τὴν θυγατέρα. The bridegroom's mother greets her brother and *his* daughter (i.e. her own niece). The sentence is obscure enough to make καὶ τὴν ἀδελφιδῆν a likely gloss; we should naturally expect the relationship of τὸν ἀδελφόν and τὴν θυγατέρα to be to the same person (the woman who has just entered).   **πάλαι ἔτρεφεν** 'was feeding all this time'.   **ἄλφιτα καὶ ἄλευρα** 'barley and wheat meal', used to sprinkle over the victim before it is killed. πεποίηται is not the natural verb: Schenkl deletes.

77 τὸν κηδεστήν 'his kinsman', i.e. his future father-in-law, who is also his uncle.   **Αὕτη μέν:** cf. Denniston (1954) 381.

78 λεπτὸς . . . λεπτότερος αὐτοῦ: the young man shows one of the classical symptoms of love, losing weight; he is also distraught and unhappy. See Nisbet and Hubbard on Hor. *Odes* 1.13.4; Ov. *Met.* 9.535ff.; C. Miralles in *Erotica antiqua*, ed. B. P. Reardon (1976) 20–1.   **λεπτότερος αὐτοῦ** 'thinner than ever'. For this 'reflexive comparative', see WS §1078. D. has other examples: 8.34, 67.5.

79 Οὐ σύ γε 'No, you didn't': sc. ὀψόμενος ἐξῆλθες.   **ἀλύων** 'in a state of distraction'. The word is mainly poetical (from Homer on) but is used by later prose writers: cf. Longus 1.28.2 λαμβάνουσι καὶ τὸν Δάφνιν ἀλύοντα ('wandering idly') περὶ τὴν θάλασσαν.   **Εἰς τρίτην** 'the day after tomorrow': WS §1686b.

80 προμνηστριῶν 'marriage-brokers', 'matchmakers'. Other words for the same office are προμνήστρις (Xen. *Mem.* 2.6.36) and νυμφεύτρια (Liban. *Decl.* 26.13). The practice of using women to bring the parties together was a feature of classical Athens (Aristoph. *Clouds* 41), and that is why it is referred to in later literature, whether or not it was current practice. An introduction that turned out badly was a source of much trouble: Xen. *ibid.* cites the opinion of Aspasia: τοὺς γὰρ ἐξαπατηθέντας ἅμα μισεῖν ἀλλήλους τε καὶ τὴν προμνησαμένην, Liban. *ibid.* represents the δύσκολος as complaining to the 'matchmaker' of having been misled about his wife's talkativeness.   **προικῶν . . . ἀπεχθειῶν** 'dowries and bride-price, promises and deceit, agreements and contracts, and, ultimately, often abuse and hatred in the marriage itself'.

81–2 'I have told this story not just to talk idly, but to show from my own experience whether thè life of the poor really is worse than that of the rich. The farmer in Euripides was wrong: the poor are actually more hospitable than the rich.'

See Introd. p. 9–10. This section clearly states that a type of life was proposed as the subject of the speech (οὕπερ ἐξ ἀρχῆς ὑπεθέμην βίου), and that the issue was the decency and 'closeness to nature' of the life of the poor.

81 ἀδολεσχεῖν: cf. D.'s comment on his πολυλογία, §1. Socrates too was accused of ἀδολεσχία (Eupolis fr. 352 Kock, τὸν πτωχὸν ἀδολέσχην); in Pl. *Phaedo* 70c he defines the charge: ὡς ἀδολεσχῶ καὶ οὐ περὶ προσηκόντων τοὺς λόγους ποιοῦμαι. D.'s protestations on this subject thus suit his Socratic pose: see also §102 and §124 below.

ὑπεθέμην 'set out', 'propounded'; Cohoon translates 'adopted', but the word can hardly mean this; and we cannot escape the conclusion that the reference is to a lost beginning.   **ὃ αὐτὸς ἠπιστάμην:** cf. §1 αὐτὸς ἰδὼν οὐ παρ' ἑτέρων ἀκούσας.   **λόγων . . . καὶ ἔργων καὶ κοινωνιῶν:** these genitives depend on παράδειγμα, and are parallel to βίου and διαγωγῆς; 'and their speech and actions and mutual relationships.'   **εὐσχημόνως καὶ κατὰ φύσιν:** cf. §103 μᾶλλον κατὰ φύσιν. 'Accordance with nature' is the basic standard of all right human behaviour in Stoic ethics.   **τῶι παντί** 'in every respect'.

82 καὶ δῆτα καί 'moreover': Denniston (1954) 278.   **τὸ τοῦ Εὐριπίδου:** D. has in mind (and must already have cited, cf. Introd. p. 9) the remarks of Electra's farmer husband, *El.* 424–31:

> ἔστιν δὲ δὴ τοσαῦτά γ' ἐν δόμοις ἔτι
> ὥσθ' ἕν γ' ἐπ' ἦμαρ τούσδε πληρῶσαι βορᾶς.
> ἐν τοῖς τοιούτοις δ' ἡνίκ' ἂν γνώμης πέσω
> σκοπῶ τὰ χρήμαθ' ὡς ἔχει μέγα σθένος
> ξένοις τε δοῦναι σῶμά τ' ἐς νόσον πεσὸν
> δαπάναισι σῶισαι· τῆς δ' ἐφ' ἡμέραν βορᾶς
> ἐς σμικρὸν ἥκει· πᾶς γὰρ ἐμπλησθεὶς ἀνὴρ
> ὁ πλούσιός τε χὠ πένης ἴσον φέρει.

This was a favourite text: Plu. *De aud. poet.* 33, Stobaeus 4.31.7. D. seems to have read ξένοις in 428, and this is the tradition of Eur., though Plu. and Stob. have φίλοις.   **αὐτοῖς:** i.e. τοῖς πένησι.   **πῦρ ἐναύοντας:** providing fire is a traditional and very essential form of help to strangers or neighbours: Hdt. 7.231, Xen. *Mem.* 2.2.12.   **ὁδῶν ἀπροφασίστους ἡγέμονας** 'guides who make no excuses', for getting out of the duty. We should not make excuses to friends: προφάσεως φασιν οὐ δεῖν πρὸς φίλους, [Phalaris], *Ep.* 83; a friend should be ἐκτενὴς καὶ ἀπροφάσιστος, Stob. 4.31.130. Cf. Matthew 5.41 καὶ ὅστις σε ἀγγαρεύσει μίλιον ἕν, ὕπαγε μετ' αὐτοῦ δύο.   **οὐδὲ πολὺ ἧττον τούτου φόρημα** 'nor yet a garment much less valuable than this'. This reading is acceptable: the preceding οὔτε is not answered, but this is not unusual (LSJ s.v. οὔτε II 5).

83–90 'Homer demonstrates this point. He represents Eumaeus as more hospitable to a stranger than the suitors are, Penelope as far from generous, Telemachus as less humane than his swineherd; it appears that in Homer's world, as today, the expectation of a return determined people's generosity. If I had time, I could expose the Phaeacians' motives similarly.'   **Εὔμαιον**: *Od.* 14.55ff. D.'s use of Homer as a moral text is in keeping with Stoic tradition: see esp. *Or.* 55, with Buffière (1956) 253–5.   **οὐ πάνυ ῥαιδίως** 'anything but readily': LSJ s.v. πάνυ I.3.   **Ἀντίνουν**: also criticized in *Or.* 55.20, but for extravagance and excess. D. here quotes *Od.* 17.455–7, with a noticeable variation: 17.457 in our text reads σίτου ἀποπροελὼν δόμεναι τὰ δὲ πολλὰ πάρεστιν. Kindstrand (1973) 42–3 regards this as a genuine variant: cf. *Or.* 74.19 for another considerable difference.

84 Καὶ ... τοιούτους 'and let us grant that they are like that, because of their other bad qualities'. See LSJ s.v. εἰμί A.v.b.   **καίτοι ... οὖσαν**: D. often (like most later authors) uses καίτοι with participle, like the classical καίπερ.   **οὐδὲ τὴν Πηνελόπην ... ἐπαγγέλλεσθαι**: not fair to Penelope's generosity in *Od.* 19.309ff., where she offers to make him presentable for dinner with Telemachus. He is perhaps thinking rather of her promise at 17.549–50, which depends on the stranger's 'telling the truth'. Such amusing – or shocking – reinterpretations of the classics are a part of D.'s appeal to his educated public.   **ἐκείνου τοῦ μηνός**: since this paraphrases τοῦδ' αὐτοῦ λυκάβαντος (*Od.* 19.306), it seems that D. took the obscure word λυκάβας as 'month'. Ancient tradition usually took it as 'year' (e.g. Ap. Rhod. 1.198, Artemidorus 2.12); P. Stengel (*Hermes* 18 (1883) 304) advocated 'month', but without citing D. as a predecessor, and his view cannot be right if *Od.* 14.158ff. are genuine.

85 καὶ ὕστερον: *Od.* 21.314ff., 333ff. Again, not quite fair, since the promise of a spear is left out; nor does Penelope make the point that the beggar is not to be considered as a possible match for her.

86 ἐξωμίδος: Penelope offers εἵματα καλά (*Od.* 21.339), but ἐξωμίς is a tunic with one sleeve, unknown to Homer, and commonly worn by slaves, the poor, and Cynic philosophers.   **ἐν ἡμέραις ῥηταῖς**: i.e.

within the month.   **τῆς σώφρονος . . . βασιλίδος:** irony at the
expense of περίφρων Πηνελόπεια. There seems to have been a tradition
about Penelope's virtue also: Sen. *Epist.* 88.8 *quid inquiris an Penelope
pudica fuerit an uerba saeculo suo dederit?* It was also suggested that she was
the mother of Pan by Hermes (Hdt. 2.145) or (because of the child's
name) by *all* the suitors; Paus. 8.12.6 reports a story that Odysseus
divorced her as unfaithful. Here it is her other traditional virtue, good
sense, that is denied.

87 ὁ Τηλέμαχος: *Od.* 17.10ff. τὴν ταχίστην is D.'s addition, but
πτωχεύσοντα reproduces Homer's verb.   **καὶ γὰρ εἰ** 'for even if . . .',
γάρ being the connective. D.'s argument is that Telemachus' instruc-
tions to Eumaeus presuppose the view that beggars and strangers should
not be *kept* long.   **ἀπανθρωπίαν** 'inhumanity'.

88 ὡς ἔθους δὴ ὄντος: δή indicates that the clause expresses
Eumaeus' supposed understanding; he knows that only the rich could
be sure of hospitality from the rich.   **ἀκριβῶς καὶ ἀνελευθέρως**
'strictly and ungenerously'. Cf. LSJ s.v. ἀκρίβεια 2, s.v. ἀκριβής
3.   **προσεδόκων . . . ἂν τυχεῖν:** an unusual construction, since
τυχεῖν, τεύξεσθαι, or τυγχάνειν (cf. below, §149) would be normal: cf.
Thuc. 7.61 for ἐλπίζω constructed with ἄν + infinitive.   **ὁποῖα . . .
προαιρέσεως** 'very much like present-day attitudes towards kindness
and good intentions'. The sense of προαίρεσις (usually 'choice', 'policy')
here (cf. LSJ s.v. 8) approximates to 'good will': cf. *OGIS* 783.49
(Eumenes II, second century B.C.): οὕτω γὰρ ὁμολογουμένην λήψεσθε
μᾶλλον δι' αὐτῶν τῶν ἔργων τῆς ἐμῆς προαιρέσεως ('good will') τὴν
ἀπόδειξιν. This is the courteous language of honorific documents.

89 φιλοφρονήσεις 'acts of kindness'.   **ἐράνων** 'contributions',
not unsolicited gifts but things given for a purpose and with expectations.   **δανείων** 'loans'. It was naturally thought bad to regard
beneficia in this light: Sen. *Ben.* 1.2.3 *turpis feneratio est beneficium expensum
ferre*, 3.14 *interituram tantae rei dignitatem si beneficium mercem facimus.*   **εἰ
μὴ . . . κακίαι:** D. corrects himself; he has implied that Homeric
attitudes resembled those of the present day, but sees that this cannot
be right: the present is much worse. Cf. *Or.* 52.13, where he describes
Aeschylus' portrayal of Odysseus in the *Philoctetes* as δριμύς and δόλιος
ὡς ἐν τοῖς τότε, but far below modern κακοήθεια. The moral inferiority
of the present is a commonplace: ἴδιον ἀνθρώπου τὸ καταμέμφεσθαι τὰ
ἀεὶ παρόντα ('Longinus' 44.6). Many of its manifestations in ancient

literature are discussed in Lovejoy and Boas (1935); it is a universal topic of satire and moral advice.

90 περὶ τῶν Φαιάκων: D. might, presumably, have argued that the Phaeacians were motivated solely by their selfish love of pleasure (cf. ps.-Heracl. *Hom. probl.* 69, 79) – or that they were anxious to get rid of him for their own safety. We do not know of any ancient interpretation that fits the circumstances more exactly.   **ἀλλὰ γάρ:** Denniston (1954) 102–3. D. 'breaks off' to turn to something more important.

91–6 'The rich are in general less generous than the poor; the poor are hospitable to the limit of their ability, and they are unlikely to have to entertain the great – so they are not liable to the problems that Menelaus encountered when Priam's son abused his hospitality and caused all the evils of the Trojan war.'

91 οὔτε πρὸς ξένους: the passage of Euripides (see on §82) is constantly in mind.   **γλίσχρους καὶ φειδώλους** 'niggardly and parsimonious'. The meanness of the rich is often noticed by moralists: see Bion of Borysthenes F34–F46 with Kindstrand's notes for a useful collection of material. For D., see esp. *Or.* 4.9ff. on the δαίμων who represents avarice.   **εἴ τις ... εὑρεθείη ... δείκνυσι ...:** for this type of condition (not uncommon in classical authors, WS §2359–60) cf. e.g. *Or.* 74.23 τοῖς πλέουσι τὸ πέλαγος συμφέρει μᾶλλον τῆς γῆς, εἰ μή τις ἐν εὐδίαι πλέοι καὶ σαφῶς εἰδὼς τοὺς τόπους.   **οὐδὲ γὰρ ... τῶν ἀπορωτέρων** 'The discovery of one rich man in 10,000 who is generous and magnanimous in his ways does not constitute a refutation of the fact that most of them are worse than the poor in these matters.' For τὸ μὴ οὐχί, WS §2749(d). The sentiment recalls the camel and the eye of the needle (Matthew 19.23; Mussies (1972) 75 compares D. 4.91, 7.82–3, 79.6, but not this passage). D. may have in mind Pl. *Laws* 742A–743A, on the incompatibility of wealth and goodness: ἀγαθὸν δὲ ὄντα διαφόρως καὶ πλούσιον εἶναι διαφερόντως ἀδύνατον.

92 'For a poor man, not bad by nature, what is at hand suffices both to restore his body, if he has been a little ill, with the sort of sickness that commonly befalls men who are not idle or stuffing themselves at every meal, and also to give guests when they come acceptable presents, offered without rousing suspicion, by a willing giver, and without causing pain.' The reference to illness again takes us to Eur. *El.* 428–9 σῶμά τ' ἐς νόσον πεσὸν δαπάναισι σῶισαι. The diseases of the poor are not those caused by excess: on these see, e.g., Sen. *Epist.* 95.18 *quid* *alios referam innumerabiles morbos, supplicia luxuriae?* Again, commonplace: Musonius 97–8 Hense enlarges on the health hazards of rich diet, Greg. Naz. σύγκρισις βίων 127–30 gives a frightening list: φῦσαι κατάρροι σπλῆνες ἐξαρθρήματα ... τῶν κόρων οὗτοι τόκοι.   **οὐδ' ἑκάστοτε ἐμπιμπλαμένοις**: cf. [Pl.] *Epist.* 7.326b δίς τε τῆς ἡμέρας ἐμπιμπλάμενον ζῆν καὶ μηδέποτε κοιμώμενον μόνον νύκτωρ.   **χωρὶς ὑποψίας**: i.e. without arousing the suspicion that the gift is intended as a bribe. **ἀλύπως**: whose 'pain' is avoided? Probably 'offence' which might be given to the recipient, rather than actual pain to the giver. Wyttenbach (on Plu. *Mor.* 38c) takes this passage differently, and translates *dona data a uolentibus nec inde penuriam metuentibus.*

93 Τηλεμάχωι: *Od.* 4.589–92, 613–19, 15.113–19. For dative depending on the noun δῶρα, cf. Pl. *Ap.* 30D ἡ τοῦ θεοῦ δόσις ὑμῖν, WS §1502.   **σατράπας ἢ βασιλέας**: see on §66.   **οἷς ... φιλίας** 'who find nothing inadequate if it comes with friendship'. A tactful remark: the great man who accepts a small gift thereby shows his virtue.   **ἀκολάστους δὲ καὶ τυραννικούς**: i.e. like Paris, who is shortly to be mentioned.

94 Μενέλεωι: Paris' breach of the rules of hospitality, his offence against Zeus Xenios, is often stressed: e.g. Aesch. *Ag.* 399–402 οἷος καὶ Πάρις ἐλθὼν | ἐς δόμον τὸν Ἀτρειδᾶν | ἤισχυνε ξενίαν τράπε|ζαν κλοπαῖσι γυναικός. According to the epic *Cypria*, Menelaus had to leave home during Paris' visit to go to Crete, and Paris took advantage of his absence to seduce Helen and elope with her and a lot of valuables (D. has πρὸς τοῖς χρήμασι τὴν γυναῖκα προσλαβών, as though the money was the main object!).

95 τὴν δὲ θυγατέρα: Hermione, then aged nine.   **ἐφθείρετο** 'drifted around', see LSJ s.v. II 4, D. *Or.* 40.7 τελευταῖον εἰς τὰ ὄρη φθείρομενος, 'finally wandering into the mountains'.   **πανταχόσε τῆς Ἑλλάδος**: he at least went to Cinyras in Cyprus, and to Delphi with Odysseus. D. has no need to be specific, only to stress the futility of it all.   **ἠναγκάσθη δὲ ἱκετεῦσαι τὸν ἀδελφόν**: again, D. wishes to make Menelaus seem as abject and dishonoured as possible. Agamemnon's submission to Calchas' advice to sacrifice Iphigenia is not usually associated so clearly with pleas from Menelaus: Odysseus is at least the main advocate (Hyginus 98.3).

96 κολακεύων ... καὶ ... ὑπομένων: the participles are parallel, the sentence being broken by the parenthesis εἰ δὲ μὴ ... ἀποπλεύσεσθαι.

δίχα: Emperius' correction for διά gives the right sense, but is not the only possibility: e.g. ⟨εἰ μὴ⟩ διά would do.

97–102 'Euripides' praise of wealth as the means of giving lavish hospitality is therefore unfounded. The poets are the spokesmen of popular attitudes, and that is why we should criticize what they say, as a great philosopher [Cleanthes] did with our passage of Euripides and with similar sentiments in Sophocles.'

97 Ἆρ' οὖν σφόδρα ἄξιον ἄγασθαι: text and connection of thought unsure. MSS have ἄρ' οὐ or ἄρ' οὖν οὐ: ἄρ' οὖν is Geel's proposal. Capps preferred οὐ σφόδρ' ἀνάξιον ('is it not most unfitting ...?'). If Geel is right (as I believe) σφόδρα goes with ἄγασθαι. 'Is it right then to admire wealth so greatly, as the poet does ...?' (Emperius' κατὰ τὸν ποιητήν also appears right: the reference is still to Euripides' *Electra, loc. cit.*, and it is very difficult to reconstruct sense on the basis of καί.) If we keep οὐ, then the whole sentence must be an imagined objection, answered in §98 by λέγομεν δὲ ταῦτα. This is not D.'s style, at least in this piece.   τοῦ πλούτου: LSJ s.v. ἄγαμαι 1 3.

98 ἀντιπαρεξάγοντες 'confronting', lit. leading out our troops against them.   ἃ δὴ ... ἐδόκει: repetitive and pleonastic after τὴν τῶν πολλῶν διάνοιαν, but this is no good reason to delete. The imperfect ἐδόκει may signify 'a truth just recognized' (WS §1902) – 'what, we find, the mass of people thinks' – so that Reiske's δοκεῖ and Geel's παλαίοις ('*sc.* iis qui inde a veteri aevo antiquos poetas legerant') are unnecessary.   ἃ θαυμάζουσι: 'wonder' or 'admiration' for the things of this world is unphilosophical. 'The other things' besides wealth will be power, prestige, fame, and the like.

99 †γενέσθαι†: the simplest solution is to delete or change to γενομένους. Wenkebach's ingenious suggestion recorded in the *app. crit.* ('seeming to be good and truthful interpreters') is needlessly complicated, and it is not clear what the point of ἐξηγητάς would be.

100 ἀπολαμβάνοντα 'taking aside'. Cf. *Or.* 13.31 ἐπειρώμην διαλέγεσθαι 'Ρωμαίοις οὐ κατὰ δύο καὶ τρεῖς ἀπολαμβάνων ... πολλοῖς δὲ καὶ ἀθρόοις εἰς ταὐτὸ συνιοῦσιν. D. seems to reject one aspect of Socratic *elenchus*, the confrontation with individuals: his critique of common opinion has to be based on more general evidence.   ἂν τύχῃς ... βασιλεύσας 'if you get rich by becoming a merchant or a king'.

101 τοὺς προφήτας ... ποιητάς 'their spokesmen and advocates, the poets'. Poets are regularly regarded as προφῆται of gods or the

Muses (for D., see *Or.* 12.47, 53.10, 36.42) but it is a little odd to use the word of their relationship to ordinary people: D. perhaps tones this down by adding συνηγόρους: the poets support the case of the ordinary man.　　**μέτροις κατακεκλεισμένας** 'enclosed in verse'. The restrictions of the verse form make the sense plainer and more memorable: Cleanthes *ap.* Sen. *Epist.* 108.10 *sensus nostros clariores carminis arta necessitas efficit.*　　**καὶ δῆτα . . . ἀποτυγχάνειν** 'and I certainly don't think we fail to find them'.

102　τῶν πάνυ φιλοσόφων τις: Cleanthes, whose philosophical use of poetry (esp. parody) was famous: *SVF* II 527, 537 (the *Hymn to Zeus*), 557, 559, 560, 562, 570, 573, 583, 586. Cleanthes' parody of Eur. *El.* 428, which D. has in mind here, is known from Plu. *De aud. poet.* 33C (= *SVF* II 562) in the form πόρναις τε δοῦναι σῶμά τ' ἐς νόσους πεσὸν | δαπάναις ἐπιτρῖψαι.　　**πάνυ:** LSJ s.v. II.　　**τοῖς ὑπὸ Σοφοκλέους . . . εἰρημένοις:** probably the passage from the *Aleadai* (fr. 85 Nauck²), quoted by Stobaeus, and clearly well known:

> τὰ χρήματ' ἀνθρώποισιν εὑρίσκει φίλους
> αὖθις δὲ τιμάς, εἶτα τῆς ὑπερτάτης
> τυραννίδος θακοῦσιν ἀγχίστην ἕδραν . . .
> καὶ γὰρ δυσειδὲς σῶμα καὶ δυσώνυμον
> γλώσσηι σοφὸν τίθησιν εὔμορφόν τ' ἰδεῖν.

(Cf. also Sen. *Epist.* 115.14 for a collection of tragic passages in praise of wealth, perhaps derived from a Stoic source.)　　**πρὸς τὸ ⟨παρα⟩χρῆμα** 'for the immediate occasion'. Extempore speech, like the present, is not constrained by the need to be concise.　　**ἐν βίβλοις:** Emperius was probably right to suspect this. Perhaps Cleanthes' constraints were not due to his writing a book but rather to his using the verse form of the passage he criticizes: ἐν ἰαμβείοις is attractive.

103–4 'So much for farming, hunting and pastoral life. I was anxious to show that poverty is no obstacle to a decent life if a man is willing to work – rather the contrary. Let us next consider what acceptable ways of earning a living can be found in the city.'

This surprising transition (Introd. p. 11) takes no account of §§81–102, but covers much more than the narrative of §§1–80. D. has not said much about farming (it could easily be praised in his sense, cf. Musonius fr. XI Hense) and his 'hunters' have more or less given up the pastoral life they enjoyed before their master's disgrace.

Cf. §§125–6 for a further 'transition' which raises problems.

103 Γεωργικοῦ . . . λελέχθω: a formal transition, marked by anastrophe of πέρι (cf. 36.33, 36.43) and perfect imperative λελέχθω. **ἀμηιγέπηι:** 'by whatever means': cf. §17. **πενίαν . . . ἐθέλουσιν** 'that poverty is not a thing incapable of achieving a decent livelihood and existence for free men willing to work for themselves'. For χρῆμα cf. §9 πενία χρῆμα . . . ἱερόν, 12.64 δαψιλὲς χρῆμα ποίησις καὶ πάντα τρόπον εὔπορον. **αὐτουργεῖν:** the word implies independence and self-reliance: cf. 1.63: the Cynic hero Heracles αὐτουργὸς ἦν καὶ τὸ σῶμα ἱκανὸς καὶ πάντων μάλιστα ἐπόνει. Electra's husband in Euripides is called αὐτουργός in the *dramatis personae* (though not in the text); note that it is his words about wealth that D.'s discussion addresses (see §82), though without taking account of his ἦθος, or supposing that the sentiments might not be Euripides' own. **μᾶλλον κατὰ φύσιν:** cf. §81.

104 εἶεν δή: common in Plato (about 100 instances), and recommended by Moeris (p. 127 Pierson) as an Attic equivalent of ἄγε δή. D. has it 18 times: cf. below §148. **τῶν ἐν ἄστει καὶ κατὰ πόλιν πενήτων** 'the town poor living an urban life'. περί governs τοῦ βίου καὶ τῶν ἐργασιῶν. Cf. *Or.* 3.125 ὅσοι δ' ἐν ἄστει διάγουσι τῶν κατὰ πόλιν τι πράττοντες. Cohoon's 'in the capital or some other city' is wrong: and no inference should be drawn from this sentence about the place where the speech is delivered (Introd. p. 13). Avezzù's remark 'è un indicazione di spazio e di fine' is correct. **ποῖ' ἄττα:** a conscious Atticism (8 occurrences in D.), see Lucian, *Lexiphanes* 21, *Rh. praec.* 16. **εὖ μάλ' ἐπισταμένων . . . ἀριθμόν:** money-lenders keep a sharp eye on the calendar: Plu. *De vitando aere alieno* 828A τῶν καλανδῶν καὶ τῆς νουμηνίας ἣν ἱερωτάτην ἡμέραν οὖσαν ἀποφράδα ποιοῦσιν οἱ δανεισταὶ καὶ στύγιον. So Horace's *fenerator Alfius* (*Epodes* 2.69–70) *omnem redegit Idibus pecuniam, | quaerit Kalendis ponere.* Seneca draws the contrast with generosity: *nemo beneficia in calendario scribit* (*Ben.* 1.2.3).

105–8 'Poor people have difficulty in providing for themselves in cities. Should they therefore be expelled? They would live a better life in the country; but there are possibilities in the city.'

105–6 Μήποτε . . . τιμίων: a difficult and confused sentence. We should accept Naber's deletion of τοῦ πυρός; there are other daily uses for wood besides fire (though this is the most essential) while φρύγανα, mentioned next, are specifically 'firewood'. I suggest δίχα γε for δίχα δέ, accept Reiske's ἀναγκάζωνται, and translate as follows, making a break in the sentence before κἂν φρυγάνων: 'It may well be that work in cities is scarce for such people and needing outside resources, since they have to pay rent for lodging and acquire other things by buying them, not only clothes and tools and food, but even wood for daily use; if they ever need firewood or leaves or any other valueless commodity, with the single exception of water, they are obliged to put down money to obtain it, because everything is locked up and nothing publicly available except all the expensive items that are on sale.'   μισθοῦ 'for rent', WS §1372.   ἢ φύλλων 'leaves' – perhaps for bedding?

106 δίχα γε ὕδατος: aqueducts were a feature of Roman city life. D. himself (*Or.* 45.12) provided water for Prusa, Pliny (*Ep.* 10.37) had plans for Nicomedia. There is nothing in this detail to make Rome the only possible venue.   τάχα γὰρ ἂν φανεῖται: D. should be allowed this irregularity, of which there are occasional cases even in classical Attic: WS §1793.   ἄλλως τε ὅταν 'especially when', LSJ s.v. ἄλλως 13.   μὴ . . . κερδᾶναι 'we do not advise them to undertake absolutely any work from which it is possible to profit, nor all in the same degree'.

107 τῶι λόγωι 'in our argument'. D. has Plato's imaginary city-founding constantly in mind (*Rep.* II 369A εἰ γιγνομένην πόλιν θεασαίμεθα λόγωι), and also his 'expulsions' of undesirables (e.g. most poets, *Rep.* III 398A).   τοὺς κομψοὺς πένητας 'the respectable poor'. Cf. 4.85 οἱ κομψοὶ τῶν δημιουργῶν, 30.23 τοὺς κομψούς τε καὶ δριμεῖς. The word has no pejorative nuance here.   πόλεις εὖ ναιεταώσας: e.g. *Il.* 2.648, *Od.* 13.285.   καθάπερ . . . Πεισιστράτου: D. means (i) before the συνοικισμός by Theseus (Thuc. 2.15, Plu. *Thes.* 24); (ii) under Pisistratus, who lent money to aid farmers ἵνα μήτε ἐν τῶι ἄστει διατρίβωσιν ἀλλὰ διεσπαρμένοι κατὰ τὴν χώραν καὶ ὅπως εὐποροῦντες τῶν μετρίων . . . μήτ' ἐπιθυμῶσι μήτε σχολάζωσιν ἐπιμελεῖσθαι τῶν κοινῶν (Aristot. Ἀθ. πολ. 16).

108 τῶν ἐν ἄστει . . . βαναύσων: Herwerden's ἀργῶν is right, since it is part of the traditional attack on Athenian democracy that it made citizens idle: cf. Pl. *Gorg.* 515E for the view that Pericles made Athenians ἀργοὺς καὶ δειλοὺς καὶ λάλους καὶ φιλαργύρους.   γραμματέων 'clerks', slightly unexpected companions for 'assemblymen' and 'jurymen'; but contempt for the γραμματεύς had a classical model in Demosthenes' attacks on Aeschines (*De corona* 127, 261).   βαναύσων: for this heavily loaded word for sedentary or mechanical workers see, e.g., Adam on Pl. *Rep.* 495E, Xen. *Oec.* 4.2, Aristot. *Pol.* 1337b8ff. D. uses it below (§111) and in 1.33 (where it means 'vulgar'); in 66.25, it is a reproach to which one is liable if one is engaged ἐπ' ἐργασίας τινός: and this is its basic sense.   **πάντα τρόπον** 'in every way'.   **ἀγροῖκοι:** see on §43.

109–13 'Some profitable occupations are not to be recommended: sedentary trades, useless occupations based on luxury and not really to be called work at all. Acceptable trades are those which do no moral or physical harm to the worker.'

109 ἵνα μὴ πολλάκις: this might mean 'lest perchance' (LSJ s.v. πολλάκις III). Cf. *Or.* 13.25 πολλάκις δὲ καὶ δὶς ἐφεξῆς ὁ αὐτός 'and possibly the same person twice in succession'; yet in both these passages the literal (and common) sense 'often' is possible, and as this is D.'s usual usage, it is safer to assume it here.   **ἀργοί ... τραπῆναι:** that 'Satan finds some mischief still/For idle hands to do' (Isaac Watts, *Divine songs for children*) is ancient wisdom also. We may compare the commonplace denunciation of the bad effects of *otium*, e.g. Catullus 51.12–16. **ἐὰν ... πρὸς ἀργύριον** 'if one judges profitability in money terms.'

110 τὴν ἀτοπίαν: the 'oddness' and vulgarity of the names of the trades, not suited to serious literature.   **ὅδε εἰρήσθω ... ἔπαινος** 'let this praise and blame be given briefly'. For the use of the perfect imperative to refer to what is now to be said, cf. e.g. Pl. *Laws* 774C εἴρηται μὲν καὶ πρότερον, εἰρήσθω δὲ πάλιν. This formal statement somewhat recalls the style of the *Laws*; D.'s familiarity with Plato is evident.   **ἑδραιότητα** 'sedentariness'; cf. ἑδραῖος, 'sedentary', Xen. *Lac. resp.* 1.3 οἱ πολλοὶ τῶν τὰς τέχνας ἐχόντων ἑδραῖοί εἰσιν.   **ὅσαι ... πόλεων** 'All such as are harmful to the body in respect of health or adequate strength because of their inactivity and sedentariness, or produce impropriety and illiberality in the mind, or are otherwise useless and devised for no useful end because of the folly and luxury of cities.' The text will stand: Wilamowitz's ἐντίκτουσαι for ἐντίκτουσι is not needed.   **τὴν ἀρχήν** 'to begin with', and so 'at all', a Platonic usage.   **τό γε ὀρθόν:** D. perhaps takes this from Pl. *Phaedrus* 261B, where it is an adverbial accusative, 'to put the facts correctly'. Here it seems to mean 'it is correct': *deest verbum*, as Emperius says. Reiske's ⟨δεῖ⟩ καλεῖν may well be right.   **Ἡσίοδος:** *WD* 311 ἔργον δ' οὐδὲν ὄνειδος, ἀεργείη δέ τ' ὄνειδος.

111 μήτε ... διδάσκειν: a slight anacoluthon. μήτε αὐτὸν μήτε τοὺς παῖδας completes the sense, διδάσκειν is then added, parallel with the other infinitives, though we should have expected a participle (διδάσκοντα).   **οὔτε καθ' 'Ησίοδον:** because Hesiod must be taken as excluding from the category of ἔργον activities which are to be deplored: they count rather as ἀεργείη.   **ἀργίας . . . ὄνειδος** 'but will earn the mean reproach of idleness combined with dirty profit'.

112 ὅσα δὲ αὖ . . . τὸν βίον 'On the other hand, all such as are not unbecoming to those who pursue them, engender no evil in the soul, and are not responsible for any disease, including in particular the weakness, cowardliness and effeminacy that develops in the body as a result of long rest, but yield adequate service for life ...'

113 ἀπόρους . . . πορισταὶ . . . ἀποροῦντες: the word-play recalls that on Πόρος in Plato's myth of the birth of Eros (*Symp.* 202D). It is difficult to translate: perhaps 'by naming them "resourceless", though they are in fact providers of resources to their cities, and have in effect no lack of any resource that is needful or useful'.   **ὀνομάζοντας** 'by naming'; the accusative (following the dative τοῖς πλουσίοις) is not abnormal (WS §1062), and no change is needed.

114–16 'What occupations do we disapprove? Orators' customary abuse of their opponents' parents on the ground of their occupation is really a sneer at poverty; but poverty is not to blame, since wealth does much more harm.'

From this point on, the argument is almost wholly negative: D. will develop the attack on various professions (culminating in the brothel-business, §§133–52), but says nothing of what can be recommended.

114 Φέρε οὖν . . . πρόσεστιν 'Come then, let us call to mind, in both categories [i.e. those τέχναι which are financially lucrative and those which are not, cf. §109], even if we don't give any very precise indications, at any rate in outline, what sorts of occupations we do not accept, and why, and what sorts we invite people to undertake with confidence, not bothering about those who bring such matters up in other ways – as they are in the habit of bringing up by way of invective not only their opponents' own trades, to which no oddity attaches ...'   **ἀλλὰ καὶ τῶν γονέων . . . παιδαγωγήσηι:** D. here confronts a passage of Demosthenes (57.45) in which Euxitheos defends his claim to citizenship against his enemy Euboulides, pointing out that his mother's occupation as a wet-nurse (τίτθη) is irrelevant to his claim to citizenship, and anyway was forced on her by poverty: ὡς γὰρ ἐγὼ ἀκούω, πολλαὶ καὶ τιτθαὶ καὶ ἔριθοι καὶ τρυγήτριαι γεγόνασιν ὑπὸ τῶν τῆς πόλεως κατ' ἐκείνους τοὺς χρόνους συμφορῶν ἀσταὶ γυναῖκες. 'Wet-nurse', 'harvest worker', and 'grape picker' are D.'s first three examples. His others – schoolmaster and παιδαγωγός – relate especially to Demosthenes' attacks on Aeschines (*De corona* 258). So this whole list is of literary origin, and should not be taken seriously as a statement of contemporary social facts.

On 'disreputable' trades in general, as a topic of ψόγος, see esp. Süss (1910) 248, Dover (1974) 32ff. **ὁμόσε ἰέναι** 'go into action'. The infinitive depends on κελεύομεν, and more or less repeats ἐπιχειρεῖν (as μηδὲν ... αἰσχυνομένους repeats θαρροῦντας).

115 πενίαν ... λοιδοροῦντες: Demosth. *loc. cit.* made the point that πενία was the cause of the choice of these ways of life. D. now repeats his own position, viz. that poverty is not a bad thing, though some ἔργα are. **οὐδὲ ... ἐκείνου** 'nor is this reproach to be taken more hardly than that'. βαρυντέον = δεῖ βαρύνεσθαι, in the sense required, e.g. in Dion. Hal. *AR* 4.14.4 ἵνα ... τὰ λυπηρὰ τῆς τύχης ἧττον βαρύνωνται.

116 εἰ γάρ τοι ... τῆς ἀργίας 'If it were necessary [Emperius' δέοι is a distinct improvement, but δοκεῖ, 'is decided', not impossible] to speak ill of the object they blame without naming it, adducing its daily consequences, they would have far more really disgraceful results of wealth to adduce, and especially the thing that Hesiod judged worthy of reproach, idleness.' The reference is again to *WD* 311 (cf. §110). **οὔτε ... οὔτ' ἀροτῆρα**: *Margites* fr. 2 (OCT *Homer* v, 152ff.); cited more fully by Aristot. *EN* 1141a12. This humorous poem was usually attributed to Homer (Aristot. *Poet.* 1448b30, [Pl.] *Alc.* ii 147B, Aristoph. *Birds* 909), sometimes to Pigres (so Suda), never to Hesiod; nor does D. here mean that is Hesiod's. See *Cambridge history of classical literature* i, ed. P. E. Easterling and B. M. W. Knox (1985) 109–10. **ἄλλως ... ἀπαλάς** 'anyway, your hands are soft and uncalloused, like the suitors' '. ἄλλως signifies that he does no other physical work either; Cohoon interprets 'in vain', 'to no purpose'. **ἀτρίπτους καὶ ἀπαλάς**: *Od.* 21.150–1 (of Leodes) πρὶν γὰρ κάμε χεῖρας ἀνέλκων | ἀτρίπτους ἀπαλάς. A familiar quotation: note D. *Or.* 16.7, Plu. *Mor.* 499D.

117–18 'The arts of adornment, whether of persons or of buildings, are unsuitable for our poor workers. Ideally, perhaps, they should not be allowed at all; but for our present purpose it is enough to say that they cannot contribute to a decent life.'

117 μυρεψούς 'perfumers'. Pollux 7.117 recommends this word as

used by the Attic classic, Critias.   **[καὶ βυρσοδέψας]:** tanners,
though disreputable (like Cleon in Aristophanes), do not belong to this
context: Pflugk was right to delete.   **διαφερούσηι:** sc. κουρικῆι
ἀνδρῶν. Reading unsure: an alternative possibility is to read
διαφέρουσι, making οὐ ... τὰ νῦν a parenthesis, '– they don't differ
much nowadays –'.   **ἐγχούσηι:** for the form cf. Xen. Oecon. 10.2
πολλῶι μὲν ψιμυθίωι ... πολλῆι δ' ἐγχούσηι. The plant ἄγχουσα or
ἔγχουσα, *Alkanna tinctoria*, was commonly used for rouge, as ψιμύθιον,
'white lead' (Lat. *cerussa*), was used to whiten the complexion.   **ὥρας
ψευδῆ καὶ νόθα εἴδωλα** 'false and spurious images of beauty'.
Emperius' re-division of words is certainly right. With ψευδεῖς, we
should have to take ὥρας as plural, 'beauties', which seems unexampled
and unlikely.   **λίθοις:** i.e. coloured marbles.   **ποικιλλόντων:** sc.
τῶν ἀνθρώπων or the like: WS §2072b. The transition from the dative
ποικιλτικῆι ... μηχανωμένηι seems natural enough.   **γλυφαῖς:** i.e.
carving of the walls themselves, not just applied ornament. Cf. the
description of the Throne of Tyranny, *Or*. 1.78: μυρίας τινας ἄλλας
ἔχοντι γλυφὰς καὶ διαθέσει χρυσοῦ καὶ ἐλέφαντος καὶ ἠλέκτρου καὶ ἐβένου
καὶ παντοδαπῶν χρωμάτων πεποικιλμένωι.

118 **τὸ δ' ⟨ἐφ'⟩ ἡμῖν ... πενήτων** 'but what it is in our power to
determine in the present context is that none of our poor people shall
be engaged in such matters'.   **περὶ τὸ τοιοῦτον γίγνεσθαι** 'to be
engaged in such matter'; LSJ s.v. γίγνομαι II c. ἄν is not needed,
and the corruption may come from a misread contraction.   **ὥσπερ
χορῶι:** D. has in mind Pl. *Rep*. IX 580B καθάπερ γὰρ εἰσῆλθον, ἔγωγε
ὥσπερ χόρους κρίνω, ἀρετῆι καὶ κακίαι καὶ εὐδαιμονίαι καὶ τῶι ἐναντίωι.
D.'s two choruses, however – the rich versus the poor – are not com-
peting in εὐδαιμονία, but only in 'a certain style and modest way of life'.
The metaphor is natural and quite common: note Plu. *De gl. Ath*. 348D,
De fort. Rom. 317E (ὁ τῆς Ἀρετῆς χόρος), both ἀγῶνες.   **οὐχ ὑπὲρ
εὐδαιμονίας:** D. may again be incidentally contrasting his topic with
Plato's aim in *Rep*., which was precisely to determine which life was
εὐδαιμονέστατος: cf. §§127–32.   **μόνης δὲ ἀρετῆς ... ἐξαίρετον** 'it
is reserved for virtue alone'. A Stoic emphasis: εὐδαιμονία can only come
from the acquisition of ἀρετή.

119–22 'Acting, tragic or comic, dancing, and music are all unsuitable, whatever complaints we receive from cities whose poets or musi-
cians have made them famous. We must hold to the point that all such

things lead to shamelessness.' This is an echo both of the Platonic banishment of such arts from his *Republic*, and of the Stoic devaluing of the arts of entertainment, which agreed with common Roman attitudes (Cic. *De off.* 1.150ff.; Introd. p. 11).

119 Καὶ τοίνυν: Denniston (1954) 578. The combination is not found in orators, but in Plato (mainly later works) and Xenophon.   **ἢ τινων . . . δημιουργούς** 'or manufacturers of the untempered laughter of certain mimes'. Cf. 2.56 γέλωτάς τε ἀκράτους καὶ τοιούτου γέλωτος ποιητὰς μετὰ σκωμμάτων (to be avoided by the good king). μῖμοι in our passage are 'mime-performances' (LSJ s.v. II).   **οὐδὲ ὀρχηστὰς . . . ὀρχουμένους** 'nor yet individual dancers or dancers in choruses (barring the sacred choruses), at any rate if they sing or dance about the misfortunes of Niobe or Thyestes'. Niobe and Thyestes are among the tragic themes selected for condemnation by Plato (*Rep.* 380A), but D's wording suggests that he has in mind pantomime performances based on tragedy, a commoner entertainment in his day: cf. Lucian, *De saltatione* 41 (Niobe), 43 (Thyestes).   **ἱερῶν χορῶν:** i.e. choruses taking part in religious festivals, a very important and respectable part of civic life, to which D. could hardly object.   **τῶν ἐνδόξων πόλεων** 'cities of note', their fame coming in part from their famous citizens: cf. Men. Rhet. 359–61.   **ἕξουσι:** WS §2238. This form of protasis 'commonly suggests something undesired or feared or intended independently of the speaker's will'.   **Σμύρνα . . . Ἄργος:** a selection of the 'seven cities' which claimed to be Homer's birthplace, a list variously given, e.g. *Anth. Pal.* 16.298 Σμύρνα Χίος Κολοφὼν Ἰθάκη Πύλος Ἄργος Ἀθῆναι. Smyrna was commonly thought to be correct, see *Vita Homeri Herodotea* (OCT Homer v 192ff.), Chios is attested by *Hymn* 3.172 οἰκεῖ δὲ Χίωι ἐνὶ παιπαλοέσσηι, and Argos was Philochorus' idea (*FGrHist* 328 F 20D). D. elsewhere (47.5–6) lists Ios, Chios, Colophon. In general, see Lefkowitz (1981) 13.   **οὐκ ἐώντων:** genitive absolute where a dative agreeing with ἡμῖν would be strictly correct: a common *constructio ad sensum*: WS §2073a.   **τὸ γοῦν ἐφ' ἡμῖν** 'to the extent of our ability'.

120 καὶ Θηβαίους . . . ἐπ' αὐλητικῆι: for this tradition, cf. Men. Rhet. 360.22, *Anth. Pal.* 16.28 (the epigram cited by D. below §121): Ἑλλὰς μὲν Θήβας προτέρας προύκρινεν ἐν αὐλοῖς | Θῆβαι δὲ Πρόνομον παῖδα τὸν Οἰνιάδου. There were many famous Boeotian αὐληταί, Pronomos being one of the later fifth century (Paus. 9.12.5).

121 ἀναστάτου ... γενομένης: Alexander, it is said, destroyed Thebes ·to the sound of *aulos*-music, but spared the house of Pindar: κατέσκαψε τὴν πόλιν πᾶσαν τηρήσας μόνην οἰκίαν τὴν Πινδάρου· φασὶ δὲ ὅτι καὶ τὸν αὐλητὴν 'Ἰσμηνίαν ἐπηνάγκασεν ἐπαυλῆσαι τῆι πόλει κατασκαπτομένηι (*Vita Alexandri* 1.27: L. Bergson, *Der griechische Alexanderroman, Rezension* β (Stockholm 1965) 41). **ἔτι νῦν ... οἰκουμένης** 'and even now remaining virtually uninhabited, except for the small area of the Cadmea'. Text is uncertain: it seems simplest to read οὐδέ for οὔσης rather than to delete οἰκουμένης or make other changes. The desolation of Thebes, and the occupation only of the old citadel, is a standard example of urban decline in this period: cf. Paus. 8.33.2 τὸ δὲ ὄνομα τῶν Θηβῶν ἐς ἀκρόπολιν μόνην καὶ οἰκήτορας καταβέβηκεν οὐ πολλούς, 9.7.6 ἡ μὲν κάτω πόλις πᾶσα ἔρημος ἦν ἐπ' ἐμοῦ πλὴν τὰ ἱερά, τὴν δὲ ἀκρόπολιν οἰκοῦσι Θήβας καὶ οὐ Καδμείαν καλουμένην. This had probably been true since the Mithridatic wars, and remained so till the modern suburbs began to encroach beyond the Cadmea-site into the area of the classical lower town. Plutarch's imaginative reconstruction of classical Thebes in *De genio Socratis*, roughly contemporary with D.'s speeches, is an exercise in romantic nostalgia. Cf. 7.34, 36.6 for other comments on the decline of cities. **τὸν δὲ Ἑρμῆν** 'the herm', i.e. a pillar with a head and erect phallos: Thuc. 6.27.1 with Gomme–Andrewes–Dover *ad loc.* **τὸ ἐπίγραμμα:** *Anth. Pal.* 16.28 (quoted on §120) is a version of this. D. is our earliest source for it.

122 οὐ δὴ φοβηθέντες: this picks up from εἰ καί τινες ... δυσχερῶς ἕξουσι, §119. The construction from §118 onwards is very loose: with τραγικοὺς ἢ κωμικούς (§119) we have to understand something like δεῖ γίγνεσθαι, and this is needed also with οὐδὲ κήρυκας at §128. There is no ambiguity, only a very informal structure. **παρὰ τοῖς Ἕλλησι:** D. 'speaks of the Greeks as if they were not present' (Brunt (1973) 17); but this is not a safe inference, since Hellenic disapproval would be a strong point also with a Hellenic audience. This passage does not itself prove delivery in Rome. **τὸ τῆς ἀναιδείας ... ὀρθότερον** 'shamelessness, too much pride on the part of the common mob – but it is better to call it audacity'. Text not quite sure: if the second μέγιστον were right, it would have to be taken as an adverb with θρασύνεσθαι, 'huge audacity'.

The theme recalls that of *Or.* 32 (*To the Alexandrians*), esp. 32.28 on δῆμοι θρασεῖς καὶ ὑπερήφανοι, and 32.55ff. D.'s attitude to unruly democracies is unrelentingly aristocratic, despite his frequent professions of a philosopher's sympathy with the poor and the common man. θρασύνεσθαι: here clearly used of a vicious attitude, in accordance with the classic grammarians' distinction between θάρσος (good, 'confidence') and θράσος (bad, 'audacity'): Ammonius, Περὶ ἀκυρολογίας p. 147 Nickau.

123–4 'Nor should they be auctioneers, advertising agents, or lawyers.'

123 κήρυκας ὠνίων: 'criers of goods for sale', 'auctioneers', Lat. *praecones*, who were often slaves or low-born, and were debarred from office (like *lenones*) by the *lex Iulia municipalis*: Juv. 3.155, 7.6, Petron. 46.7. Their coarse vulgarity and loud voice were natural objects of contempt.   **κλοπῶν . . . προτιθέντας** 'advertising rewards for information concerning thefts or runaway slaves'. Advertisements about slaves included careful physical descriptions, e.g. *P. Par.* 10 (156 B.C.: *Select papyri*, ed. A. S. Hunt and C. C. Edgar, Loeb Classical Library II 136) describes one Hermon who has a mole to the left of his nose, a scar over his mouth, and a tattoo on the right wrist. The genre could be turned to good literary purpose: Meleager (*Anth. Pal.* 5.177 = Meleager XXXVII Gow–Page) uses it beautifully of the runaway Eros, who is finally run to earth in Zenophila's eyes. Once again, D.'s detail is not specific to his own time, though not here specifically classical, as it seems to be in §114.   **συμβολαίων . . . συγγραφεῖς** 'drafters of contracts, challenges, and documents relating to court-cases and charges generally'. συμβόλαια and προκλήσεις (cf. Lysias 4.15) are terms of Attic litigation; again, no specific contemporary reference.   **τοὺς σοφούς τε . . . καὶ συνηγόρους** 'those clever and ingenious pettifoggers and advocates'. The article is unexpected (after κήρυκας, συγγραφεῖς) but D. means to point to the lawyers as a notorious class (and to distinguish them from the 'claimants to legal experience' who draft the documents: *iuris consulti*, presumably).   **δικορράφους:** since the verb δικορραφεῖν is classical (Aristoph. *Clouds* 1483), it is an accident that examples of the noun are late. LSJ cite Aristaenetus 2.3, where Glycera is apprehensive about her lawyer lover μή με δικορράφος ὢν ἀναίτιον αἰτιάσηται. συνηγόρους 'advocates', who undertake to defend even criminals for a fee, and to pull out all the stops of indignation and pathos on behalf of people with whom they have no connection.

124 γλωσσοτέχνας . . . δικοτέχνας 'tongueworkers', 'court-workers', possessors of 'tonguecraft' and 'courtcraft'. These words are

presumably coined *ad hoc*.   **Τούτων**: sc. these occupations.
ὥσπερ ταῖς νῦν οἰκουμέναις: Wilamowitz, deleting **ταῖς**, took this to
mean 'being, as it were, founded now', a reference to D.'s 'legislative'
proposals. But D. perhaps means merely 'to cities conducted like the
present ones', and it is **ταῖς** before **πόλεσι** that may have to be deleted.
κηρυγμάτων ἐνίων: as it stands, this must depend on **ἀναγραφήν**,
and this does not seem to match §123. Capps may thus be right to
suggest **ἔνια**, 'some of the proclamations'.

125 'But we are not creating an ideal city; our theme is the opportun-
ities for a respectable life open to the poor.' Cf. §§103–4, Introd.
p. 11.   **προὐθέμεθα**: cf. §103.   **οὔτε ἀσχήμονας οὔτε βλαβεράς**:
cf. πρέπουσαι καὶ ἀβλαβεῖς, §126. The pair of adjectives covers the twin
topics of καλόν and συμφέρον, *honestum* and *utile*.

126 'This is the reason for our long discussion of farming and hunting,
and now of urban occupations.'   **τοῖς μὴ κάκιστα βιωσομένοις** 'to
those who hope to live a good life'. The sense is moral, rather than
economic: Cohoon's 'low standard of living' is misleading.   **χείρους**:
i.e. morally worse than before.

127–32 'If all this is useful, our discursiveness may be excused.
Trades and businesses are important, and we should not complain at
digressions about important subjects. Neither should we complain at a
writer [Plato, in the *Republic*] who professes to discuss justice but in fact
gives a long discussion of the state, so long as what he says is germane
to his original position.'   **πρὸς πολιτείαν καὶ τὴν τοῦ προσήκοντος
αἵρεσιν** 'for public policy and the choice of a proper way of life'.
D. has left open (§124) the possibility that some of his regulations
may be useful 'to cities'; he now claims that as a justification of his
discursiveness.   **μάτην ἄλλως**: pleonasm, cf. 55.12.   **τοῖς
μετρίοις** 'people of moderate means', a euphemism for 'poor' (Lampe
s.v. 1.b).   **καὶ καθ' αὐτήν** 'even on its own', i.e. without its possible
bearing on public policy.

128 **μακραί**: the adjective should agree with ἐκτροπαί, and Reiske's
correction should be accepted. The ἐκτροπαί here seem to be the
discussions of trades, etc., just preceding.   **[λόγων]**: Casaubon's deletion seems right. The word is wrongly repeated from above.   **οὐ
προσηκόντων** 'inappropriate', 'improper'.   **ὡς οὐκ . . . διεξίηι** 'because the speaker has not abandoned the general subject so long as he
is expounding matters necessary and appropriate to philosophy'.

129′ οἵ γε . . . μετῆλθον 'who, when they have picked up the first trail and, in the course of following it, come upon a clearer and closer one, do not hesitate to follow this, and, having taken what has come in their way, subsequently go over to the other'. Text unsure: ξυνακολουθήσαντες . . . μετελθεῖν is a possible alternative. The metaphor is clear: the hunter follows a fresh trail, accidentally met with, but later returns to his original quarry. For hunting metaphors in Plato, see *Rep.* IV 432D ἰοὺ ἰοὺ ὦ Γλαύκων· κινδυνεύομέν τι ἔχειν ἴχνος, *Laws* II 654B τοῦθ' ἡμῖν αὖ καθάπερ κυσὶν ἰχνευούσαις διερευνητέον, *Parmen.* 128C ὥσπερ γε αἱ Λάκαιναι σκύλακες εὖ μεταθεῖς τε καὶ ἰχνεύεις τὰ λεχθέντα, *Lysis* 218C πάνυ ἔχαιρον, ὥσπερ θηρευτής τις, ἔχων ἀγαπητῶς ὃ ἐθηρευόμην.

130 ἐκεῖνο . . . ὅστις: WS §2510.   **περὶ . . . δικαιοσύνης:** D. clearly refers to Plato's *Republic*, which begins with this question, but diverges into the construction of an ideal state in order to answer it. It is not clear whether he is following a tradition of criticism; this need not be so, since it is better for his argument if the *Republic* is an acknowledged masterpiece. But Proclus, *In rem p.* 1.6.24ff. promises detailed discussion of unity, and (11.6ff.) discusses whether the main theme is justice or πολιτεία: he thinks the two views can be reconciled. D's view anyway seems to be that the subject is δικαιοσύνη, and the 'city' just a παράδειγμα (cf. *Rep.* 472C).   **πάσας μεταβολὰς . . . ἐπιδεικνύς:** in books VIII and IX.   **ἐναργῶς . . . μεγαλοπρεπῶς:** a good characterization of the 'vividness' and 'magniloquence' with which Plato portrays the corrupt forms of government.

131 τῆς περὶ τὸ παράδειγμα δήπουθεν 'about the model'. For δήπουθεν, see on §39. Here it is equivalent to δῆθεν (cf. Denniston (1954) 264–6), and indicates that D. does not accept the criticism he reports.   **ἀλλ' ὡς οὐδὲν . . . εὐθύνεται** 'but, on the ground that what is said is irrelevant to the proposed subject, and the question in aid of which it was brought in the first place is made no clearer by it, he is, if at all, criticized fairly'. Note the variation between acc. absolute (ὄντα . . . τὰ εἰρημένα) and gen. absolute (σαφεστέρου . . . γεγονότος): in the examples in K–G II 90 (Xen., Thuc.) the genitives precede the accusatives, so this instance is somewhat strange. For εἴπερ ἄρα, see Denniston (1954) 38: e.g. Demosth. 21.138 ἴσως μὲν οὐκ ἂν ὑβρίζοι, εἰ δ' ἄρα, ἐλάττονος ἄξιος ἔσται τοῦ μικροτάτου παρ' ὑμῖν.

132 λεγοίμεθα: φαινώμεθα (MSS) is clearly wrongly repeated from

above: λεγοίμεθα or δοκοῖμεν meets the need.   **Περὶ δὲ τῶν λοιπῶν:**
this goes back to §126, the intervening passage on digressiveness being
itself a digression.

133–52 The whole of the rest of the speech is occupied with a tirade
against prostitution and sexual licence. No argument in favour of
prostitution will stand, even (§140) the suggestion that it acts as a
preventive against adultery. Far from it, according to D.; it merely
encourages desires which lead to further immorality. Finally (§149), D.
turns to homosexuality, on which he takes a strongly disapproving line.

D.'s general view resembles that of his teacher Musonius (see esp.
63–7 Hense; A. C. van Geytenbeek, *Musonius Rufus* (1963) 51–77), and
is distanced sharply from the Cynic condonation of prostitution because
it saves us from worse sin: *cynici adulterium impugnantes processerunt eo ut
commendarent lupanar*, Bickel (1915) 361 n. 2.

133–6 (κωλύειν) 'We must legislate strongly against employment
in the trade of prostitution, which makes money from the loveless sexual
services of women or boys, slave or free, Greek or barbarian: this is a
worse business than that of the horse-breeders, and displays no respect
for the divinities that rule our sexual lives; in no city, however far from
the ideal, should such things be legal.'

133 Οὐ γὰρ δὴ . . . ἀπαγορευτέον: §124 told of occupations of
which some good can be said; of πορνοβοσκοί, *lenones*, there is nothing.
προσχρῆσθαι 'use' (LSJ s.v.).   **μήτε οὖν πένητα μήτε πλούσιον:**
Denniston (1954) 419 (a Platonic use of οὖν, not in orators). Cf. just
below (§134) μήτ' οὖν βαρβαρικὰ σώματα μήτε Ἑλλήνων. D. is primarily legislating for πένητες, but here his prohibition is universal.
ὕβρεως καὶ ἀκολασίας 'outrage and immorality'.   **ἐκλέγοντας:** *constructio ad sensum*, following the singular μηδένα.   **ἀνεράστων ἐρώτων**
'loveless loves'. For this type of oxymoron (type: ἄδωρα δῶρα) see
Wackernagel (1928) II 291. Not common in D., but Schmid (1887) I
174 cites (e.g.) ἀγνώμονι γνώμῃ (32.16), τιμῆς ἀτίμου (77/78.37). It is
especially common in tragedy (Fraenkel on *Ag.* 1142), and so a mark of
some rhetorical pretension in prose.   **συναγωγεῖς:** the commoner
and more literary form (συναγωγός as a substantive is rare), which
Emperius seems right to prefer.   **αἰχμάλωτα . . . ῥυπαρῶν** 'setting up
women or boys, prisoners of war or purchased, for disgraceful purposes
in filthy brothels . . .'   **ἄλλως:** i.e. purchased slaves are acquired in
a different way from prisoners of war. It is not implied that prisoners

are purchased.   **ἐπ' οἰκημάτων**: LSJ s.v. II 1. This euphemism for
'brothels' is common from Herodotus onwards.   **ἔν τε παρόδοις**
ἀρχόντων καὶ ἀγοραῖς 'in the rulers' entrances and in the open squares'.
πάροδος is 'entry', 'way of access', here to the presence of the ruler.

134 ἱπποφορβῶν . . . ἀποτελούσηι 'doing a fouler and more impure
deed than breeders of horses and asses, not coupling beast with beast
without compulsion, willing animals with willing animals that feel no
shame, but maddened, uncontrolled human beings with other humans
who are reluctant and ashamed, for a fruitless, barren physical copula-
tion that issues in destruction rather than in birth'. Note the polyptoton
and chiasmus (κτήνεσι κτήνη . . . ἑκόντα ἑκοῦσιν . . . οὐδὲν <u>αἰσχυνομένοις</u>
. . . ἀνθρώποις <u>αἰσχυνομένοις</u> καὶ <u>ἀκοῦσιν</u> . . . ἀνθρώπους) which mark
this elaborate outburst.   **οἰστρῶντας**: literally of madness caused by
the bite of the gadfly (οἶστρος) in cattle, but often used of violent sexual
passion (Pl. *Phaedrus* 251D).   **ἐπ' ἀτελεῖ . . . ἀποτελούσηι**: an impre-
cise reference to contraception and abortion, both common in the world
of prostitution. (ἀποτελούντων would agree with σωμάτων, or could
be taken as a loosely connected gen. abs., 'when people produce . . .';
neither seems likely, and I accept Emperius' change.)

135 The use of prostitutes offends the gods of birth and marriage:
Zeus Genethlios, Hera Gamelios, Moirai Telesphoroi, Artemis Lochia,
the Mother of the Gods, the Eileithyiai, and Aphrodite. In making his
point like this D. follows Stoic tradition. Chrysippus advised that the
wise man should marry, *ne Iouem Gamelium et Genethlium uiolet* (Jerome,
Adv. Jovinianum 2.48 = *SVF* III 727), and Musonius (p. 75 Hense) ad-
duces the presence of Hera Zygia, Eros, and Aphrodite to show the
solemnity of marriage, and in the same context emphasizes its purpose
of παιδοποιΐα.   **Δία γενέθλιον**: while θεοὶ γενέθλιοι, 'gods of birth',
are naturally invoked in marriage (cf. Hierocles ap. Stob. 4.22.24 θεοῖς
γαμηλίοις γενεθλίοις ἐφεστίοις), Ζεὺς γενέθλιος is less usual; cf. however Pind. *Ol.* 8.16; a literary rather than a cult title, it seems, and applied
to many gods, as tutelary guardians of individual lives or families.
Ἥραν γαμήλιον: the association of Zeus's wife with marriage is con-
stant (Nilsson (1941) I 401ff.); it was especially important in Plato's
ideal city of the *Laws* (774), and D. may well have this in mind.
Μοίρας τελεσφόρους: the adjective – 'bearing fulfilment' – is applied
to the Moirai in a different context, Aesch. *PV* 511; and Τελεσφόρος is
a title also of Gaia, Zeus, and Selene, and at Epidaurus the name of a

god. **λοχίαν Ἄρτεμιν** 'the virgin is also the birth goddess' (Burkert (1985) 151); she can both ease pain and kill in childbirth. **μητέρα 'Ρέαν:** the wife of Kronos and mother of Zeus and Hera, assimilated to Cybele in the Graeco-Roman world, and universally worshipped as the Great Mother, has a less specific relation to marriage, but her inclusion is not surprising. **Εἰλειθυίας:** for the plural, see *Il.* 19.119, Fraser on Apollodorus 2.4.6.

136 μὴ δὴ ἐπιτρέπειν: δή is probably resumptive (Denniston (1954) 225), and the infinitive may be regarded either as dependent on λέγοντι (§133) or, like ἐᾶν below, as used for an imperative, as often in laws (WS §2013.b). **νομοθετεῖν** 'make legal provision for …' **ἢ ὁποσταισοῦν** 'or umpteenth'. Naber is clearly right: we need the indefinite ordinal numeral, to follow δευτέραις ἢ τρίταις ἢ τετάρταις. Cf. Demosth. *De corona* 310 οὐ πρῶτος, οὐ δεύτερος … οὐχ ὁποστοσοῦν, 'not anywhere in the list'. **ἐὰν … κωλύειν** 'if it is in the power of any of them to put a stop to such things'.

137 'Deeply ingrained bad practices must be checked so far as possible; evil is never stable, but always increases.' **ἐσκιρωμένα** 'inveterate' (*inueterata*, Sen. *Epist.* 85.10), 'hardened': spelling (-ρ- or -ρρ-) uncertain, and the compound ἐνσκιρρόω (Xen. *Eq.* 4.2) is better attested than the simple verb. But cf. Olympiodorus, *In Gorgiam* 179, 32 Westerink ἐσκιρρωμένων παθῶν (Jahn, for ἐσκηρ—). **παραλάβηι:** sc. the ruler or lawgiver. **μήτοι γε … ἀκόλαστα** 'he must at any rate not allow them to go untreated or unchastised'. **ἀμηιγέπηι** 'somehow or other': see on §17. **στέλλειν** 'repress'. Though συστέλλειν is common in this sense, and στέλλειν elsewhere in D. means 'send' or 'dress', Cobet's συστέλλειν is not necessary: cf. Philo, *De spec. leg.* 2.21 παιδεία … ἀπὸ τῶν ὑψηλῶν καὶ ὑπερόγκων ἀντισπῶσα καὶ στέλλουσα καὶ τὸ ἄνισον … θεραπεύουσα. **ὡς … τυγχάνοντα:** the principle that evil is unstable and has no natural μέτρον ('measure' being a characteristic of good (cf. esp. Pl. *Phileb.* 64D)) is common to much Greek thinking. Sen. *Epist.* 47.21 *leuis est malitia, saepe mutatur, non in melius sed in aliud* provides a Stoic text to parallel the main idea here. For D., cf. *Or.* 31.142: 'You will never find any bad habit stable or stationary, until it is completely prevented. For, because it is always admitting additions and its gradual progress is hard to detect and no one easily sees how much worse the latter state is than the former, it extends infinitely, like ulcers and diseases whose natural characteristic is to keep on growing.' **μηδενὸς . . . τυγχάνοντα**: this is *not* conditional in sense: μή is used with participles in later Greek with no such limitation. Cf. note on 7.28.

138 'We should not condone sexual use of slaves or humble people, both because our common humanity implies an understanding of good and evil, and because licence in small things leads to misbehaviour in great.'   **μὴ πάνυ τι . . . ῥαιθύμως φέροντας** 'by no means tolerating, out of humane feeling or idleness . . .' Cf. the common use of οὐ πάνυ, 'not at all': LSJ s.v. πάνυ 3.   **οὐ ταύτηι μόνον . . . γέγονεν** 'not simply because the entire human race was born honoured and honoured equally by the creator god, every member of it having the same marks and tokens that it is justly honoured, namely both reason and the experience of fair and foul . . .' This is sound Stoic doctrine: we owe our share of λόγος to god, who is the source of all λόγος; we are unique in this; and we acquire our knowledge of αἰσχρόν and καλόν (to the Stoics inseparable from ἀγαθόν and κακόν: cf. Sen *Epist.* 120.1–4) by observation and experience, building on our natural and god-given potentiality for virtue: σπέρμα ἀρετῆς ἑκάστωι ἡμῶν ἐνεῖναι, says Musonius (8.2 Hense), but this seed must be made to grow in the child's development to adulthood. For a good general orientation, see Long (1974) 184–9.   **ἔντιμον καὶ ὁμότιμον**: for the figure (a type of paronomasia) cf. 12.46 ἀντίτεχνοι καὶ ὁμότεχνοι. The word ὁμότιμος is a loaded one: it may imply not only that all men are equally honoured of god but that we in some sense share his honour: cf. Theocr. 17.16 of Ptolemy τῆνον καὶ μακάρεσσι πατὴρ ὁμότιμον ἔθηκεν. Favorinus (= [D] *Or.* 37.45) knows of the ὁμότιμοι as Persian nobles (Xen. *Cyr.* 2.1.9 etc.); there may be a suggestion of this also.   **σημεῖα καὶ σύμβολα**: if there is any distinction intended, it is that σημεῖα are marks which we have in our nature (like birthmarks or brandings, cf. 36.43) and σύμβολα tokens of identification or passwords which we carry. It would be wrong to attach any technical sense to either word.   **ὅτι . . . ὑπερβαίνειν** 'that it is hard to find a limit which criminality developed by licence might begin to be afraid to transgress'.   **ἀλλ' ἀπὸ . . . λοιπῶν** 'instead, gaining an uncontrollable strength and power from practice and habituation acquired in what seem to be small and permissible matters, it no longer shrinks from anything'. Just as practice in small things enables us to form habits which will prove good in greater matters (cf. e.g. Plu. *De garrulitate* 511F, Ingenkamp (1971)

105), so the same holds for the acquisition of vicious behaviour patterns. ἀκάθεκτον: a favourite word with Philo for passions of all kinds, but apparently uncommon in pagan literature.

139 'These "open" acts of adultery are not a prophylactic against worse sins, they actually lead to them.'   παντὸς μᾶλλον 'above all', LSJ s.v. πᾶς III 4 (common in Plato).   ἀτίμους: unless this means 'unpunished' (as perhaps in Pl. *Laws* 855c, but see England *ad loc.*), it contrasts use of prostitutes, as a 'low' form of adultery, with the seduction of ἐντίμους γυναῖκας καὶ παῖδας. Cf. §138 εἰς τὰ ἄτιμα . . . σώματα. Cohoon's 'committed with outcasts' is essentially right, if awkwardly expressed.   τῶι . . . τολμᾶσθαι: D. (11.21) uses τοῦ and infin. in a final sense, but examples of the construction used to express a consequence are uncertain (K–G II 41), though there are examples in less literary Greek (Matthew 21.32, see Blass–Debrunner §400.5). τῶι for τοῦ (Selden) is a simple change: 'because such things are very lightly ventured upon when modesty is generally despised'.   ἀλλ' οὐχ . . . εὑρῆσθαι: sc. οἴεσθαι χρή.   ὑπὲρ ἀσφαλείας . . . ἁμαρτημάτων alludes to a traditional view (both Cynic and worldly-wise) that the use of prostitutes satisfies natural needs cheaply, and so keeps people from doing worse. It is common ground to ancient moralists that adultery is more heinous, both because it infringes property and because it tends to be expensive and dangerous (cf. Hor. *Sat.* 1.2). Musonius (63ff. Hense) thinks other sexual activity outside marriage is nearly as bad; the user of prostitutes demeans and sins against himself. Though D. does not make this point, his attitude is not very different. For a general survey of ancient views, see H. Herter, *RAC* s.v. Dirne.

140 'We should speak plainly to lawgivers who permit prostitution, and warn them that it leads to the very crime they wish to prevent, adultery.'   ἀγροικότερον 'rudely' – we should not mince our words. Ὦ σοφοὶ νομοθέται: alludes probably to a supposed law of Solon (Athen. XIII 569D) who διὰ τὴν τῶν νεῶν ἀκμὴν ἔστησεν ἐπὶ οἰκημάτων γύναια πριάμενος. The whole development that follows recalls rhetorical treatments of these themes: Liban. *Decl.* 25, debating 'whether Lais should be recalled to Corinth', contains similar arguments: cf. also *Rhet. Gr.* 8.409 Walz, 'prostitutes recalled because adulteries have increased owing to their absence'. Cf. 12.49ff. for D.'s including *suasoria*-material in his discourses.   σωφροσύνης φάρμακον 'medicine to ensure chastity'. Cf. Pl. *Phaedrus* 274E, LSJ s.v. φάρμακον II 2.   ὅπως . . .

μὴ . . . διώκοντας: not a final clause but a prohibition ('take care lest': subjunctive is an alternative to future indicative, *GMT* §283, 364): 'Beware lest these open, unlocked houses of ill fame throw open locked homes and inner chambers, and turn overt offenders, whose present crimes cost little, in the direction of free women of standing, at the expense of much money and many presents, because they are no longer content with the cheap and readily available, but pursue the very forbidden thing itself, in fear and at monstrous expense.'

141–2 'Where husbands are so complaisant, what confidence can we have in the virginity of girls before marriage?'

The form of this transitional passage is repeated at §149, where D. passes from girls to boys. It is implied that each stage is worse than the preceding: so the seduction of virgins of good class is worse than that of married women.

The topic of complaisant husbands is common: see esp. Juv. 6.136–41, with de Decker (1913) 23–36. τὰ τῶν μοιχειῶν μεγαλοπρεπέστερόν πως παραπέμπεται 'adultery is given a grand send-off', i.e. the husband displays magnanimity by politely letting his wife and her lover go. χρηστότητος 'good nature', here with a pejorative element: 'soft-heartedness'. τὰ δέ τινα: LSJ s.v. τις A.10.c. ξένους . . . ἀνεχομένων 'freely letting the adulterers be called guests, friends or family'.

142 ἐξενάγηται: the perfect is closer to the MS reading ἐξάγεται than Geel's ξεναγεῖται, and seems an appropriate tense. The sense is also right: 'in houses where such generous hospitality is given in relation to the wives . . .' ἐξάγεται – 'lead out', 'drive out', or 'export' in other passages of D. – is very difficult: Cohoon ventures 'where these intrigues of married women are carried on with such an air of respectability . . .' τῆς κορείας 'maidenhood', a poetical word (late epigrams and Christian poets), and a surprising feature in D. τὸν ὑμέναιον: the wedding-god and the wedding-song have the same name; he is not properly invoked unless the bride is a virgin.

143–8 'Much that happens nowadays reproduces the stories of mythology; gold flows, as for Danae; rivers and bathing-places are scenes of vice; if the bastard children were allowed to survive, the world would be full of them.'

143 δίχα γε . . . πολυπραγμοσύνης: Cohoon thinks of the angry fathers of comedy, but this does not suit the context. Acrisius, Danae's father, put her in the wooden box and launched her on the sea with her baby Perseus. †ἀλλά†: τἆλλα is perhaps the best correction: 'since many imitate the fabled loves of the gods in other respects, apart from the angry interventions of the fathers'. **χρυσοῦ ... διὰ τῶν ὀροφῶν**: this interpretation of the story of Danae is common: Menander, *Samia* 589ff., Hor. *Odes* 3.16, Ov. *Amores* 3.8.20. There are a number of epigrams in the *Greek Anthology* which use it: e.g. *Anth. Pal.* 5.34 (= Parmenion 2, *Garland of Philip* (Gow–Page, 1968) 2579): ὁ Ζεὺς τὴν Δανάην χρυσοῦ, κἀγὼ δὲ σὲ χρυσοῦ· | πλείονα γὰρ δοῦναι τοῦ Διὸς οὐ δύναμαι. Cf. also *Anth. Pal.* 5.31, 5.53.   **οὐ χαλκῶν ... τῶν οἰκημάτων**: Danae was in a tower or underground chamber of bronze (*turris aenea*, Hor. *loc. cit.*).

144 παιδαγωγῶν: Avezzù (1985) raises the unnecessary difficulty that male *paedagogi* do not have κόλπους, 'bosoms'; but though the word is chosen to suit Danae, it applies also to any fold or pocket of clothing, and especially where one keeps money (LSJ s.v. II).   **κατ' αὐτάς που τὰς κλισιάδας** 'through the doors themselves'. Gasda's correction is surely right: it makes a good contrast with 'through the roof', whereas τὰς κλισίας, 'the beds', does not, and it is hard to understand the plural.

145 ἐν ποταμοῖς καὶ ἐπὶ κρηνῶν: D. may have in mind especially the story of Tyro and Poseidon (disguised as the river-god Enipeus), *Od.* 11.235ff., a favourite with rhetoricians and poets (Men. Rhet. 402.10, with Russell–Wilson (1981)); or Polydora and Spercheios, *Il.* 16.175 (see on §146).   **κατ' οἰκίας ... ἄλσεσιν** 'in houses (? as rich as these) and luxurious lodges in parks and suburban villas, in prepared bridal chambers and wonderful groves'. The exact sense of some of these terms is unsure: why οὕτως εὐδαίμονας? If it means 'as rich as these you see', there are implications for the place of delivery of the speech. Moreover κῆποι (= *horti*, private house with park), προαστεῖα (*suburbana*), and ἄλση (*luci*) suggest a Roman setting. Cf. von Arnim (1898) 458.   **οὐ ⟨περὶ⟩ πενιχρὰς ... βασιλέων**: perhaps Nausicaa (though her father was by no means poor) or Amymone, daughter of Danaus, sent on her own by her father from Argos to Lerna to draw water, and raped by Poseidon.   **ψυχρὰ λουτρὰ ... ἀναπεπταμένοις**: certainly applies to Nausicaa. The detail is given to make a rhetorical contrast with the hot baths on private property which are the scene of present-day seductions.

146 ἐν ἐκείνηι τῆι πόλει: i.e. in the city we are talking about, which the lawgivers of §140 administer.   **Εὔδωρον**: *Il.* 16.179, son of Hermes and Polymele, daughter of Phylas: D. confuses this with *Il.* 16.175, which tells of Polydora daughter of Peleus, who bore Menesthios to the river-god Spercheios.   **ὑποκοριζόμενος** 'nicknaming' him. ὑποκορίζομαι is usually applied to euphemistic or endearing names, and so here παρθένιος is a softer equivalent for νόθος.

147 Παρθενίαι: the Spartan 'natural sons', who went with Phalanthus to Tarentum, after the Messenian wars: for the confused tradition, see Aristot. *Pol.* 1306b27; Antiochus, *FGrHist* 535 F 13; Ephorus, *FGrHist* 70 F 216; G. L. Huxley, *Early Sparta* (1962) 378; T. J. Dunbabin, *The Western Greeks* (1948) 29–31.   **εἰ μὴ διεφθείροντο**: infanticide or exposure or possibly abortion. For the association of abortion with adultery, cf. e.g. [Quint.] *Decl. min.* 277.10 *non nouimus hos mores turpissimarum feminarum, ut oderint puerperia...?*; Juv. 6.594–601; and in general, S. Pomeroy (1975) 166ff.   **ταῖς οὕτως τρυφώσαις πόλεσι**: the 'real' city, which D. describes, is τρυφῶσα πόλις, like that imagined in Pl. *Rep.* (II 372E, 399E).   **δαιμονίου ... ἐπιμελείας** 'supernatural care', such as led to the safety of illegitimate children in legend, e.g. Romulus and Remus.   **πάντα μεστὰ ἡρώων** 'the world full of heroes', i.e. of children of half-divine – in human terms, half-noble – birth. For πάντα μεστά cf. e.g. Xen. *Hell.* 3.4.18.

148 τραφῶσι: the MSS have φανῶσι, 'are revealed', 'are seen', but this contradicts κρύφα, and Schwartz's correction – 'are brought up' – is probably right.

149–52 'In such a licentious society, homosexuality will also flourish, because men will not be content with normal vices but will seek novelty in unnatural and inaccessible pleasures.'

For the condemnation of homosexuality as παρὰ φύσιν, see esp. Pl. *Laws* 841A4, with Dover (1978) 165ff. D.'s view is generally hostile: 4.102, 77/78.36. In 36.8 (q.v.) the Olbians corrupt their barbarian neighbours by introducing them to the homosexual practices they inherited from Ionia. Musonius too (63–7 Hense) treats homosexuality as a vice as bad as adultery – but not, like D., as the culminating evil.

149 οὕτως ἀμελῶς ἔχηι 'are so careless'. ἁπλῶς seems pointless, and I accept Reiske's proposal.   **τοὺς κόρους** 'the boys'. Rare word in prose, but note Pl. *Laws* 772A χορεύοντάς τε καὶ χορευούσας κόρους καὶ κόρας, and Musonius 18.4 Hense ὁμοίως κόραις καὶ κόροις.   **τό γε ἀκόλαστον γένος** 'the licentious sort' of people.   **τοῦτον ... τῆς**

φύσεως 'making nature's limit their own clear and sufficient limit'. **διακορές** 'sated'. Only here in D., but note Pl. *Laws* 629B4.

150 σὺν τῆι τοῦ Διὸς μηχανῆι: again a reference to Danae and the shower of gold.   **μετὰ χεῖρας** 'in his hand', LSJ s.v. χείρ II 6.i.   **οὐ μήποτε ἀποτυγχάνηι:** WS §2755; present subjunctive is less common than aorist in this idiom.

151 σπάνιον 'rare', and so specially valuable. Cf. Eur. *IA* 1162 σπάνιον δὲ θήρευμ' ἀνδρὶ τοιαύτην λαβεῖν | δάμαρτα· φλαύραν δ' οὐ σπάνις γυναῖκ' ἔχειν.   **ὡς ἕτοιμον δή τινα:** δή indicates the idea in their thought, not vouched for by the author: Denniston (1954) 229–36 for similar uses.   **θῆλυν:** cf. the speech of Protogenes in favour of male homosexuality in Plutarch's *Amatorius* 750F: εἰ δ' οὖν καὶ τοῦτο τὸ πάθος [love of women] δεῖ καλεῖν Ἔρωτα, θῆλυν καὶ νόθον ὥσπερ εἰς Κυνόσαργες συντελοῦντα τὴν γυναικωνῖτιν ('feminine and illegitimate, belonging to the women's quarters as its Cynosarges [the gymnasium associated with νόθοι]').   **τοὺς ἄρξοντας ... καταισχύνειν:** the corrupter of the promising young men intends to disgrace future leaders. This recalls classical διαβολή of politicians: cf. e.g. Aristoph. *Knights* 878–80 (with Dover (1978) 141). Aristophanes in Pl. *Symp.* 192A is made to say that boys who are homosexual partners of men grow up to be politicians: τελεωθέντες μόνοι ἀποβαίνουσιν εἰς τὰ πολιτικὰ ἄνδρες (*uiri*) οἱ τοιοῦτοι. D. puts a cynical gloss on all this.

152 τοῖς ἄγαν φιλοπόταις ... πάθος: the comparison with inebriates who deliberately make themselves thirsty by making themselves sweat (in hot baths) or by taking salty or sharp food, recalls practices mentioned in Roman satire and moralizing: cf. Juv. 6.425 (with Courtney *ad loc.*), Plin. *NH* 14.137ff. *bibendi causa etiam uenena concipiuntur, aliis cicutam praesumentibus ut bibere mors cogat ... cautissimos ex iis in balneis coqui uidebimus.*

12 Olympicus

Prolalia

1–16 'I am surrounded by a crowd, like the owl "admired", as they say, by the other birds. But why do the birds not rather "admire" the beautiful peacock or the singing swan? You neglect the orators and poets and sophists, and flock to hear me; am I not indeed like the owl? (§§1–5)

'It is some supernatural good fortune that gave the owl this popularity: Athena and the Athenians loved him, and Phidias included him in his portrayal of Athena Parthenos, with the consent of the *demos*, though he had to represent Pericles and himself surreptitiously. (§6)

'Yet this good fortune means nothing for the owl unless he is wise. And that is the point of Aesop's fable of how the owl warned the birds about the oak-tree, because it was one day going to produce mistletoe, and so bird-lime – and about flax, and about bows and arrows. They took no notice until too late, and only came to admire him when he had no message for them and could only moan. (§§6–8)

'So perhaps you have a tradition of the good advice Philosophy gave to the ancient Greeks, which leads their modern successors to flock around people like me, who look like philosophers. But I have no skill or knowledge. Others have, and I recommend you to leave everything else and follow them – or at least get your children taught by them! I should become their pupil myself, if I were stronger. As it is, I have to content myself with gathering bits of old wisdom. (§9–12)

'As a matter of fact, there is another way in which I resemble the owl: I could be a useful decoy to attract a crowd to any sophist who cared to employ me. Only no one does! (§13)

'I am sure you believe me when I say I have no knowledge or experience. You are so very wise yourselves. You would have believed Socrates when he said he knew nothing, and you would have thought Hippias and Polus and Gorgias wise and happy, wouldn't you? But let me tell you: the man you have come to hear really is old, ugly, feeble, and totally unqualified – all he has is his long hair. Nevertheless, I will try to satisfy you; but you will hear no grand language, and much discursiveness: I am, after all, a garrulous wanderer.' (§§14–16)

This synopsis endeavours to show this rambling *prolalia* as a whole; I have taken a line close to that of Cristofferson (1933/4) and opposed to that of Lemarchand (1929), who held that there were traces of two versions intertwined in the text we have: the original exordium consisted essentially of §§1–2 ἄστροις, §3 ὅταν … §5 γιγνομένωι, and §§14–16; the effect of this is to make everything relating to the wisdom of the owl and the comparison of ancient and modern philosophy an intrusion into the original plan. Consequential transpositions and deletions are numerous; and the theory is too involved to be at all plausible.

This is not to say there are not difficulties. D.'s ἀδολεσχία, paraded in §16, is displayed even in the formalities of his introduction. The basic difficulty lies in his use of the image of the owl. It stands both for himself, and for philosophy. Its resemblance to D. lies in its capacity to attract a crowd and consequent usefulness as a decoy. Its resemblance to philosophy is that its wise counsel was unheeded until too late, and now it is dumb. D. *looks* like a philosopher, but he is really capable of no more than the collection of a little forgotten wisdom, for philosophy now is dumb, like the owl that can only moan.

There is a close parallel in *Or.* 72.13–15. This short speech, περὶ τοῦ σχήματος, on the reactions aroused by the mere look of a 'philosopher', may itself be a προλαλία; its date is not known:

> Because they think this [sc. that 'philosophers' are wise], they come up expecting to hear from us the sort of things that Aesop or Socrates or Diogenes used to say; they importune us and cannot keep away from anyone they see so dressed – like birds when they see an owl. Aesop devised a fable about this, in which he tells how the birds came to the owl and requested him to move from his shelter in the buildings, and instead build his nest, as they did, in trees and with their branches, which gave a more conspicuous place from which to sing. In particular, they said, this oak-tree which was just planted would provide a good perch when it had developed, and one could take advantage of its green foliage. The owl, however, advised the birds not to do this, nor to take pleasure in the growth of a plant 'created to bear mistletoe, death to the winged'. But the birds did not accept the owl's advice; on the contrary, they were pleased as the oak grew and, when it was big enough, they settled on it and sang. Only when mistletoe grew, and they were easily trapped by man with its bird-lime, did they repent and begin to admire the owl for its advice. That is how they are now. They think it is clever and wise, and so they want to be close to it, thinking they may acquire some advantage from the association. And it is all in vain, or does harm. The ancient owl was indeed sensible and could give advice. Modern owls only have the wings and the eyes and the beak; in other respects they are

stupider than the other birds. They cannot even help themselves, else they wouldn't be captured and kept in captivity by fowlers. Now each of us has the clothes of Socrates or Diogenes, but in wisdom we are very far from being like those men in manner of life or in power of conversation. We are simply an object of curiosity, attracting a great crowd of birds – as they really are – as the owls do; we are fools ourselves and we are assailed by fools.

The analogy between a popular figure and the 'mobbed' owl is not new in D.: Timon of Phlius used it of Arcesilaus in his parody of Homer (Diog. Laert. 4.42, *Sillographi Graeci* (Wachsmuth) p. 119, *Suppl. Hellenist.* (Lloyd-Jones and Parsons) 808):

> ὡς εἰπὼν ὄχλοιο περίστασιν εἰσκατέδυνεν,
> οἱ δέ μιν ἠΰτε γλαῦκα πέρι σπίζαι τερατοῦντο
> ἠλέματον δεικνύντες, ὁθούνεκεν ὀχλοάρεσκος·
> οὐ μέγα πρῆγμα, τάλας· τί πλατύνεαι ἠλίθιος ὥς;

So saying, he plunged into the surrounding crowd. They marvelled at him like finches round an owl, pointing to him as a fool, because he was a crowd-pleaser. 'No big deal, poor fellow: why spread yourself out like an idiot?'

Cf. also Lucian, *Harmonides* 1, Plu. *Nicias* 19.5 (= Timaeus, *FGrHist* 566 F 100a).

1 Ἀλλ' ἦ . . . πάθος; 'Can it be, gentlemen, that I have experienced, in your company and in that of many others besides, the alleged extraordinary and paradoxical experience of the owl?' τὸ λεγόμενον goes with πάθος: the hyperbaton produces a resemblance, probably deliberate, to the beginning of Plato's *Gorgias* (447A): Ἀλλ' ἦ τὸ λεγόμενον κατόπιν ἑορτῆς . . . **τὸ τῆς γλαυκὸς . . . πάθος:** the 'mobbing' of the owl by other birds was variously interpreted. Aristotle (*HA* IX 609a) makes them pluck its feathers, and treats the phenomenon as an instance of natural enmity between species: for him, the term θαυμάζειν is a popular one, and a misnomer. In Aelian (*NA* 1.29), the birds are frightened of the owl's tricks. D., like Aristotle, contrasts his own view with 'what men say'; but his interpretation – contempt – is devised to suit the parallel with himself, given his stance of εἰρώνεια. **σοφωτέραν:** the difficulty with this reading is that D.'s owl below *is* wise, at least to begin with (§7). Hence Geel's εὐφωνοτέραν and Stich's σεμνοτέραν. But it is perhaps better to keep the manuscript reading: D. may be (inadvertently?) introducing a characteristic which belongs to him, rather than to his paradigm the owl; or we could say that he is thinking of the present state of the owl in the fable, which implies that the birds are mistaken in attributing wisdom to it. Nevertheless, the difficulty is a real one; and the price of treating the whole *prolalia* as a unit may well seem to be to accept emendation here.   αὐτῶν anticipates τὰ ὄρνεα.   τοιαύτην ὁποίαν ἴσμεν 'such as we know him to be', a euphemism for 'ugly'.   ὅταν δήποτε . . . τῆς ἀσθενείας 'the other birds gather round him, whenever he utters his painful and disagreeable cry, and indeed whenever they so much as see him, sitting near him, or flying all around, despising his inferiority and weakness, as I suppose'. Aelian *loc. cit.* has the owl's cry attracting birds and making them sit near him (καθίζει πλησίον αὐτῆς) at night, while by day he charms them by his power of mimicry. This last point is not part of D.'s picture. It would spoil it.   περιέπουσι . . . ἴδηι: cf. §8 for variation between plural and singular verbs with neuter plural subjects. K–G 1 66 gives examples from Homer onwards; it seems to be favoured by Xenophon (*Cyn.* 11.4 τὰ δὲ [*sc.* θηρία] ἀκούοντα τῆς φωνῆς . . . περιθέουσι καὶ ἐπειδὰν μὴ εὑρίσκηι δίοδον ὑπερπηδᾶι καὶ ἁλίσκεται. Schmid (1887) 1 102, ΙΙ 22 n. 80. There does not seem to be any perceptible shift in sense (i.e. from stress on individuals to mass activity, cf. WS §§958–60).

   2 τὸν ταῶ: the peacock is one of the commonest themes of sophistic ecphrasis: Ach. Tat. 1.16, Aelian, *NA* 5.21, [Liban.] 8.527–9 F, Greg. Naz. *Or.* 34.554A, Tertullian, *De pallio* 3, D'Arcy Thompson (1895) 164–7.   καλὸν οὕτω . . . ὁμοιότητα 'so beautiful and varied; raising itself moreover, and displaying the beauty of its feathers, as it shows off to the female by flexing its tail and surrounding itself with what seems like a handsome theatre or a star-studded sky represented in painting; and at the same time marvellous in the rest of its body, like gold and lapis lazuli mixed together; and, finally, in the tips of its feathers, there are eyes, as it were, or rings, so shaped and in other ways like real eyes or rings.'

   This *ecphrasis* contains some difficult details. I read σύν τε for σύν γε, taking σύν adverbially; but there may well be more corruption. Von Arnim thought σώματι concealed some form of χρῶμα; but, if so, τῶι λοιπῶι makes no sense and would have to be changed. On my reading,

there are four points to be admired: (i) the general beauty and variety
(cf. *discolor*, Tertullian *loc. cit.*); (ii) the tail display; (iii) the rest of the
body; (iv) the eyes in the tail feathers. This is less orderly than Tertullian
and [Libanius], whose *ecphrases* both follow the rhetors' rule of proceed-
ing from head systematically to tail. The divergence from this norm is
perhaps appropriate to the informality of D.'s *dialexis*.   **θέατρον:**
Geel argued for M's ἄντρον, 'cave', but θέατρον is confirmed by Ach.
Tat. *loc. cit.*: ἔτυχε γὰρ τύχηι τινὶ συμβὰν τότε τὸν ὄρνιν ἀναπετάσαι
τὸ κάλλος καὶ τὸ θέατρον ἐπιδεικνύναι τῶν πτερῶν. The point of the
metaphor is the shape: a semicircular auditorium with its segments
of seats resembles the pattern of the spreading tail.   **γραφῆι . . .
ἄστροις:** cf. Ov. *Met.* 15.385 *Iunonis uolucrem quae cauda sidera portat.*
ἐγγύτατα . . . κεκραμένου: [Liban.] 8.528 τὸ δὲ τῆς δειρῆς χρυσαυγὲς
κυανέωι συμμίσγει.   **τινων** goes ἀπὸ κοινοῦ with both ὀφθαλμῶν and
δακτυλίων.   **τὴν ἄλλην ὁμοιότητα:** i.e. in colour and brilliance as
well as shape.

3 εἰ δ' αὖ . . . ἑαυτόν 'if one wishes to consider the lightness of his
plumage, how its length does not make it painful or hard to carry, he
offers himself to public view, quiet and motionless . . .'   **ἐστι:** I adopt
Reiske's correction for εἶναι, since a consecutive clause seems awkward.
ἐν μέσωι 'in public' (usually ἐν τῶι μέσωι in D.), rather than 'in the
centre' of the circular tail (though πανταχόθεν above might support
this interpretation). cf. Aelian, *NA* 5.21 ἐᾶι γὰρ ἐμπλησθῆναι τῆς θέας
τοὺς παρεστῶτας καὶ ἑαυτὸν περιάγει δεικνὺς φιλοπόνως τὸ τῆς
πτερώσεως πολύμορφον.   **ὥσπερ ἐν πομπῆι περιστρεφόμενος:** cf.
Synesius, *Dio* 39c καθάπερ ὁ ταῶς περιαθρῶν ἑαυτόν.   **ὅταν . . .
ὕλην:** cf. Aelian *loc. cit.* ἐὰν γοῦν θελήσηι φοβῆσαί τινα, ἐγείρας τὰ
οὐραῖα εἶτα διεσείσατο καὶ ἀπέστειλεν ἦχον, καὶ ἔδεισαν οἱ παρεστῶτες
ὡς ὁπλίτου τὸν ἐκ τῶν ὅπλων πεφοβημένοι δοῦπον. D.'s peacock is
noticeably less frightening.   **ἐπορθρευομένης** 'rising early'; in popular belief, the nightingale does not sleep: Aelian, *VH* 12.20 ἀμοιρεῖν
ὕπνου καὶ διὰ τέλους ἀγρυπνεῖν.   **οὐδὲν πάσχει πρὸς αὐτήν** 'have
no special feelings towards it'.

4 τὸν κύκνον: D.'s interpretation is essentially that of Pl. *Phaedo* 84ε
(swans rejoice that in death they are going to their god) and Aelian,
NA 5.34 (the swan knows there is no pain in death). D'Arcy Thompson
(1895) 104–8 gives the (extensive) literary evidence.   **εὐγήρως:** the
variant εὔγηρυς, 'sweet-voiced', is pointless. Cf. Aristot. *Rhet.* 1361b28

εὐγηρία δ' ἐστὶ βραδύτης γήρως μετ' ἀλυπίας.   **πρὸς ὄχθην ...
νησῖδα** 'on some river's bank or broad meadow or open lake shore, or
some flowery islet in a river'. This sounds very poetical, and Emperius
printed it as verse (dividing the lines as πλατύν, λίμνης, νησῖδα). Perhaps however D. is parodying the sophists: cf. Themistius, *Or.* 27.336c
μή με ἄλλως νομίσης ὡραΐζεσθαι τῶι κύκνωι καὶ τῆι ἀηδόνι καθάπερ οἱ
κομψοὶ σοφισταὶ οἱ κομμοῦντες τοὺς λόγους οἷον φυκίωι κέχρηνται
τούτοις τοῖς ὀρνέοις. Cf. also Himerius 40.2 Colonna: the swan and the
sophist are identified, and the swan sings by Ocean or by Cayster (cf. *Il.*
2.459ff.) and Hermus, or by some translucent fountain where it washes
its wings and honours the spring. Cf. also Basil, *Epist.* 20 [the tongue]
σιωπήσει ... οὐδαμῶς, σοφιστική τε οὖσα καὶ Ἀττική, οὐ μᾶλλον γε ἢ
αἱ ἀηδόνες, ὅταν τὸ ἔαρ αὐτὰς πρὸς ὠιδὴν ἀναστήσηι.

5 ῥήτορας ... ξυγγραφέας ... ἐμμέτρων καὶ ἀμέτρων λόγων:
there were no literary competitions in the Olympic games, but the
occasion had, since the fifth century, been a favoured venue for orators,
poets and historians who sought a wide audience (Herodotus, Gorgias,
Lysias). Cf. Introd. p. 14.   **τοῦτο δὲ πολλοὺς σοφιστάς ὡς ταῶς
ποικίλους δόξηι ... πτεροῖς** 'and also many sophists, like variegated
peacocks raising themselves on the wings of their reputation and their
pupils'. Text very uncertain: I follow Reiske in assuming a transposi-
tion, the two halves of the comparison having perhaps been accidentally
reversed. If this is right, the analogy between sophists and peacocks is
explicit, since both are named. Who are D.'s σοφισταί? Elsewhere he
applies the term to Hippias, Gorgias, and Polus (54.1: cf. below §14),
to the Seven Sages (10.26), to epideictic orators (32.68, perhaps 35.8),
and in general to pretenders to wisdom (4.14, 10.32, 32.35). Here the
mention of 'pupils' suggests the epideictic orator and declaimer; and if
this is so, the people ridiculed in §§10–13 are rather different. But it is
perhaps idle to draw distinctions; in D.'s language, σοφισταί are frauds.
Where σοφισταί are named below (§13) they are in need of an audience;
and, if one carries through the bird-imagery, they correspond not to
the peacock but to the fowler.

6 σχεδὸν οὐκ ἄνευ δαιμονίας τινὸς βουλήσεως καὶ τύχης: text
again unsure. The MSS have ὑφ' ἧς, introducing the next sentence; this
is hardly intelligible. For βουλήσεως καὶ τύχης, cf. *Or.* 1.57 ὅσοι γάρ
ποτε σοφοὶ καὶ ἀληθεῖς κατ' ἀνθρώπους λόγοι ... οὐκ ἄνευ θείας ποτε
βουλήσεως καὶ τύχης ... ἐγένοντο. This emendation is strengthened by

the reference to fortune in εὐτυχήματα below. But (i) the transition from what precedes is abrupt; (ii) we expect, e.g., ⟨καὶ γάρ⟩ καὶ to link the next sentence on. It is perhaps best to mark a lacuna before σχεδόν. **οὐκ ἀπαξιώσαντος . . . τῆι θεῶι:** the great statue of Athena Parthenos included a representation of an owl (on the goddess's head, according to Fink (1950)). Cf. Aristoph. *Knights* 1092: μουδόκει ἡ θεὸς αὐτὴ | ἐκ πόλεως ἐλθεῖν καὶ γλαῦξ αὐτῆι 'πικαθῆσθαι. **Περικλέα . . . ἀσπίδος:** the allusion to Phidias' unauthorized portrayal of himself and Pericles not only brings him into the speech for the first time as the great sculptor, but suggests his trial for peculation, and this in turn perhaps hints at the imaginary 'trial' which is the subject of §49–83. The story of the self-portrait of Pericles – a splendid figure, fighting an Amazon – is told by Plutarch (*Pericles* 31.4–5), but has no basis in fact (Stadter (1989) *ad loc.*)   **εἰ μὴ . . . πλείω** 'unless she really does possess some superior wisdom after all'. Cf. Denniston (1954) 37 for this use of ἄρα. **ἔπεισι** = ἐπέρχεται: incorrect by Attic standards (indic. εἶμι should be future in sense) but cf. 35.13, 51.1, 66.11.

7 Αἴσωπος: for D.'s other version of this fable, see above p. 160. The history of the story is discussed by B. E. Perry (*T.A.P.A.* 93 (1962) 315ff.), who traces it back to Demetrius of Phalerum, whose collection of Αἰσωπεῖα (see fr. 112 Wehrli), like his interest in proverbs, shows Peripatetic interest in various forms of popular wisdom, and probably helped to make the fable popular in the Roman period. There are two traditions, it seems: one of the owl's warning about the oak (or about oak, flax, and archer) (Perry (1965) 508), and one in which the swallow gives the warnings (Hausrath 39b, Chambry 350, *P. Mich.* 457, La Fontaine 1 8). The swallow also appears as giving good advice in Hausrath 206 (= Chambry 287), where she tells a bird not to be so foolish as to sit on a snake's egg. The detail in D. *Or.* 72, where the birds ask the *owl* to move from a house to a tree, suits the swallow's nesting habits better; and there is good reason to think that the swallow-version is the original. But fables allow much variation, and every user makes his own. For D., see also *Or.* 47.20, the fox that has eaten so much meat it cannot escape: Horace's *vulpecula* (*Epist.* 1.7.29).   **ἐκλέγειν** 'pluck out', 'pull out'.   **μὴ . . . φυήσεσθαι:** in late Greek, μή is used very widely with moods other than the indicative, whatever the sense: μή with acc. and infin. is common in D. See on 7.28.

8 ἰδοῦσα τοξευτήν τινα: Aeschylus, *Myrmidons* fr. 139 Nauck:

ὧδ' ἐστὶ μύθων τῶν Λιβυστικῶν κλέος,
πληγέντ' ἀτράκτωι τοξικῶι τὸν αἰετόν
εἰπεῖν ἰδόντα μηχανὴν πτερώματος·
τάδ' οὐχ ὑπ' ἄλλων, ἀλλὰ τοῖς αὐτῶν πτεροῖς
ἁλισκόμεσθα.

This was a famous allusion; Aristophanes (*Birds* 808) had quoted
Aeschylus, and this kept the knowledge of this passage alive. (That
it is called a 'Libyan' rather than an 'Aesopic' fable has no clear
significance: see in general R. Kassel, *Kleine Pauly* s.v. Fabel; also
OCD² s.v. Fable.)   **πτηνὰ ἐπιπέμπων βέλη**: cf. Eur. *HF* 179 πτήν'
ἐναρμόσας βέλη. It would be rash to infer from this poetical phrase that
D. has a verse fable in mind.   **ἠπίστει ... ἡγοῦντο ... ἔφασκον**:
cf. on §1 (περιέπουσι ... ἴδηι).   **ὡς [πρὸς] ἅπαντα ἐπισταμένην**:
the paradosis would mean 'as having knowledge to meet all circumstances'. But πρός is probably a dittography after πρόσεισιν: cf. πάντα
ἐπισταμένους §10.   **ὀδύρεται**: not descriptive of the owl's cry, but of
its supposed emotion of sadness.

9 καί μοι προσίασι διὰ τὸ σχῆμα: D., it seems, personifies philosophy
himself. His self-portrait is further developed esp. in *Or.* 72, περὶ τοῦ
σχήματος, probably of about the same date (see above p. 160), and in
Or. 13 περὶ τῆς φυγῆς. It seems to have been only after his exile that he
adopted this stance so blatantly; but it does not follow that he had no
interest in or knowledge of philosophy before these events. Introd. p.
6.   **ἀπαρρησίαστον** 'inhibited' from free speech: [Longinus] 44.4
speaks of τὸ ἀπαρρησίαστον καὶ οἷον ἔμφρουρον ὑπὸ συνηθείας ἀεὶ
κεκονδυλισμένον in his own day, in a passage clearly relating to the
political conditions of Roman rule. There is nothing so specific here:
philosophy, like the owl, has lost her voice, because people are not
prepared to hear her message. The word is not uncommon: Cic. *Ad Att.*
9.2a.27 *deinde etiam scit* ἀπαρρησίαστα *esse in ea causa querelam suam*, 'out
of court' (Shackleton Bailey). παρρησία was a quality much admired
by Cynics (Diog. Laert. 6.69) and there is a distinctly Cynic tone to D.'s
self-presentation here.

10 ἕτεροι ... ἄνδρες: has D. any specific target? The context suggests persons with a religious and moral message, and a claim to
Oriental wisdom. Geel thought of Apollonius of Tyana; if it is he, the
tradition that he and D. were friends (Philostr. *VA* 5.27ff., 8.7.2) is a

fiction, and indeed it does not seem very likely. (The reference in *Or.* 31.121, on which Geel relied, is to Musonius, not to Apollonius (von Arnim (1898) 216).) **τἄλλα ἐάσαντες ... ξυνακολουθοῦντες:** Mussies (1972) 76 rightly compares this with Matthew 19.29 καὶ πᾶς ὅστις ἀφῆκεν οἰκίας ἢ ἀδελφοὺς ἢ ἀδελφὰς ἢ πατέρα ἢ μητέρα ἢ τέκνα ἢ ἀγροὺς ἕνεκεν τοῦ ὀνόματός μου ἑκατονταπλασίονα λήμψεται. It is not inconceivable that, a generation after St Paul's wanderings, a Christian voice should have been heard at Olympia; but we should be warned by the fact that this topos of 'abandoning all things' has antecedents in classical literature, and in very different contexts: D. could have in mind [Demosth.] 11.9 (of Philip's subjects) καταλείποντες οἴκοι τέκνα γονεῖς γυναῖκας φθείρεσθαι καὶ καθ' ἑκάστην ἡμέραν κινδυνεύειν. D.'s irony is evident throughout this passage: in the bombastic list (θεῶν ἱερὰ καὶ προγόνων τάφους), in the oriental names, and in the hyperbole εὐδαιμονέστεροι ... τῆς εὐδαιμονίας. **καθιδρυθῶσιν** 'settle'. The teachers may wander, or find a settled home in some exotic place. **εἰς τὴν Βαβυλῶνα τὴν Νίνου:** inaccurate, hence attempts to emend. In the common legend, Ninus founded Nineveh, and Semiramis Babylon. D. may just be careless. **εἴτε ἐν Βάκτροις:** Zariuspa or Bactra (Balkh) was a Hellenized city, known to the Roman world from the silk-trade; it sent an embassy to Rome in Hadrian's reign. Its claim to be a source of wisdom presumably rests on its conservative, Zoroastrian culture; this had features which were not always admired, to judge from Strabo's comments (11.11.3) on Onesicritus' report of the Bactrian practice of throwing the old and sick to the dogs. **ἢ Σούσοις:** the old Persian capital, now a Hellenized city within the Parthian empire, had a very mixed population and culture. D. again probably thinks of it as connected with the Magi; cf. Plin. *NH* 24.163 on drugs available here, and at Babylon, and *in Bactris et circa Borysthenen*; Bidez–Cumont (1938) 167. **ἢ Παλιβόθροις:** Pataliputra, capital of the kingdom of Sandacottos (Chandragupta), to whom Megasthenes was sent as envoy from Seleucus Nicator, a place where one can study with the Brahmans (*Gymnosophistai*). **ἢ ἄλληι τινὶ πόλει ... χρήματα διδόντες:** the irony is still apparent, in the categorization of ἔνδοξοι πόλεις (cf. e.g. Men. Rhet. 353ff. Spengel) and in the emphasis on money.

11 εὐδαιμονέστεροι ... τῆς εὐδαιμονίας: cf. §36 σοφώτεροι ... τῆς ἁπάσης σοφίας, satirically said of the Epicureans. **ἑκοῦσί τε ...**

πάντα τρόπον 'entrusting them to them if they are willing – or, if not, persuading or compelling them to take them by every means'. ἐπιτρέπειν is a standard word for committing people to the care of teachers: e.g. Pl. *Lach.* 200D, *Protag.* 313E, *Laws* I 650A.   ὡς ἂν ... ὦσι: WS §§2193, 2202. This construction of final clauses is rare in classical Attic prose, but common in Xenophon, whence D. no doubt learned it.   οὐ γὰρ μόνον ... ἐξ ἀνάγκης: D. starts from Hesiod, *WD* 313ff.:

> ἔργον δ' οὐδὲν ὄνειδος, ἀεργίη δέ τ' ὄνειδος·
> εἰ δέ κεν ἐργάζηι, τάχα σε ζηλώσει ἀεργός
> πλουτέοντα· πλούτωι δ' ἀρετὴ καὶ κῦδος ὀπηδεῖ.

This was a famous passage. Plutarch (*De aud. poet.* 24E) criticized it, and thought ἀρετή must be taken to mean δόξα or δύναμις or εὐτυχία, to avoid the implication that virtue can be bought for money (ὤνιον ἀργυρίου). In 7.110–11 (q.v.), D. reinterprets *WD* 313. What is his point here? (i) MSS have ἀρετὴν ... ὀπηδεῖν (ὀπηδεῖ M). Since this produces some illogicality (the ἀλλὰ καί clause states a proposition as a fact, not as a belief), Geel may be right to read ἀρετὴ ... ὀπηδεῖ. But this is a minor matter. (ii) MSS have λόγος ἀρετῆι (−ή M). This is unintelligible, and two proposals have been widely accepted: (a) λόγοις ἀρετή: Reiske, Geel. 'Virtue follows literary education': i.e. D. corrects Hesiod – it's not only wealth that brings virtue, but education. This is of course ironical. The sense is adequate; but λόγοι seems a slightly odd way of representing the revelations which the σοφοί impart to their pupils, if these are indeed of a religious and moral nature. (b) von Arnim reads πλοῦτος for λόγος. Hesiod had said that ἀρετή and κῦδος follow πλοῦτος: D. adds that πλοῦτος is bound to follow ἀρετή. Yet we have just heard that both ἀρετή and πλοῦτος are among the advantages achievable by the σοφία these people impart: and how can one of these advantages then be said to follow from another? This may be too niggling an objection: von Arnim's solution remains the likeliest.

12 Ταῦτα ... προλέγω 'this I proclaim to you before this god' – i.e. in the presence of the great statue, which they can see, if the speech is delivered from the steps of the temple (Fink (1950) 93). Cf. 12.15 and 11.6 for this solemn (or ironically solemn) use of προλέγω.   **ἀλλ' ἀγαπᾶν ἀνάγκη** 'but we must needs be satisfied' if we can pick up some crumbs of ancient wisdom. Geel's excellent correction is to be accepted (haplography of AN accounts for the corruption). διὰ τὸ κακοπαθεῖν seems to repeat τὰ τοῦ σώματος – it is part of D.'s persona to be weak and ill (7.7, 7.58) from his hardships – but need not be suspected (as by von Arnim).   ὥσπερ . . . διδασκάλων 'some stale and cast-out relic of wisdom, for lack of better, living teachers'. Reiske's brilliant ἕωλον and χήτει deserve applause (for χήτει, cf. Pl. *Phaedrus* 239D χήτει οἰκείων); ἀντί is another possible correction for δή τι (easy palaeographically), but gives much less point.

13 On the owl's use as a decoy, see Aelian, *NA* 1.29, Aristot. *HA* IX 609a οἱ ὀρνιθοθῆραι θηρεύουσιν αὐτῆι παντοδαπὰ ὀρνίθια; D'Arcy Thompson (1895) 45.   ἀνδρὶ δὲ ὀρνιθοθῆραι . . . σοφιστῆι δὲ ἀνδρί: for the idiom, WS §986, Adam on Pl. *Rep.* 620C. λυσιτελέστατον κτημάτων: Wifstrand (1934) III 14 rightly defends the text against Herwerden's addition of ἐστι, and discusses a number of passages where *variatio* between finite verb (here χρῆται) and a predicative adjective without a copula has been misunderstood by editors. οὐ γὰρ λαμβάνω μαθητάς 'I don't catch pupils', as the sophists do. The metaphor continues with διαθέσθαι τὴν ἄγραν, 'dispose of the take'. Cf. 66.12 δημαγωγοί τε καὶ ξεναγοὶ καὶ σοφισταὶ λεγόμενοι, δήμους καὶ σατράπας καὶ μαθητὰς θηρεύοντες. It is an old image: Pl. *Soph.* 223B νέων πλουσίων καὶ ἐνδόξων γιγνομένη θήρα προσρητέον . . . σοφιστική, *ibid.* 231A, [Pl.] *Def.* 415E, Xen. *Cyneg.* 13.9.   ὡς δὲ . . . ἀνδρείαν 'but to lie and deceive by promising [sc. to teach] – that's something I've not got the courage for'. Cf. 11.23 for courage in lying: ἀνδρειότατος ἀνθρώπων ἦν πρὸς τὸ ψεῦδος Ὅμηρος.   ἀλλ' οὐκ οἶδα ὅπως . . . ἀναλαμβάνει 'but, somehow or other, none of the sophists takes me up'.

14 This section is heavily ironical. D. conceives his audience as laughing at him (καταγελᾶν §12), and here as despising his folly and ignorance in the light of their own wisdom. Then he hits at them: these same people would have believed Socrates' pretence of ignorance and admired Hippias, Polus, and Gorgias.

Hippias (who was from Elis) and Gorgias made famous appearances at Olympia (Hippias A2 D–K, Pl. *Hipp. min.* 363C; Gorgias B7–8 D–K), but nothing of the kind is reported of Polus of Acragas, a pupil of Gorgias and teacher of rhetoric, and a character in Plato's *Gorgias*. κἀνεπιστημοσύνης: ἀνεπιστημοσύνη is a Platonic word (*Charm.* 170A–B, *Rep.* VIII 560B, *Theaet.* 199E, 200B), not uncommon in later Greek

(Philo). D. does not use it elsewhere, but has ἀνεπιστήμων at 12.43, 10.20, 26.6. **αὐτῶν** = ὑμῶν αὐτῶν. **πιστεύειν ἄν ... ἄν ἡγεῖσθαι**: the infinitives represent imperfect indicatives.

15 οὔτε τῶν σεμνῶν οὔτε τῶν ἐλαττόνων: the run of the sentence suggests that μαντική and σοφιστική are σεμναί (ironically of course) and rhetoric and κολακευτική are ἐλάττονες. There is a faint reminiscence of Pl. *Gorg.* 464C, where ῥητορική is the false correlate of δικαιοσύνη and σοφιστική the false correlate of νομοθετική, while κολακευτική is the genus covering all the false τέχναι. **ἀλλ' ἢ μόνον κομῶντος**: D. took the 'philosophical' line (cf. Musonius 21, pp. 114–16 Hense) that shaving was unnatural, and wrote a (lost) encomium on hair. He thought abundant hair and beard a mark of a philosopher (72.2), as of a king (47.25). In 36.17 (q.v.), he comments on a citizen of Olbia who chose to shave that he was thought to do it in order to flatter Roman manners. Cf. esp. 35.2 νῦν γὰρ ἴσως ὑπονοοῦσιν εἶναί με τῶν σοφῶν ἀνθρώπων καὶ πάντ' εἰδότων, γελοίωι καὶ ἀτόπωι τεκμηρίωι χρώμενοι τῶι κομᾶν. See in general B. Költing in *RAC* s.v. Haar. **εἰ δ' ὑμῖν δοκέει ... ἄμεινον**: *Odyssey* 1.376 = 2.141.

16 οὐ μέντοι ... ὁρᾶτε 'But you will not hear words such as you would hear from anyone else these days, but much poorer and odder ones, such indeed as you see.' (i) There is no need to question ἀτοπωτέρων (Cohoon's ἀκοπωτέρων, which he translates 'less wearisome' is pointless): D. is again claiming a Socratic trait, that of using unconventional, unliterary or downright vulgar language: e.g. Pl. *Gorg.* 491A, 494D, *Symp.* 221E. Of course, he does not do so in the rather grand speech to which this is the prelude; but he can still disclaim rhetorical sophistication. (ii) ὁποίους ... ὁρᾶτε has raised questions: Schwartz's ὁποῖον, 'like the man you see', is attractive: but ὁρᾶν may be used generally for 'perceive': cf. LSJ s.v. II 4, III. **πλανώμενος**: here again, D. claims a trait of the Platonic Socrates (cf. *Rep.* 394D), and, as often, associates discursiveness both with philosophical freedom to follow the argument wherever it leads and with his own wandering life: cf. 7.1, 7.102, 7.124; 1.56, 12.38.

16–20 'I have just returned from a journey to the Danube, to the Getae or Mysians – not as a trader, or to do anything useful to the army; but I saw all the emotions and excitement on both sides of a war of conquest against a free people, though I could not take an active part. I came here in fulfilment of a vow. Divine concerns are higher than human.'

According to Philostratus (*VS* 1.8.3), D. was at the Dacian front when he heard of Domitian's death, which was in Sept. 96. If this is true (cf. Jones (1978) 51), he can hardly have been at Borysthenes 'on his way to the Getae' (*Or.* 36.1), in summer (*loc. cit.*) 97, and then at Olympia in time for the games of that year. Text and interpretation of 36.1 are unsure (see *ad loc.*); but the dramatic date of the Borysthenes visit is probably during the exile (36.27, and so Philostratus). While there can be no certainty, the timetable is much easier if we date the Olympic visit in 101: D. will then have travelled from Rome to the Dacian front with Trajan, and back to Olympia (cf. Jones p. 53). This need not have been his first, or only, visit: Jones thinks the *Getica* (a historical and ethnographical account, cf. Tacitus' *Germania*) was written later, in connection with Trajan's second war (106). Von Arnim's (and others') arguments for 105 (eve of the second war) as the date of our speech remain strong: Introd. p. 16.   **εὐθὺ τοῦ Ἴστρου** 'as far as the Danube . . .' Cf. Xen. *Hell.* 1.4.11 εὐθὺ Γυθείου. The usage was approved as Attic (Moeris p. 130 Pierson).   **τῆς Γετῶν χώρας ἢ Μυσῶν, ὥς φησιν Ὅμηρος κατὰ τὴν νῦν ἐπίκλησιν τοῦ ἔθνους** 'the land of the Getae or Mysians, as Homer calls them, using the modern name for the nation'. Posidonius (ap. Strab. 7.3.2 = F 45 Theiler, T 88 Edelstein–Kidd (cf. F 277)) argued that Μυσῶν ἀγχεμάχων in *Iliad* 13.4ff. were a people in Thrace, not in Asia Minor (see Kidd (1989) 2.941–3). They were thus the later Moesi and were identified with the Getae, the name regularly used by the Greeks for the Dacians. D. makes the same identification in *Or.* 72.3 τῶν Θραικῶν τινες τῶν Γετῶν λεγομένων.   **σκευοφόρων ἢ βοηλατῶν**: these are genitive plurals (σκευοφόρος, βοηλάτης), not present participles.   **οὐδὲ . . . συνευχομένων** 'nor was I conducting some ambassadorial mission of allegiance or congratulation, consisting of people whose prayers come only from their lips.'   **⟨ἀλλὰ⟩ γυμνὸς . . . ἔγχος**: a connection is needed, and the passage which has to be transferred to §26 (see below *ad loc.*) begins ἄλλο, so that ἀλλὰ seems the natural choice.   **γυμνὸς . . . ἔγχος**: an adaptation of *Il.* 21.50, where Achilles kills Lycaon, who is running away:

γυμνόν, ἄτερ κόρυθός τε καὶ ἀσπίδος, οὐδ᾽ ἔχεν ἔγχος.

18 οὔτε ⟨γὰρ⟩: Wilamowitz' addition, though not certain (ὥστε . . . ὁρῶντες could be taken as a parenthesis) very much eases the sentence. **ἀλλ᾽ οὐδὲ . . . λιθοβόλος**: text unsure. Reiske deleted τὴν βαρεῖαν . . . οὐδ᾽, so that the sense is 'nor even one of the light and unarmed troops, spearman or slinger'; but it may be preferable to delete more, reading simply ἀλλ' οὐδ' ἀκοντιστὴς ἢ λιθοβόλος, 'nor even a spearman or stone-thrower', these being light-armed troops. On the other hand, the odd expression ἀνόπλων τὴν βαρεῖαν ὅπλισιν, 'unarmed with heavy weapons', may be justified as an accusative of respect.   **λιθοβόλος**: 'stone-throwers' are distinct from σφενδονῆται, 'slingers': Thuc. 6.69, Pl. *Laws* 834A, Jos. *BJ* 3.211 (τοῖς ἀπὸ τῆς Συρίας σφενδονήταις καὶ λιθοβόλοις).   **οὐδὲ ἀμῆσαι . . . πυκνὰ μεταστρεφόμενος** 'nor cut fodder from an enemy meadow, constantly turning round'. Xenophon (*Anab.* 6.1.8) describes a dance in which ὁ μὲν παραθέμενος τὰ ὅπλα σπείρει καὶ ζευγηλατεῖ πυκνὰ μεταστρεφόμενος (*v.l.* δὲ στρεφόμενος) ὡς φοβούμενος, λῃστὴς δὲ προσέρχεται. This allusion is appropriate here, for the soldier's care to watch his back when cutting an enemy field; but the phrase perhaps became a cliché, as in Basil, *Epist.* 2 (ὀφθαλμὸν) ἄνω καὶ κάτω πυκνὰ μεταστρεφόμενον.   **ἐγεῖραι** 'raise', 'construct'. Not a common meaning, but cf. *OGIS* 677.3 (Egypt, second century A.D.) οἱ ἐγείραντες τὴν οἰκοδομὴν τοῦ πυλῶνος.

19 μετεώρους 'excited', cf. 4.77, 4.118. Geel argues against this proposal of Jacobs that the word implies fear and confusion, and he prefers δριμυτέρους, 'keen'. But this is not convincing: for μετέωρος of horses cf. Xen. *Eq.* 11.1, ἢν δέ τις ἄρα βουληθῆι καὶ πομπικῶι καὶ μετεώρωι καὶ λαμπρῶι ἵππωι χρήσασθαι.   **οὐδὲ σχολὴν . . . λόγων**: contrast the Borysthenites, 36.16, who came under arms to hear D. **ἐπὶ τῶν ὑσπλήγων** 'at the starting line'. Cf., e.g., Lucian, *Timon* 20 ἅμα ἀνακηρύττομαι νενικηκώς. The runner, or the horse, leaps forward when the barrier falls.   **τὸν χρόνον** 'the delay'.   **κόπτοντας τὸ ἔδαφος ταῖς ὁπλαῖς** 'beating the ground with their hooves'. Cf. Stat. *Theb.* 6.396–401 *qui dominis, idem ardor equis . . . stare adeo miserum est, pereunt uestigia mille | ante fugam, absentemque ferit grauis ungula campum.* **πανταχοῦ . . . πανταχοῦ . . . πάντα . . . πάντα**: anaphora is a favourite figure with D. (Schmid (1887) 170), as with Plato and Xenophon: Denniston (1954) 84 draws attention to its association with vividness, force, and pathos. This suits D.'s emotive oratory.   **πάντα δὲ ὅπλων**: the argument for deleting this phrase is that it is superfluous in sense, and does not go well with 'horses' and 'armed men'. On the other hand, it makes a third clause with πάντα to balance the three with πανταχοῦ. It is perhaps corrupt: we expect some living animal – ὄνων or ὑποζυγίων? But D.'s loose and untidy style discourages emendation.   **ἀτεχνῶς** 'literally', a favourite word with D., at least in some speeches (9 occurrences in 12, 4 in 36, 3 in 53; only 8 in all the others together).

20 οὐ χρυσοῦν . . . ὁδόν: from *Iliad* 1.13–15:

> ὁ γὰρ ἦλθε θοὰς ἐπὶ νῆας Ἀχαιῶν
> λυσόμενός τε θύγατρα φέρων τ' ἀπερείσι' ἄποινα,
> στέμματ' ἔχων ἐν χερσὶν ἐκηβόλου Ἀπόλλωνος
> χρύσεωι ἀνὰ σκήπτρωι

Chryses's journey *was* a necessity, if he was to save his daughter. **ἀναγκαίαν ὁδόν:** internal accusative, WS §1567.   **ὑπὲρ ἀρχῆς καὶ δυνάμεως . . . ὑπὲρ ἐλευθερίας τε καὶ πατρίδος:** the conflict is between empire and freedom. It does not follow from this way of describing the situation that D. took a negative view of Roman Imperial rule; the whole tendency of his works on monarchy belies this (cf. Jones (1978) 123, and 34ff. on *Or.* 31), and he was 'in favour' with Nerva and Trajan. But it is an acceptable stance: cf. Tac. *Agricola* 30, where even stronger sentiments about *libertas* and the pretensions of the *pax Romana* are put into the mouth of the British rebel Calgacus (for the rhetorical background to this speech, written in A.D. 98, see Richmond–Ogilvy *ad loc.*).   **μὴ . . . μηδείς** 'let no one think that!'   **εὐχῆς . . . παλαιᾶς:** we have no other reference to this vow, presumably made in exile. **ἀπετράπην:** if pressed, this implies that D. made a detour to Olympia (? instead of going straight home).   **προὐργιαίτερα** 'more urgent', from προὔργου.   **ἡλίκα ἂν ἦι** implies that the war is a great thing, so far as human affairs go.

21–2 'Which is the more appropriate subject – a description of the manners and geography of the Getae, or an attempt to say something about the God in whose presence we stand?'   **ἢ ὡρῶν ὡς ἔχουσι κράσεων** 'how they are placed in respect of climate'; WS §1441. This clause is parallel to the accusatives τὸ μέγεθος and τὴν φύσιν, and the construction is probably continued in the following genitives γένους . . . πλήθους . . . παρασκευῆς. If this is so, Reiske's ⟨περὶ⟩ is unnecessary. Cf. [Aristot.] Περὶ κόσμου 391b4 ὡς ἕκαστον ἔχει φύσεως καὶ θέσεως καὶ κινήσεως.

In this long sentence, πότερον . . . ἢ μᾶλλον indicate the two alternatives, οὗτος . . . ἔδοξεν is a parenthesis, and ἐάν πως ἱκανοὶ γενώμεθα κ.τ.λ. depends on ἅψασθαι.

The topics enumerated – physical geography, climate, produce, inhabitants, political and military organization – are standard in ethnographic description (cf. J. G. C. Anderson, *Tacitus: Germania* (1938) xii–xix; R. F. Thomas, *Lands and peoples in Roman poetry* (1982) 1–7), and no doubt we have here something like a synopsis of the first part of D.'s *Getica*. ἱστορίας 'enquiry'.

22 οὗτος ... ἔδοξεν: this 'hymn' to Zeus (cf. §77, where many titles of the god are listed) is, as D. says, based on the poets. Zeus is πρύτανις in Pind. *Pyth.* 6.24, Aesch. *PV* 169, Eur. *Tro.* 1288, and elsewhere; he is 'father of men and gods' regularly in Homer (e.g. *Il.* 1.544); and as ταμίας of peace and war, he holds the scales of battle in *Il.* 22.210–13. Many Stoic and Platonic texts develop these ideas: note especially Cic. *ND* 2.25.64 (with Pease *ad loc.*), Plu. *Quaest. Plat.* 2 (1000Eff.), Max. Tyr. 11.9–12, 41.2; Babut (1969) 486 n. 1.   ἀποδέοντι τῆς ἀξίας 'falling short of his worth'. The orator admits inability: cf. Men. Rhet. 437.12ff. Sp. where Homer is said to have given an example of τοὺς πρὸς ἀξίαν ὕμνους ... τοῦ θεοῦ, which the orator, in his modest way, will do his best to emulate. Cf. [Longinus] 9.9 ὁ τῶν Ἰουδαίων θεσμοθέτης ... τὴν τοῦ θείου δύναμιν κατὰ τὴν ἀξίαν ἐχώρησε.   αὐτά που ταῦτα λέγοντες 'just by saying these things'. If this is right, there is emphasis on λέγειν, contrasting D.'s plain words with the 'wisdom' of the poets' hymns. The sequel suggests there is some irony.

23–6 'Hesiod was right to invoke the Muses for his hymn to Zeus. You must tell me what is most appropriate for this occasion – a hymn like Hesiod's, or to be spectators solely of the wonders of the festival, including Phidias' wonderful statue, or, finally to ask how we acquire the understanding of gods which poets and sculptors express, paying attention to nothing else except the actual games.'

D. sets out these three alternatives, foreshadowing something of his discussion, and bringing in Phidias, who is to be a chief speaker later.

23 κατὰ Ἡσίοδον: he will shortly quote *WD* 1–8. The argument is that the occasion of a hymn to their father, Zeus, is a more appropriate theme for the Muses than is the Catalogue of Ships, which is the occasion of Homer's invocation (*Il.* 2.484). This preference for the poet of peaceful pursuits and piety over the poet of war and human folly recalls the theme of the *Certamen Homeri et Hesiodi* (on this see M. L. West, *C. Q.* 17 (1967) 433–50, N. J. Richardson, *C. Q.* 31 (1981) 1–10). D. turns the comparison another way in *Or.* 2.8, where he makes

Alexander say that Hesiod is best for farmers, but Homer for kings. παρ' αὐτοῦ διανοηθείς 'thinking it up out of his own mind'. αὐτούς τε . . . τῶν νεῶν: i.e. the lists in the Catalogue of Ships. οἱ πολλοὶ ἀνόητοι: the foolishness of Homeric heroes is a favourite topic of moralists: cf. Hor. *Epist.* 1.2.8. *fabula . . . | stultorum regum et populorum continet aestus.*

24 See M. L. West (1978) 136–41.   ὅν τε διὰ 'through whom'. Note the etymological play on διὰ/Δία (certainly plain to D., even if not to Hesiod).

25 ὑπολαβόντες οὖν εἴπατε 'so answer and tell me . . .'   ὦ παῖδες 'Ηλείων: for the idiom, cf. e.g. Hdt. 1.27, Aesch. *Pers.* 402. LSJ s.v. παῖς 1 3. See also on 36.40.   ὑμεῖς . . . λόγων: D. piles on the complimentary titles. The Eleans ran and supervised the games from *c.* 570 B.C., when they took over from Pisa. The terms used – ἔφοροι, ἐπίσκοποι – have no special technical sense.   ἔργων καὶ λόγων: ἔργα will include works of art (cf. e.g. Lucian, *Pro Im.* 11, the Hellanodikai forbid statues of victors above life size) and presumably speeches or poems, though there were no literary competitions, and we do not know how this censorship was exercised.   τῆς τοῦ θεοῦ θείας καὶ τῶι ὄντι μακαρίας εἰκόνος: Geel and others rightly expect an adjective instead of the transmitted θρησκείας, 'cult', since this can hardly be a θέαμα. Choice between θείας and Kayser's θεσπεσίας is difficult. In any case, τῶι ὄντι should be taken ἀπὸ κοινοῦ with both adjectives: 'the truly divine and blessed image of the god'.   θεοφιλέστατον 'most dear to god': for this passive sense of θεοφιλής cf. Men. Rhet. 361.20 Sp., with Russell–Wilson *ad loc.*   πρὸς τὴν Ὁμηρικὴν ποίησιν . . . Φειδίου παραβαλλομένου 'wherein Phidias, they say, tried to rival Homer's poetry'. The story was well known. According to Strabo's version (354A), Phidias' brother, the painter Panainos, asked him what παράδειγμα he was going to use. Phidias replied that it was these lines of Homer (*Il.* 1.528–30); cf. also Plu. *Aem. Paull.* 28.2. The source of Phidias' inspiration formed the text of various discussions of aesthetic problems: see especially Cic. *Orator* 9, Quint. 12.10.9 (with Austin's note), Pollitt (1974) 52, 101. Cf. Introd. p. 15.   παραβαλλομένου: cf. 4.7 (Alexander) τοῖς τε ἥρωσι καὶ τοῖς ἡμιθέοις παραβαλλόμενος.   τοῦ κινήσαντος: Herwerden was right to restore the simpler word; cf. §79 κινούμενον Ὄλυμπον. Zeus did not whirl (δινεῖν) the heavens round above his head, and Homer's ἐλέλιξεν, 'shook', is perfectly well represented by κινήσαντος. The genitive depends on ποίησιν: i.e. 'Homer's poetical representation of him who, with a little nod of his eyebrows, moved all Olympus.'

26 ἐναργῶς καὶ πεποιθότως 'vividly and with conviction'. ἐνάργεια is a commonly praised literary value: see [Longinus] 15, with Russell's notes. πεποιθότως is rare (as is the perfect πέποιθα in prose) but cf. Sext. Emp. *PH* 1.60 for the corresponding noun: μετὰ πεποιθήσεως προφέρων τὴν ἀπόδειξιν. **ἢ καὶ . . . Ὄλυμπον:** *Il.* 1.528–30. **εἴ τι τοιουτότροπον . . . ἀνατυποῦν** 'any similar object which in any way fashions and represents human opinion of the divine'. **ἅτε . . . τὰ νῦν** 'as being now in a philosopher's lecture'. As it stands, this is very abrupt, and perhaps ⟨οὖσιν⟩ or ⟨γεγονόσιν⟩ should be added. But it is easier if we insert here the whole passage ἄλλο δὲ . . . ἀοίδιμον, preserved in the MSS at §17, and placed in this context by Emperius (after the quotation from Homer) and by Reiske (after ἥκοντας §25), and Kayser (after λόγων §25). Placed here, χρή carries on naturally from σκεπτέον. We may then translate from ἢ καὶ onwards: 'Or should we rather make a more careful investigation of these things themselves, the poem, the dedication, and any similar object which in any way fashions and represents human opinion of the divine, as being now in a philosopher's lecture, and take no thought for anything else, or listen to anything – except the sacred trumpet and the blessed proclamations that someone has won the boy's wrestling, or the men's, or the boxing, or the pancration, or the pentathlon, or the foot-race – made happy as it were by a single stride, and making himself and his country and his whole race fit subject for song?' Read literally, this is a concession to the Eleans and their concern for the real element in the games; but it is surely also ironical, for an alert audience must see that the athletes' vanity is ridiculed by the philosopher who has serious concerns. **ὡς ὅδε μὲν . . . γενόμενος:** not a complete list of Olympic competitions (see Paus. 5.8.6ff. for a history down to his own day), but a fair selection of the most important.

27–37 'We must speak first of the natural, universal idea of God, common to all mankind, and needing no human teacher. Primitive man was close to god, from whom he received intelligence, and admiration of the kosmos was bound to kindle the idea of the creator who provides it. The universe is a temple, the revelation of a mystery. Even animals live according to the divine law. Only foolish men reject it and make pleasure their god.'

This Stoic account of natural theology has been much discussed: commentary on the whole passage in Theiler (1982) F 368; cf. also Theiler, *Die Vorbereitung des Neuplatonismus* (1930) 100ff., 145ff.; K. Reinhardt, *RE* xxii.1, s.v. Poseidonios 811 (1954), *Poseidonios* (1921) 412ff.; Pohlenz (1949) ii 119. For a collection of Stoic texts on the whole theme, see Long and Sedley (1987) i 323–33; and for bibliography, ii 504. It is difficult to say how much of what we have here is due to Posidonius, whom D. never names; but, though the views of older scholars (Binder (1905)) who believed he was following him closely cannot be sustained, no one doubts that Posidonius was a widely read, colourful, and influential exponent of Stoic theology.

27 τοῦ πάντων ἡγεμόνος: i.e. Zeus, cf. Pl. *Phaedrus* 246E ὁ μὲν δὴ ἡγεμὼν ἐν οὐρανῷ Ζεύς, and note D.'s use of the *Phaedrus* myth in 36.39ff.   **πρῶτον μὲν καὶ ἐν πρώτοις** 'first and above all'; this type of polyptoton is a favourite with D. (Schmid (1887) 172).   **δόξα . . . γένους:** the consensus argument used to support belief in the existence of gods not only by Stoics but by Epicureans (Cic. *ND* 1.44), though Stoics and Platonists used it also to support divination, divine providence, or immortality. Cf. A. D. Nock, *Sallustius* (1926) xli.   **ὁμοίως . . . βαρβάρων:** cf. Theon, *Progymnasmata* 126.9 Spengel πάντες ἄνθρωποι Ἕλληνές τε καὶ βάρβαροι ἔννοιαν περὶ τῶν θεῶν ἔχουσιν ὡς προνοοῦσιν ἡμῶν. (This is from a rhetorical θέσις on the theme of divine providence: discussions of such things were not confined to philosophical teaching, but found a place also in the rhetorical school). Cf. also Max. Tyr. 11.5 Hobein.   **ἀναγκαία καὶ ἔμφυτος:** cf. §39, §44. D.'s argument is that, as man is kin to the gods and part of the divine universe, he cannot help having a concept of the divine from birth. This is common Stoic doctrine, at least in the later period: Cic. *ND* 2.129 *omnibus enim innatum est et in animo quasi insculptum esse deos*; Sen. *Epist.* 117.6 *omnibus insita de dis opinio est.*   **ἄνευ . . . μυσταγωγοῦ:** note the analogy with the mysteries: see on §33.   **κεκράτηκε** 'has come to prevail'. Sauppe and von Arnim rightly thought a verb to be needed; suggestions involving a noun in place of χαρᾶς (e.g. ταραχῆς Reiske, φθορᾶς Emperius, who in his edition preferred simply to delete καὶ χαρᾶς) do not meet the difficulty. Not that χαρᾶς itself is quite impossible: the mysteries involve trickery and joyful revelation (cf. Plu. fr. 178 Sandbach), though χαρά (a rational joy, according to Stoic distinction (*SVF* iii 105–6)) is not a very appropriate word; we should therefore

bear in mind the possibility that the verb has simply fallen out.   **διά**
τε τὴν ξυγγένειαν: cf. §61. The notion of a kinship with the gods as a
basis for worship is clear in Pl. *Protag.* 322A: διὰ τὴν τοῦ θεοῦ συγγένειαν
the human race is unique in believing in and worshipping the gods (see
on this passage, E. des Places, *La Religion grecque* (1969) 251); but it was
particularly attractive to the Stoics, for whom the soul (or at least
its rational part) is a fragment of the divine spirit that governs the
world. Aratus, *Phaenomena* 4–5 was a classic statement: πάντη δὲ Διὸς
κεχρήμεθα πάντες· | τοῦ γὰρ καὶ γένος εἰμέν. Cited in Acts 17.28, this
passage became famous in Christian literature. Cf. also Cleanthes, *Hymn
to Zeus* 4 ἐκ σοῦ γὰρ γένος ἐσμέν.   **καὶ πολλὰ . . . παλαιοτάτους** 'and
many evidences of the truth, not allowing the oldest and most ancient
to nod or to neglect them'. D. means the evidence of natural phenomena. That early man was specially privileged in his relationship
with god is often stated, and is no doubt implied in D.'s account here.
Cf. Pl. *Phileb.* 16c οἱ παλαιοί, κρείττονες ἡμῶν καὶ ἐγγυτέρω θεῶν
οἰκοῦντες; Sen. *Epist.* 90.44 *alti spiritus uiros a dis recentes*; Dio (?),
Charidemus (= *Or.* 30) 26ff.

28 ἄτε . . . τρόπον 'for, not being settled apart on their own, remote
from and outside the divine, but growing in the very midst of it, or
rather together with it, cleaving to it in every way …' This statement
of the intimate link between the human and the divine would be more
striking if we read θεοῦ for θείου – 'god' rather than 'the divine' – and this
would also come closer to the many parallels: Acts 17.27 καίτοιγε οὐ
μακρὰν ἀπὸ ἑνὸς ἑκάστου ἡμῶν ὑπάρχοντα [sc. τὸν κύριον]; Philo, *De
praemiis et poenis* 84 τοῦτο τὸ γένος [i.e. people whose divine precepts are
fulfilled in practice] οὐ μακρὰν ἀπώικισται θεοῦ. Cf. also Sen. *Epist.*
73.16 *deus ad homines uenit, immo quod est propius, in homines uenit*; ibid.
45.1 *prope est a te deus, tecum est, intus est.*   **οὐ μακρὰν**: cf. the hymn
to Demetrius Poliorcetes (Athen. VI 253E): ἄλλοι μὲν ἢ μακρὰν γὰρ
ἀπέχουσιν θεοί . . . σὲ δὲ παρόνθ' ὁρῶμεν.   **μᾶλλον δὲ συμπεφυκότες
ἐκείνωι**: the self-correction makes the point on which the following
argument depends.   **προσεχόμενοι** 'clinging fast to …'; Reiske's
περιεχόμενοι, 'surrounded by', is attractive; cf. Sext. Emp. *Adv. math.*
7.127ff., especially 7.129 τῆς πρὸς τὸ περιέχον συμφυῖας, in a discussion
of the views of Heraclitus, doubtless from a Stoic source.   **ἀξύνετοι**
'without understanding': perhaps an allusion, but not necessarily conscious (cf. Reinhardt (1954) 814), to Heraclitus B1, B34: cf. Sext. Emp.

loc. cit. 132. **ἄλλως τε** 'especially': cf. 7.106, LSJ s.v. ἄλλως 1 3.
[σύνεσιν . . . ἄτε δή]: omitted in much of the tradition: the phrase
simply repeats the sense of ἀξύνετοι, and it is probably best to accept
the omission. Men cannot remain 'without understanding, especially
as they are surrounded on all sides by the shining light of the great,
divine apparitions of heaven and stars'. If the fuller reading is preferred, there are two alternatives: (i) read παρά for περί (Reiske): man
then owes his knowledge to god; (ii) less plausibly, take περὶ αὐτοῦ with
ἀξύνετοι (Geel), regarding ἄλλως τε . . . εἰληφότες as a separate phrase.
νυκτός τε καὶ ἡμέρας 'by night and by day'.   **ποικίλοις . . . εἴδεσιν**
'the various and inconstant shapes of sun and moon' – i.e. their changes
of colour, phases of the moon, periodical eclipses.   **φωνὰς . . .**
θαλάττης: it is interesting that D. stresses only the wonder of these
noises, not their capacity to terrify. The terror of thunder and earth-
quakes was a common argument to explain man's consciousness of
the divine: Cleanthes in Cic. *ND* 2.14, with Pease *ad loc.* It is characteristic of D. to dwell on less alarming things.   **αὐτοί τε . . .**
παραλαμβάνοντες 'and themselves uttering the sweetest and most distinct sound, and taking pleasure in the pride and intellectuality of
human speech, stamping symbols on things that came into their perception, so as to name and point out everything they thought of, easily
acquiring thereby memories and conceptions of an infinite range of
things'.

This praise of human speech and reason, as the culmination of a list
of phenomena from which the knowledge of god is derived, is especially
appropriate to an orator's treatment of the theme. D. returns to the
subject in §65, q.v.   **γαῦρον** 'pride' is an unexpected quality: Selden
proposed **γλαφυρόν**, i.e. 'elegance', 'sweetness', which fits better with
the contrast apparently drawn between human and animal sounds. But
man's pride and his grasp of language perhaps go well together: Soph.
Antigone 354 καὶ φθέγμα καὶ ἀνεμόεν φρόνημα καὶ ἀστυνόμους ὀργὰς
ἐδιδάξατο.   **ἐπιθέμενοι σύμβολα:** cf. §65 ἐπιβάλλει . . . σφραγῖδα.
εὐμαρῶς: cf. §79 εὐμαρές. This is generally a poetic or Ionic word, but
D. had Platonic precedent (*Critias* 113E, *Laws* 706B).   **εὐμαρῶς . . .**
παραλαμβάνοντες: according to orthodox Stoic theory (*SVF* II 847:
Long and Sedley (1987) I 238) conceptions were 'stored thoughts',
derived from experience, and memories were permanent impressions
on the mind. D.'s terminology seems to reflect this.

29 ἀγνῶτες 'ignorant', cf. Xen *Oec.* 20.13. The long sentence continues to the end of §30.   ὑπόνοιαν 'inkling', 'suspicion'.   εἶναι
... ἕξειν: for *variatio* in constructions with μέλλω, cf. Thuc. 6.42.
τοῦ σπείραντος ... καὶ τρέφοντος: cf. the Stoic language in Cic.
ND 2.86, of the divine kosmos: *omnium ... rerum quae natura administrat
seminator et sator et parens, ut ita dicam, atque educator et altor est mundus.*

30–1 'The nourishment (τροφή) of primitive man came first from
the earth. They licked its moisture like a mother's milk. Then followed
fruits and herbs; they also inhaled air, which is the primary nourishment.'

This odd doctrine recalls the idea of Archelaus (60 A1, A4 D–K) that
mud (ἰλύς) provided the first nourishment, and earth was indeed,
literally, our mother. Lucr. 5.805ff. develops the idea, which had been
taken up by Epicurus (333 Usener = Censorinus, *De die natali* 4.9;
Spoerri (1959) 130–1; Guthrie (1957) 121). The fantasy does not seem
to have been confined to any one school, though Aristotle (*GA* III 762b)
ridiculed it. That the first other food was vegetable, not meat, naturally
suits D.'s general position; and this was common ground among moralists. That the air we breathe actually nourishes us (*cibus animalis*, Cic.
ND 2.136) was denied by Aristotle (*Resp.* 473a3ff.), but very commonly
held. There is no good reason to associate the idea especially with the
Cynics (cf. Gatz (1967) 160).

The text of this passage is debatable; the text printed assumes the
following readings: (1) εὐπορήσαντος (2) οἱ πρῶτοι καὶ αὐτόχθονες (3)
λιχμώμενοι, καθάπερ (4) νῦν ἕλκουσι (5) τὰ ἤδη προϊόντα for τοῖς ἤδη
προϊοῦσι. Thus εὐπορήσαντος ... θεοῦ, 'which the Ancestor God provided and made ready beforehand', goes with what precedes, οἱ ...
αὐτόχθονες is in apposition to the main subject (these are one main class
of humans), and we supply τροφήν with τὴν γεώδη. Translate: 'the
first, indigenous men licking first the earthy nourishment, as it were,
from their Mother Earth, while the mud was still soft and rich, just as
plants today draw the earth's moisture, and as second nourishment the
spontaneous plants and soft grasses that came forth, with sweet dew and
the "nymphs' potable streams" – depending also on the atmosphere,
and nourished by the continual influx of the wind, drawing in damp
air, like little children who never lack for milk while the breast is
pressed against them'.   εὐπορήσαντος: for this transitive sense, see
e.g. Isaeus 7.8 ἕως εὐπορήσειεν ἐκεῖνο τἀργύριον, 'until he made the

money available'.   **τοῦ προπάτορος θεοῦ**: Ajax in Sophocles (*Ajax* 389) addresses ὦ Ζεῦ προγόνων προπάτωρ. Zeus (the Stoic cosmic god) is the ultimate ancestor of mankind. Cf. also 39.8 Διονύσωι τῶι προπάτορι τῆσδε τῆς πόλεως (Nicaea).   **πρώτην . . . γεώδη**: note word-order (polyptoton and chiasmus), emphasizing the link between the characteristics of the men and those of the food.   **ἕλκουσι**: note plural verb with neuter plural subject.   **αὐτομάτων**: a typical trait of the 'ideal' early world: for Hesiod's 'golden generation'

καρπὸν δ' ἔφερε ζείδωρος ἄρουρα
αὐτομάτη πολλόν τε καὶ ἄφθονον (*WD* 117)

νάμασι νυμφῶν ποτίμοις: the phrase scans as two choriambs (– ∪∪ – –∪∪–), as Geel and Cohoon point out; D. uses νᾶμα elsewhere (35.20), and so do other late prose writers. So this may, but need not, be a poetical quotation: cf. §4. For the thought, note Lucr. 5.945ff.: *at sedare sitim . . . siluestria templa tenebant | nympharum*.

31 δικαιότερον: a self-correction; having alleged that man's first food was 'earthy', D. now says it would be more correct to say this of air. His argument is based on what happens in the present world: infancy provides a model for the infancy of mankind. In σχεδὸν γάρ κ.τ.λ., he develops the idea suggested by his simile ὥσπερ νήπιοι παῖδες.   **ἐπειδὰν . . . βρέφος** 'but when the infant is banished from the womb, drowsy and weak'. The helplessness of the new-born and the misery of entering life are a common topic: e.g. Lucr. 5.222ff., Sen. *Epist.* 102.26   **ἀδρανές**: not a word of classical prose, but common in Plutarch, and used by D. also at 20.24 and 40.38.   **περιψύξας** 'cooling'. This is Sonny's correction. Stoic theory was that the ψυχή was formed at birth by the cooling effect of the air, *SVF* II 804–8; see especially Plu. *Stoic rep.* 1053D γίνεσθαι μὲν γάρ φησι τὴν ψυχὴν ὅταν τὸ βρέφος ἀποτεχθῆι, καθάπερ στομώσει τῆι περιψύξει τοῦ πνεύματος μεταβαλόντος. Prior to birth the foetus was nourished φύσει, like a plant: the effect of the air is to 'temper' (στομοῦσθαι) its πνεῦμα. The word ψυχή was commonly held to be derived from ψύχω, 'cool': Pl. *Crat.* 399D, Aristot. *De anima* 405b28, *SVF* II 807–8.   **καὶ φθέγξασθαι παρέσχεν**: again, speech is the culminating achievement, cf. §28.

32 ἃ δὴ πάσχοντες: we now return to the experience of the primitives. Like children, they have acquired the ability to speak and reason. They now observe the seasons and their utility to man (a classic teleological argument: Cic. *ND* 2.49, with Pease's note), and possess the special privilege of being able to conceive god. Admiration and love of god surely follow as the next stage; the clause ἐπινοοῦντες ... τὸ δαιμόνιον is therefore out of place. It is best placed after περὶ αὐτῶν: ἐπινοοῦντες, 'by exercising thought', is subordinate to οὐκ ἐδύναντο κ.τ.λ. **πεφεισμένως ἑκατέρας τῆς ὑπερβολῆς** 'so as to be sparing with the two extremes'. Cf. Aelian, *NA* 6.24 ἡσύχως καὶ πεφεισμένως τοῦ στόματος, 'gently and so as to spare his mouth', of the fox picking up the hedgehog; Euseb. *HE* 8.17 πεφεισμένως τῶν ἀθροισμάτων ἔτι συγκροτουμένων, 'so as to spare the church groups still being formed'. For the thought here, cf. Xen. *Mem.* 4.3.8ff., [Aristot.] Περὶ κόσμου 399a22–4. **ἐξαίρετον:** i.e. chosen for man as a special honour: cf. *Il.* 2.226ff., Aesch. *Ag.* 954, etc. For man's 'special privilege', cf. especially Manil. 2.105ff.:

> quis dubitet post haec hominem coniungere caelo?
> *eximium* natura dedit linguamque capaxque
> ingenium uolucremque animum, quem denique in unum
> descendit deus atque habitat seque ipse requirit.

The whole passage gives a very similar Stoic view to D.'s. **πρὸς τὰ ἄλλα ζῷα** 'in comparison with other animals' (LSJ s.v. πρός c III 4); yet in §35 animals and even plants honour god – though of course without the rational consciousness that is man's. **θαυμάζειν καὶ ἀγαπᾶν τὸ δαιμόνιον** 'to admire and love god'. For ἀγαπᾶν as a feeling which men may have towards god, see Arndt–Gingrich s.v. 1.β, and s.v. ἀγάπη 1.b.γ. The use is common in biblical texts, in Philo and Josephus, and in the Christian fathers: but it is striking in a pagan author. In Greek thinking, god ἀγαπᾶι his human children, rather than the other way round. Note however the close association of θαυμάζειν with ἀγαπᾶν in what D. says to the Rhodians (31.163): πάντα ταῦτα σεμνὴν τὴν πόλιν ποιεῖ, διὰ ταῦτα τῶν ἄλλων διαφέρειν δοκεῖτε, ἐπὶ τούτοις ἅπασι θαυμάζεσθε, ἀγαπᾶσθε.

33 The analogy between the kosmos and a place of initiation into mysteries is widely used, but D.'s elaboration of it owes much to his own vivid writing. It probably goes back to Aristotle's picture of the wonder felt by men who dwelt long underground on suddenly seeing the upper world (Περὶ φιλοσοφίας fr. 12 Rose = Cic. *ND* 2.95; Festugière, *RHT* II 223–8, where our passage is translated), but it was particularly popular with the Stoics. Cleanthes (*SVF* I 538) makes the κόσμος a mystery, the sun a 'torchbearer', δαιδοῦχος. For Seneca (*Epist.* 90.28, see Blankert (1940) *ad loc.*), the world is a temple and *sapientia* reveals the mysteries. Cf. also Plutarch, *Tranq. an.* 477C: ἱερὸν μὲν γὰρ ἁγιώτατον ὁ κόσμος ἐστὶ καὶ θεοπρεπέστατον. εἰς δὲ τοῦτον ὁ ἄνθρωπος εἰσάγεται διὰ τῆς γενέσεως οὐ χειροκμήτων οὐδ' ἀκινήτων ἀγαλμάτων θεατής, ἀλλ' οἷα νοῦς θεῖος αἰσθητὰ μιμήματα νοητῶν ... ἔμφυτον ἀρχὴν ζωῆς ἔχοντα καὶ κινήσεως ἔφηνεν, ἥλιον καὶ σελήνην καὶ ἄστρα καὶ ποταμοὺς νέον ὕδωρ ἐξιέντας ἀεὶ καὶ γῆν φυτοῖς τε και ζώιοις τροφὰς ἀναπέμπουσαν. ὧν τὸν βίον μύησιν ὄντα καὶ τελετὴν τελειοτάτην εὐθυμίας δεῖ μεστὸν εἶναι καὶ γήθους. See further P. Boyancé, *R.E.G.* 75 (1962) 460–82; Reinhardt (1954) 809.   **σχεδὸν οὖν ὅμοιον ὥσπερ εἴ τις ...** 'It is almost as though one ...' For the omission of ἐστι, cf. 32.10 ὅμοιον γὰρ ὥσπερ εἰ ... The construction is classical: Pl. *Laws* 628D ὅμοιον ὡς εἰ κάμνον σῶμα ἰατρικῆς καθάρσεως τυχὸν ἡγοῖτο.   **μυεῖσθαι ... ⟨εἰσάγοι⟩**: text debatable, but Reiske's view that a verb should be supplied seems right, and εἰσάγειν is the natural one (cf. Plu. *loc. cit.*). The only other change required is then an optative instead of περιχορεύειν, as Selden and Theiler propose. **μυχόν**: Selden's μυχόν ('inner chamber', 'grotto') is closer than P's οἶκον to the μῦθον of the other principal MSS, and has been widely accepted, probably rightly.   **σκότους τε καὶ φωτὸς ἐναλλὰξ αὐτῶι φαινομένων**: though the secrets of the mysteries have been well kept, it is plain that, both at Eleusis and elsewhere, the terrors of darkness and the reassurance of revelation by light were an essential part. See, in general, Burkert (1985) 276ff. Cf. especially Plu. *De anima* fr. 178 Sandbach διὰ σκότους τινὲς ὕποπτοι πορεῖαι καὶ ἀτέλεστοι ... ἐκ δὲ τούτου φῶς τι θαυμάσιον ἀπήντησεν καὶ τόποι καθαροὶ καὶ λειμῶνες ἐδέξαντο, φωνὰς καὶ χορείας καὶ σεμνότητας ἀκουσμάτων ἱερῶν καὶ φασμάτων ἁγίων ἔχοντες.   **ἔτι δὲ ... περιχορεύοιεν** 'and if, moreover, the celebrants made their initiates sit down, and danced around them, as they do in the "enthronement"'. Plato (*Euthyd.* 277D) made the θρόνωσις of the Corybantic mysteries familiar, in terms like D.'s: καὶ γὰρ ἐκεῖ χορεία τις ἐστι καὶ παιδιά ... καὶ νῦν τούτω [the two sophists] οὐδὲν ἄλλο ἢ χορεύετον περὶ σὲ οἶον ὀρχεῖσθον παίζοντε, ὡς μετὰ τοῦτο τελοῦντε. Rituals of the same kind occurred in other cults, such as those of the Magna Mater (θρονισμοὶ μητρῶιοι was the title of an 'Orphic' book, O. Kern, *Orphica* (1922) 298) and the Cabiri.   **ἆρά γε ... ἔχων;** 'Is it likely that this man would have no psychological experience and no suspicion that what was going on was due to intentions and preparations wiser than his own, even if he was a remote and obscure barbarian, with no exegete or interpreter to hand, so long as he possessed the mind of a man?' **ἀνωνύμων**: cf. 11.138 οὐ σμικρῶν οὐδ' ἀνωνύμων χωρίων. 'Undistinguished': cf. Eur. *Hipp.* 1, *Hel.* 16. **ἐξηγητοῦ**: the ἐξηγηταί were official 'expounders' of oracles; at Eleusis the Eumolpidae fulfilled these functions: Nilsson (1941) 1 636ff. The rhetor Sopatros (8.110ff. Walz = case 20, Innes and Winterbottom (1988) 93ff.) works out the case of a man who claimed to have been initiated in a dream, and not by a human initiator; such divine guidance was more holy.

34 ἢ τοῦτο μὲν οὐκ ἀνυστόν, κοινῆι δὲ ξύμπαν τὸ τῶν ἀνθρώπων γένος ... τούτων ξυμπάντων μηδεμίαν αἴσθησιν ... λαβεῖν: an *a fortiori* argument, expressed typically in a complex question: can it be that *this* is impossible (viz. that any individual human being should be unaffected by the spectacle of the universe) but that the whole human race should be unable to perceive the marvels of our initiation? **τῶι ὄντι τελείαν τελετήν**: τέλειος is an adjective loaded with religious significance (used of sacrifice, ritual, vows, dreams, auguries, initiates (cf. Arndt–Gingrich s.v. 2b)). For its conjunction with the etymologically related τελετή, see especially Pl. *Phaedrus* 249c7 τέλεος ἀεὶ τελετὰς τελούμενος τέλεος ὄντως μόνον γίγνεται, with de Vries (1969) *ad loc.*, and Hermias 172–3 Couvreur ὡς τῶι ὄντι τότε τῆς ψυχῆς τελείαν καὶ ὁλόκληρον ἑαυτῆς ἀπολαμβανούσης τὴν οὐσίαν; Plu. *Tranq. an.* 477c (quoted above §32). 'Charondas' moralizes the idea, 60 Thesleff = Stob. 4.2.24.: τελεῖσθαί τε τὴν μεγίστην καὶ τελειοτάτην τελετήν, ἀνδραγαθίαν ... οὐδεὶς γὰρ ἀνὴρ τέλειος ἄνευ ταύτης. **μικρῶι ... ὄχλου βραχέος**: though thousands were initiated at Eleusis, this was insignificant compared with the mystery of the kosmos, open to all mankind. **θαυμαστῶν**: Reiske's θαυμάτων is perhaps more elegant, but unnecessary. **ἔτι δὲ ... τελούντων** 'and moreover with the initiation performed not by men like those who are being initiated, but by immortal gods initiating mortals ...' **περιχορευόντων**: this picks up the image of the θρονισμός, but is also suggestive of the 'dance' of the stars: cf. e.g. [Pl.] *Epinomis* 982e τὴν τῶν ἄστρων φύσιν, ἰδεῖν μὲν καλλίστην, πορείαν δὲ καὶ χορείαν πάντων χορῶν καλλίστην καὶ μεγαλοπρεπεστάτην χορεύοντα πᾶσι τοῖς ζῶσι τὸ δέον ἀποτελεῖν. **νυκτί τε ... καὶ ἄστροις** 'by night and day, by light and stars'. If the

text is right, these are the mode of our initiation; but the phrase is
pleonastic and awkward, and von Arnim reasonably questioned it. But
note the 'abundance' of the whole passage.   τούτων: resumptive.
μάλιστα δὲ 'and above all'. Von Arnim's objection that logic requires
μηδέ is strictly right; but his deletion of μάλιστα δέ leads into further
difficulties. We should keep the text: 'and especially (have no perception
or suspicion of) the leader of the dance, who presides over the universe
and directs the whole heaven and ordered world, like a wise helmsman
who captains a beautifully and completely equipped ship'. The dance
metaphor continues in κορυφαίου: cf. [Aristot.] Περὶ κόσμου 399a18
κατὰ γὰρ τὸ ἄνωθεν ἐνδόσιμον ὑπὸ τοῦ φερωνύμως ἂν κορυφαίου
προσαγορευθέντος κινεῖται μὲν τὰ ἄστρα ἀεὶ καὶ ὁ σύμπας οὐρανός, 'the
stars and the whole heavens move continually as the keynote is given
on high by Him who might well be called the Leader of the Dance'.
κυβερνήτου: this image too is traditional, and a favourite with all
schools. Cf. [Aristot.] Περὶ κόσμου 400b6 ἐν νηὶ μὲν κυβερνήτης, ἐν
ἄρμασι δὲ ἡνίοχος, ἐν χορῶι δὲ κορυφαῖος, ἐν πόλει δὲ νόμος, ἐν
στρατοπέδωι δὲ ἡγέμων.   ἀνενδεῶς 'completely', cf. 1.8 ἀνενδεὴς
καὶ τέλειος ἡγέμων (of wise λόγος).

35 τὸ τοιοῦτον γιγνόμενον: i.e. that man should have a concept
of the government of god.   μέχρι τῶν θηρίων . . . θεσμόν: D.
seems to pass tacitly from the common idea that all living things live
according to divine law ([Aristot.] Περὶ κόσμου 401a9 τῶν τε ζώιων τά
τε ἄγρια καὶ ἥμερα . . . γίνεται καὶ ἀκμάζει καὶ φθείρεται τοῖς τοῦ θεοῦ
πειθόμενα θεσμοῖς, Epict. 1.14.3 (plants), M. Aur. 5.1 τὰ φυτάρια τὰ
στρουθάρια τοὺς μύρμηκας τοὺς ἀράχνας τὰς μελίσσας . . . τὸ καθ' αὑτὰς
συγκροτούσας κόσμον) to the more specific notion that they do so
voluntarily and show cognizance of god (cf. Manil. 2.99ff. *pecudes et muta
animalia . . . | natura tamen ad mundum reuocante parentem | attollunt animos
caelumque et sidera seruant*; Simplicius, *In enchiridion Epicteti* 95 Dübner οὐκ
ἄνθρωποι μόνον ἀλλὰ καὶ τὰ ἄλογα ζῶια καὶ τὰ φυτὰ καὶ λίθοι καὶ
πάντα ἁπλῶς τὰ ὄντα κατὰ τὴν ἑκάστου δύναμιν ἕκαστα ἐπέστραπται
πρὸς τὸν θεόν). He may have in mind some examples, real or fictional,
which were often alleged: the elephant worships the sun and the moon
(Aelian, *NA* 7.44, 4.10); the heliotrope turns towards the sun (Plin. *NH*
2.109). These 'phenomena' illustrated not only the 'sympatheia' between different parts of the universe but the recognition of the divine
power throughout the whole system. This was specially important to

Posidonius (Sandbach (1975) 130 gives a balanced account) and D. here is certainly influenced by this strain of Stoicism. **ἀπεοικότως** 'improbably', 'unexpectedly'. **ἁπλῆι τινι φύσει διοικούμενα**: Stoic doctrine is that plants have no ψυχή (as Aristotle held) but only φύσις (*SVF* II 204). So this is orthodox: but it is less orthodox to add that they produce their fruit ἑκουσίως καὶ βουλόμενα, unless this simply means that their obedience to cosmic law must be 'voluntary' in a sense, as is ours, because the service of the divine kosmos, i.e. of Zeus, is also the expression of our freedom. **ὡς δὴ καὶ ταῦτα . . . ἑκάστωι:** this clause, loosely constructed, depends on οὐ . . . θαυμάσαι τις ἄν. There is no need to emend. **τοῦδε τοῦ θεοῦ:** i.e. Zeus, whose statue was perhaps visible to D.'s audience from where they stood. Introd. p. 15. **γνώμη** 'intention'.

36 ἀρχαῖοι 'primitive', 'unsophisticated': cf. 33.63 καταγελᾶται . . . ἡ τῆς φύσεως τέχνη, καθάπερ ἀρχαία τις οὖσα καὶ σφόδρα εὐήθης. **ἐγγυτέρω . . . ἄγνοιαν** 'if we say that this kind of understanding is nearer to animals and trees than inexperience and ignorance are to us'. An involved way of introducing the following instance of human folly, namely the impiety of the Epicureans. **σοφώτεροι . . . τῆς ἁπάσης σοφίας:** cf. §11 εὐδαιμονέστεροι . . . αὐτῆς τῆς εὐδαιμονίας. For the idea that some pretended σοφία is not so at all, cf. Eur. *Bacch.* 395, Hor. *Odes* 1.34.2 insanientis . . . sapientiae (of Epicureans, see Nisbet–Hubbard *ad loc.*). **οὐ κηρὸν . . . ὠιδῆς:** *Od.* 12.173ff. **ὑπὲρ τοῦ μὴ κατακοῦσαι** 'so as not to hear': LSJ s.v. ὑπέρ II 5. **μολύβδου . . . φύσιν** 'a lead substance, soft and also impenetrable to the voice'. μολύβδου . . . φύσιν is little more than a periphrasis for 'lead' (LSJ s.v. φύσις II 5), and lead has natural associations with stupidity: Terence, *Heauton.* 877 quae sunt dicta in stulto: caudex stipes asinus plumbeus. **σκότος . . . καὶ ἀχλύν:** in *Il.* 14.342, Zeus covers Hera and himself with a cloud. **μίαν . . . δαίμονα πονηρὰν καὶ †ἄλυπον†:** ἄλυπον cannot be right (nor can any reconstruction involving ἀλυπία, e.g. πονηράν, ἀλυπίαν καὶ τρυφήν τινα), since ἀλυπία ('painlessness') is a good thing. Choice of emendation is difficult: the best perhaps is ἀνόσιον, 'unholy'. By δαίμονα, D. means merely 'god'; his usage of the word covers both this sense (e.g. 36.38) and that of 'personal *daimon*' (e.g. 3.5.6); occasionally (33.4, 3.54) he seems to regard δαίμονες as intermediate between the divine and the human. See J. Puiggali, *L.E.C.* 52 (1984) 103–14. **τρυφήν . . . ὕβριν** 'a lavish luxury and ease and uncontrolled wanton-

ness'.   **γυναικείαν τῶι ὄντι θεόν** 'truly a womanish divinity'. Cf. *Or.*
4.101ff., where D. describes the δαίμων of the life of pleasure (but
without reference to Epicurus): ὁ τὰ τῆς ἡδονῆς ἀναφαίνων ὄργια καὶ
τὴν θεὸν ταύτην θαυμάζων καὶ προτιμῶν, ἀτεχνῶς γυναικείαν θεόν. In
Fronto (*Ad M. Caes.* 2.15.3) Ἀπάτη is γυναικεία θεός: the term is
also used (Plu. *Caesar* 9.4) for the Roman Bona Dea.   **κυμβάλοις**
. . . αὐλουμένοις 'with tinkling cymbals and pipes played in the dark'.
Cf. *Or.* 4.112 αἱ δὲ [*sc.* γυναῖκες ἀκόλαστοι] μετὰ πατάγου κυμβάλων
τε καὶ αὐλῶν φέρουσαι μαινόμενον αὐτὸν σπουδῆι προΐτωσαν. In our
passage, D. benefits from the association of cymbals with Isis, pipes with
Cybele, and music of all kinds with dissolute living.   **ὑποψοφοῦσι:**
this is Capps's proposal: an adjective or participle is certainly needed. ἢ
ψόφοις, 'or noises', is out of place between the two named instruments.
εὐωχίας: D. distorts Epicurean ethics by implying that Epicurus approved elaborate dinners: in fact, of course, *uoluptatis assertor omnes libros*
suos repleuit oleribus et pomis (Jerome, *Adv. Jovinianum* 2.11 and Usener
466), and this vulgar view of him is unfair.   **οὐδεὶς . . . φθόνος** 'I
do not grudge . . .', a common Atticism (Plato, Lucian), oddly not
elsewhere in D.

37 εἰ . . . ἦν: 'if their "wisdom" was limited to singing'.   **τοὺς**
θεοὺς . . . εἴς τινας . . . ἐρήμους: Epicurus held that the gods existed
in the *intermundia*, the spaces between the innumerable worlds, where
they lived in perfect tranquillity. It was easy to represent this in ridiculous
terms: Cic. *De div.* 2.40 *deos enim ipsos iocandi causa induxit Epicurus per-*
lucidos et perflabilis et habitantis tamquam inter duos lucos sic inter duos mundos
propter metum ruinarum; Sen. *Ben.* 4.19.2, *Epist.* 90.35; Atticus ap. Euseb.
PE xv 800b (= Usener 362) καθάπερ εἰς ἀλλοδαπὴν ἀπώικισε καὶ ἔξω
που τοῦ κόσμου καθίδρυσεν.   **ἐκ τῆς αὐτῶν πόλεώς τε καὶ ἀρχῆς**
[ἐκ] τοῦδε τοῦ κόσμου παντός 'from this whole world, which is their
own city and realm'. Geel's small correction seems right.   **εἴς τινας**
νήσους ἐρήμους: islands were typical places of exile: 'the Siberia of the
empire' (Mayor's rich note on Juv. 1.73 *breuibus Gyaris et carcere dignus*).
Gyara was especially so used: Musonius was sent there by Nero (Tac.
Ann. 15.71, Philostr. *VA* 7.16).   **μηδὲ ὥσπερ . . . φέρεσθαι** 'not even
in the sense that children set their hoops in motion and then let them
roll on their own'. Epicurus denied not only a divine plan and continuous divine control of the universe, but even the possibility that a creator
once set it all going and then let go: cf. Pl. *Politicus* 269c τὸ γὰρ πᾶν

τόδε τοτὲ μὲν αὐτὸς ὁ θεὸς συμποδηγεῖ πορευόμενον καὶ συγκυκλεῖ, τοτὲ
δὲ ἀνῆκεν, ὅταν αἱ περίοδοι τοῦ προσήκοντος αὐτῶι μέτρον εἰλήφωσιν
ἤδη χρόνου.

38 'This digression arose out of the run of my argument. Philosophers
are freer than orators who speak in court for limited time.' Cf. 7.102,
124, 128 for apologies for digression.   **τυχὸν γὰρ ... τοῖς
ἀκροωμένοις** 'for it is perhaps not easy to restrain the mind and argument of the philosopher, whatever direction it takes, if what meets it at
any moment appears useful or necessary to the hearer'. τυχόν here (like
ἴσως often) merely makes a dogmatic statement more modest, it does
not imply any doubt.   **ἔνθα ἂν ὁρμήσηι:** cf. Pl. *Rep.* 394D οὐ γὰρ ...
πω οἶδα, ἀλλ' ὅπηι ἂν ὁ λόγος ὥσπερ πνεῦμα φέρηι, ταύτηι ἰτέον; *ibid.*
365D ὡς τὰ ἴχνη τῶν λόγων φέρει.   **οὐ μελετηθέντα ... ἀδείας** 'it
has not been prepared with an eye to the clock and the constraints of
the court as someone once put it, but with great freedom and licence'.
Cf. Pl. *Theaet.* 172D–E οἱ ἐν δικαστηρίοις ... πρὸς τοὺς ἐν φιλοσοφίαι
... ὡς οἰκέται πρὸς ἐλευθέρους ... οἱ δὲ ἐν ἀσχολίαι τε ἀεὶ λέγουσι –
κατεπείγει γὰρ ὕδωρ ῥέον ... ἀνάγκην ἔχων ὁ ἀντίδικος παρέστηκεν;
ibid. 201B πρὸς ὕδωρ σμικρόν.   **ὥσπερ ... παραλλάξασι** 'as for
competent pilots on a voyage, who have not strayed from their course'.

39–48 'As well as the innate conception of the divine, which we have
just described, there are acquired conceptions – some acquired voluntarily from the poets, some under compulsion from lawgivers. Without
discussing the relative priority of these, we should perhaps think it right
to regard the poets' teaching as primary, since the basis of it, as of our
innate concepts, is respect and affection for a father to whom we owe
our beginning.

'We should discuss these things patiently and with care. (§43).

'To the three sources of belief already set out – the innate, the poetic,
and the legal – we should add the visual arts. (§§44–6)

'And (?) in addition both to the innate and to the three acquired
sources we have now named – poetic, legal, artistic – we must add a
fourth: the philosopher. (§47)

'Let us pass over the lawgiver, and select representatives of the others.
In fact they all agree. The true philosopher (?might need) special help
in a comparison with poets and sculptors before an audience at a
festival. (§48)

'Suppose, first of all, we summon Phidias to account for himself . . .'

Such a synopsis reveals the awkwardness of the argument. The philosopher (§47) seems an afterthought; he is not discussed. Nor are the poets discussed in any detail, though Phidias will make a comparison later between his art and theirs. D.'s purpose is evidently to lead into the question of the validity of sculpture as an expression of the divine; and he has therefore distorted the traditional 'tripartite theology', which we know from Roman sources (Scaevola, Varro, reported, e.g. in Tertullian, *Ad nationes* 2, Augustine, *CD* 4.27: but see also, e.g., Plu. *Amat.* 753B–C; see in general Pépin (1958), Lieberg in *A.N.R.W.* 1.3 (1973) 63–115, Theiler (1982) 280–1) and which sharply distinguished *theologia ciuilis, poetica*, and *philosophica*. It has been thought (Pohlenz (1949) II 119, Pépin (1958) 281) that D. equates the 'innate conception' with that of the philosophers. If this is so, he does not make it clear; and we should expect the 'philosophers' to say something more specifically Stoic: i.e. to identify kosmos, all-pervasive divinity, and fire (cf., e.g., the passages cited by Long and Sedley, 1 323–31). When D. proposes (§48) to select representatives of all teachers except lawgivers, he is perhaps leaving himself the option of making a longer speech: whether he did so or not, we cannot know. Cf. Introd. p. 18.

39 οὐ κατὰ πλάνην συστᾶσαν οὐδὲ ὡς ἔτυχεν 'not formed in error or accidentally'.   **ἀέναον** 'perennial': cf. 2.41 κρήναις ἀενάοις. The choice of adjective continues the metaphor in πηγήν.   **σχεδόν τε ... γένους** 'in effect, the common public property of the rational species'.   **τοῖς μὲν ἀδεσπότοις ... τοὺς κυρίους:** this distinction between the anonymous and the attributable beliefs is not used in what follows. The whole phrase is thus not much more than a 'polar' expression conveying the total field of acquired belief (cf., e.g., Barrett on Eur. *Hipp.* 441–2). The following distinction, into voluntary and obligatory, by contrast, *is* pursued.

40 παραμυθητικὴν ... προστακτικήν 'hortatory ... imperative'. Posidonius thought that laws should be purely designed to command, not to instruct (Sen. *Epist.* 94.38 (= F178, E–K)), and this seems to be D.'s position here.   **τὰ μὲν ... τῶν δὲ:** both pronouns are neuter. τὰ μέν is needed instead of τῶν μέν because D. means that poets and lawgivers make some points correctly and in accordance with our basic, innate understanding, but in other respects 'wander' from it. He cannot mean that *some* poets and lawgivers are always right, and others sometimes wrong: this is what would be meant if we read τῶν μέν.

41 ἀμφοῖν . . . λεγομένοιν: feminine duals. The dual is always an 'Attic' feature: cf. Moeris p. 244 Pierson νῶι δυϊκῶς Ἀττικῶς, ἡμεῖς Ἑλληνικῶς. It is not rare in D., but commoner with nouns than with verbs. Cf. 7.69.   **παρά γε ἡμῖν**: because Homer and Hesiod taught the Greeks about the gods (cf. Hdt. 2.53), whereas other nations (e.g. the Jews) obtained their religion from lawgivers.   **πρέπει**: the argument is one of propriety. It is better, because more respectful of human nature and its worth, to think the more humane method is also the older. **παραμυθητικόν**: this (which picks up §40) or (less likely) Koehler's πειστικόν ('persuasive') must be what D. wrote. We need a word to contrast with μετὰ . . . προστάξεως.

42 σχεδὸν οὖν . . . γονέων 'so far, there is a similarity between human attitudes to the first, immortal parent . . . and to mortal, human parents.'   **τοῦ πρώτου καὶ ἀθανάτου γόνεως**: cf. §22.   **πατρῷον Δία**: the cult of Zeus Patroos is quite widely attested (Nilsson (1940) 1 524), as a family or tribal god, though the title more often belongs to Apollo. D. here interprets it of the universal fatherhood of Zeus.   **οἱ τῆς Ἑλλάδος κοινωνοῦντες**: i.e. Hellenes, wherever they are; or, possibly, Greek speakers, cf. Aelian, *VH* 9.16 αὐτὸ δὲ τοὔνομα εἰς τὴν Ἑλλάδα, φασιν, ἱππομιγὴς δύναται, 'the name itself ["Mares"], translated into Greek, means "horse-hybrid"'.

43 ἄνευ τοῦ διασαφεῖν . . . μὴ ἀνέκτιτον ἐᾶν 'without explaining and showing what parents are like and what the benefits are which give rise to the debt which they command us not to leave unpaid'. Note again (cf. §40) the assumption that lawgivers give no reasons for their commands.   †**ἐν τοῖς . . . γιγνόμενον**†: a vexed passage. We should consider reading: τοῦτο ἰδεῖν ἔστιν ἐπ' ἀμφοτέρων γιγνόμενον, μᾶλλον δὲ ἐν τοῖς περὶ θεῶν λόγοις καὶ μύθοις. Then τοῦτο is the 'lack of clarity' about 'what parents are like', and this is evident in laws about duties to parents, and still more in laws relating to religion. In any case, this sentence belongs with what precedes.   **Ὁρῶ μὲν οὖν . . . λόγους**: another methodological section, not really in place here: cf. §26 (to which Emperius wished to move this passage). 'I observe that many people find accuracy a troublesome thing, and not least in words, who concern themselves only with quantity, and make no preliminary statement or division of the subject, nor begin from any proper beginning, but simply go through the bare, obvious points, "with unwashed feet", as the saying goes. Now there is no great harm in unwashed feet if one's path lies through mud and filth, but an unskilled tongue is seriously damaging to the hearers.' **πλήθους**: probably 'quantity', i.e. they are concerned only with the length of their speech, not with its organization, rather than 'the multitude', 'the size of their audience'. **ἀπλύτοις ποσί** 'with unwashed feet', i.e. without having got ready for the party: cf. A Gell. 1.9.8 for the application to learning: *nunc autem ... isti qui repente pedibus illotis ad philosophos deuertunt, non est hoc satis, quod sunt omnino* ἀθεώρητοι ἄμουσοι ἀγεωμέτρητοι *sed legem etiam dant qua philosophari discant*. The phrase is proverbial: Zenobius 1.95, Diogenianus 1.49, Otto (1890) 274–5. **γυμνότατα** 'barest', 'baldest' points: Wilamowitz felt doubtful; Sonny proposed ἑτοιμότατα, 'readiest', which fits the other adjective better. **συνεξανύειν καὶ συνεκπονεῖν** 'keep up with us and share the labour to the end'. Cf. Plu. *Mor.* 137D συνεξαμιλλᾶσθαι. M. B. Trapp well compares Max. Tyr. 1.6 συναγωνιστής ... συγκονιόμενος καὶ συμπονῶν. In all these passages, note the strong affective force of repeated συν- compounds: the same effect is sought by St Paul, Romans 8.22 πᾶσα ἡ κτίσις συστενάζει καὶ συνωδίνει ἄχρι τοῦ νῦν. **τοὺς πεπαιδευμένους**: D. implies that his present audience is 'educated' in this sense: for the term, see Anderson (1989) 105, with his references. **ὧν λόγον τινὰ ἔχειν ἄξιον** 'of whom one ought to take some notice'. Note the exclusiveness implied: this audience is élite, not vulgar. **ἐκ καμπῆς τινος καὶ δυσχωρίας** 'from windings and rough ground'. D. uses καμπή of a winding river (35.13), a crooked measuring rod (67.1), and a musical flourish (2.56).

44 προχειμένων 'having been set out' (in the preceding sections). ⟨**τοῦ**⟩ **δαιμονίου**: the article is surely necessary, cf. §39 τῆς περὶ τὸ θεῖον δόξης καὶ ὑπολήψεως. **τὴν πλαστικὴν ... φύσεως** 'the plastic and creative skill of statues and images of the divine: I mean the skill of painters, sculptors, workers in stone and in general everyone who claims to prove himself an imitator of the divine nature in art.' **ἀνδριαντοποιῶν**: perhaps specifically of workers in bronze, as opposed to stone: cf. Aristot. *EN* 1141a11, Φειδίαν λιθουργὸν σοφὸν καὶ Πολύκλειτον ἀνδριαντοποιόν. **εἴτε σκιαγραφίαι ... πρὸς ὄψιν** 'whether by shaded drawing, weak and visually deceptive ...' The phrase is from Pl. *Critias* 107D ἅτε οὐδὲν εἰδότες ἀκριβὲς περὶ τῶν τοιούτων [mountains, rivers, etc.] οὔτε ἐξετάζομεν οὔτε ἐλέγχομεν τὰ γεγραμμένα, σκιαγραφίαι δὲ ἀσαφεῖ καὶ ἀπατηλῶι χρώμεθα περὶ αὐτῶν. Pollitt (1974) 123, 247 discusses the meaning of σκιαγραφία – 'outline

drawing' or 'shading' – and seems to prefer 'shading' in this passage.
Trimpi (1983) 186, in a careful discussion, favours 'rough sketch'.
⟨εἴτε⟩ χρωμάτων μίξει . . . περιλαμβανούσης 'or by a mixture of
colours and the definition of a line embracing the most exact form
possible'. Pl. *loc. cit* contrasts ἀκριβείᾳ with σκιαγραφία: and this con-
firms Capps' suggestion. D. in fact enumerates six different arts:
σκιαγραφία, coloured drawing, stone, wood, bronze and wax statuary.
Pollitt (1974) 396 sees here a 'hint of a controversy over the relative
merits of draftsmanship and σκιαγραφία', comparing Quint. 12.10.4,
and suggesting that Parrhasius stressed precise drawing, and Zeuxis and
Apollodorus the use of light and shade. D.'s list of media anyway
seems to proceed from the least realistic towards the most plastic and
malleable.   ξοάνων: probably 'wooden statues'.   κατ' ὀλίγον
. . . εἶδος: the view that the statue is inherent in the piece of marble,
and the sculptor reveals it by chipping away the rest, is set out by
Cicero, *De div.* 2.48 *quasi . . . non in omni marmore necesse sit inesse uel
Praxitelia capita! illa enim ipsa efficiuntur detractione* (= ἀφαιρέσει) *neque
quicquam illuc adfertur a Praxiteli; sed cum multa sunt detracta et ad liniamenta
oris peruentum est, tum intellegas illud quod iam expolitum sit intus fuisse.* It
became a common idea: cf. Addison, *Spectator* 215: 'Aristotle [where?
Met. 1013b6–8 is not to the point] . . . tells us that a statue lies hid in a
Block of Marble, and that the Art of the Statuary only clears away
the superfluous Matter and removes the Rubbish.' And Michelangelo
wrote to Benedetto Varchi in 1547 'by sculpture I mean that which is
fashioned by the effort of cutting away', and in all his thinking on
sculpture respected the block of stone from which his work was to come:
but whether this and other similarities with our speech show that he
knew D. (as is suggested by D. Summers, *Michelangelo and the language
of art* (Princeton 1981) 273 and 487 n. 26) is debatable. Introd. p. 19.
τὸ φαινόμενον εἶδος: i.e. the form that we see.   εἴτε χωνείαι . . .
τύπους 'or by the founding of bronze or similar valuable materials
beaten out in fire or flowing into moulds'. See LSJ s.v. ἐλαύνω III 1.
πλεῖστον ἐπιδεχομένου τὸ τῆς μετανοίας 'most readily permitting a
change of mind'. So *pentimenti*, 'repentances', is the term used by art-
critics for original lines of a painting which has been over-painted as a
result of the artist's second thoughts.

45 Φειδίας . . . Δαίδαλος: the list naturally begins with Phidias and
his pupil Alcamenes, who are coupled together, e.g., in Quint. 12.10.8

(see Austin *ad loc.*), in a context also praising Phidias' power of adding *aliquid etiam receptae religioni* in his Athena and Zeus. Polyclitus is the other unavoidable classic sculptor; Aglaophon, his pupil Polygnotus, and Zeuxis represent the painters. The mythic Daedalus, traditionally regarded as the inventor of archaic statuary, completes the list. No Praxiteles (despite his Hermes), no Apelles, no Lysippus, though he worked at Olympia. This is a classicizing, if not archaizing, selection. **καὶ διαθέσεις παντοδαπάς** 'subjects of all kinds'. Cf. Polemo (ap. Athen. v 210D) ἐξηγούμενος διάθεσιν ἐν Φλιοῦντι ... γεγραμμένην. **χορηγούς** 'patrons'.   **πολλῆς ... ὑπονοίας καὶ ποικίλης** 'a rich and varied notion' of the divine.   **ταῖς ἐπικειμέναις ... ζημίαις:** penalties for ἀσέβεια were a standard feature of Greek cities. **προκατειλημμένους αὐτοὺς ... εἰδωλοποιΐαν** 'that they had been anticipated by the poets, and their representation was the older'. The reflexive αὐτούς seems best.   **εἰδωλοποιΐαν** 'image-making'. Here a faculty common to poets and painters: see [Longinus] 15.1 (with Russell's note) for other usages.

46 καινοποιοῦντες 'by making innovations'. Novelty in religion is suspect: it was introducing καινὰ δαιμόνια that Socrates was accused of.   **τοῖς μύθοις ... συνηγοροῦντες** 'following and lending support to the myths'. They were the poets' συνήγοροι, 'advocates'. **ἀντίτεχνοι καὶ ὁμότεχνοι** 'professional rivals and professional colleagues'.   **ὡς ἐκεῖνοι ... θεαταῖς** 'actually explaining religious matters visually to the ignorant majority of spectators, as the poets displayed them to the ear'. In order to emphasize the likeness between poets and painters, D., somewhat paradoxically, uses 'display' of poets and 'explain' of painters. For the traditional comparison between poetry and the visual arts see, e.g., Brink on Hor. *AP* 361–5. Basic texts: Plu. *Mor.* 17F, 58B, 346F (Simonides' dictum that painting is silent poetry), *Ad Herennium* 4.39, Quint. 12.10.   **πάντα ... τοῦ δαιμονίου** 'all these activities, which are done for the honour and pleasure of the divine power, acquire their strength from the original first principle' – i.e. the innate conception we all have.

47 δίχα γε 'setting aside'. Von Arnim deleted these words: and it is true that the poets etc. are in fact 'interpreters' of the natural instinct. Deletion does not solve the problems of this section. He is however right to delete the ungrammatical ποιητικῆς ... δημιουργικῆς below.   **ἅμα τῶι λόγωι** 'together with reason'. The conception of god is not born with us, though our capacity to form it is, but develops as our reason develops.   **οὐδὲ ἀπείρως . . . ὑπὲρ αὐτῶν** 'nor believing that one ought to remain inexperienced about them'. ἡγούμενον, sc. δεῖν: LSJ s.v. ἡγέομαι III 4. ὑπέρ is a little odd, and ἀπείρως . . . αὐτῶν, 'without experience of them', would be more natural.   **τὸν φιλόσοφον ἄνδρα:** it is only here and in next section that we hear of this 'interpreter'.   **†τῆι λόγωντ:** no suggestion convinces. Perhaps we should read: ἔχειν ⟨τῶν⟩ ὑπὲρ αὐτῶν λόγων, λέγω . . . ἄνδρα, ἐξηγητὴν κ.τ.λ. **ἐξηγητὴν καὶ προφήτην** 'expositor and prophet'. Both words carry religious overtones: ἐξηγηταί were interpreters of oracles (cf. 12.33n.) προφῆται were spokesmen who pronounced them.

48 **Τὸν μὲν οὖν . . . ἀσχολίας** 'let us forbear to call the lawgiver to account – he is a stern person who calls others to account – for I probably ought to spare myself and your busy lives'. ἐᾶν + infinitive is not common, but see LSJ s.v. II 1. The point of the last clause is that neither D.'s strength nor his audience's other concerns permit a long speech. But there may also be some suggestion that it would be inexpedient to criticize the lawgiver.   **τὸν ἄκρον** 'the top man', in each class. No philosopher is presented, however, and the top poet, Homer, does not answer for himself, but is discussed by the top sculptor, Phidias, who alone is going to be 'called to account'.   **ἢ καί:** Wilamowitz' correction should be accepted, since the question is to be asked of each defendant is whether he has done good or harm.   **ὅπως τε . . . ἀλλήλοις** 'and how they are placed in regard to agreement or difference with each other'. Note the *variatio* (abstract noun, infinitive); for ἔχω + genitive, see WS §1441.   **τῆι πρώτηι καὶ ἀδόλωι γνώμηι:** the 'first, sincere, judgement' is that provided by our natural instincts.   **†τοιγαροῦν†:** omitted by first hand in M. There is serious corruption here, and Emperius may be right simply to delete the whole sentence. D. normally has τοιγαροῦν as first word, though postponement is found in Ionic and Hellenistic Greek (Blomquist (1969) 130); in any case, its sense ('therefore', 'and that is why . . .') is quite inappropriate. The sentence would however make sense after §46 τοῦ δαιμονίου: but the problems of the train of thought in this passage are not solved by this means either. **ξυνάιδουσιν . . . ἴχνους:** note the clumsy mixture of metaphors, from choral singing to hunting.   **οὐ γὰρ ἂν . . . δικαστῶν;** 'For perhaps the true philosopher would not need an excuse, if he were brought into comparison with the makers of statues or verses, even in a festival

crowd of judges favourable to them.' This gives a reason for not pro-
ceeding with the case of the philosopher: it has not been stated that
this is to be the procedure, and the train of thought seems elliptical.
⟨ἀλλ'⟩ οὐ γὰρ κ.τ.λ. would be an improvement (Denniston (1954) 101
for similar examples), but in so confused a passage it seems vain to
'improve'.

49–54 'Let us suppose that Phidias was made to appear before a jury
of all Greeks, not to answer for his financial management, but for
venturing to represent Zeus in human form, something which earlier
artists did not dare to do.'

49 οὐ τῶν χρημάτων λόγον ἀπαιτῶν: there is here an allusion to
the story that Phidias was prosecuted by the Eleans for misappropriat-
ing gold destined for the statue, and was either excused or had his
hands cut off. This was a known declamation theme (Sen. *Contr.* 8.2,
[Cornutus] §215 p. 390 Sp.-H., p. 42 Graeven). Philochorus (*FGrHist*
328 F121) perhaps gave the basis for it. Somewhat more reliable is the
account of Phidias' alleged trial for malpractice in Athens, in connection with the statue of Athena Parthenos: Plu. *Per.* 31.2–5, with Stadter
(1989) *ad loc.* Declamation themes relating to artists are not uncommon:
note Sen. *Contr.* 10.5, on Parrhasius' crime in torturing a captive from
Olynthus to give himself a model, and Sopatros (8.126 Walz = case 22,
Innes and Winterbottom (1988)) on Micon's offence in representing
the barbarians as bigger than the Greeks in a picture of the battle of
Marathon.   **κυπάριττος . . . ἀδιάφθορος** 'and cypress and thyine
wood, durable and incorruptible material for the inner construction'.
The core of the statue was of hard woods: θύον (Theophr. *HP* 5.3.7)
was a valuable timber, imported from Cyrene, and used in statues.
Cypress too is ἀσαπὴς φύσει (*ibid.* 5.4.2, Hor. *AP* 332). Meiggs (1982)
316 says the core was of cypress and lotus ('nettlewood', *Celtis australis*, a
Greek timber), but this is not what D. says, and is much less likely.
⟨ἀπολαβόντι⟩: von Arnim's addition, or something like it, is necessary. τελεώτατον however may be kept (cf. §52 μισθὸν . . . μείζω καὶ
τελειότερον).

50 εἰ οὖν δή resumes εἰ γάρ τις at the beginning of §49. The apodosis
does not follow till §55 εἴποι ἄν.   **οὖν δή:** a common combination in
Herodotus and late Plato (Denniston (1954) 468), not much found in
other classical prose. Here it is clearly resumptive.   **ὡς μὲν οὐχ:**
answered by εἰ δ' αὖ, §52. If οὖν is right, it is 'emphasizing a prospective

μέν' (Denniston 473); but οὐδεὶς ἀντερεῖ leads us to expect a redundant οὐ: WS §2743, Demosth, 8.31 ὡς μὲν οὐκ ἀληθῆ ταῦτ' ἐστίν, οὐχ ἕξετ' ἀντιλέγειν, 'you will not be in a position to deny that this *is* true', i.e. 'to say in opposition that it is *not* true'.   **ἡδὺ . . . θέας** 'a pleasing and attractive spectacle, an infinite visual delight'. Note the 'abundance' throughout this sentence, which introduces a rather formal speech.

51 ταύρων τε . . . χάριν 'the bulls which at any time are brought to this altar, so that they would voluntarily submit to the sacrifices, if by so doing they would be giving the god some pleasure'. **κατάρχεσθαι,** strictly to cut off the hair as the first part of the sacrificial rite, is also used of the whole procedure.   **ὡς = ὥστε.   ἰκτίνων**: ἵππων will not do, for horses are not wild things like eagles and lions. Jacobs' conjecture (= 'kites') is based on Paus. 5.14.1, where it is said that no kite ever interferes with sacrifices at Olympia.   **ἐπίπονος τὴν ψυχήν** 'in mental distress'.   **ἀναντλήσας** 'having endured', ἀπ- cannot be right: it would mean 'having drawn off'.   **μηδὲ ὕπνον ἡδὺν ἐπιβαλλόμενος** 'without even wrapping himself in sweet sleep'. The unusual sense of the verb and the *epitheton ornans* ἡδὺν (cf. Eur. *Hec.* 915) suggest that this is a poetical allusion.   **καὶ ὅς** 'even he'.

52 νηπενθές . . . ἁπάντων: *Od.* 4.221, of a drug 'that banishes grief and anger, and brings forgetfulness of all troubles'. Both the direct and the indirect tradition of Homer vary between ἐπίληθες and ἐπίληθον. **τοσοῦτον . . . τέχνης** 'such light and such charm rests upon it through your art'.   **κρίνοντα . . . ὄψεως** 'if he were to judge it on human pleasure and delight'.   **ἀνδρός τε . . . πλὴν ἀνδρός** 'and displaying the form of a man, preeminent in size and beauty, but still the form of a man'. The three participles χρησάμενος, δείξας, ποιήσας, are parallel to each other and subordinate to ἐδημιούργησας.

53 ὁρᾶις γὰρ . . . ὁ κίνδυνος ἡμῖν: such emphasis on the importance of a theme is not only a common rhetorical move (πηλικότης: see Russell (1983), Index, s.v.) but also reminiscent of Platonic passages (e.g. *Gorg.* 472C) where the vital importance of being right in a philosophical matter is underlined.   **πᾶν τὸ θνητόν** 'all mankind'. If this reading is right, the words should be taken with ἀνεπλάττομεν (so Emperius) rather than with ἰνδαλλόμενοι καὶ ὀνειρώττοντες. Emendation, on the lines of περὶ τὸ ἀθάνατον (Wenkebach) or πᾶν τὸ θεῖον (Capps), is attractive (i) because the *constructio ad sensum* is awkward; (ii) because, although we can easily understand that the dim apprehension described is apprehension of the divine, this is not explicit. Since πᾶν has little point with τὸ θεῖον, Wenkebach's suggestion is better.   **ἰνδαλλόμενοι**: apparently 'picturing', 'imagining', though this is not the sense of the word in Plato (who uses it to mean 'resemble' or 'seem'), but cf. Sext. Emp. *Adv. math.* 11.122 ὁ τὸν πλοῦτον μέγιστον ἀγαθὸν ἰνδαλλόμενος, 'the man who imagines wealth to be the greatest good'.   **ὀνειρώττοντες**: dream-experience was generally held to be a major source of our knowledge of god: Sext. Emp. *Adv. math.* 9.45 ἡ ... ἀρχὴ τῆς νοήσεως τοῦ εἶναι θεὸν γέγονεν ἀπὸ τῶν κατὰ τοὺς ὕπνους ἰνδαλλομένων. Even Epicureans held this: cf. Lucr. 5.1170–1. But it is of course a dim and unsure vision, and D. here contrasts it with the clear revelation given by Phidias' genius.   **ξυνέλεξας** 'gathered together'. This seems weak after ἐνίκησας, and Emperius conjectured ξυνήλλαξας, 'reconciled', perhaps rightly.   **ὡς μηδένα ... ῥαιδίως** 'so that no-one who saw it could easily thereafter form any different opinion'.

54 τὸν Ἴφιτον: the king of Elis who reorganized the Olympic games with the collaboration of the Spartan lawgiver Lycurgus, according to a tradition accepted by Aristotle and discussed by Plutarch (*Lycurgus* 1.2). D. seems to follow Aristotle.   **ἢ μᾶλλον**: the real reason why the early Eleans did not erect a statue was, says D., that they 'feared they would not be able to reproduce the supreme and perfect nature by means of mortal art'.

55–83 Phidias' long reply is carefully composed. (i) He stresses the importance of the issue (§55); (ii) he rebuts the allegation that it was he who established the anthropomorphic concept: it was already old (§§56–7); (iii) 'representations of heavenly bodies allow no ἦθος and διάνοια: only the human form can represent intelligence to our eyes (§§58–9); (iv) contemplation of the heavens does not satisfy our longing to stretch out our hands to a Father (§§60–1); (v) blame Homer, not me, for anthropomorphic images (§§62–3); (vi) Homer has vast resources of language, metaphor, simile, onomatopoeia (§§64–9); whereas (vii) the sculptor is restricted by the nature of his material and his difficulty in keeping the same model in his mind so long (§§70–2); (viii) Homer's god is sometimes gentle, sometimes terrible: mine is our common Father and Protector (§§73–4); (ix) this concept accords with the traditional titles of Zeus (§§75–7); (x) the god of storm and strife, whose nod made Olympus tremble, is beyond my power to delineate, even if I wanted to do so (§§78–9); but do not think this is the fault of my materials, for no better can be handled by man; it is Zeus himself, who made the world of the elements, who is the supreme craftsman' (§§80–3).

Dio makes many points in this: but central to it is the position that Phidias' gentle and clement Zeus is a worthier representation than Homer's. See Introd. p. 15, 18–19.

55 **ἀνὴρ οὐκ ἄγλωττος οὐδὲ ἀγλώττου πόλεως** 'no uneloquent man, nor from an uneloquent city'. Note the polyptoton.   **συνήθης καὶ ἑταῖρος Περικλέους**: cf. Plu. *Pericles* 31. Pericles' fame as an orator, though he left no written work, was very great: cf. Plu. *Pericles* 8, with Stadter (1989) 101ff.   **ὁ μὲν ἀγὼν τῶν πώποτε μέγιστος** 'this is the greatest case there has ever been'.   **ὁμοιότητος** 'likeness' – cf. Plu. *Alex.* 1 οἱ ζωιγράφοι τὰς ὁμοιότητας ἀπὸ τοῦ προσώπου ... ἀναλαμβάνουσιν.

56 **τῆς ἀληθείας**: Phidias pre-empts the question by calling the doctrine he expounds 'the truth'.   **ἔτι** goes with what follows: in the beginning, Greece *still* had as yet no clear opinions.   **σαφῆ καὶ ἀραρότα δόγματα** 'clear, fixed opinions'. Cf. 3.79 ἀσφαλῶς καὶ ἀραρότως.   **πεπεισμένης καὶ νομιζούσης ἰσχυρῶς** 'being convinced and firmly holding' its beliefs about the gods.   **σύμφωνα ἦσαν**: note plural verb with neuter subject. Cf. 12.1n.   **κατὰ τὴν ἀκρίβειαν τῆς ποιήσεως** 'in the exactness of the execution'.

57 **παλαιὰς ἀκινήτους**: ἀκινήτους is predicative, παλαιάς attributive with δόξας. This is clearer if we read ⟨τὰς⟩ παλαιὰς. Alternatively, we may read παλαιὰς ⟨καὶ⟩ ἀκινήτους.   **μόνην ... εἰκασίαν** 'having only this one adequate likeness', i.e. the human form, cf. §59.

58 **ἡλίου καὶ σελήνης**: Clerc (1915) 206 compares Lucian, *De dea Syria* 34: there are no images of Sun and Moon in the goddess's temple at Hierapolis, though each has a throne. This is because 'they are plain and all men see them; and what reason is there for sculpture of things that are visible in the air?'   **ἄτεχνος** 'making no demands on art'. **ἔτι δὲ ... τοῖς Ἕλλησι** 'again, though they are indeed themselves full of moral and intellectual character, they display nothing like that in representations. This is perhaps why the Greeks held this view even in early times' – viz. the view that the gods should be represented anthropomorphically. ὅθεν κ.τ.λ. explains what was said in §56, namely that Phidias had predecessors in anthropomorphism. This has caused difficulties: Capps read οὔπω for οὔτως, 'this is why the Greeks did not yet hold this view in the beginning', i.e. that the sun and the moon were divine. This makes nonsense of καί.

ἦθος καὶ διάνοια, the two sources of action according to Aristotle (e.g. *Poet.* 6.1450a2), are the signs that the gods act as persons: cf. 53.12, on how Homer displays the ἦθος, δύναμις, and διάνοια of Zeus.

59 While intellect cannot be represented in itself (cf. Xen. *Mem.* 3.10.3, where Parrhasius argues that ἦθος has no proportion or colour, and so you cannot draw it), the vehicle which carries it, the human body, is totally familiar to us.   **οὐχ ὑπονοοῦντες ἀλλ' εἰδότες** 'knowing, not merely suspecting'.   **ἀνθρώπινον . . . προσάπτοντες** 'attaching a human body to god, as the container of wisdom and reason'. **ἀγγεῖον** 'vessel', an emotive and somewhat pejorative term: it is the contents, not the 'container', that have value. Cf. Cic. *TD* 1.52 *uas aut aliquod animi receptaculum*; M. Aur. 3.3.6.   **τῶι φανερῶι . . . ἀφανές:** chiasmus.   **συμβόλου δυνάμει χρώμενοι:** cf. §77 ἐν εἴδει συμβόλου; 'using the force of a symbol'. A σύμβολον is a token of recognition, originally half an object which has to be put together with the other half (like a torn postcard); it comes to mean any sign which puts us in mind of something else, in particular a visible object which stands for an idea. See in general Buffière (1956) ch. 3, 'Allégorie et symbolisme'. **ζώιοις:** criticism of animal gods (especially those of the Egyptians) is common in Greek writers: cf. especially Plu. *Isis and Osiris* 71–6, where all kinds of reasons for the worship of animals are advanced and refuted. See Juv. 15, with Mayor's or Courtney's notes.   **ὁ δὲ πλεῖστον . . . ἀγαλμάτων:** Phidias must here be saying that the noblest model is the best for images of the gods: κάλλος must be a quality of the object, not of the artist. Hence the need for Schwartz's δημιουργοῖς ⟨τύπος⟩: 'the pattern that excels in beauty, dignity and grandeur, is the best pattern for artists of statues of the gods'.

60 Phidias next rebuts the view that it is better not to have statues, because our religious belief should derive from contemplation of the heavens. This view may have been held by Zeno, who forbade temple building and perhaps statues: *SVF* 1.246–7, especially the passage of Theodoret, *Therapeutica* 3.75 ἐν τῶι τῆς πολιτείας ἀπαγορεύει βιβλίωι καὶ ναοὺς οἰκοδομεῖν καὶ ἀγάλματα τεκταίνειν· οὐδὲν γὰρ εἶναι τούτων φησὶν θεῶν ἄξιον κατασκεύασμα. D.'s more moderate attitude was perhaps that of Posidonius (fr. 369 Theiler); in any case, the present context demands the rejection of Zeno's radicalism. See des Places (1969) 337–40 for a general discussion, based on Acts 17.24 ὁ θεὸς ὁ ποιήσας τὸν κόσμον ... οὐκ ἐν χειροποιητοῖς ναοῖς κατοικεῖ. For a general discussion of D.'s view, see Clerc (1915) 192–230.   **μακρόθεν ὁρῶν**: contrasted with ἐγγύθεν τιμᾶν just below.   **ὁρμήν**: Wilamowitz' conjecture is supported by Philo, *De spec. leg.* 1.66 (cf. Theiler (1982) 284): the highest temple is the κόσμος, but there is also one made by hands: ἔδει γὰρ ὁρμὰς ἀνθρώπων μὴ ἀνακόψαι φορὰς τὰς εἰς εὐσέβειαν συντελούντων καὶ θυσίαις βουλομένων ἢ ἐπὶ τοῖς συμβαίνουσιν ἀγαθοῖς εὐχαριστεῖν ἢ ἐφ' οἷς ἂν ἁμαρτάνωσι συγγνώμην καὶ παραίτησιν αἰτεῖσθαι, 'it was necessary not to cut short the urges of men who contribute the payments for cult, and want by sacrifices either to give thanks for the good things that happen to them or to beg pardon and forgiveness for their sins'. This is quite like the motivation that D. gives, though less emotional.   **μετὰ πειθοῦς** 'with persuasiveness', i.e. in the hope of persuading gods to help or relent.

61 θεοῖς: sc. ὀρέγουσι χεῖρας. Reiske's conjecture seems right. Translate: 'As infants wrested from father or mother, having a great longing and desire for them, often stretch out their hands to them in their dreams, though they are not there, so do men to gods, justly loving them for their benefits and kinship to us, anxious to be with them and converse with them in any way.' Theiler compares a Neoplatonist discussion of prayer (Porphyry, in Proclus, *In Timaeum* 1.208 Diehl): 'as children wrested (ἀποσπασθέντας) from fathers we are bound to pray for our return to our true fathers, the gods: those who do not think it right to pray and turn to the higher powers (τοὺς κρείττονας) are fatherless and motherless'.   **ὀρέγουσι χεῖρας:** the common gesture of prayer: *Il.* 1.351 etc.   **πολλοὶ τῶν βαρβάρων ...:** this *topos* is worked out elaborately in Max. Tyr. 2 Hobein: Persians worship fire, Libyans mountains (i.e. Mount Atlas), Cappadocians also a mountain, the Celts a tall oak, the Arabs a square stone, and so on. So also in Christian apologetics: Arnobius, *Adv. nat.* 6.11: *ridetis temporibus priscis Persas fluuios coluisse ... informem Arabas lapidem, acinacem Scythiae nationes.*   **δένδρα ἀργά** 'unworked trees': cf. Paus. 3.12.3 ἀντεδίδοσαν ἀργὸν τὸν ἄργυρον καὶ χρυσόν ('unstamped', 'unmarked').   **ἀσήμους λίθους** 'unshapen stones': cf. Opp. *Cyn.* 3.160 (of the bear cub) σάρκα δ' ἄσημον, ἄναρθρον.   **οὐδαμῆι οὐδαμῶς:** cf., e.g., Pl. *Phaedo* 78D.

τὴν μορφήν 'in shape'. Cohoon's correction is right, but his translation ('than is the human form') disregards it.

62 οὐκ ἂν φθάνοιτε ... ἔχοντες: see on 7.29.   χαίτας ...
ἀνθερεῶνα: *Il.* 1.529, 501. This passage perhaps gives colour to Lessing's view (*Laokoon* ch. xxii) that the lesson Phidias claimed to have learned from Homer's description of Zeus's 'nod' was that eyebrows and hair were important; he therefore developed the representation of hair. πρὸς δὲ τούτοις ... μίξεις: the human activities of the Homeric gods include conversation, deliberation, orations, journeys from Ida to heaven and Olympus, sleep, drink, and sex. Again, a common *topos*: cf. Max. Tyr. 4.9 πίνει μὲν καὶ παρ' Ὁμήρωι ὁ Ζεύς, ἀλλὰ καὶ δημηγορεῖ καὶ βουλεύεται. A verb is surely needed, and Capps' ἔνεμε meets the case. καὶ δή γε καὶ 'and especially ...' Denniston (1954) 256.   ὄμματα
... τερπικεραύνωι: *Il.* 2.478.

63 τὸ δέ γε ... συνεξεταζόμενον: some uncertainty in the text; Emperius however seems right in deleting θεοῦ. 'As to my work, not even a madman would compare it to any mortal being, if it is judged by its beauty and grandeur.' As Geel explains, Phidias finds fault with Homer for constructing a picture of Zeus such that one could compare a mortal man with him; Phidias' conception allows no such thing.   ἀφ' οὗ γε
... ἐγώ 'Hence I am prepared to suffer any penalty you choose if I do not prove myself much superior to and wiser than Homer, whom you believe to be godlike in his wisdom.'   εἰ μὴ ... φανῶ: εἰ + subjunctive (not in classical Attic prose: WS §2327) is common in later Greek, but there seems to be no clear case in D. It may be a 'vulgarism' (Radermacher, *NTG* 199); the simplest correction here is to read φανοῦμαι.   σοφώτερος: Wenkebach's conjecture gives more point to the following σοφία, and there seems no sense in attributing σωφροσύνη to Phidias here.   ἕτοιμος ... ἐγώ: ellipse of εἰμι is particularly common with ἕτοιμος. Cf. Adam on Pl. *Rep.* 499D.

64 δαψιλὲς ... αὐτόνομον 'for poetry is a lavish thing, universally resourceful and independent'.   χρῆμα: for the idiom, cf. 7.9.
εὔπορον: similar praises of poets' licence can be found in comparisons between poetry and oratory or history: e.g. Aristides 45.1 εὔδαιμόν γε τὸ τῶν ποιητῶν γένος καὶ πραγμάτων ἀπήλλακται πανταχῆ, Lucian, *Conscr. hist.* 8: see Russell (1990) 201ff. For a general note on the ancient views of 'poetic licence', see Brink on Hor. *AP* 9–10.   τὰ τῆς ψυχῆς

βουλήματα: i.e. whatever the poet wants (so Geel).   κἂν ὁποιονοῦν
. . . ἕκαστα 'and, whatever shape or action or disaster or magnitude it
conceives, it will never be at a loss for a messenger, a voice that plainly
indicates everything'. Cohoon thinks there is a reference to the messen-
gers of tragedy, but this is irrelevant. With σχῆμα and μέγεθος, D. means
us to think of monstrous and giant forms, such as only poets can
conceive.   στρεπτὴ . . . καὶ ἔνθα: Il. 20.248–9. The context (Aeneas
speaks to Achilles, against bandying words) is not relevant here.
αὐτός = ipse, emphatic, because Homer is Phidias' rival.

  65 οὐδὲν γοῦν . . . τἀληθοῦς 'Man has left nothing of what comes
into the range of his senses unexpressed in sound or unlabelled, but
instantly attaches to his thoughts the clear identifying mark of a name,
often giving several sounds for one thing; and when he utters any one
of these he produces an impression not much weaker than that of the
object itself.' D. does not elaborate on the process by which language
was developed, but accepts the view that names were given deliberately
(θέσει rather than φύσει), though not by any one or particularly wise
lawgiver. For a brief general note on ancient theory on this subject, see
Costa (1984) on Lucr. 5.1028–90; more detailed discussion, e.g., in Cole
(1967) 60–9.   σφραγῖδα: a σφραγίς is a means of identification
rather than a secure way of keeping something safe.   πλείους . . .
πράγματος: Geel and others take this to refer to different languages and
dialects; this hardly seems relevant, but D.'s point (however vaguely
made) is to emphasize the πλοῦτος φωνῆς which man possesses.
περὶ λόγον 'in respect of speech', to be taken with ἐξουσία καὶ δύναμις.
τὸ παραστάν 'what is presented to the mind'.

  66 αὐθάδης καὶ ἀνεπίληπτος 'independent and uncensored'.   ὃς
οὐχ ἕνα εἵλετο χαρακτῆρα . . . οἱ βαφεῖς: the first proof of Homer's
exceptional liberty is that he chose to use all the dialects of his time. The
point is often made (cf. Max. Tyr. 3.4, [Plu.] De vita et poesi Homeri 8);
it was supposed that the mixture made Homer universally acceptable,
or that it showed the extent of his travels. The tradition usually
(and rightly) mentions Aeolic elements; hence Reiske's supplement.
ἀνέμιξε: cf. Max. Tyr. loc. cit.: ἀθροίσας ἀναμὶξ τὴν Ἑλλάδα φωνὴν καὶ
ἀνακερασάμενος.   οὐ μόνον . . . διὰ φιλορρηματίαν: a second point,
Homer's archaism; 'not only of his contemporaries, but also of his
predecessors, picking up any obsolete word, like an old coin out of some
unclaimed treasure, through his avarice for words'. [Plu.] De vita et poesi

Homeri 14 has a note on Homer's ξέναι καὶ ἀρχαῖαι λέξεις. The analogy between words and coins is common: see especially Hor. *AP* 59 (with Brink *ad loc.*), Quint. 1.6.8 *utendumque plane sermone ut nummo*. D. takes it further than usual, imagining a 'word miser' discovering an unclaimed hoard. (Geel's suggestion φιλορρηματίαν, adopted by most recent editors, is an *ad hoc* coinage, based on φιλοχρηματίαν, 'love of money': the alternative is to delete διὰ φιλοχρηματίαν, as indeed Geel preferred to do in his own text.)

67 βαρβάρων ὀνόματα: i.e. (a third point) γλῶσσαι, words not in the author's normal language.   **ἡδονὴν ἢ σφοδρότητα** 'charm or vehemence', two contrasting stylistic qualities.   **μεταφέρων:** the fourth peculiarity of Homer's language is his 'far-fetched' metaphors. Cf. Demetrius, Περὶ ἑρμηνείας 78 μεταφοραῖς χρηστέον ... μήτε μὴν πόρρωθεν μετενηνεγμέναις, ἀλλ' αὐτόθεν καὶ ἐκ τοῦ ὁμοίου, οἷον ἔοικεν ἀλλήλοις στρατηγός, κυβερνήτης, ἡνίοχος.   **ὅπως ... καταγοητεύσας** 'so as to charm and fascinate the hearer by astounding him'. For ἔκπληξις, see [Longinus] 15.2 with Russell's note, R. Heinze, *Virgils epische Technik* (Stuttgart 1957), 466 n. 1.   **καὶ οὐδὲ ταῦτα ... παρατρέπων** 'not even leaving these words as they are, but lengthening some, shortening others, or otherwise distorting'. This is a fifth set of devices: D. is thinking of diektasis (ὁρόων = ὁρῶν), shortening (δῶ for δῶμα) and adaptation to metre (ἀθάνατος). These things were often observed by ancient readers of Homer; Aristot. *Poet.* 1458a1ff. gives examples. The same three principles were adduced by Plato (*Crat.* 393D) to explain the development of language.

68 Τελευτῶν 'in the end'. The final resource is the invention of new words. Like metaphor and γλῶσσαι, πεποιημένα are traditionally part of the poets' resources (Aristot. *Poet.* 1457b 33).   **τὰ μὲν ... εὔδηλον** the distinction is between coining words for things hitherto unnamed, and inventing new and more vivid terms to replace or supplement τὰ κύρια (i.e. the current terms). The following examples are all in our sense onomatopoeic, i.e. imitative of natural sounds: cf. Dion. Hal. *CV* 16, who explains how Nature (φύσις) taught us ταύρων τε μυκήματα λέγειν καὶ χρεμετισμοὺς ἵππων καὶ φριμαγμοὺς τράγων πυρός τε βρόμον καὶ πάταγον ἀνέμων καὶ συριγμὸν κάλων. For Stoic concern with such things, see Barwick (1957) chs. 5–6. D. here follows well established tradition.   **καναχάς** 'clang': *Il.* 16.105, 794; 19.365, *Od.* 6.82.   **βόμβους** 'boom': βομβέω is in *Il.* 13.520, 16.118, *Od.* 8.190, 12.204.

([Plu.] *De vita et poesi Homeri* 16 also cites βόμβος, though the noun is not attested in Homer.) **κτύπον** 'crash': e.g. *Il.* 10.535, 15.379. **δοῦπον** 'thud': e.g. *Il.* 4.455, 11.364; *Od.* 5.401. **ἄραβον** 'chatter': *Il.* 10.373. **μορμύροντας** 'roaring': *Il.* 5.590, 18.403, 21.325. **βέλη κλάζοντα:** *Il.* 1.46. **βοῶντα κύματα:** *Il.* 14.394. **χαλεπαίνοντας ἀνέμους:** *Il.* 14.399; *Od.* 5.485. ⟨καὶ⟩ τῶι ὄντι θαύματα 'and truly "marvels"'. It seems desirable to add καί, because D. probably has in mind Aeschines' famous critique of Demosthenes, *Contra Ctesiphontem* 167 ταῦτα δὲ [some strange words] τί ἐστιν, ὦ κίναδος; ῥήματα ἢ θαύματα;

69 φοβερῶν: Reiske's conjecture gives a contrast with ἡδέων, parallel to that between λείων and τραχέων. Homer's skill gives him command of both ranges of effect. **ἤχοις** 'sound effects'. **ἐποποιΐας:** this word normally means 'versification' or 'composition of poems'. If it is right here, it must cover all the resources listed in §§66–9; but it is tempting to propose ὀνοματοποιΐας: this often means what we call 'onomatopoeia', cf. Quint. 1.5.72: *sed minime nobis concessa est* ὀνοματοποιΐα, *quis enim ferat si quid simile illis merito laudatis* λίγξε βίος *et* σίζ' ὀφθαλμός *fingere audeamus?* **τὸ χειρωνακτικόν** 'the tribe of manufacturers and craftsmen'. Phidias uses slightly derogatory terms: cf. [Pl.] *Axiochus* 368в τὰς χειρωνακτικὰς [sc. τέχνας] ... καὶ βαναύσας. So Cohoon's paraphrase, 'dependent on the workman's hand and the artist's creative touch' is misleading. **πορισθῆναί τε οὐ ῥαιδίας** 'and not easy to procure'.

70 καὶ ... τοῦ χρόνου: very difficult. (i) If προσέτι is right (and D. uses the word elsewhere), τὸ ... χρόνου should be *either* something which the poet can represent, parallel to the 'many shapes and various forms', *or* something which the poet can attribute to his figures, parallel to 'movement and rest', 'deeds and words'. On the second (more probable) hypothesis, 'deceit' makes sense, but 'time' is difficult. (ii) If P's πρόσεστιν is right, a fresh start is made: 'time' then refers to the short time the poet needs to accomplish his task, and this is further developed in the following γάρ-sentence, but 'deceit' presents difficulty. The balance of probability seems to favour πρόσετι and Geel's δαπάνης: 'They also, of course, have an advantage in cost and time.' **ἐπιπνοίαι** 'inspiration'. So Selden; and this goes better with ὁρμή. The poet is 'carried away by a single mental inspiration and urge'. **πολύ τι ... ὑπερβλύσαντος** 'draws a great quantity of lines, as it were, from a spring

whose water overflows'. That the poet draws his inspiration from holy
fountains is a familiar idea (Pl. *Ion* 534A, Virgil, *Georg.* 2.174, Propertius
3.3, etc.; J. Cousin, *Etudes sur la poésie latine*, (Paris 1945) 237); here,
the welling spring comes from within, and one is reminded of A. E.
Housman's description in his lecture on *The name and nature of poetry* of
thoughts that 'bubble up . . . from the pit of the stomach'.   ἐπιλιπεῖν
αὐτὸν καὶ διαρρυῆναι 'fails him and dissolves'. We may compare the
stories of Virgil, who composed many verses in the morning, and then
dictated them; and whose ὁρμή could overtake him in the midst of a
recitation (Donatus, *Vita Vergilii* §§22, 34).   πετρώδει . . . ὕληι
'labouring as it does with its stony, solid material'.

71 ἀνάγκη παραμένειν: cf. Cic. *Orator* 8 *ipsius* [sc. *Phidiae*] *in mente
insidebat species pulchritudinis eximia quaedam, quam intuens in eaque defixus ad
illius similitudinem artem et manum derigebat.* Phidias' point in our passage
is to emphasize again the difficulty of his task. Nothing is said – and D.
would not have thought – of the Platonist doctrine that art 'does not
imitate the visible, but goes back to the principles from which nature
comes' and 'adds anything lacking, because it has beauty in it', so that
Phidias 'made Zeus to no standard perceived by the sense, but by
grasping what he would be like if he chose to appear to our eyes'
(Plotinus, *Enn.* 5.8.1). D. does not explain how Phidias proceeded from
reflection on Homer to forming his stable mental image of Zeus. Cf.
Introd. pp. 15–16.   ἀκοῆς πιστότερα ὄμματα: proverbial, cf. Herod.
1.8, Sen. *Epist.* 6.5, Otto (1890) 251. Cf. 7.1, note.   δυσπειστότερα
'harder to convince'.   ἀναπτερῶσαι καὶ παραλογίσασθαι 'arouse
and deceive'.   ῥήματα . . . ἤχοις 'words bewitched by metre and
sound'. Geel and others doubt this text, but it is probably sound.

72 καὶ μὴν . . . μεγέθους 'moreover, the standards of art for us are
binding in respect of quantity and size', i.e. sculptors have to keep to
the scale imposed by their commission and the available material,
whereas poets can invent monstrous beings of any size they choose.
τῆς Ἔριδος: *Il.* 4.443, adversely criticized by [Longinus] 9.5.   ἢ
Ἀθηναίων alludes to his work on the Athena Parthenos at Athens.

73 Σὺ μὲν οὖν . . . δεινάς 'You will agree [sc. with my evaluation
of poets' powers], most wise of poets, Homer, first in time and in the
power of your poetry, for you were the first to display to the Greeks
many beautiful images of all the gods and indeed of the greatest of them,
some peaceful, some dread and frightening.' We should accept ἐπέδειξας

and σχεδὸν γάρ: in any case φήσεις must mean 'you will agree', for it is irrelevant to say that Homer 'will claim to have displayed ...'

74 εἰρηνικὸς ... πρᾶιος: this emphasis is important for D.'s interpretation of the statue, which, for him, gives a juster representation of the gods than Homer.   ἀστασιάστου καὶ ὁμονοούσης: the statue was made in peacetime, before the Peloponnesian War, and the games were always a time of truce. But it is hard to think that D. did not also here have in mind the internal peace and harmony of Greece which Roman rule ensured in his day.   ἐν ἀλύπωι σχήματι 'in an undisturbing attitude'.   σωτῆρα 'Saviour'. There was a famous cult of Zeus Soter and Athena Soteira at Piraeus: but the title was commonly given to Zeus, as to Asclepius and the Dioscuri, in connection with any rescue from danger: Amann (1931) 104, Deubner (1956) 174.

75-6 The long litany of Zeus's titles is repeated in *Or.* 1.39ff., and has parallels in many other texts: e.g. [Aristot.] Περὶ κόσμου 401b, Max. Tyr. 41.4, Aelius Aristides, *Hymn to Zeus* (= *Or.* 43) §30, Themistius, *Or.* 6.79d, and especially Cornutus 9, p. 9, 14 Lang καὶ σωτῆρα καὶ ἕρκειον καὶ πολιέα καὶ πατρῶιον καὶ ὁμόγνιον καὶ ξένιον καὶ κτήσιον καὶ βουλαῖον καὶ τροπαιοῦχον καὶ ἐλευθέριον αὐτὸν προσαγορεύουσιν, ἀπεριλήπτων ὅσων ὀνομασιῶν αὐτοῦ τοιούτων οὐσῶν, ἐπειδὴ διατέτακεν εἰς πᾶσαν δύναμιν καὶ σχέσιν καὶ πάντων αἴτιος καὶ ἐπόπτης ἐστιν. As des Places (1969) 28 observes, such lists exploit the 'many names' of the god whom Cleanthes (*SVF* I 537 = Long and Sedley (1987) II 326) addressed:

κύδιστ' ἀθανάτων, πολυώνυμε ...

Wentzel (1889) held that there was a single source of these lists of ἐπικλήσεις, in which the titles were organized – weather-god, god of places and races, protector, god of war, saviour – but this is very unsure. What is certain is that the accumulation of titles fulfilled a religious need: it is evident in Cleanthes' hymn, and in many later hymns to many gods. A philosopher, or philosophizing sophist like D., uses the device to emphasize his concept of divine power or (like D.'s teacher Musonius, p. 78 Hense) to relate human duties to divine sanctions; in prayer, it is more a precautionary measure, designed to make sure of pleasing the god, and often followed by the saving formula 'or by whatever name thou wouldst be known': cf. Aesch. *Ag.* 160 (with Fraenkel's note), Pl. *Crat.* 400E, and especially Norden (1913) 144. See also Amann (1931) 99ff., who has useful notes on many ἐπικλήσεις.

Here D. first lists titles, then explains them. The explanation contains items not in the text of the list: hence Reiske's proposed supplements. There are similar problems in *Or.* 1.39ff. In *Or.* 1, the context requires emphasis on Zeus as King; here, it is on his fatherly and gentler qualities. No title representing his aspect as a storm- or sky-god is included: cf. §79.

75 Βασιλεύς: Zeus is 'king' of gods and men in Hesiod (*Theog.* 886, 923, *WD* 668), and kings derive their power from him (*Theog.* 96). Many cults are known.   **Πολιεύς** 'City-holder'. Zeus Polieus and Athena Polias were both tutelary deities of Athens. Similar titles are πολιοῦχος, πολιάρχης. Note that D. stresses not the security of a citadel, but 'law' and 'common benefit'. Cf. his doctrine of the heavenly city in *Bor.*   **Φίλιος:** ναὶ τὸν Φίλιον, 'by Friendship's god', is an adjuration found in classical texts (e.g. Pl. *Euthyph.* 6B), but Zeus Philios is less often named: but cf. Pl. *Phaedrus* 234E2 πρὸς Διὸς Φιλίου, Musonius 78 Hense ὁ περὶ φίλους [*sc.* ἄδικος] εἰς τὸν Φίλιον [*sc.* ἁμαρτάνει Δία]. **'Εταιρεῖος:** cf. Hdt. 1.44: Croesus calls on Zeus ἐπίστιόν (= ἐφέστιον) τε καὶ ἑταιρήιον, τὸν αὐτὸν ὀνομάζων θεόν, ... τὸν δὲ ἑταιρήιον ὡς φύλακα συμπέμψας αὐτὸν εὑρήκοι πολεμιώτατον (Adrastus, whom Croesus had sent to the hunt with his son, accidentally killed the young man: so he has betrayed the duties of a ἑταῖρος).   **'Ικέσιος** 'God of Suppliants'. A common title both in literature and in inscriptions (Nilsson (1940) I 392), representing an idea familiar already in Homer: *Od.* 9.270 Ζεὺς δ' ἐπιτιμήτωρ ἱκετάων τε ξείνων τε.   **Ξένιος** 'God of Strangers'. These too are under Zeus's protection. Musonius *loc. cit* ὁ περὶ ξένους ἄδικος εἰς τὸν ξένιον ἁμαρτάνει Δία.   **'Επικάρπιος** 'Fruit-giver'. Cf. Cornutus *loc. cit.* ὑέτιος καὶ ἐπικάρπιος καὶ καταιβάτης καὶ ἀστραπαῖος. This is the only one of these 'weather-god' names that D. makes Phidias select. It is the only one relevant to the picture of a benevolent Zeus.   **'Ομόγνιος** 'Family God'. Cf. especially Musonius *loc. cit.* ὅστις εἰς τὸ ἑαυτοῦ γένος (family) ἄδικος, εἰς τοὺς πατρῴους ἁμαρτάνει θεοὺς καὶ εἰς τὸν ὁμόγνιον Δία, τὸν ἐπόπτην τῶν ἁμαρτημάτων τῶν περὶ τὰ γένη. The title is ancient: Aristoph. *Frogs* 750, Pl. *Laws* 881D.

76 Φύξιος δὲ διὰ τὴν τῶν κακῶν ἀπόφυξιν 'Escaper, because we escape evil through him'. D. gives a general moral interpretation: Zeus Phyxios, who had an altar at Corinth (Paus. 2.21.2), seems rather to be thought of as a protector of refugees, or of the defeated; cf. Lycophron 286ff. (the Greek army at Troy, when the Trojans burn the ships) καλῶν ἐπ' εὐχαῖς πλεῖστα Φύξιον Δία | πορθουμένοισι κῆρας ἀρκέσαι πικράς. In Ap. Rhod. 2.1147 (and cf. 4.119) Phrixus has sacrificed his ram to Zeus Phyxios. The scholiast tells us this was a Thessalian cult 'either because they escaped Deucalion's flood or because Phrixus escaped to him'. All this has little to do with D.'s meaning.   **Κτήσιος** 'Possessor'. In his rôle as a house-god, Zeus represents the possessions of the household: Πάσιος is the corresponding Doric form: Nilsson (1940) 1 378.

77 Ὅτου δὲ . . . τέχνην 'Is not the man in whose power it was to display these things without speech an adequate artist?'   **τὸ αὐστηρόν** 'severity'. A metaphor from taste: αὐστηρός is 'dry' (of wine), 'astringent': its metaphorical use of style is usually favourable (Dion. Hal. *CV* 22, *Isaeus* 20).   **ἐν εἴδει συμβόλου:** see on §59. The anthropomorphism itself demonstrates the kinship between god and man. But von Arnim is right to doubt the text; the phrase spoils the symmetry of the sentence.   **προσομοιοῖ** 'reflects', 'reproduces'.   **ἁπλότης** 'simplicity', 'frankness'. D.'s point is a moral one: the expression suggests a being who is straightforward and generous with those he benefits. **ἀτεχνῶς . . . τἀγαθά** 'he looks exactly like one who offers and bestows blessings'.

78 συνεχῶς . . . ἐπὶ πολέμωι: *Il.* 17.547ff.

> ἠΰτε πορφυρέην Ἶριν θνητοῖσι τανύσσῃ
> Ζεὺς ἐξ οὐρανόθεν, τέρας ἔμμεναι ἢ πολέμοιο
> ἢ καὶ χειμῶνος δυσθαλπέος, ὅς ῥά τε ἔργων
> ἀνθρώπους ἀνέπαυσεν ἐπὶ χθονί . . .

ἢ ὄμβρων ὑπερβολὴν ⟨τεύχοντα⟩: a participle is needed, and τεύχοντα is suggested by *Il.* 10.5–8:

> ὡς δ' ὅτ' ἂν ἀστράπτηι πόσις Ἥρης ἠϋκόμοιο
> τεύχων ἢ πολὺν ὄμβρον ἀθέσφατον ἠὲ χάλαζαν
> ἢ νιφετόν, ὅτε πέρ τε χιὼν ἐπάλυνεν ἀρούρας
> ἠέ ποθι πτολέμοιο μέγα στόμα πευκεδανοῖο.

ἢ τανύοντα κυανῆν ἶριν: *Il.* 17.547 again.   **στρατιώταις ⟨ἢ⟩:** *Il.* 4.75ff.:

> οἷον δ' ἀστέρα ἧκε Κρόνου πάϊς ἀγκυλομήτεω,
> ἢ ναύτηισι τέρας ἠὲ στρατῶι εὐρέϊ λαῶν,
> λαμπρόν· τοῦ δέ τε πολλοὶ ἀπὸ σπινθῆρες ἵενται.

ἔριν ἀργαλέαν: *Il.* 11.3–4:

Ζεὺς δ' Ἔριδα προΐαλλε θοὰς ἐπὶ νῆας Ἀχαιῶν
ἀργαλέην, πολέμοιο τέρας μετὰ χερσὶν ἔχουσαν

⟨ὥστε⟩ ἔρωτα ἐμβάλλειν: the infinitive is certainly needed, ὥστε perhaps not essential: 'sending Eris to implant love of war'. Not only does Homer use infinitives like this with πέμπειν, but it is an occasional Attic prose usage: *GMT* §770.   οὐκ ἦν διὰ τῆς τέχνης μιμεῖσθαι: von Arnim was right to transpose this phrase from after κρινομένας to after ἀπειρηκόσιν. Then οὐδέ γε, following οὐ, becomes intelligible, and the construction of the whole sentence is revealed at an earlier stage. οὐδέ γε ἱστάντα . . . κῆρας: the famous image of the scales, *Il.* 8.69ff. (cf. *Il.* 22.209ff.):

καὶ τότε δὴ χρύσεια πατὴρ ἐτίταινε τάλαντα,
ἐν δὲ τίθει δύο κῆρε τανηλέγεος θανάτοιο,
ἕλκε δὲ μέσσα λαβών · ῥέπε δ' Ἕκτορος αἴσιμον ἦμαρ.

οὐ μὴν οὐδὲ παρὸν ἠθέλησά γ' ἄν ποτε: an important new point. Not only was Phidias' art unable to reproduce these portents, he would not have wished to do so; they have impious implications.

79 βροντῆς . . . γένοιτο; 'For what noiseless image of thunder, what fireless image of lightning flash or bolt could come out of the mines here on earth?' The εἴκασμα would have to represent thunder without making a noise, and lightning without a flash. ἀστραπή and κεραυνός are distinct: if either word is to be deleted, it should perhaps be κεραυνοῦ, which gives an ugly hiatus with εἴκασμα.   τῆιδε 'here on earth': ἐπιγείων explains this, and should probably be deleted as a gloss.   ἔτι δὲ γῆν σειομένην: it is of course Poseidon who shakes the earth; but in the conflict of the gods (*Il.* 20.54ff.) the earthquake follows hard on Zeus's thunder. D. may well be thinking of this passage, which was a stumbling-block to the pious (cf. [Longinus] 9.6).   καὶ κινούμενον Ὄλυμπον ὑπὸ νεύματι βραχεῖ: *Il.* 1.528. Phidias here in effect denies what D., speaking in his own person, said was alleged of him (§26).   ἢ τινα νέφους περὶ τῆι κεφαλῆι στέφανον: *Il.* 15.153: ἀμφὶ δε μιν θυόεν νέφος ἐστεφάνωτο.   ἐγγύθεν . . . ὄψεως 'because it has the test of sight close at hand and plain'.

80 ἀσημότερον 'too undistinguished'.   τὸν ἑλόμενον καὶ δοκιμάσαντα 'the person who chose and approved' the material, i.e. the sculptor himself.   **φύσις** 'substance'.

81 τὴν ἄφθονον πηγὴν ὕδατος 'water's generous fount' sounds a poetical phrase.   **[ἔν τισι θνητοῖς ὀργάνοις]:** Emperius did well to delete this. Emendation is tempting – e.g. ἔντεσι θνητοῖς [ὀργάνοις], 'by mortal gear' (glossed 'tools') – but the logic of the sentence is against this: Phidias seems to enumerate the elements – air, fire, water, earth – and argues that only the creator god is able to construct a universe out of these. (This brief reference to creation by combining elements should be compared with 36.39ff.)   **ὅσον ... ἕρμα** 'and whatever solid support there is in all these things' – i.e. in the world we see. The phrase is perhaps from Eur. *Hel.* 854 κακοὺς ἐφ' ἕρμα στερεὸν ἐκβάλλουσα γῆς. The word ἕρμα has many meanings: 'support', 'reef', 'ballast'; it is hard to see exactly which is dominant here, but there is no need to question Morel's emendation. D. does, it seems, mean 'earth', as the fourth element, and also describes it by τὴν ... οὐσίαν below. But he is not very clear: M. B. Trapp suggests that the meaning is 'all the solid, recalcitrant substance in any of the elements': and βαρεῖα ... οὐσία would, in Stoic terms, describe water as well as earth.   **εἰς [ταὐτὸ] γένεσιν ζῴων καὶ φυτῶν** 'to create living animals and plants'. Text unsure: note Capps's ingenious rewriting: 'to separate each kind and weave them together and so compose every species of animal and plant, is something that not even all gods could do ...'   **ἕτερος:** Pindar, fr. 57 Snell: 'Mighty Father of Dodona, best of craftsmen'. This passage (probably from a Paean) was naturally popular with writers who looked in the poets for confirmation of the idea that Zeus was the great 'demiurge' who made the world: Plutarch cites it five times.

82 Πολύκλειτον: he also worked at Olympia.   **καὶ ταῦτα:** i.e. 'the gold and stone which human sculptors use is capable of being worked by divine craftsmen, as Homer shows'.

83 εὐπόρησεν 'had at hand', cf. §29.   **οὐκ ἐφίκετο εὑρεῖν** 'did not succeed in inventing'.   **χαλκὸν δ' ... ἄργυρον:** *Il.* 18.474–5.

84–5 A puzzling conclusion: (i) ταῦτ' οὖν ... στεφανῶσαι ἄν – a sufficient conclusion in itself; (ii) ἴσως δὲ ... πολὺ ἄμεινον, a recapitulation of the main lessons of the earlier part of the speech and of §§75–7 of Phidias' reply; (iii) τῷ γὰρ ὄντι ... ἀεικέα ἔσσαι, a moving prosopopoeia of the god, who is imagined as congratulating Greece on the lavishness of the cult and the games, but commenting sorrowfully on her old age and poverty. Section (ii) was bracketed by von Arnim, and can hardly be part of D.'s speech as delivered. If it is removed, there must be something lost before Section (iii), since τῶι ὄντι is not explained, and it is not absolutely clear what τοιοῦτος means, or that it refers to Zeus – though no doubt a gesture in the direction of the statue would suffice for this.   **στεφανῶσαι ἄν:** i.e., so far from punishing him, they would give him an honour.   **εἰ δὲ μετ' εὐφημίας . . . ἄμεινον:** obscure. 'If it has all been said to the honour of the statue and those who have had it set up, so much the better.'   **†Ἠλεῖοι δὲ καὶ† ἡ σύμπασα Ἑλλάς:** corrupt. Von Arnim and Cohoon, in their reconstructions, assume that the statue is made to address the Greeks, and read ἐπιτελεῖς, διαφυλάττεις and σ' for γ' in the quotation from Homer (who does indeed have σ', *Od.* 24.249). This is not convincing. Perhaps Ἠλείοις should be considered: the whole of Greece does this for the Eleans, who run the festival.   **⟨ὡς⟩ ἀπ' ἀρχῆς** 'as in the beginning'.   **αὐτήν γ' οὐκ ἀγαθὴ κομιδὴ ἔχει:** old Laertes symbolizes Greece, old and ill-kept. Cf. 7.34, 121; 36.6; 31.158. An oddly pessimistic note on which to end a speech of celebration.

36 Borystheniticus

1 'On a visit to Borysthenes, I was walking in the morning by the Hypanis, outside the city.'   **Ἐτύγχανον μέν:** for this beginning, see on 7.2.   **ὡς τότε εἰσέπλευσα** 'as I had arrived there at that season'. **[μετὰ τὴν φυγήν]:** this must mean 'after (the end of) my exile', cf. 40.12 μετὰ φυγὴν οὕτως μακράν, rather than 'after I went into exile' (as Desideri takes it). It seems likely that we have here a phrase which really belongs to the title: Synesius (*Dio* ch. 2, 38B–39A) says that πρὸ τῆς φυγῆς and μετὰ τὴν φυγήν were added to some speeches in his text, and ought to be added generally (Introd. p. 5).   **εἰς Γέτας:** in 12.16 (q.v.) D. represents himself as just returned from the Getae, who are in a state of war, defending themselves against Rome. This seems likeliest to refer to one of Trajan's Dacian Wars, probably the first, in 101. But Philostratus (*VS* 1.7) says that he visited the Getae ὅτ' ἠλᾶτο, i.e. during his exile, which ended in 96. The visit which is the background of this speech seems to be during the exile, to judge from the *post eventum* prophecy of safe return in §27. There is no reason why D. should not have travelled in these parts more than once, returning later to obtain

more information for his *Getica* (*FGrHist* 707).   **περὶ πλήθουσαν
ἀγοράν:** i.e. in the middle of the morning. A standard classical expression (Hdt. 4.181, Xen. *Anab.* 1.8.1; cf. Dio, *Or.* 67.4), chosen for preference over the use of numbered hours, which was normal contemporary
usage, but disapproved of by classicizing writers (I. Düring, *Chion of
Heraclea* (Gothenburg 1951; Arno Press, New York, 1979), on *Epist.*
13.1; Athen. 1 1E).   **παρὰ τὸν Ὕπανιν:** the setting, outside the city,
faintly recalls Pl. *Phaedrus* 227A (M. B. Trapp, in Russell (1990) 150).
ἡ γὰρ πόλις . . . ἐν τῶι κατ' ἀντικρύ: Olbia lay on the right bank
of the Hypanis (Bug), near to its junction with the estuary of the
Borysthenes (Dnieper). It was not the earliest Greek settlement in the
area, for that was Berezan (= Borysthenes), an island (though in early
times joined to the mainland) commanding the entrance to the estuary.
Milesians were established here from the middle of the seventh century
B.C., and the site of Olbia was established not much later. Olbia
displaced Berezan as a trading centre (corn, fish, slaves) and a point of
contact with the Scythian tribes. It declined in the late fourth century
B.C., but revived in Hellenistic times, until evil days set in *c.* 150 B.C.
There followed a period of Scythian domination (coins bear the name
of a Scythian king), a brief subjection to Mithridates, and (worst of all)
destruction by the Getae, under their aggressive ruler Burebistas, about
150 years before D.'s visit (see §4). In D.'s time, the city and the
surrounding settlements were clearly under threat, while Berezan had
recovered some importance as the centre of the cult of Achilles Pontarches, apparently displacing Achilles' other island, Leuke, off the
Danube delta (Wasowicz (1975) 124); cf. §9. Not long after D.'s time,
a Roman garrison was installed. By the end of the second century, Olbia
was part of Moesia Inferior.

   D.'s description is in traditional style: cf. especially Hdt. 4.53 ἀγχοῦ
τε δὴ θαλάσσης ὁ Βορυσθένης ῥέων γίνεται καί οἱ συμμίσγεται ὁ Ὕπανις
ἐς τὠυτὸ ἕλος ἐκδιδούς. τὸ δὲ μεταξὺ τῶν ποταμῶν τούτων ἐὸν ἔμβολον
τῆς χώρης Ἱππόλεω ἄκρη καλέεται, ἐν δὲ αὐτῶι ἱερὸν Δήμητρος ἐνίδ-
ρυται · πέρην δὲ τοῦ ἱροῦ ἐπὶ τῶι Ὑπάνι Βορυσθενεῖται κατοίκηνται.
So D. takes 'the Point of Hippolaus' and the 'beak' of land (ἔμβολον)
from Herodotus. The 'Point' is the headland between the two rivers,
near Stanislav. The metaphor in ἔμβολον is from the beak or ram of a
ship.

2–6 Description of the estuary, history of the town (§§4–5), and its present condition.

2 ταῖς εὐδίαις 'in fine weather', cf. Pl. *Laws* 961F.   **σταθερά** 'settled': LSJ s.v. 3. But there is something to be said for Reiske's **σταθερᾶι**, 'stagnant', LSJ s.v. 1.   **ἐν δὲ τοῖς δεξίοις . . . τὸ βάθος** 'to the right, it is seen to be a river, and sailors coming in judge the depth by the current.'   **ὅθενπερ καὶ ἐξίησι** 'And it is on this side that it makes its outfall.'   **ἂν ἐφράττετο:** ἂν is needed, and the simple verb φράττειν, 'block', suffices (Hdt. 2.99, Thuc. 4.13).

3 ὑλώδης 'woody', the vegetation being trees and reeds. Emperius conjectured ἑλώδης (cf. ἕλος in Hdt. *loc. cit.*), thinking that ὑλώδης was redundant, δασεία . . . δένδροις conveying the same sense.   **ὡς ἱστοῖς προσεοικέναι** 'so as to look like masts'. D.'s observation shows that the sea was encroaching on the land, as it has done ever since. Olbia had been founded at a more favourable moment, when the sea had retreated (Wasowicz (1975) 43).   **καὶ ἤδη . . . ἐπέχοντες** 'inexperienced navigators have been known to go wrong, imagining they were steering towards ships', Hdt. 9.59 has ἐπέχω in a related sense: ἐπεῖχέ ('he bore down upon') τε ἐπὶ Λακεδαιμονίους τε καὶ Τεγεήτας.   **τῶν ἁλῶν:** Hdt. 4.53 also mentions the salt-pans. They were not very near the city, but probably around the outfall of the Dnieper–Bug liman.   **τῶν Ἑλλήνων . . . τὴν Ταυρικήν:** the Crimean region, an important centre of Greek influence and the source of corn for classical Athens, was by this time effectively under Roman control, and had been so since the defeat of Mithridates. D., so far as we know, never visited it, but its economic and political importance was a familiar fact.   **παρὰ φρούριον Ἀλέκτορος:** unknown, presumably the headland on the northern side of the outlet. Alector is a not uncommon name in myth (a king of Argos, Apollod. 3.6.2; a king of Elis, Diod. 4.69; the father of Iphiloche, *Od.* 4.10 with scholia). The Sauromatae or Sarmatians were the Iranian people who moved into southern Russia in the second century B.C., and later into the Danube plain; they included the Iazyges and Roxolani, frequent and ferocious enemies of the Romans.

4 ἑάλωκεν·⟨ἑάλω δὲ⟩: this supplement assumes a haplography. For the internal accusative, see G §1051.   **πεντήκοντα καὶ ἑκατὸν ἐτῶν:** this fits the date of Burebistas' aggressions. Cf. n. on §1.   **μέχρι Ἀπολλωνίας:** Apollonia Pontica (Sozopol) was a Milesian colony, prosperous in classical times, but sacked by Lucullus after the Mithridatic war. See Ch. Danoff, *RE* Suppl. IX 1069.

5 καὶ . . . συρρυέντων 'and most of them with a large influx of barbarians', sc. οἰκισθεισῶν. But this is a little awkward: it is tempting to delete καὶ τῶν, and translate 'large numbers of barbarians having flowed into them'. **πολλαὶ . . . διεσπαρμένης:** a general statement applying to the whole Greek world ('Ελλάς), illustrated by the fate of the Pontic cities; Olbia itself, by its recovery, is something of an exception. **ἐθελόντων . . . τῶν Σκυθῶν:** D.'s conjecture that the Scyths collaborated in the revival after Burebistas seems very credible. There is evidence for fresh Greek settlements around Olbia after the crisis period, and this implies native help.

6 μέρει γάρ τινι . . . ἀσθενές: text and sense uncertain, but I retain the MSS reading, and translate: 'For it is built up against a certain stretch of the perimeter wall, where a few towers remain, quite out of scale with the size and strength of the city, while the gap is filled by the houses, which have no intervals between them thereabouts, and a low, weak wall has been added.' Casaubon's reading (see app. crit.) – i.e. 'the houses are continuous where there is a gap' in the wall – is clearer, and may well be right. D.'s description broadly corresponds with what is known from excavations, but the details are naturally hard to confirm, and allowance has to be made for some conventional elements (see on 7.34 for the *topos* of the city in decline). For a somewhat different view, see Wasowicz (1975) 119; he takes τὸ μεταξύ to mean 'la superficie de la ville actuelle', but it is more natural to take it as the space between the surviving towers in the built-up area. T's περιβέβληται, 'has been put round the city', may well be right. **ὅτι μιᾶς ἦσαν πόλεως** 'that they once belonged to one city'. **ὑγιές** 'undamaged', cf. Lysias 6.12 ἤ μὴν τὸν 'Ερμῆν ὑγιᾶ τε καὶ ὅλον εἶναι.

7–17 'I was approached by some friends, including the young beauty Callistratus, a devotee of philosophy who had already distinguished himself in war. Knowing he was a lover of Homer, I teased him by asking him whether he thought Homer or Phocylides the better poet. He had never heard of Phocylides; so I explained, and quoted him verses about "the little city on a rock well-governed" being better than Nineveh. Those present resented my depreciation of Homer; but, despite an alert for a Sarmatian raid, they were anxious to hear me on Phocylides. In view of the danger, we moved to the forecourt of the

temple of Zeus. They were all well-bearded, except for one, who followed Roman fashion, and was disliked accordingly.'

7 Ὅπερ οὖν ἔφην: in §1. D. returns from his historical and geographical description, which has set the scene in this remote, threatened,
half-ruined outpost of Hellas.   **πρὸς ἐμέ** 'to meet me'. Cf. Xen. *Anab.*
7.6.6 αὔριον ὑμᾶς πρῷ ἄξομεν πρὸς αὐτούς, 'we will take you to meet
them early tomorrow'.   **Καλλίστρατος:** the name is given without
explanation. A description follows (§8). It is a common name: an Olbian
example (*Inscriptiones Olbiae* (Leningrad 1968) 83.7) is the father of a
Ναύτιμος who is one of a college of στρατηγοί offering thanks to Apollo
Prostates. We should assume he is a real character.   **πάνυ κοσμίως**
... ὑποστείλας: traditional good manners. So orators were not supposed to let their hands wander outside their clothes: Aeschin. *In
Timarchum* 52, Quint. 12.10.21 (with Austin's note). Plutarch reports
that Phocion (*Phocion* 4), a model of propriety, never laughed or cried
or showed his hands outside his clothes. Callistratus was armed; perhaps
his restraint was to show that he came in peace.   **μάχαιραν ... τῶν**
ἱππικῶν: if D. is choosing his words carefully (and this phrase looks
precise), this is a long, curved sword, for close combat: cf. Xen. *Eq.*
12.11 μάχαιραν ... μᾶλλον ἢ ξίφος ἐπαινοῦμεν· ἐφ' ὑψηλοῦ γὰρ ὄντι
τῶι ἱππεῖ κοπίδος μᾶλλον ἡ πληγὴ ἢ ξίφους ἀρκέσει.   **ἀναξυρίδας**
'trousers', a word of foreign origin denoting the garment thought by
the Greeks particularly characteristic of eastern people, especially Persians and nomads like the Scythians: first found in Herodotus (e.g.
1.71) and Hippocrates (*Airs, waters, places* 22), who rightly associates
this dress with horse-riding, but goes on to regard it as a cause of
impotence.   **χρῶνται ... μελαίνηι** 'the rest of their clothing is
also black'. The 'Melanchlainoi', 'Black-cloaks', were known from
Herodotus (4.20, 100–2, 107, 119, 125), who believed them not to
be Scythian but to practise Scythian customs.

8 πολὺ ἔχων Ἰωνικὸν τοῦ εἴδους 'with many Ionic features in his
appearance'. The implication is partly that he is of old Milesian colonial
stock, partly that he is somewhat effeminate in appearance: cf. perhaps
Aristoph. *Thesmo.* 160ff., where Ibycus, Anacreon, and Alcaeus
ἐμιτροφόρουν τε καὶ διεκλῶντ' Ἰωνικῶς, and this life-style determined
the style of their poetry.   **ὥστε καὶ ἐκπλεῦσαι σὺν ἐμοὶ ἐπεθύμει:**
D. represents himself as a philosopher ready to acquire a disciple who
would accompany him on his travels.   **ἐμμεμένηκεν αὐτοῖς** 'has

persisted among them', cf. 38.5 ἡ στάσις . . . ἐμμεμένηκεν ὑμῖν. Note that homosexuality is here regarded as an inheritance from Miletus, though Ionia was not a primary area of homosexual society in early times (Dover (1978) 81, 194). Homosexual references in the poets (Ibycus and Anacreon) are presumably the basis for this version of history. D.'s attitude to homosexuality is uniformly hostile (see 7.149, 151), so that his portrait of Callistratus is not of an ideal young man, but of one who seems (mutatis mutandis) to be like a typical character in a Platonic dialogue. βαρβαρικῶς καὶ οὐκ ἄνευ ὕβρεως: when βάρβαροι learn these practices, they naturally implement them βαρβαρικῶς; D. explains that this involves ὕβρις, i.e. the kind of violent behaviour that shows total disregard for the other person, here presumably homosexual acts committed on an unwilling partner. See in general Dover (1978) 34ff.

9 Εἰδώς . . . ἐπυνθανόμην 'Knowing him to be a lover of Homer, I began by questioning him about this.' διὰ τὸ πολεμικοὶ εἶναι ἔτι νῦν: Homer is the poet of warriors: cf. 12.74. πολεμικοί is nom. because, although the articular infinitive is in the accusative after διά, the infinitive expresses a state of the subject of the main verb: WS §1973a. ἄρα: 'denotes that the hypothesis is one of which the possibility has only just been realized' (Denniston (1954) 37). τὴν πρὸς τὸν Ἀχιλλέα . . . ἐν τῆι πόλει: the cult of Achilles, both as a hero and as a god, was widespread in the Black Sea region (Pfister (1909) 15, n. 33; G. Hirst, J.H.S. 23 (1909) 45ff.; Roscher I 58–9) and various places were specially associated with him. Both Olbia and Berezan were seats of a cult of Achilles Pontarches, and it is probably Berezan that is meant here by 'the island of Achilles', not the more famous but more distant Leuke which lies off the mouth of the Danube (J. N. Treščeva, Das Altertum 32 (1986) 186–9, is wrong about this). Another holy site was the Dromos (Race-course) of Achilles (Hdt. 4.55), which is a long tongue of land now called Tendra, quite near the Borysthenes area; but this cannot be meant here. οὐκέτι σαφῶς ἑλληνίζοντες 'no longer possessing an accurate knowledge of Greek'. Cf. Or. 15.15: Callias' groom (a slave) was captured at Acanthus, enslaved by the Thracians, and subsequently returned to Athens to contest Callias' inheritance, pretending to be his son, who had in fact been killed in the battle. The evidence he offered for his impersonation was that ἡλλήνιζεν ἀκριβῶς καὶ γράμματα ἠπίστατο. τὴν Ἰλιάδα . . . ἀπὸ στόματος: not too uncommon an accomplishment in classical times, to judge from Xen. *Symp.* 3.5–6, where Niceratus explains that he was made by his father to learn both *Il.* and *Od.* by heart, in order to become καλὸς κἀγαθός; he now listens to rhapsodes every day. The dominance of Homer in Hellenistic and later literary education made memorization common and much admired: cities organized official competitions, in which one pupil took up the text where another left off, and so on. It is the Borysthenites' excessive attention to Homer which D. is to criticize.

10 προσπαίζων 'teasing'.   **Φωκυλίδης:** the type of the 'gnomic poet' (West, *J.H.S.* 98 (1978) 161–7), traditionally dated mid-sixth century, but perhaps earlier, if the capture of Nineveh (612) is a contemporary event. Cf. *Or.* 2.5, where Alexander is made to contrast Homer, the poet for kings, with Phocylides and Theognis, who wrote δημοτικά, suitable advice for τοῖς πολλοῖς καὶ ἰδιώταις.   **οἶμαι δὲ . . . μηδένα:** for the use of μή-negatives with infinitives of *oratio obliqua*, see on 7.28.   **μόνου . . . ἐλέγετο:** text and interpretation unsure. (i) αὐτῶν (better than αὑτῶν) probably depends on μόνου: 'the only one of themselves whom poets mention in their poems is Homer'. Alternatively (with αὑτῶν), 'the poets among them', i.e. the Borysthenites: but this seems very implausible. (ii) We should accept Emperius' correction, and translate: 'and they are in the habit of mentioning him on various occasions, but invariably when they are giving encouragement to their people when they are going into battle'. (iii) The added words 'as Tyrtaeus' poems were delivered in Sparta' are, as Emperius says, *aliena a persona loquentis*, since Callistratus is not supposed to know other poets besides Homer. For the regular association of Tyrtaeus with Homer, cf. Hor. *AP* 401–3 *Homerus | Tyrtaeusque mares animos in Martia bella | uersibus exacuit*; Quint. 10.1.56. But Cobet may be right to expunge even more.   **εἰσὶ δὲ πάντες οὗτοι τυφλοί** 'all these [i.e. all poets] are blind'. In *Il.* 2.594, Thamyris is blind; in *Od.* 8.64, so is Demodocus; in the Homeric *Hymn to Apollo* (172), the author himself is blind. So was Tiresias. The tradition was marvellously exploited by the blind Milton, *PL* 3.32–6. Cf. in general C. M. Bowra, *Heroic poetry* (1952) 420–2.

11 [οἱ ποιηταὶ αὐτῶν]: probably wrongly repeated from the previous section.   **πάνυ δὲ τῶν ἐνδόξων γέγονε ποιητῶν** 'he is one of the very famous poets'. For the word-order, cf. Hyper. *Pro Euxen.* 3 νυνὶ δὲ τὸ γιγνόμενον ἐν τῆι πόλει, 'what is now happening in the city': Wifstrand (1930) 1 16.   **καταπλεύσηι** 'sails in', 'arrives'.   **οὐ**

πρότερον ⟨παρα⟩γεγονώς 'who has never been here before'. The supplement is necessary, since D. regularly uses γεγονώς only, of 'being born' or the like.   ἠτιμάσατε 'gnomic' aorist, here parallel to the presents ὠνεῖσθε, ἐᾶτε: *GMT* §§154ff. Aorist and present together, e.g., in Pl. *Rep.* 566E, Demosth. *Or.* 21.72: see WS §1931.   τοῦ οἴνου: a typical, important import, whether from Aegean Greece (Rhodes, Chios, Samos) or from the Crimea.   δεῖγμα 'a sample'.

12 τῶν ... εἰρόντων 'one of those who string together a long, continuous poem'. εἴρειν in this sense seems to be post-classical: cf., e.g., Jos. *BJ* 6.5.3 εἴρειν θρῆνον. As often, ποίησις here (and just below, where it has ἀρχή and πέρας) means a whole poem, a 'literary unity' (Brink (1963) 63); just above (τῆς τοῦ Φωκυλίδου ποιήσεως), it means 'poetic art' or the like. D. does not use such terms with technical exactness, but συνεχῆ ποίησιν (= *carmen perpetuum,* cf. Hor. *Odes* 1.7.6) is noticeable: cf. Varro, *Men.* 398 *poesis est perpetuum argumentum ... ut Ilias Homeri.* See now Heath (1989) 67–8.   μίαν ... ἔπεσιν: books 11–17 of the *Iliad* are devoted to a single battle, and total 5,052 lines.   δύο καὶ τρία 'two or three': cf. Denniston (1954) 292 for this use of καί 'in numerical approximations, where the two alternative estimates are given'. In fact, Phocylides' *gnomai* are normally two hexameters, though one elegiac couplet is known (spurious; West (1972) 93).   ἀρχὴν ... καὶ πέρας: that which has a beginning and an end is a unity, and complete. προστίθησι τὸ ὄνομα αὐτοῦ: in the phrase καὶ τόδε Φωκυλίδου, which modern scholars (not the ancient authors) call a σφραγίς, 'seal', 'identification mark': M. L. West, *J.H.S.* 98 (1978) 164 n. 4.   οὐχ ὥσπερ Ὅμηρος ... αὐτόν: cf. *Or.* 53.9, where D. praises Homer's ἀνδρεία and μεγαλοφροσύνη on two grounds: (i) that he had lived a hard, wandering life; (ii) that he never mentioned himself, but was content, like oracles, to speak ἐξ ἀφανοῦς καὶ ἀδύτου ποθέν.

13 ἀποφάσει 'statement' (= ἀπόφανσις, from ἀποφαίνω). The passage is fr. 2 Bergk.   πόλις ... ἀφραινούσης 'a little city on a rock, well-governed, is better than Nineveh in its folly'. Notice the association between mountains and virtue, between the city of the plains and vice: Nineveh, which fell before the attack of Medes and Babylonians in 612, was proverbial for luxury and effeminacy (see especially the story of Sardanapalus, first in Hdt. 2.150).   πρός 'equivalent to', 'as good as': LSJ s.v. II 4.   τοῖς μὴ παρέργως ἀκροωμένοις 'to readers who gave it their full attention'. Cf. 1.10, 18.6, 60.5.   πηδήσεών τε καὶ

ὀρούσεων 'leaps and rushes'. These nouns are rare, but ὄρουσις has a technical use in Stoic psychology: Stob. 2.7.9. (=2.87 Wachsmuth) ὄρουσιν φοράν διανοίας ἐπὶ τὸ μέλλον. So Philo (*De mutatione nominum* 160) uses it of the preliminary ὁρμή of a bull in the arena. For the conjunction of the two words, cf. Aesch. *Ag.* 826 (of the Trojan Horse that 'leaps the wall') πήδημ' ὀρούσας.   τῆς φωνῆς: a satirical reference to Achilles' shouting over the ditch, *Il.* 18.228–9 τρὶς μὲν ὑπὲρ τάφρου μεγάλ' ἴαχε δῖος Ἀχιλλεύς, | τρὶς δὲ κυκήθησαν Τρῶες.

14 οὐ μάλα ἡδέως 'badly'.   **ὅτι . . . αἰδούμεθα:** there seems to be an ellipse; he means 'I listen to you because we love you and respect you very much.' Dr Innes suggests ⟨οἶσθ'⟩ὅτι, which gives good sense. **ὡς ὁρᾳς:** there was a temple in the city, then, as well as on the island. **μετὰ τοὺς θεούς** 'second only to the gods'. Cf. 7.58.   **εἴ τι . . . εἴρηται:** *Il.* 4.362–3.   **ἐπαινεσόμεθα . . . λέγειν:** as a philosopher (cf. Pl. *Symp.* 198D), D. will only praise where praise is due. He is willing to criticize Homer – indeed, he has to, in view of his own moral and philosophical attitudes, cf. Phidias' speech in *Ol.* – and Kindstrand (1973) 31–9 seems to underestimate this in his general view of D.'s reception of Homer.

15 καίτοι . . . ἔχοντας 'though they are by no means without cause for alarm'. Cf. 7.84. οὐ with a negative adj. or adv. with α-privative (cf. οὐκ ἀηδῶς 7.1, οὐκ ἀγεννές 7.67) is a common form of litotes: the speaker here means that they are actually very much alarmed. οὐκ ἀθορύβως is similarly found in Plato (*Laws* 640c). The addition of πάνυ also contributes to the litotes: LSJ s.v. πάνυ 3.   **μεσημβρίας:** it is summer (§1), and the midday siesta presumably gives the enemy their chance. **ἅτε . . . φεύγουσιν** 'since they do not escape towards the city', 'since the city isn't on their escape route'. 'Seemingly a touch of humour', as Crosby says.

16 τὸ σημεῖον ἦρτο: cf. Thuc. 1.49.1, or 1.63.2 τὰ σημεῖα ἤρθη. Presumably some kind of flag is hoisted, or a shield is flashed in the sun. Arrian (*Tactica* 27) and Asclepiodotus (*Tactica* 10) speak vaguely of σημεῖα ὁρατά, to be given when noise or high wind interferes with trumpets or shouted commands. This is clearly a regular alarm signal (τὸ σημεῖον . . . τὸ πολεμικόν).   **ἀγάμενος . . . προθυμίαν** 'admiring their zeal'. Cf. 44.6 ἀγάμενος τῶν ἀνδρῶν τό τε ἄφθονον καὶ τὴν προθυμίαν.   **Βούλεσθε . . . καθιζώμεθα:** cf. G §1358.   **τυχὸν γὰρ . . . προσελθεῖν** 'Maybe, as we are now, they don't all hear equally

well, as we walk around, but those behind have trouble, and cause
trouble to those in front of them, because they are anxious to get nearer.'
The scene recalls Pl. *Protag.* 315B, where a discussion goes on during a
walk, and Protagoras' listeners are drilled to turn round in a disciplined
fashion whenever he turns. The Borysthenites are not up to this.
πράγματα ἔχουσι καὶ παρέχουσι: a classic instance of this play on
words is Epicurus, *Kuriai doxai* 1: the Epicurean god οὔτε πράγματα
ἔχει οὔτε ἄλλωι παρέχει.

17 τὸ τοῦ Διὸς ἱερόν: Wasowicz (1975) 97 n. 44 points out that the
Hellenistic agora had been destroyed, so that this area, where a temple
serves also as a council-chamber, is distinct from it. No trace of D.'s
'temple of Zeus' seems to have been found.   **γνωριμώτατοι** 'nota-
bles'. γνώριμος in D. seems normally to mean 'famous' or 'an acquaintance', but here it has a clearly social sense (cf. 34.1), in accordance
with a common classical usage (Xen. *Hell.* 2.2.6, Aristot. *Pol.* 1291b18,
etc.).   **τὸ δὲ λοιπὸν πλῆθος ἐφεστήκεσαν:** for the *constructio ad sensum*
see on 7.30.   **φιλόσοφος ἀνήρ:** cf. 12.8 τοξευτὴν τινα ἄνδρα. This is
a classical idiom (first in Homer, *Il.* 11.514 ἰητρὸς ... ἀνήρ) and
common in all kinds of prose.   **κομῶντες:** Homer's Achaeans are
κάρη κομόωντες (*Il.* 3.43). For D.'s approval of beards and long hair,
see 7.4, 12.15.   **ἐξυρημένος:** first-century Romans generally shaved
(though they often kept a close-clipped beard till about 40: Courtney
on Juv. 4.130) but Hadrian popularized the growing fashion for full
beards. The apparent anti-Roman tone of this passage is remarkable,
and is taken by some (Palm (1959) 18) as indicative of D.'s feelings: cf.
12.20, for his assessment of the Dacians' fight for liberty. But his general
attitude is clearly favourable to the empire: he had Roman citizenship
from his grandfather (41.6), he was proud of his reputation at Rome
(44.1) and of his friendship with Nerva and Trajan (47.22, *Or.* 1–4).
He can even say (38.38) that the Romans are often right to criticize or
ridicule Greek vanities. It is of course true (13.31–2) that they need
Hellenic culture.

Does this passage imply an actual Roman presence at Olbia? There
was a garrison in a new fort in the second century (Wasowicz (1975)
126, de Ballu (1972) 173), but no evidence for the time of D.'s visit:
earlier military occupations of sites on the N. coast of the Black Sea,
and in the Crimea, had apparently ceased because of the wars on the
Danube frontier.

18–23 D.'s first long speech. 'We must define what we mean by a city (πόλις) before speaking of it: it is "a multitude of human beings living in the same place, controlled by law". A "city" not so controlled is no real city. But there is no perfect city on earth, only in heaven, where the star-gods and planet-gods dwell in order and harmony. Men are citizens of this city in the same sense that children are immature citizens of a human city where adults have full rights. Yet some human societies are less badly flawed than others.'

18 γνῶναι depends on βουλόμενοι. They have not however asked for a definition, and it is possible that (e.g.) δεῖ has fallen out: 'First, one must clearly understand what it is that we are discussing.'

19 πεπαιδευμένοι: cf. 12.43 for the implication that the 'educated' are philosophically serious. Here, the point is that they expect definitions by genus and differentia.   οἱ ἑλληνίζοντες 'Greek speakers'. λέγω δὲ . . . ταὐτόν 'i.e., what sort of thing it is and in what respects it is different from everything else'.   ἀλλ' ἢ . . . βάρβαροι 'other than to point to himself or someone else, as barbarians do'. The question has deprived the uneducated person of his use of language, and he is no better than a foreigner. Cf. Aesch. *Ag.* 1061–2, Clytemnestra to Cassandra: εἰ δ' ἀξυνήμων οὖσα μὴ δέχει λόγον, | σὺ δ' ἀντὶ φωνῆς φράζε καρβάνωι χερί (Fraenkel *ad loc.* dispels misinterpretations of this passage).   ζῶιον λογικὸν θνητόν: a model definition common to many schools: cf. Sext. Emp. *Adv. math.* 11.8 = *SVF* II 224.

20 πλῆθος . . . διοικούμενον: cf. §29. This is a Stoic formulation (*SVF* III 80, 81, Long and Sedley (1987) I 431 (=67J)), and the emphasis on law should be noted. Cicero's version (*De rep.* 1.39) is classic: *populus . . . coetus multitudinis iuris consensu et utilitatis communione sociatus.*   ἤδη . . . ἀνόμων 'so it is clear just from this that no foolish or lawless "city" has anything to do with [*or* 'has no claim on'] this name'. Cf. Xen. *Anab.* 3.1.31 ἀλλὰ τούτωι γε οὔτε τῆς Βοιωτίας προσήκει οὐδὲν οὔτε τῆς Ἑλλάδος παντάπασιν, ἐπεὶ ἐγὼ αὐτὸν εἶδον ὥσπερ Λυδὸν ἀμφότερα τὰ ὦτα τετρυπημένον.   οὔκουν . . . αὐτῆς 'so the poet won't have spoken of Nineveh either as a city, since it was "foolish"'. This is to interpret Phocylides in a Stoic sense: since τὸ φρόνιμον and τὸ νόμιμον are necessary characteristics of a πόλις, a place that does not possess them cannot be one. 'Law' and 'reason' are inseparable, and both are embodied in the 'order' of the universe: human 'cities' reflect, as far as they can, these features of the heavenly city.

21 ἀπὸ τῶν διοικούντων 'on the basis of its managers'. Again, the analogy between κόσμος and πόλις is clear; and D.'s model of a πόλις involves a governing class and a 'mass' (πλῆθος); how he saw this in practice can be observed in his political speeches (especially 38, 40, 42).   ὥσπερ χορὸν . . . ἀδήλως 'just as we would say that a choir is musical, if the choir-leader is musical, and the others follow him and make no sound out of tune, or only occasionally and not so as to be noticed'. This image is also appropriate to the κόσμος: see below on §22.

22 ἀγαθὴν ἐξ ἀπάντων ἀγαθῶν πόλιν 'a good city made up wholly of good elements'. But ἀγαθῶν may be questioned: ἐξ ἀπάντων, 'wholly', would give the expected sense. D. here (against Plato, and perhaps against the early Stoics?) denies even the bare possibility (ἄξιον διανοηθῆναι) of a perfect πόλις upon earth. (See in general Devine (1970) 323–36). θνητήν should probably be retained, though it is redundant and slightly illogical in view of the following exclusion clause πλὴν εἰ μὴ . . . κατ' οὐρανόν.   οὐδαμῶς ἀκίνητον . . . τοῦ ξύμπαντος οὐρανοῦ ' . . . which is neither motionless nor inactive, but vigorous and in motion, one set of gods being in the lead and first, the others second and following, without any strife or defeat, since it is wrong for gods to strive or be defeated by one another – for they are friends – or by any other superior being: they have to do their work unhindered, in total, universal, and perpetual friendship; the most conspicuous go each their own way, not pointlessly errant in foolish error, but dancing a blessed dance with reason and supreme wisdom, while the mass besides are driven in a single plan and impluse by the common motion of the whole heaven.'   ⟨τῶν δὲ δευτέρων τε καὶ ἑπομένων⟩: some such supplement is needed, since ἥττης requires a reference to what might be supposed to be a 'defeated' or 'inferior' set of gods. It follows from the next remarks that the 'first' gods are the planets, the 'second' the fixed stars.   οὐ πλανωμένων . . . πλάνην: the planets – though their name means 'wanderers' – do not really wander. This is a commonplace in authors praising the order of the universe: cf. Pl. *Laws* 821B, Cic. *ND* 2.51 (with Pease's parallels), Philo, *De decalogo* 103–4.   χορείαν εὐδαίμονα χορευόντων: this analogy has a long history. Note Eur. *El.* 467 ἄστρων αἰθέριοι χοροί, *Ion* 1078–9, Soph. *Ant.* 1147; of philosophical texts the most significant are *Timaeus* 40C (χορείας), *Epinomis* 982D (quoted above, on 12.84), [Onatas] (Thesleff (1965) 139–40: τοὶ δ' ἄλλοι θεοὶ ποτὶ πρᾶτον θεὸν καὶ νοατὸν οὕτως ἔχοντι ὥσπερ χορευταὶ ποτὶ κορυφαῖον), and [Aristot.] Περὶ κόσμου 399a12–24 (μία ἐκ πάντων ἁρμονία συναιδόντων καὶ χορευόντων κατὰ τὸν οὐρανὸν). For D., see 12.84, 40.39: τῶν πλανωμένων ἄστρων τὴν ἄπαυστον χορείαν. Various notions come into the development of this imagery: the movements of the stars, the patterns of the constellations, the 'music of the spheres'.

23 καθαρῶς εὐδαίμονα 'happy without a stain', 'possessing unalloyed happiness'.   **πολιτείαν εἴτε καὶ πόλιν χρὴ καλεῖν:** cf. §27 εἴτε πόλεως εἴτε διακοσμήσεως. D. seems to anticipate the argument of §27, where he treats the existence of a πολιτεία – ordered government – as evidence for the existence of an actual πόλις as defined above (§20). Plutarch (*Mor.* 826) speaks of several different senses of πολιτεία, of which 'form of government' is one; Isocrates (*Areop.* 14) calls it ψυχὴ πόλεως, its basic principles or inner structure, and that seems near to D.'s sense here.

Planets and stars are thus the true πολῖται of the heavenly city. Plutarch (*Mor.* 1076E) makes fun of this Stoic fancy: ἀλλὰ μὴν τὸ τὸν κόσμον εἶναι πόλιν καὶ πολίτας τοὺς ἀστέρας, εἰ δὲ τοῦτο, καὶ φυλέτας καὶ ἄρχοντας δηλονότι καὶ βουλευτὴν τὸν ἥλιον καὶ τὸν ἕσπερον πρύτανιν ἢ ἀστυνόμον, οὐκ οἶδ’ εἰ μὴ τοὺς ἐλέγχοντας τὰ τοιαῦτα τῶν λεγόντων καὶ ἀποφαινομένων ἀποδείκνουσιν ἀτοπωτέρους (see Cherniss *ad loc.*, *Plutarch: Moralia* (Loeb) XIII 2.795).   **ὡς παῖδες . . . αὐτοῦ** 'just as boys are said to have a share in a city, along with adult men, because they are citizens by nature [i.e. by birth], not in virtue of having the mind or actions of citizens or participating in the law, of which they have no understanding'. Male children are πως πολῖται, 'citizens in a sense' (Aristot. *Pol.* 1275a13), because they do not yet have full rights or duties. The citizens of the heavenly city, in contrast to those of the human world, act with νοῦς and φρόνησις, and invariably obey the divine law. For ἀξύνετος, cf. Heraclitus fr. B1 τοῦ δὲ λόγου τοῦδ’ ἐόντος αἰεὶ ἀξύνετοι γίνονται ἄνθρωποι. Heraclitus was an important source of ideas for the Stoics; their identification of god, *logos*, and fire is very much a development of his basic concepts.   **πασῶν σχεδὸν ἁπλῶς** 'practically all without exception'.   **ἡμαρτημένων τε καὶ φαύλων:** cf. *SVF* III 80 (=324): Chrysippus says τοὺς κειμένους νόμους ἡμαρτῆσθαι . . . ἅπαντας καὶ τὰς πολιτείας.   **πρὸς τὴν ἄκραν εὐθύτητα** 'in comparison with the supreme rectitude'.   **ὅμως δὲ . . . διεφθαρμένην** 'yet for our present purposes we shall be in a position to provide a model of the constitution which is comparatively good in relation to the totally depraved'. For this use of εὐπορεῖν with the accusative, cf. 12.29, 12.83. D. now offers to expound the least bad human constitution, but his hearers do not want to be told for the moment (§27). He would no doubt advocate monarchy (cf. 3.43), which represents on earth the reign of Zeus in the kosmos.

παράδειγμα must be right: παραδειγμάτων – i.e. 'we shall have plenty of examples' – would contradict D.'s clear view that even comparative goodness is rare.   ὡς ... παραβάλλοντες 'as it were comparing the most comfortable with the worst off, when all are sick'.

24–9 'I was interrupted by the elderly Hieroson, who (as a devotee of Plato) was anxious to hear my views on the heavenly order, if I would consent to postpone the subject of the best human constitution to another day. I agreed to do this, but not to vie with Plato or Homer.'

This interlude serves to prepare for the unusually elevated tone of the closing myths, in which D., despite his disclaimer, attempts something like a Platonic myth, though with a Stoic message.

24 τῶν ⟨ἐκ⟩ φιλοσοφίας λόγων: cf. 27.7, 8; 3.16.   ὥσπερ τέρας τι: a striking simile; D.'s appearance seems an almost supernatural visitation.

25 ἔμποροι καὶ ἀγοραῖοι: if D. (who was a keen reader of Xenophon) has in mind Xen. Πόροι 3.13, he distinguishes these two classes, ἔμποροι needing no more than a place to buy and sell, ἀγοραῖοι being given lodging and shops in the town.   ἀπὸ τῆς νήσου: probably Berezan rather than Leuke. See §9.   κατελθεῖν: this sounds like a prophecy of safe return *from exile*, not just a prosperous voyage.

26 ἀνεπτέρωμαι 'I am all up in the air', i.e. 'excited'. Cf. Xen. *Hell.* 3.4.2, *Symp.* 9.5, Pl. *Phaedrus* 255c, etc. Cf. 12.71.   ὀργῶντας 'eager', a metaphor from sexual excitement.   τῶν ποιητῶν: Heinze's conjecture is apt. In the speaker, it is a *naïveté* to call Plato a 'poet', as though all writers were 'poets'; but D. may wish to recall that Plato's work was in many ways poetical (cf. Aristot. *Poet.* 1447b9, Quint. 10.1.81, etc.). In any case, πολιτῶν can hardly be right: (i) if we take βαρβαρίζοντα ... μάλιστα together, the old man would be saying he is more barbaric in speech than his fellow citizens, which is absurd; (ii) taking τῶν πολιτῶν (as is natural) as dependent on τῶι ... σοφωτάτωι, it would have to be made to refer to Plato's own fellow citizens, i.e. the Athenians: very obscure. In fact, μάλιστα probably qualifies χαίρειν καὶ ξυνεῖναι:

'it is absurd for a barbarous speaker to delight in and consort most of all with the most Hellenic and wisest of poets'.   **καθάπερ ...** **ἀναβλέποι:** cf. Max. Tyr. 11.1 εἰ γάρ τις ἐς τὰς Πλάτωνος φωνὰς ἐμπεσὼν ἑτέρων δεῖται λόγων, καὶ εἴ τωι τὸ ἐκεῖθεν φῶς ἀμαυρὸν δοκεῖ ... οὗτος οὐδ' ἂν τὸν ἥλιον ἴδοι ἀνίσχοντα (I owe this parallel to M. B. Trapp).

27 προσγυμνάζεσθαι αὐτοῖς 'exercise ourselves on them', an ironical way of referring to the fighting which is in prospect.   **περὶ δὲ τῆς θείας ... διακοσμήσεως:** Hieroson's proposal is D.'s way of limiting the subject of this speech. Conversely, in *Or.* 1.37, he expresses a preference for the divine theme, but passes over it in an elaborate *praeteritio* (37–47), in favour of something more germane to Trajan and the Roman *imperium*.   **τῆς τοῦ Πλάτωνος ἐλευθερίας περὶ τὴν φράσιν** 'Plato's freedom of style'. In Dion. Hal. *CV* 22 and in [Longinus] 39.1 (if μετ' ἐλευθερίας is the right reading), ἐλευθερία in style implies the avoidance of regular periods or contrived figures in the interest of producing natural emotive effects. This is certainly what the old man means here; D. has given a specimen of the free grand style in §§19–23. From the point of view of D.'s relation to his audience in Prusa, this amounts to a promise of a non-rhetorical, rather bizarre performance.   **οὐ σμικρὸν ... φθέγγεται** 'his utterance is grand and not far off Homer'. It is a common idea that Plato is 'Homeric' in the grandeur of his language or in thought: cf. [Longinus] 13.3, with Russell's note. But the ostensible meaning of Hieroson's remark is not quite this: it is that, having got used to Homer's language, they find it easy to understand Plato.

28 τῆι ἁπλότητι 'the frankness'.   **Ἱεροσῶν:** Hieroson is a name attested at Olbia (e.g. *Inscr. Olb.* 87). Boeckh was right to restore it here. Note the technique of introducing a name casually, not when the character first appears: cf. Sotades 7.59. Plutarch uses a similar device in *Pyth. or.* (Diogenianus) and *De defectu* (Lamprias), perhaps also in *De facie*, though the beginning of that dialogue is missing.   **ἀνδράσι ... οὐκ ἐθελήσω:** *Od.* 8.223. Odysseus there claims to be a better archer than any of the present day, though he will not contend with the heroes of old, Heracles and that Eurytus of Oechalia, who challenged Apollo and was killed. If D. means us to recall the context, he is claiming to surpass his contemporaries; but quotations like this do not usually imply their contexts. He is in any case more modest than Longinus, who thinks

(13.4) that Plato did seek to rival Homer ἴσως μὲν φιλονικότερον καὶ οἱονεὶ διαδορατιζόμενος, οὐκ ἀνωφελῶς δέ, and that this ἀγών is a noble one, even if you are bound to be beaten by your great predecessors.

29 πρὸς ἐκεῖνον 'in answer to him'. **ὑπεκίνουν καὶ ἀνεφερόμην τρόπον τινα** 'I was somehow moved and raised up'. Despite his disclaimer, he is inspired by Homer and Plato. In Pl. *Rep.* 573c ὑποκεκινηκώς means 'somewhat deranged': in Xen. *Cyr.* 3.6 ὑποκινοῦσα means 'stirring', of a hare. These intransitive uses are not rare.

29–30 'It is the present world-order (*diakosmēsis*), not the kosmos as an eternal order, which is properly compared to a city, because of the controlling reason which makes a unity of its many diverse elements.' **οὐκ ἄντικρυς τῶν ἡμετέρων [ζῷον] τὸν κόσμον ἀποφαινομένων [ἢ] πόλιν:** text and interpretation unsure. Emperius' τῶν ἡμετέρων (i.e. Stoics) seems certain, but choice between the tradition of UB, which includes ζῷον and ἤ, and that of M, which omits these words, is difficult. For a more adventurous approach, see L. François, *Essai* (1922) 199. On the basis of UB (followed by von der Mühll) we should translate: 'One must take what is said about the city on the basis that our people do not say outright that the kosmos is an animal or [?that it is] a city.' (Note the ambiguity here: does D. mean the definition runs ζῷον ἢ πόλις, or that there are two alternative definitions? That the κόσμος is a 'rational' animal is indeed standard Stoic doctrine (texts in *SVF* II pp. 191ff.) derived from earlier thinking (see especially Pl. *Tim.* 30B).) 'This would be contrary to their argument about the city, which, as I said [§20], they defined as a "system" of men; and at the same time it would perhaps be improper and implausible, having said that the kosmos is strictly an animal, then to assert that it is a city.' (τοῦτο is again ambiguous: is it just the last word (πόλις), or is it the whole preceding statement?)

On the basis of M's readings, we have a simpler connection with what precedes. The argument runs: (i) Stoics do not assert that the κόσμος is a city, because (ii) a city is an exclusively human system (the kosmos being a system of 'men and gods and all things created for their sake' (*SVF* II 527 = p. 168)), and (iii) it would be inconsistent with the doctrine that the kosmos is an animal (ζῷον λογικόν). The main difficulty with this interpretation is the abrupt introduction of this last doctrine; but on balance it seems less tortuous, and therefore to be preferred.   ὑπῆρχε: for the omission of ἄν, cf. WS §§2313–20; emendation is unnecessary.

30 τὴν νῦν διακόσμησιν: this is the present 'dispensation' or state of the κόσμος, composed of various elements brought into a unity, but destined to be destroyed when one or other element predominates (*SVF* II pp. 168, 182). The myth will illustrate this. It is this that can be reasonably compared to a city, because its existence depends on the organization and harmony of its constituent parts; the eternal κόσμος, living and divine, of which the successive 'dispensations' are phases or manifestations, does not allow any such analysis.   ὁπηνίκα . . . διεπόμενον 'when the Whole is divided and separated into many shapes of plants and animals, both mortal and immortal, and also air, earth, water, and fire, though it is none the less a unity in all this and controlled by a single soul and force'.   τὸ πᾶν: Stoic usage (*SVF* II p. 167) was to differentiate τὸ πᾶν from τὸ ὅλον, as embracing not only the κόσμος but the void (κενόν). D. does not seem to use this distinction here, since what he goes on to say could not be predicated of τὸ πᾶν in this sense, of which we cannot say whether it is corporeal or not, is movement or not, or indeed anything about it (*SVF* I 95, Baudry (1931) 230). His terminology comes rather from Plato, who uses both terms similarly: e.g. *Gorg.* 508A, *Tim.* 30B; cf. §37, where τὸ ὅλον and τὸ πᾶν are clearly synonymous.   ζώιων θνητῶν καὶ ἀθανάτων: i.e. men on the one hand, daimones, heroes and gods on the other (*SVF* II nos. 1101–5).   ἀμηιγέπηι 'in some sense', a self-conscious Atticism, cf. 7.17, 103, 137.   γιγνομένων τε καὶ ἀπογιγνομένων 'coming into being and ceasing to be'.

31–2 (καταστάσεως) 'This doctrine embraces both humanity and the divine: the divine law-giver sets the pattern of beneficent monarchy, for he rules over a true "city".'   ἔμβραχυ 'in brief'. Cf. 12.16, 12.68.   τῶι θείωι: sc. γένει. Geel's correction is right, because the community is of all gods and all men; in this context, the essential monotheism of Stoic religion is not to the fore.   τὸ λογικὸν . . . εὑρίσκων: the possession of reason is the only sure bond of a just community: cf. §22, where the common φιλία of the heavenly bodies is associated with the νοῦς or φρόνησις displayed in their movements.   τυράννων . . . ὀλιγαρχιῶν: δεκαρχίαι (or δεκαδαρχίαι M: the form δεκαταρχίαι also occurs) are an odd item in a list which otherwise enumerates the classic three types of constitution. Though the word is used of the Roman decemvirate and of the office of the Latin *decurio* in various contexts, it is most likely that D. is here talking not of contemporary life but of classical history: the word was used of the 'commissions of ten' established by Sparta in various cities after the end of the Peloponnesian War (Isocr. *Paneg.* 110, *Panath.* 68, Xen. *Hell.* 3.5.13). They stand for imposed, unrepresentative power.   **ἀρρωστημάτων** 'infirmities'. Cf. 32.7 τὰ τῆς πόλεως ἀρρωστήματα. The word is medical (=illness involving lack of strength, and so illness in general; cf. ἀσθένεια), but was commonly used of vicious attitudes, e.g. the conviction that money is the greatest good.   **διαφορουμένη** 'torn asunder'. Cf. 4.138 ψυχὴν διαφορουμένην τε καὶ διασπωμένην, ἀεί ποτε ἐν μάχηι καὶ στάσει διηνεκεῖ πρὸς αὐτὴν οὖσαν.   **τῆι σωφρονεστάτηι καὶ ἀρίστηι βασιλείαι:** for D., as for many Stoics under the Empire, monarchy, not a 'mixed constitution' is the best political order attainable (Devine (1970) 323–36). Cf. especially 1.37, 1.42, 40.35ff. for the analogy between the cosmic and the imperial order: see Introd. p. 23. Cohoon's 'noblest form of kingship' is wrong: βασιλεία is altogether good, tyranny being the bad form of monarchy.

32 ὁ τοῦ ξύμπαντος ἡγεμὼν οὐρανοῦ: an echo (one of many: M. B. Trapp in Russell (1990) 148ff.) of Plato's *Phaedrus*: 264E ὁ μὲν δὴ μέγας ἡγεμὼν ἐν οὐρανῶι Ζεύς. For the hyperbaton (also in τῆς ὅλης δεσπότης οὐσίας) cf. J. D. Denniston, *Greek prose style* (1952) 55–6.   **ἐξηγούμενος** 'expounding' the true meaning of kingship, and so giving a model to mortal rulers.

32–5 'The poets – at least the earliest poets – have a certain understanding of this, which they communicate to their hearers, though they are not the true initiates. They all proclaim Zeus King and Father of gods and men.'

On this passage, see Luzzatto (1983) 73–7.

32 οἱ θεῖοι ποιηταί: as appears from §34, D. does not here mean that all poets are θεῖοι – as though it were a stock epithet and used ironically – but that some poets were inspired, others not.

33 τὸ ποιητικὸν γένος 'the poetic tribe'. Cf. Pl. *Soph.* 224C (τὸ σοφιστικὸν γένος), *Laws* 801B (τὸ τῶν ποιητῶν γένος), *Tim.* 19E, etc. Such periphrases, being a little grandiose, may also be ironical.   **οὐ πάνυ ἄστοχον . . . οὐδὲ ἀπὸ στόχου:** the repetition causes one to suspect the text. ἄστοχον (see below) may be guaranteed by the Platonic allusion; ἀπὸ σκοποῦ, 'beside the mark', would give the expected sense in the second half of the clause.   **οὐ πάνυ ἄστοχον ... τῶν ἱερῶν λόγων:** 'not at all failing to understand the Holy Words'. D. may be thinking of Pl. *Tim.* 19E τὸ τῶν σοφιστῶν γένος ... μή πως ... ἄστοχον ἅμα φιλοσόφων ἀνδρῶν ἧι καὶ πολιτικῶν, ὅσ' ἄν ... πράττοιεν καὶ λέγοιεν. D.'s λόγων has no specific reference: it anticipates the extended metaphor of 'mysteries' which follows next.   **κατὰ θεσμὸν καὶ νόμον ... τοῦ ξύμπαντος πέρι:** the pleonasm, the solemn word θεσμός, and the anastrophe of πέρι give an effect of elevation. All this is high, Platonic style, as D. promised.   **ἀτεχνῶς δὲ ... παριοῦσιν** 'And it [i.e. 'the poetic tribe'] really resembles the outside servants of the mysteries, who stand at the door, ornamenting the entrance and the public altars, and making other preparations, never entering within.' **θεράποντας Μουσῶν:** e.g. Hes. *Theog.* 100 (see West *ad loc.*), *Hymn Hom.* 32.20; it is an ancient cliché, ridiculed in Aristoph. *Birds* 909.

34 τοὺς πλησίον ... ὑπερφανέντος 'it is likely enough that people moving around near some initiatory ceremony, by the entrance, should to this extent be aware of something inside, if a mystic cry has been uttered, or a fire seen above the building ...' Ritual cries and the use of fire or bright light in the revelation of the mysteries are natural features of such rites; and there is no doubt that exposure to a dazzling light after being in the dark was a part of the initiates' experience at Eleusis and elsewhere (P. Boyancé, *R.E.G.* 75 (1962) 460–82).   **τοῖς πάνυ ἀρχαίοις:** cf. *Or.* 18.3 for the idea that the oldest poets had a special revelation (τῶν ποιητῶν οἱ ἀρχαιότατοι καὶ παρὰ θεῶν τὴν ποίησιν λαβόντες οὔτε τοὺς ἰσχυροὺς οὔτε τοὺς καλοὺς ὡς θεοὺς ἔφασαν ὁρᾶθαι, ἀλλὰ τοὺς λέγοντας, a reference to *Odyssey* 8.170–7). In *Or.* 53, D. discusses the Stoic theory (Zeno's, but anticipated – D. says – by Antisthenes) that Homer wrote sometimes κατὰ δόξαν and sometimes κατὰ ἀλήθειαν. He himself (53.7) bases his belief on Homer's inspiration by Apollo and the Muses on his fame among barbarians who know nothing else of Greek civilization. So Homer should be among the ἀρχαῖοι here regarded as inspired; that Hesiod goes with him is suggested by §40, where 'Homer and Hesiod' know nothing of the 'chariot of Zeus' described by Zoroaster and the Magi. There is thus no reason to suspect ἃ ἔπασχον ... Ἡσίοδος on the ground that Homer and Hesiod should not be named. The construction (ἔπασχον ... καὶ κατείχοντο = πάσχοντες κατείχοντο) seems a natural parataxis. (It is true, however, that some Stoics regarded Hesiod as a corrupter of ancient wisdom by his own 'fabulous additions': Cornutus 17, p. 31, 12–18 Lang.)

35 οἱ δὲ μετ' ἐκείνους: the tragedians generally, not (as Luzzatto (1983) 75) specifically Euripides. Traditional objections to the myths in tragedy extend to Aeschylus and Sophocles also (Plato found much impiety in Aeschylus). **ἐπὶ σκήνας καὶ θέατρα:** cf. Max. Tyr. 37.4, where the Athenian μοῦσα is said originally to have been confined to honest, rustic choruses of boys and men, but then μεταπεσοῦσα ... ἡσυχῆ ἐπὶ τέχνην ἀκορέστου χάριτος ἐν σκηνῆι καὶ θεάτροις ἀρχὴ τῆς περὶ πολιτείαν αὐτοῖς πλημμελείας ἐγένετο.   **τὴν αὐτῶν σοφίαν** 'their *own* wisdom', contrasted with the divine inspiration of their predecessors.   **ἀμύητοι ἀμυήτοις:** polyptoton, cf. §22, §42.   **ἀτελῆ** 'incomplete', but also 'uninitiated'.   **τῶι ὄντι . . . τριόδοις** 'in truth constructing open booths for bacchic rites at a sort of tragic crossroads'. D. has in mind (i) the association of σκηναί both with tragedy (as in Pl. *Laws* 817c, where the tragic poets build their σκηναί in the agora) and with Dionysiac worship, (ii) the ambiguity of ἀκαλύπτους ('open to the sky', but also 'openly revealed', the insinuation being that they illicitly revealed a mystery), and perhaps (iii) the association of τρίοδοι with the worship of Hecate as well as with ordinary, vulgar life.

36–8 'Hence men speak of Zeus as King and Father; as Father, he has the kosmos as his household; as King, it is his city. This doctrine shows us gods and men dwelling in a community of reason; it is a juster and better dispensation than that of Sparta, whose Helots plot against her.'

36 Διὸς βασιλέως: see on 12.75. The cult existed at Olbia too (Hirst (1903) 36ff.).   **ἐν ταῖς εὐχαῖς:** so frequently in Homer, Ζεῦ πάτερ: e.g. *Il.* 1.503, 2.371, 3.276.   **οἶκον . . . τὸν ἅπαντα κόσμον:** cf. *SVF* II p. 169, 23 (Arius) λέγεσθαι δὲ κόσμον καὶ τὸ οἰκητήριον θεῶν καὶ ἀνθρώπων, i.e. one of the various senses given to κόσμος by the Stoics is that of the 'dwelling' of gods and men. D. here associates this with the 'fatherhood' of Zeus; as πατήρ, he is head of the household.   **κατὰ τὴν μείζονα ἀρχήν** 'having regard to his larger sphere of rule'. He is not only Father, but King; and this carries with it the idea that his power is over a 'city'.

37 οὐ γὰρ δὴ . . . τὸ πολιτευόμενον 'For if they [i.e. the worshippers of Zeus the King] say that the ruler of all things is a king, they cannot fail to admit that the sum of things is governed as a kingdom, and

having said that, they cannot say that it is not constitutionally governed
or that there is no constitution of the whole. Admitting this, moreover,
they will not be deterred from saying that that which is "constitutionally governed" is a city, or something very like a city.' The run of the
argument, which requires simply that βασιλεύεσθαι entails πολιτεύεσθαι
(βασιλεία being one species of πολιτεία) supports von Arnim's deletion
of βασιλικήν.

38 δαιμόνων here = θεῶν: cf. 12.36, 32.76.   **οὐ τοῖς τυχοῦσι** 'not
to absolutely *any* . . .'   **πολὺ . . . εἰσηγούμενος** 'introducing a legislative system much better and fairer than the Laconian . . .' Spartan laws,
as devised by Lycurgus, were proverbially good and wise; but the divine
lawgiver is much better.   **καθ' ἣν . . . Σπαρτιάταις** 'according to
which not even the Helots [*sc.* though inhabitants of Laconia] can
become Spartiates'.

Were there still Helots in Roman times? Strabo (8.365) says the
institution lasted μέχρι τῆς Ῥωμαίων ἐπικρατείας, but implies it was
defunct by his time. Many had been freed in the time of the 'tyrant'
Nabis (207–192 B.C.); and the *perioikoi* were independent of Sparta
under Roman rule. It looks as if D.'s statement that 'they continue to
plot against Sparta' is untrue of his own day. For his general views on
Sparta, see Rawson (1969) 110.

39–61 *The 'myth of the Magi'*. The remainder of the speech is occupied
by a colourful myth concerning the conflagration (ἐκπύρωσις) of the
world and its rebirth (παλιγγενεσία). This is attributed to 'Zoroaster
and the Magi', and D. insists more than once on its bizarre nature. It
is plainly an imitation of Plato (there are particularly many echoes of
the *Phaedrus* myth, the source of the dominant image of the chariot and
horses), and so a fulfilment of Hieroson's request for 'Plato's liberty of
style' (§27). Its doctrine however is by no means Platonic, but distinctly
Stoic. It raises many problems.

(i) Is it really 'Zoroastrian', or in any way indebted to Mithraic or
similar rites? Or is it rather just an exotic presentation of familiar Stoic
cosmology? For Bidez–Cumont (1938) it was a 'hymn', a precious
testimony to the Magusaean beliefs which D. knew in Asia Minor; but
that this is at least very much exaggerated is clearly made out, e.g., by
Pohlenz (1949) II 45–7 and R. L. Gordon (see notes on §43). There are
two themes – the connection of horses with the worship of the sun (§39),
and the worship of fire (§§39–40) – which are certainly close to Persian

beliefs: but both were known from earlier Greek sources (Herodotus, Xenophon), and they seem to be present primarily to motivate the use of the chariot-image and the exposition of the Stoic ἐκπύρωσις. This involves a totally different eschatology from that usual in Mithraism: no succession of planetary ages culminating in the age of the sun, but a cycle of destruction and rebirth, ending in a total repetition of the preceding cycle. The symbols in §43 (see note) are the closest to real oriental influence of any detail in the story. Why then did D. so emphasize its 'non-Hellenic' qualities? Partly no doubt because of the long tradition of claiming such authority (the pseudo-Platonic *Axiochus* (371A) is a good parallel to the use of the Magi in this way: and see in general Festugière's chapter on 'Les prophètes de l'orient' in *RHT* I² (1950) 19–44). But we should also think of D.'s fictitious audience and his real one. The Borysthenites, in the front line against the Sarmatians, who were Iranian nomads, expected Hellenic culture from D., and look at what they got! No wonder he had to apologize (§§51, 54). Back home in Prusa, it was different: D. was a returning traveller, expected to have exotic tales to tell. (§1). He excites attention and interest by proclaiming that he has one to tell. Yet it turns out to be no such thing, but straight out of the Stoic school.

(ii) There remains, however, a great difficulty. D. clearly distinguishes (§§50–1) between two 'horse-races'. One represents the destruction of *large* parts of the *earth* by fire or flood, catastrophes remembered in the myths of Phaethon and Deucalion, and so survived by at least a remnant of humanity; the other represents the final fusion of all the elements into the cosmic fire, which then takes on the rôle of World Soul or Intellect, and, by a mysterious process, engenders a new world. Now the first of these types of disaster – the partial catastrophe to the earth – has a long history in Greek thought, and indeed in Oriental myth also (Caduff (1986), H. Schwabe (*RE* Suppl. xv, s.v. Weltalter)). There are traces of it in pre-Socratic texts (Anaximander B1, Xenophanes A33) and it was familiar to Plato (*Tim.* 22A) and to Aristotle (*Protrepticus* fr. 19 Ross, *Meteor.* 1.14), who took the flood to mark the winter, and the fire the summer 'solstice' of a supposed 'Great Year', defined as the period required for all the stars (or all the planets) to return to the relative positions in which they were at the start (ἀποκατάστασις). Many calculations of this period were made (van der Waerden (1952));

none appears in D., nor any hint, except the vague phrase in §47 ἐν μήκει χρόνου καὶ πολλαῖς περιόδοις. D. in fact does not explain how this danger of fire and flood on earth relates to the universal destruction by the ἐκπύρωσις. Presumably, we live in a world subject to both fates. Yet, in many Stoic accounts, Phaethon and Deucalion are taken as models of the ἐκπύρωσις and a final flood is as decisive as a final conflagration (cf. [Heraclitus] *Qu. Hom.* 25, quoted on §47 below, Manilius 4.832, Sen. *NQ* 3.27ff.). They also often involve the time-scale of the ἀποκατάστασις and the Great Year. D.'s account of the ἐκπύρωσις is more consistent and probably closer to the ideas of Chrysippus and Cleanthes, which Posidonius probably followed (Diog. Laert. 7.142-3, with Kidd (1988) on Posidonius F5 and 13). I have tried to explain in the notes how closely the myth follows the doctrine; details such as D.'s correct use of the terms τόπος and χώρα (§53) are significant. It is important to note that the doctrine is an optimistic one: none of these calamities is a punishment for man's wickedness, all are inevitable in the course of nature, and the ultimate event is a new world, better (at least to begin with) than the one we live in.

Even if we accept this general view, two puzzles remain. (i) How does D. conceive the relationship between the partial and the total destruction? This remains unclear. (ii) Why is the myth given, and how does it relate to the earlier themes of the speech? A tentative answer to this may be hazarded: in the story of the παλιγγενεσία (§55), stress is laid on the desire of the cosmic intellect for concord (ὁμόνοια) and rule over an ordered universe. This has a possible political application, at least in a broad sense. Both in this speech and elsewhere (*Or.* 1-4, 40), D. shows an interest in the analogies between earthly and cosmic monar-chy; his theology is, in a sense, the servant of his political message. After all, he wrote this speech in the dawn of a new era, which could be seen as a sort of παλιγγενεσία, not long after *primo statim beatissimi saeculi ortu Nerua Caesar res olim dissociabiles miscuerit, principatum ac libertatem ...* (Tac. *Agr.* 3) The Stoic god – Reason or Fire or whatever we call him – does just this, out of his own desire to re-create the world. See also Introd. p. 22-3.

39-41 'The Magi, in their secret ceremonies, praise God as the supreme charioteer. The chariot of the sun is known to all; but the chariot of Zeus was praised worthily only by Zoroaster, who came unscathed from the burning mountain and taught the Magi how to serve God. They maintain a team of Nisaean horses for Zeus, and a single horse for the sun.'

39 ἐν ἀπορρήτοις τελεταῖς 'in secret rituals', not to be taken as implying Mithraic rites; but note Plu. *Pomp.* 24.7 (Cilician pirates) τελετάς τινας ἀπορρήτους ἐτέλουν ὧν ἡ τοῦ Μίθρου καὶ μέχρι δεῦρο διασώζεται. Cf. §56.   **ὑπὸ μάγων ἀνδρῶν:** cf. [Pl.] *Axiochus* 371A ἀνὴρ μάγος. This sense of μάγος – 'wise man' – is found in Herodotus (7.37), and is common later: cf. on §41.   **τὸν θεὸν τοῦτον:** the cosmic king and lawgiver just decribed, who is also Zeus, near whose temple the conversation takes place (§17).   **τέλειον:** with the sense of 'the Fulfiller', this is a common cult-title of Zeus (cf. Fraenkel on Aesch. *Ag.* 973), but here it clearly means 'perfect', 'complete', and so 'supreme'. **τοῦ τελειοτάτου ἅρματος** 'the most perfect team'. A τέλειον ἅρμα (cf. Lucian, *Timon* 50) is a team of grown horses, not πῶλοι; so there is here also some play on the word, and νεώτερον, 'younger', has added point: the sun is a young colt in the race.   **ἡνίοχον:** cf. §42 ἡνιόχησιν. This image is an important one in the myth. It is suggested, in part, by Plato's use of it, *Phaedrus* 246E (μέγας ἡγεμὼν ἐν οὐρανῶι Ζεύς, ἐλαύνων πτηνὸν ἅρμα), 253Dff. (the soul has two 'horses' and one 'charioteer', reason); and the image of god as the world's charioteer is obvious and banal (cf. Philo, *De aeternitate mundi* 85 ἡνιόχου καὶ κυβερνήτου τρόπον ἡνιοχεῖ καὶ πηδαλιουχεῖ τὰ σύμπαντα). But the force of the image is enhanced by its association with Persian things: Xen. *Cyr.* 8.3.12, a ἅρμα sacred to Zeus is followed in procession by one sacred to Helios: Q. Curt. 3.3.11, a procession led by chanting Magi, in which the horse of the sun follows the chariot sacred to Jupiter, drawn by white horses (cf. below §41). Bidez–Cumont (1938) II 142 cite Avestan and Mithraic evidence for 'white horses': and no doubt D. has these picturesque associations in mind.   **ὅθεν . . . τοῦ δίφρου** 'beginning, in effect, with the poets, who, every time they describe risings and settings, all expound in the same way the yoking of the horses and Helios himself mounting his chariot'. D. is thinking of the many descriptions of sunrise in Homer, but also of passages like Mimnermus fr. 12 West, a splendid and colourful account of the labours of Helios as charioteer.

40 οὐδεὶς ἄρα ὕμνησεν ἀξίως τῶν τῇδε: an echo of Pl. *Phaedrus* 247C τὸν δὲ ὑπερουράνιον τόπον οὔτε τις ὕμνησέ πω τῶν τῇδε ποιητὴς οὔτε ποτὲ ὑμνήσει κατ' ἀξίαν. ἄρα indicates that this is part of the views of the Magi: Denniston (1954) 38–9. By τῶν τῆιδε, D. means 'Greek' poets etc.; Plato meant 'poets on this earth'.   **Ζωροάστρης:** this is the normal Greek form of the name Zarathuštra, the great prophet whom the Greeks believed to have lived many thousands of years ago – 5,000 years before the sack of Troy, according to the Platonist Hermodorus (Diog. Laert. *prooem.* 2)! – but who in fact flourished in the seventh or sixth century B.C. There were many legends about him: born perhaps in Bactria, he spent many years in solitude and fasting in the desert, and later came to the court of king Vistaspa (Hystaspes), probably a prince in N.W. Iran. He was a great religious reformer, opposed to animal sacrifice, much concerned with prayer and morality. Plutarch (*De Is. et Osir.* 46, 369D) summarizes what the Greeks regarded as his essential doctrine: that Horomazes (Ahura-mazda) was the creator of good, and a god, and Areimanios (Ahriman) the creator of evil, an inferior power, to whom only apotropaic sacrifices should be made. See in general Gwyn Griffiths (1970) *ad loc.* Greek sources for Zoroastrianism are collected in Clemen (1920), and (with elaborate discussion) in Bidez–Cumont (1938).   **μάγων παῖδες . . . μαθόντες:** phrases like μάγων (σοφῶν, ἰατρῶν) παῖδες are simply periphrases (so [Plu.] *De vita et poesi Homeri* 29, on υἷας Ἀχαιῶν) for μάγοι (σοφοί, ἰατροί): see Stevens on Eur. *Androm.* 1124, Pl. *Rep.* 407E, 408B, *Laws* 769B. See also on 12.25. Bidez–Cumont should not have inferred that D. is thinking of the handing down of wisdom from father to son. Nevertheless ἄιδουσι . . . μαθόντες suits an oral tradition: note that St Basil (*Epist.* 258 = Clemen p. 86) states that the Magusaeans had no books but depended on the oral transmission of their learning.   **ἀποχωρήσαντα:** the story of the retreat of Zoroaster is well attested in classical literature: Plin. *NH* 11.242, Porph. *Ant. nymph.* 5, Schol. Pl. *Alcib.* 122A, pp. 99–100 Greene. He is said to have lived 20 or 30 years in the desert or in a mountain cave; some said he lived on a special cheese which lasted indefinitely.   **τῶν ἀνθρώπων:** the corruption of ἀνθρώπων to ἄλλων probably arises from use of the contraction ΑΝΩΝ, one of a group of contractions of *nomina sacra* (God, man, Christ, etc.) originally used in Christian texts, but later also quite freely in texts of pagan authors: see esp. C. H. Roberts, *Manuscript, society and belief in early Christian Egypt* (Oxford 1979) 26–48.   **ἔπειτα . . . κάεσθαι** 'then the mountain caught alight, a great fire striking down from on high, and burned continually'. No oriental version of this story seems to be known, but

Bidez–Cumont (1 30) connect it with the custom of lighting fire on mountain tops, practised by the Persian and Pontic kings.   **τὸν οὖν βασιλέα:** Hystaspes (Vistaspa).   **ἐξελθεῖν ἐκ τοῦ πυρὸς ἀπαθῆ:** it is natural to compare the narratives of the Transfiguration (Matthew 17.1–8, Mark 9.2–8, Luke 9.28–36) in which Jesus goes up alone on to a mountain and μετεμορφώθη, his face shining like the sun, and his clothes miraculously whitened, and he commands his disciples not to be afraid (cf. θαρρεῖν here).   **ὡς ... τοῦ θεοῦ** 'because God had come to the place'.

41 τοῖς ἄριστα ... γόητας 'to those best endowed by nature for the truth and capable of understanding god – persons whom the Persians call *magi*, who understand how to serve the divine power, not sorcerers, as the Greeks ignorantly use the word'. Pl. *Alcib.* 1.121E–122A is the primary authority for the description of Zoroaster's μαγεία as θεῶν θεραπεία: cf. Dio, *Or.* 49.7 τοὺς καλουμένους παρ' αὐτοῖς μάγους, οἳ τῆς φύσεως ἦσαν ἔμπειροι καὶ τοὺς θεοὺς ᾔδεσαν ὡς δεῖ θεραπεύειν. Cf. Apuleius, *Apol.* 26, citing Plato, and Apoll. Tyan. *Epist.* 16–17, where Apollonius agrees that Pythagoreans and others deserve the name μάγοι, because the Persians used this word of the servants of god. So in N.T. μάγος is used (a) of the 'wise men from the East' (Matthew 2.1), (b) of a 'sorcerer' (Acts 8.11, 13.6, 13.8).   **τὸ δαιμόνιον:** not here distinct from τὸ θεῖον.   **Νισαίων ἵππων:** famous horses from Armenia, where the satrap was supposed to send 20,000 foals a year to the Persian king (Strabo 11.14.9, 530c). Cf. Himerius 12.36, 25.30.   **ἕνα ἵππον:** as in the processions described by Xenophon and Q. Curtius (see on §39).

42–7 'Their explanation of the myth is extraordinary: they say that the motion of the whole universe is beyond human observation, and the motions of the sun and moon, which we do see, are only motions of parts of the whole. There are, they say, four horses in a team: the horse of Zeus, in which the sun and moon and stars can be seen; the horse of Hera; the horse of Poseidon; and the horse of Hestia, who does not move at all.'

This allegory of the elements is sometimes held to betray Mithraic influence; worship of the elements is certainly something which the Greeks themselves saw as characteristic of Iranian religion: Hdt. 1.131 θύουσι δὲ [the Persians] ἡλίωι τε καὶ σελήνηι καὶ γῆι καὶ πυρὶ καὶ ὕδατι καὶ ἀνέμοισι. But what is said here, in preparation for the account of the ἐκπύρωσις (§48ff.) is explicable in Greek, and particularly Stoic, terms. 'Fire' is the element of which all the heavenly bodies are composed; 'air' (ἀήρ, an anagram of ῞Ηρα) is 'dark' or 'black' except where illuminated by the sun; water tends downwards; earth is characterized by its central position and its centripetal force (§47).

42 προφῆται τῶν Μουσῶν: cf. 53.10 (of Homer) τῶι ὄντι ὥσπερ οἱ προφῆται τῶν θεῶν ἐξ ἀφανοῦς καὶ ἀδύτου ποθεν φθεγγόμενος. The Muse is the goddess whose oracle the poet speaks forth: Pindar fr. 150 μαντεύεο Μοῖσα, προφατεύσω δ᾽ ἐγώ, *Paean* 6.6 Πιερίδων προφάταν. **αὐθαδῶς** 'boldly', 'wilfully'. The contrast with μετὰ πολλῆς πειθοῦς conveys the idea that, while Greek poets are concerned to convince their audience, the Magi say what they believe outright and without caring to ingratiate. Cf. 52.4 on τὸ αὐθαδὲς τῆς διανοίας καὶ φράσεως in Aeschylus, contrasted with Sophocles and Euripides. **ἀγωγήν τε καὶ ἡνιόχησιν . . . γιγνομένην ἀεί** 'a single guidance and driving of the chariot, perpetually conducted by supreme experience and strength'. **ἄπαυστον . . . περιόδοις** 'unceasing, in unceasing cycles of eternity'. For the polyptoton, cf. §35. For the language cf. [Aristot.] Περὶ κόσμου 391b18 οὐρανὸς . . . κινούμενος κίνησιν ἀίδιον, μιᾶι περιαγωγῆι καὶ κύκλωι συναναχορεύει πᾶσι τούτοις [i.e. the stars] ἀπαύστως δι᾽ αἰῶνος. **καθάπερ εἶπον:** this must be a reference back to §39, where the doctrine of the Magi was said to be that the sun's chariot is 'younger', and owes its fame to its visibility. It is not an exact reference, however: the Moon was not mentioned in §39, and the notion of 'parts' was not expressed there. **ὑπ᾽ ἀνθρώπων:** von Arnim's correction is probably right. The meaning seems to be that these 'motions of parts' are discernible because the sun and the moon can be seen to move relatively to the fixed stars; they have their own motion, in addition to that of the whole heaven. (So M. B. Trapp.) **κινήσεως καὶ φορᾶς:** φορά is locomotion, κίνησις movement generally: *SVF* II 161.3, Aristot. *Phys.* 260a28, etc. **ἀγῶνος** 'race'.

43 οὐ πάνυ τι . . . τὸ τῆς εἰκόνος 'not caring in the least whether their image is in all respects a good likeness'. D. develops this criticism in §46. **παρὰ Ἑλληνικὰ . . . ἐπάιδων** 'singing a barbarian song to follow songs that were elegant and Greek': the 'Greek song' was the exposition of the 'city of the kosmos', §§29–38. Neither passage is strictly a 'song': cf. 12.23. **Φασὶ . . . ἀλλοῖα** 'They say that the uppermost horse is infinitely superior to the others in beauty, size, and speed, for he runs on the outside, the longest track of the course, and he is sacred to Zeus himself. He is winged, brilliant in colouring, of the purest light. The Sun and the Moon are seen as visible marks on him, like the marks on horses in our world, some of which are crescent-shaped, some of other forms.'   τὸν δὲ Ἥλιον ... ἀλλοῖα: some Oriental ideas may lie behind this curious analogy. The fiery horse bears two symbols of fire, one masculine, one feminine, Sun and Moon, corresponding perhaps to the Iranian Mithras and the goddess Anahita, often his companion. It is noticeable that in his analogy with the marks or blazes on the horses we know, D. specifies 'crescent-shaped' marks: a lunar crescent is sometimes a symbol of Anahita, though we also hear (Plu. *Lucullus* 24.4) of cows reared in her honour, branded with the sign of a torch (Turcan (1975) 92, 96, 101). But D. makes no attempt to give more than vague hints, and to attach his myth in any way to Mithraic rites is made virtually impossible (i) by his failure to mention Mithras at all, (ii) by the incompatibility of his doctrine of ἐκπύρωσις with the Mithraic conception of successive ages, dominated by the several planets, and culminating in the age of the Sun (Gordon (1971) 237ff.).

44 ταῦτα ... μορφάς 'These are seen by us gathered together (?), like powerful sparks circulating in the bright light of a flame, but they have their own separate movements. The other stars are also seen through him and are all parts of him, some revolving with him with one motion, others running on separate tracks. These each have separate names among men, but the others only when they are together in groups, divided into certain figures and shapes.'

This potted astronomy is not very plain. (i) συνεστραμμένα must mean 'concentrated', 'gathered together', 'forming a συστροφή'. This is not an apt description of the sun and moon. We should *either* (a) read συστρεφόμενα, i.e. 'turning together' with the universal fire, *or* (b) transpose ταῦτα ... διαθέοντας to follow μορφάς, where the sentence would form a possible description of the constellations. (ii) What are the 'other stars' which are subdivided into those which share the horse's motion and those which have separate courses? There are two possibilities: (*a*) the planets, subdivided into Venus and Mercury (which revolve with the same speed as the sun; cf. Geminus, *Isagoge* 1.28–9) and the rest; (*b*) all the heavenly bodies except sun and moon, subdivided into the fixed stars and the planets. (*b*) is right; then the next sentence takes up the two classes in reverse order, ταῦτα μέν being the last mentioned, i.e. the planets, and τὰ ἄλλα the fixed stars which revolve 'with' the horse of fire.

45 πρῶτος . . . πρώτας: polyptoton (cf. 7.134n.). D. is thinking of Zoroastrian fire-worship.   **Ἥρας ἐπώνυμος:** Empedocles is supposed to have made this identification (the anagram ἀήρ = Ἥρα is powerfully suggestive), but it is common in later texts, especially Stoic: Kirk–Raven–Schofield (1983) 286, Cornutus 3 (p. 3, 16 Lang), etc. **εὐήνιος καὶ μαλακός** 'obedient to the rein and soft'. **μέλας:** air is 'black', i.e. colourless, unless suffused by light.   **φαιδρύνεται . . . ἰδέαν** 'the part that Helios shines upon is bright, but the part cast in shadow in its revolution resumes its own natural colour'.

46 εἴδωλον: D. suggests that Pegasus is an 'image' of the Horse of Poseidon, i.e. the element water. In myth, he was the child of Poseidon; his name is said to derive from πηγαί, 'springs' (Cornutus 22, p. 44.9 Lang). He is here said to have opened with his hoof not (as in most versions) the fountain of Hippocrene on Helicon, but Peirene, the fountain at Corinth (cf. Stat. *Theb.* 4.60 *uatum qua conscius amnis | Gorgoneo concussus equo*). In the common form of the story, it was at Peirene that Bellerophon bridled Pegasus.   **οὐχ ὅπως πτερωτός** 'far from being winged'. The position of the οὐχ ὅπως clause, following the contrasting phrase instead of preceding it, is uncommon: but see Jebb on Soph. *El.* 796 (πεπαύμεθ᾽ ἡμεῖς, οὐχ ὅπως σε παύσομεν) and his quotation from Lucian, *Charon* 8: ὅταν πλέηι μηδ᾽ ἐμπίδ᾽, οὐχ ὅπως ταῦρον, ἔτι ἄρασθαι δυνάμενος.   **χαλινὸν . . . ἐνδακόντα:** another echo of Pl. *Phaedrus*, 254D ἐνδακὼν τὸν χαλινόν.

47 συνερείδειν . . . μέρεσι 'he presses in upon himself with all his parts from every side', i.e. earth has its own centripetal force.   **καὶ τὼ δύο . . . φέρεσθαι:** i.e. the Horses of Air and Water lean over towards the Horse of Earth and jostle it, only the Horse of Fire moving round, as though Earth was the νύσσα, 'turning-point, of the race-course.

47 Τὸ μὲν οὖν πολύ – 50 'The horses generally get on together, but periodically the heat of the Horse of Fire burns the others, especially Earth. The story of Phaethon reflects this. At other times, the sweat of the Horse of Water produces a cataclysm, as in the time of Deucalion. These apparent disasters are in fact part of the divine plan, a necessary discipline to keep the horses in order.'

D. here gives a straightforward allegory of the theory that the earth is subject to periodical conflagrations and floods, which cause great damage, but not its destruction. (See above, p. 232.) Other mythical floods were associated with Ogygus, king of Thebes, and with Dardanus; but the story of Deucalion, so like that of Noah, is much the most important. (See Caduff (1986), van der Waerden (1952), Schwabl, *RE* Suppl. xv, s.v. Weltalter.) It is important to keep in mind (cf. p. 233) that D. makes a clear distinction between these catastrophes and the final triump of Fire which marks the end of the existing διακόσμησις, which he describes below (§§51–60). Many Stoic writers are less precise: e.g. [Heraclitus], *Qu. Hom.* 25 φασὶ τοίνυν οἱ δοκιμώτατοι φιλόσοφοι ταῦτα περὶ τῆς διανομῆς τῶν ὅλων· ἕως μὲν ἂν ἀφιλόνεικος ἁρμονία τὰ τέτταρα στοιχεῖα διακρατῆι ... ἀκινήτως ἕκαστα μένειν. εἰ δ᾽ ἐπικρατήσειέ τι τῶν ἐν αὑτοῖς ... τὰ λοιπὰ συγχυθέντα τῆι τοῦ κρατοῦντος ἰσχύϊ μετ᾽ ἀνάγκης ὑπείξειν. πυρὸς μὲν οὖν αἰφνιδίως ἐκζέσαντος ἁπάντων ἔσεσθαι κοινὴν ἐκπύρωσιν, εἰ δ᾽ ἁθροῦν ὕδωρ ἐκραγείη, κατακλυσμῶι τὸν κόσμον ἀπολεῖσθαι. This implies that either fire or flood may produce the destruction of the whole universe.   **θυμοειδοῦς** 'spirited', Plato's word for one of the three elements of the soul, but also appropriate to horses: Dio, *Or.* 8.3, 15.30.   **τήν τε δὴ χαίτην ... καὶ τὸν ἅπαντα κόσμον** 'its hair, in which it took great pride, and all its adornment'. Not 'the whole world', because this is not destroyed in this way; but D. presumably is aware of the possible misunderstanding. For the metaphor in χαίτην (i.e. forests), cf. Callim. *Hymn* 4.81 ὡς ἴδε χαίτην σειομένην Ἑλικῶν, [Aristot.] Περὶ κόσμου 397a24 ἡ ... γῆ φυτοῖς κομῶσα παντοδαποῖς. So *coma* in Latin poetry: Austin on V. *Aen.* 2.629.

48 Φαέθοντι: for a good account of the development of the myth, see J. Diggle, *Euripides: Phaethon* (Cambridge 1970) 4–32. It was used by Plato (*Timaeus* 22c) as a symbol of the supposed periodical destruction, and this is how D. uses it here, no doubt with Plato in mind; but it is often used by other writers as a symbol of total destruction (Manil. 4.831, [Aristot.] Περὶ κόσμου 400a29).   **οὐκ ἐθέλοντας ψέγειν:** it would be impious to blame a god for this disaster, so the story of a mortal charioteer is invented. 'They therefore say that a younger charioteer, the Sun's mortal son, took a fancy for a difficult game, one that was to do all mortals harm [note the repetition θνητὸν ... θνητοῖς], asked his father to let him drive the chariot, scorched up all living animals and all plants in his uncontrolled flight, and finally perished himself, laid low by a greater fire.'

49 διὰ πλειόνων ἐτῶν: presumably at the 'winter' of the Great Year.
Pl. *Tim.* 22E also recognizes destruction by flood, but does not adduce
Deucalion.   **παρὰ τὸ σύνηθες ἀγωνιάσας** 'distressed and disturbed
contrary to his wont': he is a 'slow' horse as a rule (§46).   **ἱδρῶτι**
. . . ὁμόζυγα 'swamps that very same horse [i.e. the Horse of Earth]
with floods of sweat, as he is yoked to him.'   **ὁμόζυγα:** again a
Phaedrus reminiscence (256A).   **πειρᾶται** 'experiences'. Cf. 68.2 οἱ
μὲν οὐ πάνυ τι φροντίζουσι τῶν ἡδέων, ἀρχὴν δ' οὐδὲ πειρῶνται
ἀπάντων.   **ὑπὸ νεότητός τε καὶ μνήμης ἀσθενοῦς:** an allusion to Pl.
Tim. 22B, where the Egyptian priest says that all Greeks are children:
νέοι ἐστε . . . τὰς ψυχὰς πάντες· οὐδεμίαν γὰρ ἐν αὐταῖς ἔχετε δι' ἀρχαίαν
ἀκοὴν παλαιὰν δόξαν οὐδὲ μάθημα χρόνωι οὐδέν. (This is in the context
of the periodical 'destruction' by fire and water.)   **Δευκαλίωνα:** the
hero of the commonest Greek flood-legend, very like Noah: a son of
Prometheus, he built a boat, and rode the flood nine days, sent out
a dove (Plu. *Soll. an.* 968), and landed on a mountain (Othrys or
Parnassus). How he and Pyrrha repeopled the world is best told in
Ovid's rendering (*Met.* 1.314-415). For other versions, see Apollod.
1.7.2, and Lucian, *De dea Syria* 12-13, where the influence of the
Hebrew story is clear.   **βασιλεύοντα:** king of the 'parts around
Phthia', according to Apollodorus *loc. cit.*   **σφισὶν ἀρκέσαι πρὸ**
τῆς παντελοῦς φθορᾶς 'sufficed them as a protection against total
destruction'.

50 δοκεῖν: still part of *oratio obliqua.*   **εἶναι γὰρ ὅμοιον:** cf. 12.33.
ὁ δ' ἐσκίρτησε καὶ ἐταράχθη: this is the main sentence, ὅταν . . .
ἀψάμενος being the subordinate clause. For the gnomic aorist, cf.
κατέκλυσε §49; for δέ *in apodosi,* Denniston (1954) 179.

51-60 'They also describe the change in the elements and their
ultimate fusion into fire by the same image of the chariot and horses,
moulded together into one! On their view, however, it is the nature of
the Horse of Fire that determines his victory; when he has absorbed the
rest, he is bigger than they all were before. He is, they say, the mind of
the charioteer; and, having reached this state, he begins to desire the
old harmonious universe. So he marvellously re-creates it, and the new
universe is more beautiful than the old.'

This elaborate passage puts in colourful terms a doctrine generally
held in Stoicism: that the world is to be resolved into one of its elements,
fire, and then re-created, to run its course again: *SVF* II pp. 183-191,

and especially Pohlenz (1949) II 45–7. Formally, the description is a cosmogony, an account of how the world was made: the past tenses are true, not gnomic. But as the cycle is infinitely repeated, it is also a statement of what is to be.   **συνέλθηι:** the (neuter) subject must be εἴδη. (τῶν τεττάρων above may be neuter, but more likely = τῶν τεττάρων ἵππων.)   **ἀτοπωτέρας . . . εἰκόνος** 'when they need their image to be odder'. τῆς makes ἀτοπωτέρας predicative. Perhaps we should insert ⟨τέτταρας⟩: the image surely requires *four* wax models, and D. has been emphasizing this.   **θαυματοποιός** 'toy-maker'.   **ἐκ κηροῦ:** cf. κηρίνους §53. The same image in Plutarch's hostile report of Stoic views (*Comm. not.* 31, 1075C): διαρρήδην λέγουσι τοὺς ἄλλους θεοὺς [i.e. except Zeus] ἅπαντας εἶναι γεγονότας καὶ διαφθαρησομένους ὑπὸ πυρός, τηκτοὺς κατ' αὐτοὺς ὥσπερ κηρίνους ἢ καττιτερίνους ὄντας. **ἔπειτα . . . ἐργάζοιτο** 'and then removed or scraped off bits of each to add now to one and now to another, until ultimately he had used them all up and made a single shape out of all his material'.

52 τοῦ δημιουργοῦ: the process is not the act of a 'craftsman' shaping 'material' (note the overtones of the words: creator god as well as doll-maker, 'matter' as well as 'raw material') but is something which arises from the nature of the 'horse', i.e. from the structure of the universe, which is itself divine. This is in accordance with Stoic 'immanentism'.   **ἐν ἀγῶνι μεγάλωι τε καὶ ἀληθινῶι** 'a real race, and a great one'. The implication is that, in real competitions, the urge to win comes from within.   **ἀλκῆι** 'strength', a poetical word: used by D. elsewhere of animals (2.67, 5.14, 32.64) or with a poetical allusion (11.84, 52.10). Here picked up by ἀλκιμώτατον.   **ἐν ἀρχῆι:** §43, §45.

53 ἐν οὐ πολλῶι τινι χρόνωι: what seems an infinite time to us is brief to God: 'A thousand ages in Thy sight / Are like an evening gone . . .'   **ἀναλαβόντα:** 'taking back'. In this final conflagration, the divine fire, from which all things came, takes them back: cf. *SVF* II 599 (p. 184.31ff.): ὁ κοινὸς λόγος καὶ ⟨ἡ⟩ κοινὴ φύσις μείζων καὶ πλείων γενομένη, τέλος ἀναξηράνασα πάντα καὶ εἰς ἑαυτὴν ἀναλαβοῦσα ἐν τῆι πάσηι οὐσίαι γίνεται . . .   **ὑπ' οὐδενὸς ἄλλου θνητῶν οὐδὲ ἀθανάτων ἀλλ' αὐτὸν ὑφ' αὐτοῦ νικηφόρον γενόμενον . . .** 'made victor in the greatest race not by any mortal or immortal but by himself'. An emphatic statement of the principle stated in §52 that all the force comes from the divine Fire itself: note the polar expression (see Barrett on Eur. *Hipp.* 441–2) and the use of negative and positive in

parallel (WS §3042: also called σχῆμα κατ' ἄρσιν καὶ θέσιν).   **στάντα**
... **μένους** 'High and proud he stood, exulting in his victory; he
occupied as much room as may be, and needed more space because of
his strength and energy.'

This too is good doctrine: when the world is dissolved in fire, it
occupies more room, like vaporised solids. It thus extends into what has
been void (Cleomedes 6, 11ff. Ziegler = 1.1.43ff. Todd). The Stoics
thus conceived of void (κενόν) as a condition of the cosmic cycle. They
also distinguished between τόπος, 'place', and χώρα, 'room'; τόπος is
the space occupied wholly by body, χώρα is space partly contained by
a body (e.g. the unfilled part of a wine-jar). Thus the expanded world
in the conflagration occupies as much τόπος as it can, and needs more
χώρα – hitherto unfilled, but potentially occupiable space – to do so.
D. uses his terms correctly. *SVF* ΙΙ pp. 162ff., Long and Sedley (1987)
I 296–7.   **μένους** 'strength', a word rare in prose, used by D. only
in 2.48, where he explains the Homeric μενοεικέα δαῖτα as τὴν οἵαν
παρέχειν μένος, τουτέστιν ἰσχύν. Xenophon does however use it: *Cyr.*
3.3.81 προθυμίας καὶ μένους καὶ τοῦ σπεύδειν συμμεῖξαι; there it seems
nearer to its Homeric sense of 'warlike passion'.

54 δυσωποῦνται 'they are embarrassed'. Cf. 32.7 δυσωπεῖσθαι
ἐξειπεῖν Πηνίκα παύσεται;   **τὴν τοῦ ἡνιόχου ... αὐτῆς:** the Horse
of Fire is now revealed as the ψυχή, or rather the νοῦς or ἡγεμονικόν,
of the universe. Again, this is the pure doctrine of Cleanthes or
Chrysippus: *SVF* ΙΙ 605 (p. 186) διόλου μὲν γὰρ ὢν ὁ κόσμος πυρώδης,
εὐθὺς καὶ ψυχή ἐστιν ἑαυτοῦ καὶ ἡγεμονικόν. 'When the kosmos is fiery
throughout, it is at once its own soul and control.'   **[οὕτως ...
εὐφήμοις]** 'So do we also speak, honouring and venerating the greatest
god with good actions and pious words.' This sentence is certainly
interpolated; it does not suit the context to contrast ἡμεῖς with the Magi
who propound all this. But it is not necessarily a Christian interpolation.
To say that the Greatest God is the Soul or Intellect of the World is
more like some form of Platonic theology.

55 λειφθείς ... βίον 'So Nous was left alone. Diffused evenly in all
directions, it filled a vast space with itself. Nothing dense remained in
it, but openness of texture everywhere prevailed. When it was thus at
its most beautiful, having acquired the purest nature of unsullied light,
it at once began to long for its original life.' I take it that οὐδενὸς ...
μανότητος is subordinate to κεχυμένος, that ὅτε ... φύσιν constitutes a

fresh subordinate clause, and that εὐθὺς ... βίον is the (paradoxical) main sentence.

Orthodox Stoicism saw the παλιγγενεσία of the world after the ἐκπύρωσις as a phase in the eternally recurring cycle. The elements changed in a certain order – fire to air, air to water, water to earth (*SVF* II 579). But it was of course difficult to explain just how the purified Fire, now pure Intellect, came to initiate the next cycle. It was held that it contained λόγος σπερματικός, a seminal principle, which, once united with other elements, produced the entire universe. It is hard to make sense of this: the version here given is of course a myth, with the implausibility of attributing ἔρως, ὁρμή, and πόθος to a pure Intellect. Why should the creator fire want to go through it all again? D.'s answer, that it desired ἀρχὴ καὶ ὁμόνοια, recalls perhaps Plato's insight that a good creator wished to make other things good (*Tim.* 29A, 30A); but it also has perhaps some political resonance, given D.'s concern with the analogy between the human and cosmic orders.   **πυκνοῦ ...**
μανότητος: the densest element is earth, the least dense fire: in the pure fire which is now Nous, the quality of μανότης is totally dominant (ἐπικρατούσης).   **τῶν τριῶν φύσεων:** i.e. air, water, and earth. **ὥρμησεν ἐπὶ τὸ γεννᾶν:** cf. the definition of Ἔρως as ὁρμὴ ἐπὶ τὸ γεννᾶν in the Stoic Cornutus (17, p. 28.18 Lang).   **πολὺ κρείττω ... ἅτε νεώτερον** 'our present world, much better and more splendid in the beginning because younger'.

56 ἀστράψας δὲ ... τῆι νοήσει 'Delivering, with his whole being, a flash of lightning, that is not disorderly or foul, like that which in storms often darts through violently colliding clouds, but pure, and with no taint of the dark in it, he made the change with ease, in the instant of thought.'   **ἀστράψας ... ἀστραπήν:** WS §§1564ff. The themes of Cleanthes' *Hymn to Zeus*, in which the traditional epithets and functions of the God of Thunder and Lightning are applied to the Stoic divine fire (D.'s *Nous*) are echoed in this, as in many other, later treatments of these themes. Cf. Cleanthes 9–12:

> τοῖον ἔχεις ὑποεργὸν ἀνικήτοις ἐνὶ χερσὶν
> ἀμφήκη πυρόεντ' αἰειζώοντα κεραυνόν·
> τοῦ γὰρ ὑπὸ πληγῆις φύσεως πάντ' ἔργα βέβηκεν,
> ὧι σὺ κατευθύνεις κοινὸν λόγον ...

(Text in Long and Sedley (1987) II 326.)   **ὅλος:** von Arnim is doubt-less right; the whole substance of the Fire produces the marvellous flash, which (unlike ordinary lightning) has no impurity or darkness in it because it is not yet mixed with air, and air is dark (§45) (*aer spissus* is a feature of thunder-clouds: Sen. *NQ* 2.26.1), and does not arise from the collision of clouds (*nubes in nubem incitatae*, Sen. *NQ* 2.23.1) but (like all the action of the Divine Fire) from itself.   χειμέριος 'stormy', as opposed to χειμερινός, 'wintry'. οἷα, as Casaubon saw, is the case required.   ἅμα τῆι νοήσει: to produce an effect instantaneously on a thought is a divine trait: Callim. *Hymn* 1.87–8 (of Ptolemy) ἑσπέριος κεῖνός γε τελεῖ τά κεν ἦρι νοήσηι, | ἑσπέριος τὰ μέγιστα, τὰ μείονα δ᾽ εὖτε νοήσηι.   εἰς ἀέρα . . . ἠπίου 'turns into fiery air, whose fire is gentle.' This is meant to explain how the 'pure' fire of the Nous is modified into the fire which can create the world (πῦρ τεχνικόν, ὁδῶι βαδίζον ἐπὶ γένεσιν κόσμου, a definition of god, *SVF* II 1027 (p. 306)). For doubts about the text and sense of this passage, see Scott, *Hermetica* (1924–36) II 123ff. (on *CH* III 2a). His restorations seem unnecessary.   μιχθεὶς . . . λέχους 'He then, jointly with Hera, shared that most perfect bed, and on going to rest, released once again the whole seed of the universe.' τρέπεται . . . ἀφίησι are presumably historic presents: but, once again, this is a process infinitely repeated in history. Cf. πλάττει . . . τυποῖ in §57. τελειότατον is a significant word: the ἱερὸς γάμος (alluded to more distinctly just below) is connected with the cult of Zeus Teleios and Hera Teleia. This union – sometimes interpreted as an allegory of the 'marriage' of Heaven and Earth – was a favourite subject of art (a metope of the Heraion at Selinus, fifth century, is one of the earliest and most famous depictions of Hera's unveiling before Zeus) and a powerful emotive symbol of marriage. Chrysippus (*SVF* II 1071–4, p. 314) is supposed to have written at length about a representation of the union at Samos, where the cult of Hera was very important; Hera, he argued, represented matter into which Zeus was inserting his seed – apparently by putting his penis in her mouth, if we are to believe our witnesses. Such allegorization of popular cult was typical of Stoic efforts to enlist traditional belief in the cause of their world-view.   τοῦτον . . . γάμον 'This is what wise men sing of in secret rituals, as the blessed marriage of Hera and Zeus.' Though there is some evidence for a place for the Hieros Gamos in mystery cults (J. Schmid, *RAC* II 537), D.'s language here should not be so interpreted: παῖδες σοφῶν (cf. §40) are philosophers, and their 'secret rites' are probably simply their teachings (cf. §39).

57 ὑγρὰν δὲ . . . εὐπετῶς 'And, making his entire substance liquid, one single Seed of the Whole, himself circulating within it, like the Breath that forms and fashions within the semen, he was then most like the structure of other animals, inasmuch as he could properly be said to consist of Soul and Body; and so he easily forms and shapes the rest, diffusing around himself his substance, which is smooth and soft and easily yielding in its entirety.' Cf. *SVF* II 580 (p. 179) = Diog. Laert. 7.136 = Long and Sedley (1987) II 272 (46B): κατ' ἀρχὰς μὲν οὖν καθ' αὑτὸν ὄντα [sc. τὸν Δία] τρέπειν τὴν πᾶσαν οὐσίαν δι' ἀέρος εἰς ὕδωρ. καὶ ὥσπερ ἐν τῆι γονῆι τὸ σπέρμα περιέχεται, οὕτω καὶ τοῦτον σπερματικὸν λόγον ὄντα τοῦ κόσμου, τοιόνδε ὑπολείπεσθαι ἐν τῶι ὑγρῶι, εὐεργὸν αὑτῶι ποιοῦντα τὴν ὕλην πρὸς τὴν τῶν ἑξῆς γένεσιν. Stoic cosmogony was obviously much influenced by the biological model of conception and impregnation; D.'s account is somewhat more detailed than others, but it is perhaps unwise to press its detail.

58 Ἐργασάμενος . . . νῦν 'having worked and perfected our existing world he displayed it in the beginning, indescribably fair and beautiful, much more brilliant than we see it today.' The notion that the world produced better things when it was young is common (e.g. Sen. *Epist.* 90.44, Lucr. 5.799), and naturally suits the widespread attitude of 'chronological primitivism', holding that 'that age is best which is the first' in the world as in human life. Our passage is quoted to illustrate this in Lovejoy and Boas (1935) 100, who give many parallels. **καινὰ . . . τοῦ ποιήσαντος** 'fresh from the skill and the maker's hands, at the first moment . . .' **ὅλα τε βλαστοῖς ἐοικότα:** i.e. the whole plant has the freshness and pliancy of new wood.

59 ἡ μὲν γὰρ ἀνθρώπων φύσις: man is thus the exception to the rule that 'first is best'. The feebleness of the infant is a common theme; Lucr. 5.222ff. expresses it best:

> Tum porro puer, ut saeuis proiectus ab undis
> nauita, nudus humi iacet, infans, indigus omni
> uitali auxilio.

For D. here, this is not a pessimistic thought: man's capacity to develop to maturity sets him apart as a superior being. **ὑδαρής** 'watery', and so 'feeble'. **Δημητρὸς ἀτελεῖ χλόηι** 'unripe green shoots of corn', an elevated and perhaps poetical phrase. **παμφαίνων** 'radiant', an epic word (e.g. *Il.* 19.398), and clearly an indication of the lofty tone of all this passage.

60 ἤσθη . . . πάθος 'was indeed not *pleased*, for that is a low emotion of low creatures'. Stoic theory distinguished ἡδονή, as ἄλογος ἔπαρσις, from χαρά, which was εὔλογος ἔπαρσις ('reasonable sense of elevation'): *SVF* III 434. τέρψις was also sometimes regarded as good: *SVF* III 432. So D.'s choice of words here is appropriate. For the thought, cf. especially Pl. *Tim.* 370D, on the joy felt by the demiurge in his creation (ἠγάσθη . . . εὐφρανθείς). So too the creator in Genesis I (Septuagint) εἶδεν ὅτι καλόν, at each stage of his creation.   ἥμενος . . . θεούς: *Il.* 21.389–90.   εἰ μὴ . . . ἁρμονίας 'save only the Muses and Apollo with the divine rhythm of their pure and supreme harmony'. Presumably an allusion to the music of the spheres.

61 'Let us stop here. If it all seems fantastic, blame the Borysthenites, not me.'   ἐξίτηλον 'vanishing from sight': from ἐξιέναι, so often of faded colours or obsolete practices. In 30.38 D. uses it of the flavour of wine which is lost because it is too weak a mixture. So it is an unexpected word to couple with ὑψηλόν: only the image makes it clear – the bird soars out of sight, and the augur can make nothing of it.   ὥσπερ . . . ποιεῖν 'as experts in bird-lore say that the bird that goes too high and hides itself in the clouds invalidates the augury'.

BIBLIOGRAPHY

Amann, J. (1931) *Die Zeusrede des Ailios Aristides*. Stuttgart.

Anderson, G. (1976) *Studies in Lucian's comic fiction*. Leiden.

   (1989) 'The pepaideumenos in action', *A.N.R.W.* 33.1:79–208.

Anderson, J. K. (1985) *Hunting in the ancient world*. Berkeley and Los Angeles.

von Arnim, H. (1891) 'Die Entstehung und Anordnung der Schriftsammlung Dios von Prusa', *Hermes* 26:366–407.

   (1898) *Dio von Prusa*. Berlin.

Avezzù, E. (1985) *Dione di Prusa, Il Cacciatore*, ed. E. A. and F. Donadi. Venice.

Babut, D. (1969) *Plutarque et le stoïcisme*. Paris.

Barwick, K. (1957) 'Probleme der stoischen Sprachlehre und Rhetorik', *Abh. der sächsischen Akademie, phil.-hist. Klasse* 49.3. Berlin.

Baudry, J. (1931) *Le Problème de l'origine et de l'éternité du monde*. Paris.

de Ballu, E. Belin (1972) *Olbia*. Leiden.

Bickel, E. (1915) *Diatribe in Senecae philosophi fragmenta* I. Leipzig.

Bidez, J., and F. Cumont (1938) *Les mages hellénisés*. Paris.

Binder, H. (1905) *Dio Chrysostomus und Posidonius*. Tübingen.

Blankert, S. (1940) *Seneca (Epist. 90) over Natuur en Cultuur*. Amsterdam.

Blomquist, J. (1969) *Greek particles in Hellenistic prose*. Lund.

Bodson, A. (1967) *La Morale sociale des derniers Stoïciens*. Paris.

Bompaire, J. (1958) *Lucien écrivain*. Paris.

Bowersock, G. W. (1965) *Augustus and the Greek world*. Oxford.

Brancacci, A. (1986) *Rhetorike philosophousa: Dione Crisostomo nella cultura antica e bizantina*. Naples.

Brink, C. O. (1963) *Horace on poetry: prolegomena to the literary epistles*. Cambridge.

Brunt, P. A. (1973) 'Aspects of the social thought of Dio Chrysostom and of the Stoics', *P.C.P.S.* 199 (N.S. 19):9–34.

Buffière, F. (1956) *Les Mythes d'Homère et la pensée grecque*. Paris.

Bühler, W. (1964) *Beiträge zur Erklärung der Schrift vom Erhabenen*. Göttingen.

Burgess, T. C. (1902) *Epideictic literature*. Chicago. (Repr. Ann Arbor, 1980.)

Burkert, W. (1985) *Greek religion*. Oxford (Blackwell) and Cambridge, Mass.

Caduff, G. A. (1986) *Antike Sintflutssagen* (Hypomnemata 82). Göttingen.

Chirassi, Ileana (1963) 'Il significato religioso del XII discorso di Dione Crisostomo,' *Riv. di cult. class. e med.* 5:266–85.

Clemen, C. (1920) *Fontes historiae religionis Persicae*. Bonn.

Clerc, C. (1915) *Les Théories relatives au culte des images chez les auteurs grecs du 11e siècle après J.-C.* Paris.

Cole, T. (1967) *Democritus and the sources of Greek anthropology*. Yale.

Costa, C. D. N. (1984) *Lucretius V*. Oxford.

Cristofferson, T. (1933–4) *Bemerkungen zu Dion von Prusa* (Kungl. Humanistika Vetenskapssamfundet i Lund 3). Lund.

Cumont, F. (1938) 'La fin du monde selon les mages occidentaux', *Revue d'Histoire des Religions* 103:29–96.

Day, J. (1951) 'The value of Dio Chrysostom's Euboean discourse for the economic historian', *Studies ... in honour of A. C. Johnson*, 209–35. Princeton.

de Decker, J. (1913) *Iuvenalis declamans*. Gand.

Denniston, J. D. (1954) *Greek particles*[2]. Oxford.

des Places, E. (1969) *La Religion grecque*. Paris.

Desideri, P. (1978) *Dione de Prusa: un'intellettuale greco nell'impero romano*. Messina.

Deubner, L. (1956) *Attische Feste*. Berlin.

Devine, F. E. (1970) 'Stoicism on the best régime', *J.H.I.* 31:323–36.

de Vries, G. J. (1969) *A commentary on the Phaedrus of Plato*. Amsterdam.

Döring, K. (1979) *Exemplum Socratis* (*Hermes* Einzelschriften 42). Wiesbaden.

Dover, K. J. (1974) *Greek popular morality in the time of Plato and Aristotle*. Oxford.

(1978) *Greek homosexuality*. London.

Duncan-Jones, R. (1982) *The economy of the Roman Empire*[2]. London.

Elorduy, E. (1936) 'Die Sozialphilosophie der Stoa,' *Philol.* Suppl. 283, Leipzig.

Ferri, S. (1936) 'Il discorso di Fidia in Dione Crisostomo,' *Ann. Sc. Norm. Pisa* 2.5:237ff.

Festugière, A. J. *La Révélation d'Hermès Trismégiste* I–IV, Paris 1950–4. (= *RHT*)

Fink, J. (1950) 'Die Eule der Athena Parthenos,' *Mitt. d. deutsch. Arch. Inst., Athen. Abt.* 71:90–7.

François, L. (1917) 'Dion Chrysostome critique d'art,' *R.E.G.* 30 (1917), 105–16.

(1922) *Dion Chrysostome: deux Diogéniques.* Paris.

Garnsey, P. D. (1968) 'Trajan's Alimenta,' *Historia* 17 (1968), 367–81.

(1988) *Famine and food supply in the Graeco-Roman world.* Cambridge.

Gatz, B. (1967) *Weltalter, goldene Zeit und sinnverwandte Vorstellungen.* Hildesheim. (= *Spudasmata* 16)

R. L. Gordon, (1971) 'Cumont and the doctrine of Mithraism', in *Mithraic studies*, ed. J. R. Hinnells. Manchester.

Griffith, J. Gwyn (1970) *Plutarch's De Iside et Osiride.* University of Wales Press.

Guthrie, W. K. C. (1957) *In the beginning.* Cambridge.

Heath, M. (1989) *Unity in Greek poetics.* Oxford.

Highet, G. (1973) 'The Huntsman and the Castaway', *G.R.B.S.* 14:35–40.

Hirst, G. (1903) 'Cults of Olbia', *J.H.S.* 23:24–53.

Hirzel, R. (1985) *Der Dialog.* Leipzig.

Hunter, R. L. (1983) *A study of* Daphnis & Chloe. Cambridge.

Ingenkamp, H. G. (1971) *Plutarchs Schriften über die Heilung der Seele.* Göttingen.

Innes, D. C., and M. Winterbottom (1988) *Sopatros the rhetor* (*B.I.C.S.* Supplement 48). London.

Jebb, R. (1888) *Attic orators.* London.

Jones, C. P. (1978) *The Roman world of Dio Chrysostom.* Cambridge, Mass.

Jouan, F. (1977) 'Les thèmes romanesques dans l'Euboicus de Dion,' *R.E.G.* 90:38–46.

Kennedy, G. A. (1972) *The art of rhetoric in the Roman world.* Princeton.

Kidd, I. G. (1989) *Posidonius: the fragments* II, *Commentary.* Cambridge.

Kirk, G. S., Raven, J. E., and Schofield, M. (1983) *The Presocratic philosophers*, ed. 2. Cambridge.

Kindstrand, J. F. (1973) *Homer in der zweiten Sophistik.* Uppsala.

(1976) *Bion of Borysthenes.* Uppsala.

Koolmeister, R., and T. Tallmeister (1981) *An index to Dio Chrysostom.* Uppsala.

Lefkowitz, M. R. (1981) *The lives of the Greek poets.* London.

Lemarchand, L. (1926) *Dion de Pruse*. Paris. (And see *R.Ph.* 55 (1929) 13–29.)

Lieberg, G. (1973) 'Die *theologia tripertita* in Forschung und Bezeugung', *A.N.R.W.* 1.4:63–115.

Liegle, J. (1952) *Der Zeus des Pheidias*. Berlin.

Long, A. A. (1974) *Hellenistic philosophy*. London.

Long, A. A., and D. N. Sedley (1987) *The Hellenistic philosophers* I–II. Cambridge.

Lovejoy, A. O., and G. Boas (1935) *Primitivism and related ideas in antiquity*. Baltimore.

Luzzatto, M. T. (1983) *Tragedia greca e cultura ellenistica: l'or. 52 di Dione di Prusa*. Bologna.

Marrou, H. I. (1950) *Histoire de l'éducation dans l'antiquité*. Paris.

Mazon, P. (1943) 'Dion de Pruse et la politique agraire de Trajan,' *C.R.A.I.* (1943) 74–85.

Meiggs, R. (1982) *Trees and timber in the ancient world*. Oxford.

Moles, J. L. (1978) 'The career and conversion of Dio Chrysostom,' *J.H.S.* 98:79–100.

Mortenthaler, M. (1979) 'Der Olympicus des Dio von Prusa als literarhistorisches und geistesgeschichtliches Dokument', diss. Vienna.

Mrás, K. (1949) 'Die προλαλιά bei den griechischen Schriftstellern', *W.S.* 64:71ff.

Mussies, G. M. (1972) *Dio Chrysostom and the New Testament*. Leiden.

Nilsson, M. P. (1940–50) *Geschichte der griechischen Religion* I–II Munich.

Norden, E. (1913) *Agnostos theos*. Leipzig–Berlin.

Otto, A. (1890) *Die Sprichwörter und sprichwörtlichen Redensarten der Römer*. Leipzig.

Palm, J. (1959) *Rom, Römertum und Imperium in der griechischen Literatur der Kaiserzeit*. Lund.

Pépin, J. (1958) *Mythe et allégorie*. Paris.

Perry, B. E. (1965) *Babrius and Phaedrus*. Loeb Classical Library.
  (1967) *The ancient romances*. Berkeley and Los Angeles.

Pfister, F. (1909) *Der Reliquienkult im Altertum* (Religionsgeschichtliche Versuche und Vorarbeiten 5). Giessen.

Pohlenz, M. (1939) 'Plutarchs Schriften gegen die Stoiker,' *Hermes* 74:1–33.
  (1947–9) *Die Stoa* I–II. Göttingen.

Pollitt, J. J. (1974) *The ancient view of Greek art*. New Haven and London.

Pomeroy, S. B. (1975) *Goddesses, whores, wives and slaves*. New York.

Puiggali, J. (1984) 'La démonologie de Dion Chrysostome', *L.E.C.* 52:103–14.

Rawson, E. (1969) *The Spartan tradition in European thought*. Oxford.

Reardon, B. P. (1983) 'Travaux récents sur Dion de Pruse', *R.E.G.* 96:286–92.

Reesor, M. E. (1951) *The political theory of the Old and Middle Stoa*. New York 1951.

Reinhardt, K. (1921) *Poseidonios*. Munich.

   (1953) *RE* xxii.1, 558–826 Poseidonios.

Reuter, D. (1932) *Untersuchungen zum Euboikos des Dion von Prusa*. Leipzig.

Ros, J. G. A., S. J. (1938) *Die Μεταβολή* (*Variatio*) *als Stilprinzip des Thukydides*. Nijmegen (repr. Amsterdam 1968).

Russell, D. A. (1983) *Greek declamation*. Cambridge.

   (ed.) (1990) *Antonine literature*. Oxford.

Russell, D. A., and N. G. Wilson (1981) *Menander Rhetor*, edited with translation and commentary. Oxford.

Salmeri, G. (1980) 'Per una biografia di Dione di Prusa', *Siculorum Gymnasium* (1980) 671–715.

Sandbach, F. H. (1975) *The Stoics*. London.

Schwabl, H. (1978a) Zeus, *RE* Suppl. xx 994–1481 (esp. §§49, 90, 125, 130).

   (1978b) Weltalter, *RE* Suppl. xv 840–50.

Schmid, W. (1887–96) *Der Atticismus* i–iv. Stuttgart.

Sonny, A. (1896) *Ad Dionem Chrysostomum Analecta*. Kiev.

Spoerri, W. (1959) *Die späthellenistischen Berichte über Welt, Kultur und Götter*. Basel.

Stadter, P. A. (1989) *A commentary on Plutarch's Pericles*. Chapel Hill, N.C.

Süss, W. (1910) *Ethos*. Leipzig.

Thesleff, H. (1954) *Studies on intensification in early and classical Greek*. Copenhagen and Helsingfors.

   (1965) *The Pythagorean texts of the Hellenistic period*. Åbo.

Theiler, W. (1982) *Poseidonios: die Fragmente*. Berlin.

Thompson, D'Arcy W. (1895) *A glossary of Greek birds*. Oxford.

Treu, K. (1961) 'Zur Borysthenitica des Dio Chrysostomus', in *Griechische Städte und einheimische Völker des Schwarzmeergebietes*, ed. J. Irmscher. Berlin.

Trimpi, W. (1983) *Muses of one mind*. Princeton.

Turcan, R. (1975) *Mithras Platonicus*. Leiden.

Vischer, R. (1965) *Das einfache Leben*. Göttingen.

Wackernagel, J. (1928) *Vorlesungen über Syntax*. Basel.

Wasowicz, A. (1975) *Olbia pontique et son territoire*. Paris.

van der Waerden, B. L. (1952) 'Das Grosse Jahr und die ewige Wiederkehr', *Hermes* 80:129–55.

Wenkebach, E. (1940) 'Beiträge zur Textkritik Dions von Prusa', *Philologus* 94:86–124. (And see also *Hermes* 43 (1908) 77–103.)

(1944) 'Die Ueberlieferung der Schriften des Dion von Prusa', *Hermes* 79:40–65.

Wentzel, G. (1889) Ἐπικλήσεις, diss. Göttingen.

West, M. L. (1978) (ed.) *Hesiod, Works and Days*. Oxford.

(1989) (ed.) *Iambi et elegi Graeci*. Oxford.

Wifstrand, A. (1930–4) *Eikota* I–III (Kungl. Humanistika Vetenskapssamfundet i Lund).

von Wilamowitz-Moellendorf, U. (1902) *Griechisches Lesebuch*[2]. Berlin.

(1928) 'Lesefrüchte', *Hermes* 63:382.

INDEXES

References are to the sections of the speeches, or to pages of the Introduction.

1 General

254

2 Proper names in the text

3 Greek words discussed in the Commentary

4 Passages cited in Introduction and Commentary